Praise for *Confi*

"As a long-time admirer of Kanter's pio[neering work,] this book is a masterpiece. But reader, [fasten your safety] belt and get ready to be thrown for a loop by the originality, and heretofore uncovered insights and a fresh perspective that will enliven, if not transform, your mind set of how business is done. An astonishing piece of scholarly work written with grace and lucidity."
—Warren Bennis, distinguished professor of business administration, USC, and author of *On Becoming a Leader*

"What a completely original way to look at organizations! I found myself nodding in agreement as I read each page. And as much as I believe that confidence and success are inextricably linked, I've never seen a how-to book on the subject of confidence. Thank you, Rosabeth, for articulating and illustrating for all of us what we instinctively know to be true . . . success comes to those who believe they will be successful. Congratulations on this important new book."
—Shelly Lazarus, chairman and CEO, Ogilvy & Mather Worldwide

"A novel and very thoughtful approach, this exciting work documents what successful organizations and people learn during the course of their careers: work hard every day, have high standards, demand excellence around you, and stick to your values. The surprising thing is if everybody in an organization does one little thing better than they thought they could, the collective power and positive energy can be astounding. Kanter's extensive research shows what that kind of confidence looks like and how great leaders inspire it in others."
—Ivan Seidenberg, chairman and CEO, Verizon

"*Confidence* is a riveting account of how winning and losing streaks begin and end. With fascinating examples from the realms of business and sports, this is actionable advice that every business leader can benefit from."
—Pamela Thomas Graham, president and CEO, CNBC

"This book is packed with real-life examples providing important and profound new insights into the psychology of continuing success or repeated failure. *Confidence* will make a lasting difference to leaders, and it can help improve the state of the world and the lives of individuals."
—Dr. Daniel Vasella, chairman and CEO of Novartis

"*Confidence* provides a fascinating analysis of real-world behavior that creates self-reinforcing cycles of winning and losing. Kanter goes behind the scenes to show how companies, sports teams, and even governments foster winning streaks and succumb to losing streaks. Systems have momentum, yet as Kanter demonstrates, leaders make choices that affect the odds of success, propelling a winning streak or reversing a losing one. Her work demonstrates the critical role of effective leadership in setting high-expectations and instilling confidence in organizations. Her message about the importance of confidence in success makes inspirational reading."
—Laura D'Andrea Tyson, dean, London Business School, former economic adviser to President Clinton, and *Business Week* columnist

"You don't need a crystal ball to predict who will succeed at the next big challenge—just read this remarkable book, and see for yourself how confidence separates winners from losers. From avoiding doom loops to the chemistry of teamwork, everyone from novices to the most experienced leaders can learn from a world-renowned expert's brilliant new theory about how to shed losers' curses and maintain winners' advantages. *Confidence* provides big ideas of the highest intellectual value and brings them down to earth through engaging, practical stories. It's a winner!"
—Sir Martin Sorrell, CEO, WPP

"*Confidence* is the right book for our times . . . a thought-provoking must-read for anyone recharging their organization."
—Ann Fudge, chairman and CEO, Young & Rubicam

Confidence

Confidence

HOW WINNING STREAKS

AND LOSING STREAKS

BEGIN AND END

Rosabeth Moss Kanter

RANDOM HOUSE

BUSINESS BOOKS

Published by Random House Business Books in 2004

3 5 7 9 10 8 6 4

Copyright © 2004 Rosabeth Moss Kanter

The right of Moss Kanter has asserted her right under the Copyright, Design and
Patents Act, 1988 to be identified as the author of this work

First published in the United States by Crown Business, a member of the Crown
Publishing Group, a division of Random House Inc. in 2004

Random House Business Books
The Random House Group Limited
20 Vauxhall Bridge Road, London SW1V 2SA

Random House Australia (Pty) Limited
20 Alfred Street, Milsons Point, Sydney, New South Wales 2061, Australia

Random House New Zealand Limited
18 Poland Road, Glenfield, Auckland 10, New Zealand

Random House South Africa (Pty) Limited
Endulini, 5a Jubilee Road, Parktown, 2193, South Africa

Random House UK Limited Reg. No. 954009

A CIP catalogue record for this book is available from the British Library

Papers used by Random House UK Limited are natural, recyclable products made
from wood grown in sustainable forests. The manufacturing processes conform
to the environmental regulations of the country of origin.

Printed and bound in Great Britain by
Mackays of Chatham PLC, Chatham, Kent

ISBN 978 1 8441 3592 9

To Barry and Matthew, of course

Contents

Part III

IMPLICATIONS AND LIFE LESSONS

Preface

MY SON THINKS I WROTE THIS BOOK SO I WOULD FINALLY KNOW ENOUGH ABOUT SPORTS TO SWAP STORIES AND WATCH BALL GAMES TOGETHER. MY CORPORATE CLIENTS AND SENIOR EXecutive audiences think I wrote it to give them a roadmap for how to get to the top and stay there, especially if they need to turn around unproductive cycles to get in shape for high performance and growth. My civic and nonprofit boards think I wrote it to help them manage through turbulent times and develop strong community leadership.

My Harvard colleagues think I wrote the book to weave my past work on innovation and change into a new theory of organizational cycles and dynamics. My MBA students think I wrote it to make lessons about teamwork in business more interesting by drawing from the best sports teams. My husband thinks I wrote it so I would learn how to persevere even when the roof crumbles over me (which it did, because of the unfortunate timing of renovations).

There is truth in all these professional and personal reasons for writing *Confidence*. But if I think back on what I had in mind at the beginning, my first goal was empowerment.

I wanted to give more people the tools and the confidence to avoid the destructive patterns of losing streaks and get onto winning paths—whether they are executives concerned with business strategy, managers and employees looking for ways to foster teamwork and a creative work environment, coaches and fans cheering their favorite teams to victory, professionals interested in success trajectories, or community activists seeking to improve the quality of life at home.

I wanted to understand confidence in order to spread it.

The mission of Harvard Business School, where I work, is to "educate leaders who make a difference in the world." I get to spend time with people in the highest circles of business and government and advise them. (For example, I was one of a handful of American experts invited to the Economic Summits of both President Clinton in Little Rock, Arkansas, in 1992 and President Bush in Waco, Texas, in 2002.) But my students these days are not interested just in business per se; they might wind up being business consultants by day and nonprofit volunteers by night, or working to develop better leadership for public schools, or heading organizations to improve health care or make a dent in global poverty.

I believe in leadership to make a difference at all levels, so I help social entrepreneurs create new grassroots organizations to change the world corner by corner. Among other boards, I have served for a decade on the national board of City Year, the model for Americorps, which mobilizes young people in teams to perform a year of national and community service in schools, community centers, or wherever they are needed.

So when I decided to write this book, I wanted it to be relevant across a wide spectrum and apply not just to corporate cultures and business turnarounds (such as Gillette's), but also to all the institutions that we must turn around to make the world a safer, saner place. And to make our lives more fulfilling.

In addition to going inside a wide range of organizations in several countries, I focus a portion of the book on sports. I chose this area not just for its intrinsic interest (I am a big fan myself) but also for widely applicable lessons from the great or faltering teams I examined. (Among the great ones, I am pleased to say, are two tremendous women's teams.) Sports is a near-universal source of metaphors for leadership and management, because it is a good microcosm for examining patterns of winning and losing and see-ing the elements of exceptional leadership and teamwork.

I know that everyone who loves sports will resonate immediately with the stories I have drawn from that realm and will see immedi-ately the applicability to other areas. But one does not have to be passionate or even knowledgeable about sports to understand the relevance of the stories I tell about success, setbacks, and turn-arounds in many walks of life.

Ultimately, the lessons I draw are all about people and how they work together (or don't) to produce better (or worse) results. These truths about people, and the systems that surround them, hold across all sorts of games—whether they are simple ball games, complex business situations, community problems, or the personal game of life.

Rosabeth Moss Kanter,
Boston, Cambridge, and Edgartown,
Massachusetts, March 1, 2004

Part I

WINNERS AND LOSERS:
HOW CONFIDENCE GROWS OR ERODES

The Locker Room and
the Playing Field:
Booms, Busts, Streaks, and Cycles

SOMETIMES IT SEEMS AS IF THERE ARE ONLY TWO STATES OF BEING: *BOOM* OR *BUST.* WHEN THINGS ARE UP, IT FEELS AS IF THEY WILL ALWAYS BE UP. PEOPLE COME TO BELIEVE THEY CAN SUCCEED AT anything they try; companies proffer grand visions of innovative futures; and investment is easy to attract. When things are down, it seems as if they will always be down. That's how depressed people feel; that's why recession-dominated economies find recovery elusive; that's why teams or businesses or schools can stay in decade-long slumps.

Any company, any group, any person can be swept along by one of these fortunate or unfortunate cycles. What causes them to rise or to fall is often a matter of confidence. Confidence is the bridge connecting expectations and performance, investment and results. It is a familiar term used every day to indicate future prospects in a wide variety of circumstances—the self-confidence of athletes, consumer confidence in the economy, public confidence in leaders, or votes of no confidence at board meetings. But there is remarkably little understanding of what lies behind it. Consider the following dramatic examples, and the questions they raise about how confidence builds or erodes.

The women's basketball team at the University of Connecticut consistently broke records, winning ten Big East conference championships and chalking up a seventy-game winning streak. For the

2002–2003 season, the individual talent level of the team was well below that of its predecessors and many of its opponents, yet the team of valiant women continued to rack up victories. They were confident that they could win, even without the very best players. Why?

Although its competitors canceled hundreds of flights and lost millions of dollars during America's Great Blackout of August 2003, Continental Airlines kept flying and even made money, despite power outages at its Newark and Cleveland hubs. Within minutes after the Northeast electric power grid went down, employees were on cell phones sharing ideas about dealing with the crisis. Far from losing money and passenger goodwill, Continental increased both, exceeding forecasts by $4 million for the two days following the blackout. The company's employees had confidence in one another that enabled them to spring into action as a team. Where did it come from?

The Philadelphia Eagles were roundly booed by fans for picking rookie quarterback Donovan McNabb over a more highly rated running back who was seen as a better athlete. The mayor of Philadelphia even introduced a city council resolution urging the other choice. Recruiting players such as McNabb for "character," not just for raw athleticism, gave the once-mediocre Eagles the confidence to bounce back from losses and win more regular season games from 2000 to 2003 than any other professional football franchise. The New England Patriots were even better at converting character into championships. In terms of individual ability, quarterback Tom Brady was not considered the best in the National Football League, yet through strength of character he led his team to two Super Bowl wins in three years and an almost-unprecedented fifteen-game winning streak in 2003. What was the connection between character, team culture, and top performance?

After one of the highest-performing decades in its hundred-year history, Gillette, the global consumer products company, slipped badly in the mid-1990s. Poor business practices and over-promising to Wall Street resulted in fifteen quarters of missed earnings estimates before a new leader turned the company around and restored accountability. Gillette once had confidence, then lost it, then got it back. Why did they fall into a "circle of doom" in the first place, and how did they break out of it?

At De La Salle High School in Concord, California, successive generations of student athletes won every single football game for over twelve years, even when they faced the toughest national competition. But at Prairie View A&M University in Texas, no matter how hard the spunky student athletes tried, or how much talent was on the team, they lost all but a mere handful of games over the same period. What happened to confidence during these winning or losing streaks to make further success or further failure seem inevitable?

On January 29, 2004, thousands of British Broadcasting Corporation (BBC) employees mobbed the streets outside television studios in one of Britain's largest industrial actions ever. But this wasn't a protest of labor against management—far from it. The crowds were protesting the resignation of their boss following a report faulting a BBC News account of British government intelligence about weapons of mass destruction in Iraq. Over a four-year period, the BBC's chief had moved a demoralized organization to renewed initiative and innovation through leadership actions that his now-empowered executive team vowed to continue and extend. What had awakened the passion of the people and produced this unusual show of commitment and confidence?

Nelson Mandela spent twenty-seven years in prison under the apartheid government of the old South Africa. Yet, after being released and becoming the new South Africa's first democratically elected president, he resisted the temptation to take revenge. Instead he led the divided country out of a cycle of decline to one of hope and enterprise. He extended his personal confidence in people, even those who had wronged him, into a national culture of respect and inclusion. How did he do that?

• • •

In this book I go inside these stories, and many others, to show how confidence shapes the outcomes of many contests of life—from simple ball games to complex enterprises, from individual performance to national culture. I describe what confidence is and where it comes from. I explain the culture of success and failure, why winning streaks and losing streaks perpetuate themselves, and how to shift the dynamics of decline to a cycle of success.

Confidence helps people take control of circumstances rather than be dragged along by them. By illuminating the roots and role of confidence at many levels—confidence in oneself, in one another, and in the system—I offer insights and tools for guiding people and organizations onto productive and healthy paths.

CYCLES OF CONFIDENCE

On the way up, success creates positive momentum. People who believe they are likely to win are also likely to put in the extra effort at difficult moments to ensure that victory. On the way down, failure feeds on itself. As performance starts running on a positive or a negative path, the momentum can be hard to stop. Growth cycles produce optimism, decline cycles produce pessimism. These dispositions help predict the recovery of problem-ridden businesses, low-performing urban schools, or even patients on their deathbeds. We encapsulate this in slogans. When people or groups are "on a roll," they go "from strength to strength." "Losers," on the other hand, seem doomed always to lose, because no one believes in them, no one invests in them, no one helps them improve. That's how the rich get richer and the poor get poorer—or the sick get sicker, the vulnerable become victims, and things start looking rundown because momentum is running down.

Persistent patterns of winning and losing are familiar in sports as well as business. When I was a young baseball fan, the New York Yankees always seemed to win, and the New York Mets always seemed to lose. It didn't matter who the particular players were, or even that legendary Yankees manager Casey Stengel moved to the

Mets. Winning teams become "dynasties" that seem to win most of the time regardless of who is on the field—the Yankees in professional baseball, Miami of Florida in college football, North Carolina in women's college soccer, the Australian national team in international cricket. Teams that lose most of the time can start sliding into patterns of perpetual disappointment—the Chicago Cubs, for example, didn't have back-to-back winning seasons in over fifty years.

As patterns develop, streaks start to run on their own momentum, producing conditions that make further success or failure more likely. Winning creates a positive aura around everything, a "halo" effect that encourages positive team behavior that makes further wins more likely. Winning makes it easier to attract the best talent, the most loyal fans, the biggest revenues to reinvest in perpetuating victory. Losing has a repellent effect. It is harder for the team to bond, harder for it to attract new talent, easier for it to fall behind. Winners get the benefit of the doubt. Losing breeds qualms. In the midst of a winning streak, winners are assumed to have made brilliant moves when perhaps they were just lucky. In the midst of a losing streak, if losers eke out a victory, sometimes they are assumed to have cheated.

In short, confidence grows in winning streaks and helps propel a tradition of success. Confidence erodes in losing streaks, and its absence makes it hard to stop losing.

CONFIDENCE AND SELF-FULFILLING PROPHECIES

Confidence consists of positive expectations for favorable outcomes. Confidence influences the willingness to invest—to commit money, time, reputation, emotional energy, or other resources—or to withhold or hedge investment. This investment, or its absence, shapes the ability to perform. In that sense, confidence lies at the heart of civilization. Everything about an economy, a society, an organization, or a team depends on it. Every step we take, every investment we make, is based on whether we feel we can count on ourselves and others to accomplish what has been promised. Confidence determines whether our steps—individually or collectively—are tiny and tentative or big and bold.

Confidence is a sweet spot between arrogance and despair. Arrogance involves the failure to see any flaws or weaknesses, despair the failure to acknowledge any strengths. Overconfidence leads people to overshoot, to overbuild, to become irrationally exuberant or delusionally optimistic, and to assume they are invulnerable. That's what induces people to become complacent, leaders to neglect fundamental disciplines, investors to turn into gamblers. But underconfidence is just as bad, and perhaps worse. It leads people to underinvest, to under-innovate, and to assume that everything is stacked against them, so there's no point in trying.

It is human nature to set expectations based on assumptions about whether conditions seem to be improving or deteriorating, about whether the game can be won or will inevitably be lost. We seek patterns and trends even in events that are random, like gamblers who believe that when they hold a few good hands of cards, they must be "hot," and that the next hands will be equally good. And for nonrandom activities, where human effort and skill make a difference, success and failure easily become self-fulfilling prophecies.

Patterns, apparent or real, become enshrined in myths and superstitions that have an effect on those playing the game. In baseball, the Chicago Cubs always seemed to go downhill during the "June swoon," making June a psychological hurdle. The Boston Red Sox always seemed to play well during the season and disappoint their fans by losing at the end. The New York Yankees always seemed to beat the Red Sox. This was blamed on the "Curse of the Bambino" imposed on Boston when baseball star Babe Ruth left the Red Sox for the Yankees.

In the 2003 playoffs, the Red Sox lost to the Yankees in the eighth inning of the last game of the series when manager Grady Little left pitcher Pedro Martinez in the game, even though he had already thrown more than 100 pitches and (in hindsight) was fatigued. Little, who was later fired (but not because of that call, Red Sox owners said), became the symbol of the curse in action, and fans called for his departure even though he had led the team to a winning season, as though serving him up as a scapegoat would purge the team of its past. But fans' extreme anger reinforced the image of the Red Sox and their extended family as inevitable losers, and sore losers at that. "In Boston, only the World Series counts as winning," Little said. Such reactions undermined confidence that the Red Sox would ever break their curse. In February 2004, when the Yankees landed Alex Rodriguez, considered the best player in baseball, after the Sox failed to make a deal with him, the "curse" was said to continue.

Failure and success are not episodes, they are trajectories. They are tendencies, directions, pathways. Each decision, each time at bat, each tennis serve, each business quarter, each school year seems like a new event, but the next performance is shaped by what happened last time out, unless something breaks the streak. The meaning of any particular event is shaped by what's come before. The same $10,000 in someone's bank account can make him feel rich and getting richer if he had only $5,000 the day before and $1,000 the day before that, or poor and getting poorer if he had $50,000 the previous day and $100,000 two days earlier. History and context shape interpretations and expectations.

In sports, each game starts at zero in a strictly technical sense. Statistically, each player is no more likely to sink the same number of baskets in the next game as in the last game. And unanticipated events pop up: For an airline, weather problems or national emergencies; for the BBC, the suicide of a government source for a news report about intelligence in the war in Iraq; for a sports team, injuries. But many things are carried over from game to game and shape the mood in the locker room; that mood can then follow players out onto the field. The list starts with the quality of players' relationships, the availability of workout equipment, the continuity or turnover of coaches, the size of crowds, the nature of press accounts. (Nearly all coaches say that they tell players not to pay attention to the media. They also say that the players do it anyway.)

The context that creates expectations affects outcomes. American professional football is just a game, but many millions of fans imbue it with meaning as the most-watched national sport. Was it thus inevitable that the New England Patriots would win the first Super Bowl after the terrorist attacks of 9/11? The name alone might have shaped the mood. Perhaps the team bearing the name "Patriots" felt an obligation not to be defeated in front of a U.S. television audience of more than 137 million and another estimated 700 million people in 225 countries. From the first moment they appeared, the Patriots' behavior symbolized national solidarity. At the beginning of the game they ran out onto the field as a team, rather than one by one, with no individual names called in the usual way, signaling their unity—the United Team of America. This was a tradition the Patriots had started in the third week of the season, after losing the first two games. Head coach Bill Belichick, who had come a year earlier to lead a successful turnaround of the Patriots, preached a passion for teamwork and told the players they had to subsume their egotistic instincts in order to win. Then-co-captain Lawyer Milloy and another veteran player introduced the idea of the players running out as a team. For the Super Bowl, this was a hard sell to the league and television producers, Patriots' vice-chairman Jonathon Kraft told me, but the team captains were firm on this point. "Announce us any way you want to," Kraft recalled that they said, "but we will run out as a team." That team confidence gave the Patriots the margin of victory.

People are likely to bet on a team that believes in itself and digs deep at critical moments. Those assumed to be successful have no trouble attracting the investment that ensures their success. But if people who must invest their time or resources in an enterprise believe that it is failing, they withhold effort and investment, and that deepens the state of decline. Self-fueling cycles of advantage or disadvantage can become growth engines or death spirals. It is sometimes hard to disentangle cause and effect. Previous wins can create enthusiasm for high performance, which helps produce victory, and losses can cause poor performance as much as poor performance can cause the next loss. Success provides the resources, the pride, the enthusiasm that make it easier to succeed the next time—that build confidence.

At the most basic level of daily activity, confidence can be manifested in body language, in demeanor, and in personal surroundings. Chris Wallace, general manager of the Boston Celtics, used the toes and shoulders test to see whether professional basketball players were likely to win: whether players are sticking close to the ground or up on their toes, whether shoulders are sagging or players are standing tall.

Demeanor sends signals that shape other people's confidence in the team or the business. Jeanette Sarkisian Wagner felt she could have predicted Target's rise and Kmart's fall years before they materialized, just by walking in the doors of the corporate headquarters of the two retail chains. Then vice-chairman of Estée Lauder, she visited them with a sales team in 1999 to discuss distribution of a new mass-market cosmetic label Lauder had acquired. Consider what a difference company appearances made:

- The Target building was bright, clean, and colorful. Senior executives were on hand to greet the Lauder delegation. People were welcoming, enthusiastic, and well prepared. The Target team members introduced themselves by describing their roles and points of pride in their work. Though Lauder was the supplier and Target the buyer, Target was "selling *us* on a relationship," Wagner said. "They wanted us to know the quality of their work. They were open to our ideas."
- Kmart headquarters was a forbidding fortress, austere outside, dirty and disheveled inside. A receptionist escorted the Lauder group to a dark conference room that held "two faceless people who looked depressed, with no water, and no offer of coffee," Wagner said. The visitors from Lauder felt dragged down by the

palpable absence of pride. Wagner remembered thinking, "This is not a place for us to do anything."

The contrast was clear, as each company sent signals about where it was heading. Target was on a winning streak, and the Target team's confidence helped them establish a relationship with a high-prestige supplier, reinforcing Target's strategy for winning with consumers. For the lethargic Kmart staff, failure was a self-fulfilling prophecy. By acting like losers in front of a supplier, they lost. Kmart declared bankruptcy in 2002. "Everything you do sends a message," Wagner liked to say.

PERSONAL CONFIDENCE AND NATIONAL INVESTMENT: THE CRICKET SAGA

Messages about confidence are sent at many levels. On the playing field, confidence is embodied in whether people feel they can count on themselves and count on other members of their team to do their part. In the locker room or behind the scenes, confidence stems from a reliance on leaders and the system itself—the structure of the larger organization—to provide resources and support that make it possible to play the game, and play it well. And further beyond, confidence on the part of investors (or customers, consumers, and fans) shapes their decisions about whether they will supply what is needed for success to continue—or not—into the future, including money, time, talent, attention, or loyalty. All of these levels are intertwined and reinforce one another. The confidence of fans shapes the emotions of players. The confidence of players shapes outcomes for investors, and sometimes for the stature of nations.

These connections are visible in the history of international cricket competitions.

Cricket is not a familiar sport to Americans, but it is tremendously important to the countries of the former British Empire that send teams to world cricket championships—Australia, Bangladesh, England, India, New Zealand, Pakistan, South Africa,

Sri Lanka, Zimbabwe, and a fourteen-country coalition from the West Indies. Like the New England Patriots at the U.S. football Super Bowl, cricket carries the weight of national attitudes and aspirations, and even national subsidies. Teams compete for the glory of their countries (and themselves) in competitions of three to six matches, each several days in length, or about twenty-five days of cricket.

Over the past two decades, there were two historically unparalleled winning streaks and one long losing streak in international cricket competitions. First the West Indies, then Australia dominated the game, while England, where the game was invented, languished near the bottom of the pile. In the West Indies, cricket was traditionally a game of the people, played anywhere there were young boys and sticks. This ensured a large talent pool, enthusiastic and committed fans, and cricket stars who became symbols of national pride. When the prime minister of Grenada—an idyllic but poverty-stricken island of 100,000 people—asked citizens to choose between a new hospital and a cricket stadium, they opted for the stadium, which cost about 10 percent of the country's gross domestic product. The prime minister won the next election in a landslide.

During the West Indies' winning streak, the team had strong leadership and discipline. Old hands mentored novices. Instead of glorifying one star bowler (bowlers are similar to pitchers in American baseball), the team tended to "share the wickets around" (equivalent to giving everyone a chance to get on base). Innovations, such as fast bowling, changed the game from gentlemanly to aggressive. Great players became tour managers or coaches, ensuring continuity. Legendary figures emerged, such as the bowler with a fractured left thumb who batted one-handed and bowled England out in a famous West Indies victory.

When the longtime West Indies captain was replaced by a parade of warring leaders less able to forge a coalition of fourteen countries, team spirit disintegrated, and the West Indies began its slide into cricket oblivion. Tougher international competition raised standards of play, but the growing popularity of basketball (courtesy of U.S. television) meant that cricket talent no longer emerged naturally from the grassroots. As the West Indies lost, they became a less popular team. They could not command high fees for touring matches, which meant less money for training new players, for the upkeep of grounds, and promoting the sport. Youngsters turned away from cricket.

The team once called a byword for professionalism, organization, fitness, and ruthlessness was now described by sportswriters as negligent, careless, and indifferent. Defeat led to defeatism. Instead of solving the problem, the team blamed administrators, administrators blamed the captain, and everyone blamed American television for corrupting the culture. Cricket's decline was seen as a metaphor for the region. In 1999 a journalist bemoaned the fact that the nations of the West Indies had shifted from cricket and bananas to relying on drugs and tourists.

Australia's rise started with the Australian Cricket Board's decision in 1984 to build a winning national team. Strong new leadership brought stability and innovative approaches to both game tactics and team organization. Once chosen, players were allowed to mature, rather than being cycled through, which helped build a cohesive team. To invest in younger players, the ACB founded the National Cricket Academy in 1987. The academy leveraged partnerships with football clubs and sports institutes to coach and mentor promising talent, offering scholarships to four-month programs, week-long targeted programs, and camps for younger players. As the number of world-class players increased, other countries sought Australians to help them create similar programs. The *Sydney Morning Herald* contrasted the sharp Australian team, "crackling like electricity whenever it takes the field," with languid England.

Winning made cricket more popular. Attendance at games increased, and money poured into the ACB from both turnstiles and sponsors, enabling increased investment in developing the game.

The Australians livened up the game through colorful World Series matches, which attracted corporate sponsors—a cricketing innovation. Good press increased cricket's attractiveness to youngsters, thus improving the pipeline. Australian cricket enjoyed a virtuous cycle of success.

Once-dominant England, in contrast, was on a two-decade losing streak. "Where and when did it all go wrong?" asked a columnist in *The Independent* in 1999. "How is it that [England], which invented almost every sport on the planet, is now rubbish? Why do we keep producing crap teams liable to get stuffed by almost any Johnny foreigner? At football, rugby and cricket, our three main team sports, England are currently also-rans, way down the world pecking-order." One answer was weak leadership—a high turnover of captains, who were discredited for poor form, poor results, and scandal in their public and private lives. Another was over-reliance on a few stars such as Geoffrey Boycott or Ian Botham (all-time best all-rounder in the modern game). Though cricket was a game that could not be won by one star player—length of matches alone precluded this—England failed to focus on building a cohesive team.

As losses mounted, cricket was watched and played by a smaller and less representative portion of the British population than in its heyday. It was a game of the elite and became more so as cash-strapped local authorities sold off public and school cricket fields, reducing the pool of potential cricketers. As other nations invested in young talent and improved play, England fell behind, perhaps another sign of post-imperial malaise.

Those with the power to change the situation denied the magnitude of the problem, saying "it's just one bad game." Officials complained that Australia had destroyed the game through its fast bowling and lobbied for regulation against such innovations. The public blamed umpires' bad decisions. Batters blamed bowlers and vice versa. Some players blamed other countries for "raising their game when they play England." (How jolly unfair of them!) The media attacked the team rather than cheering it on, using words such as "dark night," "acute anguish," "drearily predictable," or "capitulation." Expectations of failure made failure more likely.

Once set in motion, streaks have a way of hardening. But, as the Australian case demonstrates, they can be turned around, if leaders build a foundation for confidence.

TAKING CONFIDENCE SKY-HIGH

To shift a cycle from decline to success, leaders must restore people's confidence in the system, in the organization, in the group, and in themselves.

Between 1983 and 1994, Continental Airlines had been on a major losing streak that nearly killed it. The streak started with its acquisition by Frank Lorenzo (whom Barbara Walters once called the "most hated man in America"). It featured a decade of deteriorating customer service, hostile labor relations, financial losses every year after 1986, two bankruptcies, and a parade of ten CEOs. Continental was generally at the bottom of its league (major U.S.-based carriers with international service). A culture of blame, disrespect, and turf protection further undermined confidence.

In 1994, Gordon Bethune was named CEO and began the turnaround that transformed the Continental team from losers to winners—a story I tell in detail in Chapter 8. Under Bethune (who was still CEO ten years later), Continental won numerous awards for customer service and workplace excellence. It outperformed its competitors to remain on top of its league even during one of the worst periods in the industry, when no one could make any money (and the definition of success was losing less than anyone else).

"An airline is the biggest team sport there is," Bethune was fond of saying. The value of renewed confidence helped Continental win the game that everyone else lost—the power blackout I mentioned at the beginning of this chapter.

On August 14, 2003, at 4:06 p.m. Eastern Daylight Time, the worst blackout in American history began with a power surge near Akron, Ohio. Within seven minutes more than 263 power plants in the Northeast power grid went down, which cut off electricity to 50 million people in eight states and Canada. Cleveland and Detroit went completely dark. The blackout eventually caused an estimated $6 billion in economic and other losses. Airports suffered serious disruptions, and airlines absorbed the high costs of canceled flights and payments to stranded passengers. Because its Newark and Cleveland hubs lost power, analysts imagined that Continental would suffer some of the most severe losses.

The Continental team defied expectations. They made both money and friends. Continental canceled only thirty flights, compared with Northwest's 216 and American's 141. Continental canceled only fifteen flights on August 15 while American cancelled another 182. On August 15 and 16, Continental was the only major airline running in the New York City area. Its crews flew several special sections to accommodate customers and to reposition aircraft. For the two days after the blackout, Continental's gross revenues were $4.34 million above normal forecasts.

Initially, no one knew what was happening—just that there was a massive blackout of unknown origin, and power outages were cascading. Within fifteen minutes of the first outages, the Continental team was in action, even before news bulletins were issued. No one waited to be told what to do; they felt empowered to take initiative and believed their extra efforts would pay off. They trusted one another to do the right thing.

Larry Kellner, Continental's president, was in his nineteenth-floor office at Continental headquarters in downtown Houston when the phone rang, shortly before 4:30 p.m. Eastern time, 3:30 p.m. in Houston. The caller was Jay Salter, who ran systems control. Salter was calling from the systems operations coordination center (SOCC) on the thirteenth floor, the nerve center of the airline. Salter rattled off a list of cities served by Continental that had suffered power outages. Kellner clicked onto the *New York Times* website and then glanced at CNN, which was running on a television set in his office. Nothing about power failures.

A few minutes later, Salter called back with an update. Then

Charles Scully, hub vice-president for Newark Liberty Airport, called to inform Kellner that the airport people wanted to keep the flights moving. They were talking with the Transportation Security Administration (TSA) about how to keep running passengers through security. Martin Hand called from California about the reservations centers; he had been on the phone to stop people from going home, as they would be needed for the anticipated high volume of calls. There was an update from the marketing group, which had capped all flights to avoid problems stemming from the usual practice of overbooking. Dante Marzetta, senior vice-president of airport services, responsible for airports worldwide, happened to be at headquarters and walked into Kellner's office to confer.

Deborah McCoy was on a flight to Louisville, Kentucky, when the blackout began. A pilot and now senior vice-president of flight operations, she was responsible for approximately 5,200 pilots and more than 9,600 flight attendants, as well as in-flight functions related to more than 2,200 daily departures reaching 223 airports on five continents. When she landed, there was a message on her cell phone from the duty director on shift at the SOCC. She spoke with Jay Salter and members of the tactical group about making sure that the planes en route could continue. There was backup power in Newark, and the weather was good, meaning that special devices were not required on the ground. Once that decision was made, the question was how to successfully complete the flights. They needed the commitment of air traffic control. The primary issue was safety. "The pilots are on the scene and empowered; they will tell us what they can and can't do," McCoy said.

Kellner, McCoy, and Salter were the switchboards through which information passed. But callers weren't asking permission, they were indicating what they had done. "They bounced ideas off me, they updated me," McCoy said. "I don't think I would have been doing anything any differently if I had been in the office. I did not have to be down on the field managing, because the people out there knew what they were doing."

There was no panic, just calm, steady professionalism. "No one was worrying. Everyone knew their job and went to work. And they had confidence that everyone else knew their job," Kellner said. "They knew they could count on everyone else," echoed Deborah Larza, vice-president of airport service operations.

Newark and Cleveland crews pushed aircraft back, loaded them, and pulled people off, all without power. In Cleveland the power stayed out until 7:30 a.m. the next day. This meant no lights, computer access, or baggage carousels. Employees used daylight through windows in the concourses until sundown, and after dark they used ingenuity to figure out how to get the flights to move. They called Houston on cell phones for passenger information. All but one of the forty-five flight attendants scheduled to check in at Cleveland on August 15 made it to the airport that morning—choosing not to take a perfect excuse to avoid work. McCoy stayed on her cell phone at thirty-minute intervals through midnight to monitor operations. At headquarters, Kellner's phone-call volume was back to normal within two hours of the first power outage, and he could turn his attention to business opportunities, such as running extra sections for stranded New York and New Jersey passengers.

Years of investment in a culture of collaboration, communication, responsibility, and initiative produced the confidence that made Continental a winner. (Later in the book I'll show how this was accomplished.) Continental's culture was as resolutely upbeat in the Gordon Bethune years as it had been depressingly downbeat in the previous era. People who had once thought failure was inevitable now thought success was unstoppable. Even in a disaster.

FROM LOSERS' CURSE TO WINNERS' CONFIDENCE: INVESTIGATING CYCLES, STREAKS, AND TURNAROUNDS

Confidence underlies the performance of individuals, teams, businesses, schools, economies, and nations. The fundamental task of leaders is to develop confidence in advance of victory, in order to attract the investments that make victory possible—money, talent, support, loyalty, attention, effort, or people's best thinking.

I am an expert on leadership, innovation, transformation, and change. I have devoted my career to understanding cycles of advantage and disadvantage: the dynamic interplay of situation, behavior, attitude, system performance, and results. For example, I have explored how opportunity shapes ambition and explains differences in the career paths of men and women; why powerlessness corrupts and empowerment is vital to high performance; how a culture of pride differs from a culture of mediocrity in encouraging or stifling innovation; and how strategies determine effectiveness in dealing with new threats and opportunities.

In *Confidence*, I have set out to explain the culture of success or failure, why winning streaks and losing streaks perpetuate themselves, and how to shift the dynamics of decline to a cycle of success. I took a broad and deep look in many realms and in many kinds of competitions to find the most revealing examples and identify universal principles. My stories and lessons are based on well over 300 original interviews, two surveys with 2,754 responses, firsthand observations, and unusual insider access to leaders and organizations in North America, Europe, Asia, Australia, South Africa, and elsewhere around the world.

My research team and I were on the spot in boardrooms, conference rooms, locker rooms, classrooms, emergency rooms, stadiums, fields, factories, and back offices to see the action behind the scenes. We captured the details of particular episodes or games—a key decision or meeting, a fumble on the field, a winning play, a successful project—and we also tapped people with long historical memories to take us through the ups and downs of booms, busts, and turnarounds over long periods of time. I was deliberately seeking variety, to find the examples that would best represent the nature of confidence for individuals, teams, and even countries.

For prominent international companies such as Gillette, which carries one of the world's most respected brand names, I traveled to China, Singapore, and spots in Europe to meet with people on the ground, as well as spending time with CEO Jim Kilts and top executives at American headquarters; our reach extended to the

Middle East and Latin America. In London, I went inside the BBC's cultural turnaround and subsequent political events. We were in California and Minnesota with Seagate, a leading manufacturer of hard-disk drives for personal computers; in Germany with a Siemens subsidiary; and around the international system with Continental Airlines. I looked at a General Electric division that exemplified the struggle to achieve excellence, and I watched the sad decline of other organizations that I keep anonymous. Some of the most inspiring stories I encountered were also the most exotic. Akin Öngör, a former Turkish national basketball player, led Garanti Bank, once a backwater financial institution in Istanbul, to become *Euromoney* magazine's "best small bank in the world."

In health care, I found innovations with the potential to reverse a decade of pessimism about decline in the U.S. health-care system. In Washington, D.C., Dr. Craig Feied and Dr. Mark Smith transformed the emergency department at Washington Hospital Center from the city's worst to the city's best. Their Insight system, a tool that empowers physicians through information, proved so valuable in the aftermath of 9/11 and the subsequent anthrax scare in Washington that Dr. Feied was asked to run major portions of the U.S. public health data base, invaluable for tracking viral epidemics. I looked at the problems of low-performing public primary and secondary schools, and how leaders in New Jersey, Tennessee, and elsewhere had turned around inner-city schools, some of them using tools developed by IBM and my own partnership with IBM's Reinventing Education initiative. I returned from these visits more optimistic about the potential to develop leadership that can shift the dynamics of low-performing schools from decline to success.

The same principles of leadership to restore confidence can work for a whole country. I traveled to South Africa to begin an exploration of how former president Nelson Mandela had turned around a cycle of decline and shaped a culture of hope in a place that might otherwise have sunk into despair—or worse. I learned about the country from the ground up through young "Clinton Democracy Fellows" who came from South Africa to learn from American social entrepreneurs. Euvin Naidoo, a native of Johannesburg and a Harvard MBA, later collaborated with me in examining Mandela's accomplishments.

To put winning streaks, losing streaks, and turnaround leadership into sharper relief, I turned to sports—professional and college teams in baseball, basketball, football (American-style), soccer, hockey, and cricket. Sports is an ideal realm in which to see confidence at work, in the games themselves and in the businesses that surround them.

In the sports world alone, we conducted more than sixty-five interviews focused on twenty-four major professional and college teams, studied their games and statistics, and compiled dossiers on twenty others across a deliberately varied range of sports. We chose three kinds of teams: those with long unbroken winning streaks, those with long unbroken losing streaks, and those that had successfully turned around a pattern of losing. This took us to interviews with the Chicago Cubs, the Boston Red Sox, the Montreal Expos, and the Oakland Athletics in Major League Baseball; the Boston Celtics, the Memphis Grizzlies, and the Dallas Mavericks in professional basketball; the Philadelphia Eagles and the New England Patriots in professional football; the Anaheim Mighty Ducks in professional hockey. But some of the best and most revealing sports stories came from college teams, including two perpetually winning women's teams—the University of Connecticut women's basketball team and the University of North Carolina women's soccer team—and coaches such as Larry Coker (Miami), Anson Dorrance (North Carolina), and Mike Krzyzewski (Duke's "Coach K"). We reached back in history in a few cases to look at the forces involved in famous streaks of the past, and we included one high school football team, De La Salle, a Christian Brothers school in California, because it has won every single game for twelve years, with only a handful of losses for the ten years before that—a feat for the record books.

To augment the 300-plus interviews and make sure that my ideas applied across an even wider number of organizations and teams, I conducted two surveys in May 2003. More than 1,243 companies in a range of industries responded to my online survey about their corporate cultures and financial results during the economic down-turn of 2001–3. By separating out those companies that were solid "winners" (self-reported revenues and profit growth during this pe-riod, stronger position vis-à-vis competitors, and a position at the top of the industry) from solid "losers" (with the opposite record), I could compare the subset of 183 companies on a clear success cycle with the 92 firmly in decline. My second online survey included 1,511 high school sports coaches and athletes reporting about the behavior and performance of their teams. Using a similar method, I compared the "winners"—the 952 teams that always or generally won their games in the current season—with the 250 that always or generally lost. All of the differences between winning streaks and losing streaks on both surveys confirmed my developing picture of the behaviors and structures that build or undermine confidence.

SUPPORTING SUCCESS:
SECRETS OF WALKING ON WATER

"Confidence is what it's all about," comedian Chris Tucker said to me at a summer gathering on Martha's Vineyard, when he heard about my project. He meant his own self-confidence: striding out onto the stage with head held high, ready to face large audiences directly, certain he could win them over with his first words, posi-tive that he could handle hecklers or microphone failures. I learned that he went out alone only in the strictest technical sense. Backing him up were his brother, his manager, his track record, positive media coverage, and a big fan network.

Even for individuals who rise or fall on the strength of their own talent, what happens backstage in the boardroom, the conference room, or the locker room builds or undermines the confidence to perform. And the results of each performance make that surround-ing system stronger or weaker, increasing or decreasing confidence at many other levels.

Success derives from the broader context that surrounds the

players. Individual players must cross a threshold of talent, whether that talent is a genius for comedy, natural athletic ability, or mental dexterity. But continuing success is not a matter of raw talent. Winning on the playing field is influenced heavily by what goes on off the field—the nature of the system to attract people, develop people, build bonds among team members, gather external support, and do all the other behind-the-scenes work, before and after each game, before and after each season. Powerful historical, economic, and organizational forces accumulate to shape the likelihood of winning the game.

Confidence is not just in people's heads. There are certainly differences between individuals in character, mood, and interpretation of situations. The heroes of the Continental blackout victory, such as Deborah McCoy, Larry Kellner, and Gordon Bethune, seem to be positive, upbeat, optimistic people. But confidence is not an artificial mental construct, solely dependent on what people decide to believe; it reflects reasonable reactions to circumstances. People are caught in cycles, and they interpret events based on what they see happening, on how they are treated by others around them. Winning and losing are not just functions of the talents of the people individually, and they cannot be predicted by adding up individuals' IQs or grade-point averages or years of advanced schooling. The momentum of the systems people are in shapes a culture that shapes perceptions that shapes the confidence to invest—or not.

One of my favorite corporate expressions describes people with high potential who are destined to gain the top positions. They are called "water walkers." I first heard this expression years ago in the leadership development group of one of the world's largest companies. Every company seemed to have its own term for high-potential employees, but "water walkers" resonated with me. Water walkers are the ones assumed to have extraordinary talent, enabling them to perform miracles (like walking on water). They are sure bets for success, so other people fall in line behind them, hoping to follow in their footsteps.

The identification of water walkers is well understood in many realms; Bill Clinton, for example, was described early in his career as a future American president. The characteristics and achievements of water walkers are the subject of long conversations, as other people seek to emulate them and companies seek to duplicate them. It is assumed that their talent alone is responsible for success.

However, I remember, at one meeting in New York, a discussion about whether some of the big corporation's emerging leaders had become too arrogant. Suddenly there was a profound insight from a senior executive: "The problem with water walkers," he said, "is that they forget that there are stones holding them up when they walk across the water."

Every water walker needs a few stones. Rocks give people a solid place to stand. When supported by a firm foundation, people can indeed keep moving on a positive path, heading from victory to victory. When people can rely on themselves and one another to be accountable, to collaborate, and to take initiative, they can perform extraordinary feats. These lessons are relevant for leading teams, businesses, countries, and life.

2

Winning Streaks: The Cycle of Success

It's a very simple dynamic that you're working under. Losing begets losing, winning begets winning. Players want to be on winning teams. They want to be champions. So as you win, things come together. Your chemistry becomes better. Your team relationships are better. It's hard to have all this great chemistry and wonderful interpersonal relationships when you're losing fifteen out of twenty games, when your team is year after year out of the playoffs and getting drubbed and is ridiculed by the fans and your local media. So when things come around, you start to win, and you start to receive more media attention, the crowds are bigger, then all those interpersonal dynamics and chemistry facets of the team become enhanced.

—*Chris Wallace, general manager, Boston Celtics*

AKIN ÖNGÖR LEARNED ABOUT WINNING AT BANKING FROM WINNING AT BASKETBALL. A FORMER STAR ON TURKEY'S NATIONAL TEAM, ÖNGÖR WORKED FOR SEVERAL MULTINATIONAL COMPANIES BEfore serving as CEO of Garanti Bank from 1991 to 2000. "Sports are important for ideas, motivation, and values," he explained to me in Istanbul, in a luxury hotel near the Bosphorus during a break in a seminar. "Basketball teaches teamwork."

Istanbul was an unlikely setting for a company eventually named the world's best small bank (by *Euromoney*) and one of Europe's fifty most respected companies of any kind (by the *Financial Times*). Only a few years before Öngör arrived, timid employees routed customers to competing banks rather than risk punishment for errors in complicated transactions; bells rang at noon for lunch and at 6:00 p.m. to send everyone home; and a former CEO's mail was delivered not to his office but to a local bar he frequented across the street.

Öngör led a significant winning streak. During his tenure, Garanti was the fastest-growing of Turkey's four major private banks. Market capitalization soared from $150 million to $5 billion. Annual profits grew from $85 million to $500 million without increasing the number of branches, while income per branch increased tenfold, from $258,000 to $2 million. Productivity skyrocketed from $15,000 to $110,000 per employee. Innovation flourished, including the first debit cards for lower-income Turks and extensive Internet banking. Garanti expanded to Luxembourg, the Netherlands, Russia, and beyond.

Öngör attributed success to good people, good systems, and the harmony to perform under pressure. The first step was assembling the right team and getting them to play together. With human resources head Saide Kuzeyli, Öngör established mandatory communication seminars for management, "to build an understanding of 'we,' " he said. "We are all together a team, we share the glory and the pain. There's not 'I,' 'they,' 'them.' The leader's job is to harmonize the people. We would have dinners together, or an offsite meeting, just to brainstorm and let everyone say whatever they want to say, but not to hurt each other." People who couldn't play the new game were helped to learn or were replaced. Under Kuzeyli, training days per employee grew eightfold. She was also proud that the number of women employees increased to 50 percent.

"Relax under pressure" was one of Öngör's basketball lessons. The 1991 Gulf War crisis had hardly affected Garanti, but drastic devaluation of Turkey's currency in 1994 caused losses at many branches whose customers held foreign exchange loans. "People started to blame each other, and Mr. Öngör stopped them," Kuzeyli said. Garanti's leaders supported rather than reprimanded managers in losing branches. One manager recalled, "Our top management never panicked. They backed us and helped us in getting through this crisis. This confidence was so valuable."

"In basketball, sometimes you're back twenty points in a game, but you never give up. Sometimes it's impossible to win, but you never give up," Öngör emphasized. "You relax under this pressure, you try to encourage them. Rather than focus on the losses, what is the next step that we can do to take advantage of this environment?" Garanti acquired a failing bank, a move widely viewed as having helped to save the national banking industry, which added to Garanti's prestige, and, in another virtuous circle of success, helped Garanti attract more investment and top recruits, which fueled further wins. By the end of 1994, Garanti had continued its streak of annual profit increases.

Öngör held large all-employee forums, modeled after General Electric (one of his earlier employers). At a twelve-hour session in Ankara in 1999, Öngör heard hundreds of proposals. A manager argued that the bank should provide leadership in creating a healthy, smoke-free work environment. Although many employees smoked (Turkey was a cigarette capital), 75 percent of attendees approved the motion. A female trainee proposed allowing women to wear trousers, which was also approved. Such dialogues taught people to believe in their ideas, however small. Energy and initiative increased everywhere, further fueling the winning streak.

Ambitious "quantum leap" projects included forming new teams to win business, armed with computerized tools to track their own performance. By 1997, 286 portfolio teams worked from 143 branches, each responsible for 120 commercial customers, visiting an average of three customers or prospects a day. The number of customers doubled in the first year alone.

Winning made it easier to attract talent. Garanti received more than 10,000 applications a year for about 100 vacancies (lower odds than getting into Harvard, I thought, as Kuzeyli related the statistics on a visit to my Harvard office). Talent was applauded. When Garanti's financial safety rating was raised from C to A by an international agency (a first for Turkey), the bank sent a leaflet with a big bold *A* to all employees, along with a letter from Öngör urging them to share the glory with their spouses: "Show them that they should be proud of you, because you got 'A' in banking."

"I don't want the star alone, I want the star in the team," he declared. "My model is the Dream Team in American basketball. Each one is a fantastic star, but they operate very well as a team."

TALENT AND THE TEAM: LEVELS OF CONFIDENCE

At the beginning of every winning streak is a story with elements like that of Garanti Bank. Leaders have created a foundation for confidence that permits unexpected people to achieve high levels of performance, and to do it as part of a successful team. Each time the team or the organization wins a victory, support for confidence is increased. An occasional win turns into a long winning streak.

Winning begets winning, because it produces confidence at four levels.

Self-confidence: an emotional climate of high expectations

Winning feels good, and good moods are contagious. Success makes it easier to view events in a positive light, to generate optimism. It produces energy and promotes morale. It is easier to aim high and expect to reach the target. It is easier to find the energy to work hard because it looks as if the hard work will pay off. These attitudes reinforce top performance.

Confidence in one another: positive, supportive, team-oriented behavior

Winning makes people feel more engaged with their tasks and with one another. It makes people like one another more, want to spend more time together, feel more generous, and therefore want to practice, prepare, and help one another succeed. It breeds respect, which then makes people more willing to take responsibility and admit mistakes, because they feel secure. These behaviors make it more likely that problems will be caught and solved, because people share information, take responsibility and admit mistakes, pull together and find solutions.

Confidence in the system: organizational structures and routines reinforcing accountability, collaboration, and innovation

Winning makes it likely to turn informal tendencies into formal traditions, by building winners' habits of responsibility, teamwork, and initiative into routines, processes, and practices that encourage and perpetuate them. It makes it more likely that leaders will remain in place so that there can be continuity of strategy and approach, institutionalizing systems for producing winners' behavior. Winning provides the resources for investing in training and tools to ensure that people can be responsible members of the team. This makes it possible to transmit problem-solving and team-enhancing behavior to new people and, thus, to keep the winning streak going.

External confidence: a network to provide resources

Winning makes it easier to attract financial backers, loyal customers, enthusiastic fans, talented recruits, media attention, opinion leader support, and political goodwill. Continuing to win stimulates this network to grow in size, scope, and magnitude of investment. Having a flow of valuable resources from the network makes it easier to invest internally in conditions associated with victory, including facilities and staff. And knowledge on the part of the team that there is external support for winning circles back to fuel positive expectations, further strengthening the cycle of success.

At each level—emotional, behavioral, organizational, environmental—confidence both feeds winning and feeds off of it. Momentum builds because each success in a sequence of successes makes it easier to generate self-confidence, confidence in colleagues, confidence in the system, and investor confidence. All those aspects of confidence converge to prepare the people who must deliver victory on the field, even if the team is a different set of people every year. Winning becomes an ingrained tradition, embedded in the culture and supported by powerful external networks, even if individual talent comes and goes.

That is how leading companies such as General Electric, Toyota, Wal-Mart, and IBM, or leading universities such as Oxford, Yale, and Harvard succeed year after year, and how some of the historic winners in professional sports created dynasties like that of the New York Yankees. Consider the impressive records of three of the most successful sports teams I encountered in my research:

- From its beginning in 1979 through this past 2003 season, the University of North Carolina women's soccer team, the Tar Heels, had a record of 559 wins, 25 losses, and 15 ties. Successive teams won 18 national championships and enjoyed two streaks of over 100 undefeated games. In 1996, *Fortune* magazine named the North Carolina women's soccer program to a list of seven high-performance groups, along with the U.S. Navy SEALS and Massachusetts General Hospital's trauma unit.
- Between 1984, when a turnaround began, through the spring of 2003, the University of Connecticut women's basketball team, the Huskies, won 501 games and lost 99—but 39 of those losses were in the early years. Connecticut won 10 Big East conference championships and, between 2001 and 2003, enjoyed a 70-game unbroken winning streak. The team won the 2004 national championship.
- For twenty years, starting in 1983, the University of Miami Hurricanes was one of three teams that dominated college football, earning five national championships. They were ranked number one or number two in the nation every year between 2000 and 2003, holding the NCAA (National Collegiate Athletic Association) record for a home-game winning streak of 58 undefeated

games between 1985 and 1994. Between 2000 and 2002, the Hurricanes had 34 straight wins.

What makes these streaks even more dramatic and attention-worthy is that winning is hard work. Really hard work. Losing is so much easier. Winners may have the advantage of multiple layers of confidence as they go into each game, but winning is still not guaranteed. Regardless of what happened in the last game and how it was won, people must walk out onto the playing field—again—and deliver top performance—again. It's possible to win once or a few times because of lucky breaks or competitors' mistakes. It's sometimes possible to coast for a while. But without the next touchdown pass, the next hit film, the next product innovation, or just continued flawless execution, momentum slows, and it's impossible to keep winning. Teams or organizations on winning streaks get a boost, but they cannot take winning for granted.

That is made clear by looking at all the factors surrounding one big game of one of my long-term sports winners—Connecticut versus Duke in February 2003.

FROM PRAYING TO WIN TO EXPECTING TO WIN

At the start of the 2002–3 season, the Duke University women's basketball team, the Blue Devils, was ranked nationally as the number-one U.S. team. Head coach Gail Goestenkors told us how expectations had grown in her ten years working with the team, and how each successive winning season took confidence up a notch. Over the years, she said, the Duke Blue Devils went from "praying to win, to hoping to win, to knowing they could win, to expecting to win."

And win they did—for the most part. But winners become eligible to play against formidable competition. So it was actually a Duke *loss* that players on a rival team remember best, as one of their best wins as a team and a powerful demonstration of their winners' habits. Members of the University of Connecticut women's basketball team told us about defeating Duke on February 1, 2003, to illustrate how they win against even the toughest competition. The story of their victory over Duke encapsulates the high expectations of self and others that make it possible for people to rise to the highest standards.

Roots of Connecticut's Confidence

The Connecticut Huskies that beat Duke 77–65 on the Blue Devils' home court that winter Saturday was the latest collective incarnation of a sports dynasty built by head coach Geno Auriemma and associate head coach Christine Dailey. The Connecticut Huskies had had ten losing seasons in the eleven years prior to Auriemma's and Dailey's arrival in 1984, and there had been so little interest in women's basketball that only one set of aluminum bleachers was needed for home games. Officials recalled attendance topping out at fifty—if the janitors were enticed to come. But in 1984 the university promised Auriemma the resources of a broad-based athletic program, and he in turn committed to produce a top women's basketball program. As the team started winning, the school became even more interested in investing resources to continue building the foundation for success. By 1991 the Huskies made the prestigious NCAA Final Four, and a luxurious new facility opened for basketball.

Fans became devoted to the Huskies. From 1997 on, all home games were sold out in advance—more than ninety straight games. Connecticut topped attendance records in its sport. No other women's basketball team came close to getting as much attention as was showered on the Huskies. They even attracted their own pack of seven full-time beat reporters, nicknamed the Horde. Every game was broadcast on a high-wattage radio station and televised live starting in 1995, either on national network or cable channels; Connecticut Public Television paid $1 million a year for the privilege and received some of the highest public TV ratings in the U.S. "Husky Nan" (Nancy Pfaff of Wallingford, Connecticut) ran a website and an Internet chat room about the Huskies, with, 1,300 registered users. Players were stopped for autographs on the street.

"We're like a traveling circus. People want to see us," Sue Bird, a junior guard in 2001, told reporters.

This translated not just into enthusiasm—a positive emotional climate—but into dollars. Many women's programs generated no revenues at all, and when they did, they couldn't make a profit. In 2001 only six NCAA (National Collegiate Athletic Association) Division I women's basketball programs (a mere 5 percent of the total) reported operating at a profit (with an average of just $510,000). The Huskies were off the scale, generating $4 million in profits in 2001. The team traveled by chartered airplane and stayed in the same upscale hotels as men's teams. In 2003, new donors to the Connecticut athletic program paid up to $50,000 for four season tickets to the women's games. No one else came close to numbers like these. Because of the Huskies, Connecticut was slated to get a professional WNBA (Women's National Basketball Association) team, the first in an area without a men's NBA (National Basketball Association) team.

A TEAM BETTER THAN ITS TALENT

All these winners' advantages filtered down to the team in the form of signals about the high expectations the wider world held for the Huskies. Of course, individual players still had to play winning basketball. The Huskies that went out on the court at Duke's home arena on February 1, 2003, to play the number-one-ranked Blue Devils had to be able to play to win, and that wasn't at all a slam dunk.

The 2002–3 Huskies had nowhere near the best talent in the country. The previous year's graduating seniors were snatched by the WNBA, as draft picks number one, two, four, and six. But the '02–'03 team lacked speed, size, and experience, having lost those star seniors and added many freshmen newcomers. A low preseason ranking out of the top ten made them feel "disrespected" compared with their predecessors. They even lost an exhibition game (but it didn't count against the streak). No one outside of the Huskies family expected much, and they had to decide whether to use that as an excuse to be mediocre, or rise to the occasion and show that they deserved to bear the proud name of the team.

"People were doubting us a lot this season, and nobody thought that we could beat them on their home court," said Ashley Battle, a junior guard on that team. No one, that is, except Auriemma, Dailey, and the players. Choosing to live by their own expectations, instead of by what the media expected, was a key to their success. "If you have expectations that are higher than everyone else's, you're more likely to meet those expectations," team member Ann Strother said. "We expect great things out of each other whenever we put on the uniform," teammate Maria Conlon agreed.

Auriemma often said that too many people who coach women don't demand enough from them, but he expected his recruits to play at a high level immediately. He expected mental and physical toughness. Practices were more intense and difficult than the hardest games; sometimes he would set up practice games of five against eight. Auriemma felt that "the way you feel good about yourself is when somebody forces you to do something you didn't think you could do." Though Connecticut's winning tradition was a spur to high performance, Auriemma told them to forget the streak, and just focus on playing the game.

However limited the '02–'03 team was individually, they became winners collectively. Auriemma likened his women's team (without recognizing the gender irony) to "a band of brothers, to the troops fighting in Iraq," saying that how prepared they were made a difference in survival, as though teammates' lives depended on everyone taking responsibility for doing their jobs and covering all the details.

One thing the '02–'03 team had going into the Duke game was tremendous chemistry between the players, a feeling that they liked and respected one another. Creating that chemistry had been a challenge, because in addition to the fact that there were so many newcomers who didn't know one another very well, the team was unusually diverse in terms of backgrounds and personalities. Two of the freshmen had been on rival teams in high school and had to overcome mutual antagonism. But a summer of practice in a college town with not much else to do forged friendships over pickup games. Team events to let off steam encouraged bonding. And watching one another master the challenges of unrelenting practices raised respect, which turned into the desire to draw closer, which turned into high performance.

Practice strategy adjusted to team composition. Players felt respected for their strengths, not trashed for their weaknesses. Players knew that they lacked speed, so they looked for other tactics that worked to their advantage. Maria Conlon said that they focused on finding their own identity and roles, rather than on trying to fill the shoes of last year's team. Then, as the season opened and the team started winning, respect and solidarity grew exponentially. Ashley Battle felt that the Huskies' ability to win came from knowing one another off the court, "because we know each other's tendencies, we know where we like the ball, we know what ticks each other off." Winning made team members want to be together even more of the time.

The word most often used to describe the team was "unselfish." Auriemma's standards reinforced this. There were no individual names on the backs of uniforms, and no prima donna behavior. Also no headbands, no visible tattoos, no headphones in public, no backward baseball caps, no shirts untucked even in practice. The coach was known to bench even star players if they failed to give their maximum effort in practice. In his remarks to the media, he downplayed the stars and talked up the whole team. He didn't want to talk about the obvious things like how much someone scored but preferred to mention the unseen things that helped win the game, such as a rebound that somebody grabbed at a crucial time. It was those little things on the part of everyone that separated a win from a loss.

Confidence in the team was boosted by a victory over Boston College early in the season, to which every player contributed. The players saw they could count on one another. If an experienced player was injured, as Nicole Wolfe was, somebody else stepped up.

If the star shooter, Diana Taurasi, didn't have a great game, others filled the gap. The players never knew who was going to have the big game that night. So the whole team had to be ready.

By the time they went into the Duke game, the players had taken initiative to ensure that they were well prepared. Ashley Battle reported, "Our coaches give us scouting reports, and we'll go over what they run and how we should defend. A lot of it comes from us, too. We'll talk about the game or how we should defend someone, or if they do this, what should we do. Just a nice little game plan within ourselves in addition to what our coaches have already told us."

Calm and Confident: Playing Under Pressure

The Huskies' mood in the Duke visitors' locker room before the game was calm and confident, despite Duke's number-one ranking. Because they had practiced in basically the same way as for any game, they could trust the routine and one another. Confidence was high, and it was contagious. "Going into the Duke game we were having awesome practices," Battle said, "and usually how we practice is how we play in a game. We knew we were going to beat them. It was in everyone's eyes, and everyone was on the same page."

They walked onto the court that day like winners, just as Auriemma had taught them. "Look them in the eye. Be the first out there waiting at half-court when it's time to start the game. Show them how ready we are. Have a really good warm-up. Teams are already intimidated playing Connecticut, and they watch what we do in warm-ups. We confirm all their fears by being on top of every shot, every pass, every rebound."

Duke was having one of its first sellouts for a women's basketball home game. For the Huskies, this was business as usual, but they thought the Duke team was not accustomed to the pressure of such a big crowd and so much media attention. (That's exactly what the Duke coaches told us later about that game, when explaining why they lost.) The Connecticut strategy echoed the Akin Öngör principle "relax under pressure": stay calm, take an early lead, and increase the pressure on Duke. For the first half, it seemed to be working. Diana Taurasi made three three-point shots right off the bat. Connecticut took a lead that swelled to 28 points.

Then the referees called a technical foul against Auriemma at the start of the second half. The Duke crowd got so enthused that the floor was literally shaking. The Blue Devils started picking up. Now the pressure was on the Huskies. "You feel like you're in a car wash," Auriemma said. "Everything's happening around you, and you have no idea where to find a handle."

There were two dangers at that point. First, the team could panic and forget the drills, forget the plan. Ashley Battle, the junior guard, said they knew how to avoid that trap. "You've got to relax a little bit because you can't get really anxious because that's when you start making mistakes. We'll come out victorious if we keep to our game plan." The second danger was that people would play at such a high level that they would run out of steam. But the players knew how to encourage and count on one another. They looked one another in the eye during time-outs and said they'd win. Those looks at one another must have been reassuring. "It wasn't like one person just stood out," Battle observed. "I think a group of people played really well at the right time." Later, when the team returned to the locker room after the Huskies' victory, they told Auriemma they had known they would win.

Twenty minutes into the game, one of the Duke coaches started to think Connecticut could win, too. "They were very confident," La Vonda Wagner, a Duke assistant coach, explained to us. "They were very sure about what they needed to do, because they've been there many, many times before, whereas our team was not real sure about themselves. In the first twenty minutes, our players did not want to make mistakes, and all they did was make mistake after mistake after mistake."

What made the Connecticut players so confident? After all, the match was Best versus Best. Duke was a formidable competitor, well-led by coach Gail Goestenkors and known for its talent and teamwork, but winning was a more recent habit. Each Connecticut Husky had a potential edge as she walked out onto the court, from the emotional and behavioral advantages that surround a long-term cycle of success. Let's look at this level of confidence first.

GREAT EXPECTATIONS:
EMOTIONAL CLIMATE AND SELF-CONFIDENCE

The Connecticut-Duke game provides an example of a clear and well-documented relationship between expectations and performance that is at the heart of self-confidence. People who believe in themselves are likely to try harder and longer, thus increasing their chances of eventual success. But it is also true that causality can run in the opposite direction, and might even be more powerful in that situation: People who succeed are more likely to believe that their efforts in the future will pay off.

Expectations about the likelihood of eventual success determine the amount of effort people are willing to put in. Those who are convinced that they can be successful in carrying out the actions required for a successful outcome—who have "self-efficacy"—are likely to try harder and to persist longer when they face obstacles. Consider this scientific test of athletes' endurance: Athletes engaged in a leg-stretching contest were told that they had lost the first round either to a varsity track athlete or to someone with a knee injury. They tried harder in future rounds (stretching their leg farther) if they thought they were losing to strong competition (which made them feel they still had the potential to win) than if they thought they had been beaten by an injured player (which made them feel like losers).

Athletes and coaches, entertainers and professionals, know the value of positive "self-talk"—those silent pep talks in the head that keep spirits up and encourage peak performance. Top performers get good at screening out messages that could interfere with their internal pep talk. They concentrate on the task at hand and shut their ears, literally and mentally, to anything else. This is a great deal easier to do when the messages from other people are positive, as there is less danger when the inevitable leak occurs, and external messages penetrate. The experience of winning makes positive self-talk more credible.

A great deal of self-talk is undoubtedly instant replays of others'-talk. The voices in one's head are louder when the people piped in are in a position to give or withhold approval. For example, if teachers think students are in a top group (even if they were put there randomly), and thus treat them like high achievers, their performance improves—a self-fulfilling prophecy known as the Pygmalion Effect. When bosses assume anyone hired by their organization must be awfully good to get through the hiring process, even if the personnel department was asleep at the switch or desperate to meet recruitment quotas that day, they hold higher expectations and get higher performance. When coaches set high expectations even for less talented players, as Geno Auriemma did for the 2002–3 team at Connecticut, they can produce winning teams.

Assuming that people are capable of winning is not just a mental exercise. Concrete things happen that translate expectations into investments of resources or effort that actually improve performance—a mini–virtuous cycle. Thinking that someone is a potential high performer encourages leaders and colleagues to look more closely at her, to invest more time, to pass on more tips, to find the positives that surely must be there and mention them, ignoring the negatives because surely they cannot be true.

Positive expectations by leaders make people want to rise to the occasion, but people need proof that there is some reality to the expectations. Pep talks without convincing content are devoid of credibility. People see right through them. "Irrational exuberance" based on nothing but fantasy and hype doesn't last very long. That's why winning—or its close approximation—is often necessary before people believe they can win. The best pep talks include evidence.

When Losing Is Grounds for Confidence:
The Miami-versus-Florida Game

The pivotal game of the 1983 season that began the University of Miami Hurricanes' winning tradition was one the team lost badly. It was the opening game against the archrival Florida Gators, and the score was a pitiful Florida 28, Miami 3. Miami's team started without a reservoir of confidence. The university had almost dropped football in the 1970s. As a small private university, it had neither the resources nor the huge alumni and fan base of Notre Dame or the large state universities that tended to be the football powerhouses, so there was not a great deal of external confidence in the team. Head coach Howard Schnellenberger called the 1983 team "overachievers," and David Heffernan, who was one of them, agreed, calling himself (from the safe vantage point of his Miami law firm twenty years later) "a skinny defensive end out of a local high school that Schnellenberger decided to make into a center over a weekend." Still, the team had high expectations, because they had just gone through "the training camp from hell," with three practice periods a day and extreme pressure from Schnellenberger.

The players were despondent after losing the game, and they were a little scared, ready to be defensive. "Schnellenberger was beating the hell out of us before, what was he going to do now?" Heffernan recalled wondering. Confidence was shaken, and they were all ready to lower their expectations. But the coach surprised them by exuding optimism and pushing for even tougher training because he knew the team could do it. The staff used film of the game to show how much talent and potential this team had. What helped them decide they could win were the tough tests they mastered in practices. The coaches worked them to the point of exhaustion. Then, after being on the field all day, the team spent evening hours going through films of themselves and the other team, looking for an edge. Schnellenberger gave them his "Roger Bannister speech" about how Bannister, the first man to break the four-minute mile, collapsed when he crossed the finish line. Players got the message that they shouldn't hold anything back, but they were also flattered by the comparison and heartened by the positive expectations.

"It was such a positive week going into the next game that things started to roll from there," Heffernan said. Self-confidence and team confidence blossomed. Expectations transformed into experience, as the Hurricanes began to feel they could handle anything. Miami won the season and the national championship in the New Year's Day Orange Bowl Classic against Nebraska, the top team in the country that year. It was a close victory, 31–30, but it proved that Miami could win without superior talent in every position. Beating Nebraska was the impetus needed for the football program to attract support from the university. "We got a bid to the Orange Bowl and won, and the school realized, 'Oh, there's a nice check that comes from the Orange Bowl, maybe football's not so bad,'" Heffernan reminisced.

That started the momentum that created one of the great college football dynasties of all time. From then on, expectations that "we can do it" were supported by the knowledge that "we have done it."

Permission to Win: Verizon's Game Plan

"The impact on an organization is amazing when you give people permission to win," declared Ivan Seidenberg, chairman and CEO of Verizon Communications, early in 2004. He was describing the mindset behind Verizon's success spiral, even through the bust years of turbulence in the telecommunications industry.

Seidenberg found insights in sports similar to Schnellenberger's for Miami or Auriemma's for Connecticut: that thinking like winners was based on knowledge of strengths and grew with each victory in intensely competitive games.

In 2002, telecom giant Verizon had risen to number ten on the *Fortune* 500. That year included some of the largest losses in corporate history. Verizon earned net profits of over $4 billion on revenues of $67.6 billion, while the top 25 companies collectively lost over $63 billion. Verizon had long surpassed its former parent

AT&T (number 22 on the *Fortune* list) in revenues and market capitalization. Since 1984, when Verizon predecessors Bell Atlantic and NYNEX were spun off in the AT&T divestiture, it had become a fierce competitor striving to beat AT&T in every match.

The company was once thought to have little chance to win long term, because it was running out of room to grow and was locked in to a network of wires in its core regional operations. But it reinvested cash from the traditional phone business in new technologies, winning 30–40 percent of the wireless market from a standing start. Such victories reinforced the self-confidence of executives and encouraged them to put the interests of the team above their own narrow interests, which is a mark of confident people. In two major mergers between 1996 and 2000—Bell Atlantic with NYNEX and then both with GTE to form Verizon—Seidenberg, originally CEO of NYNEX, twice gave up his solo CEO position, first becoming number two to Bell Atlantic's Ray Smith and later co-CEO with GTE's Charles "Chuck" Lee until Lee's retirement. Such power-sharing ensured smooth integrations, defying conventional wisdom that corporate marriages-of-equals are impossible. That in itself was a victory.

"The institution is larger than any one person," Seidenberg told me in his New York City office in October 2002. The office was not fancy, and neither was he. In the dozen years I had known him, he always appeared unassuming and down-to-earth. He had a tough core and a sharp intellect but was definitely not an imperial CEO. Like New England Patriots coach Bill Belichick, Seidenberg stressed teamwork and shied away from personal publicity. At a large funeral of a Verizon manager's son who had died when the World Trade Center collapsed in the terrorist attacks of 9/11, Seidenberg waited patiently in the back of the line for over two hours so he could pay his respects to the family. "People couldn't believe the the CEO would wait with everyone else," a former Verizon executive recalled. Seidenberg's message—that the important thing is winning, not who's in charge—set a tone at Verizon.

Two beliefs shape a positive emotional climate in the workplace:

first, that it is possible to meet high standards, and second, that there is a purpose worth achieving.

Verizon set high standards while making success attainable. Jobs were broken down into actionable, measurable components, so that every day people knew exactly what to do to add value to the business. Measurable goals ensured that performance would be objective, not political—an emphasis that was particularly important after a series of mergers, to prevent any hint that one group was favored over another.

A sense of greater purpose was codified in a values statement that featured service first, followed by integrity, respect, imagination, and passion. Over thirty years ago, Seidenberg had learned on day one that service was an ingrained value, when he joined the company as a cable splicer's assistant and was told that afternoon to call home, because cable needed to be fixed, and the team could be working all night. Being tested in the trenches on a task considered important—maintaining telephone service—built confidence in people that they could handle anything. From September 11 to 17, 2001, as the telecom provider for Wall Street, Verizon people worked extraordinarily long hours to repair damage in the terrorist attacks so that the financial markets could function again.

In February 2004, Cingular grabbed AT&T Wireless, defeating Vodafone in the final minutes of a bidding battle for the AT&T spinoff, emerging as a more formidable competitor. Seidenberg claimed to welcome the competition, because that gave Verizon a clear target to beat. He looked ahead to Verizon's next championship game. Seidenberg knew that Verizon would need a greater rollout of broadband capacity and that Verizon was further behind than he wanted it to be, but he told everyone—employees, analysts, the press, public audiences, his executives—that he was confident Verizon could succeed.

"The worst thing we could do is lose our nerve and not move aggressively enough," Seidenberg said. His job was to keep the mood positive and expectations high. The Verizon team had won in the past, and they could do it again.

Good Moods: Winning Is Contagious

Through their confidence in the team, leaders can set an emotional tone and shape expectations that produce initial wins. Winning certainly puts people in a good mood. Then emotional contagion kicks in to spread that mood and reinforce positive expectations. Winning begets winning.

Moods are catching, especially among people who know they depend on one another. Moods spread from person to person in surprisingly subtle ways, yet they have a big influence. "Primitive emotional contagion" is the unconscious tendency to mimic another person's facial expressions, tone of voice, posture, and movements, even when one is focused on other things and is seemingly unaware of the model for the mood. This synchronizing of a sad or happy tone of voice, for example, is often unconscious, as though the human brain is hard-wired to get in tune with other people, because it is more pleasant to have a sense of rapport. Being out of tune is jarring and makes people feel isolated.

Happiness clues that spread positive moods seem to be a little stronger than sadness signals, but that depends on circumstances. Anger contagion is certainly strong in real life, leading to mob behavior as people incite one another to violence. Emotional contagion can even be mediated by technology. Television producers must believe that their laugh tracks work, but auto horns were the mediator of an irritation contagion I witnessed the other night in a traffic jam. Still, since positive emotions draw people together and negative emotions tend to push them apart, as people want to withdraw from sad situations, it is not surprising that contagion effects are stronger for good moods.

Good moods are both causes and effects. Winning puts people in a good mood, and being in a good mood makes it easier to win. The contagion of positive emotions can help improve cooperation, decrease conflict, and underscore more-positive perceptions of everyone's task performance. Negative emotions have the reverse effect. These associations are stronger for people already well connected to one another, because they've worked together in the past and expect to continue to be together. Emotional contagion has been confirmed in scientific measurement of the moods of English professional cricket teams during matches. (Note to Americans: Cricket is a really slow game, so there is ample time for research.) Not surprisingly, everyone played better when the whole team was in a good mood. Or perhaps they were in a good mood because they were playing well for a change.

DOING WHAT COMES NATURALLY: WINNERS' BEHAVIOR AND CONFIDENCE IN THE SYSTEM

The positive emotional climate surrounding success makes it more likely for people to behave in ways that bring them closer together, that create the chemistry the Connecticut Huskies found was so vital to winning. In the Connecticut victory over Duke, we caught glimpses of that behavior in action—the way the team communicated, respected one another, bonded, shared responsibility, exercised initiative. Liking one another seems important to women's teams, but men are equally inclined to use metaphors of "family" to describe the chemistry that makes their teams win. Whatever the basis for bonding, success stems from high engagement of people with their tasks, with their responsibilities, and with one another. They come to feel they can count on one another, the way the Verizon team pulled together after 9/11 and the Continental team did after the Great Blackout. Confidence is reflected in behavior that propels winning.

The pattern is consistent everywhere, from the sports world to the business world to education, and to every realm in which individuals perform to high standards. In the midst of winning cycles, people naturally gravitate toward behaving in ways that support confidence.

- *Accountability.* People want to share information and take responsibility; they have nothing to hide. They seek feedback and self-improvement. Because they feel committed, they communicate more often and make higher-quality decisions. They set high aspirations and respect each other for meeting high standards. They avoid excuses and try self-scrutiny before blaming others.

- *Collaboration.* People want to work together. Mutual attraction is high, interpersonal bonds are strong, and relationships are multifaceted because people take the time to know one another in a variety of settings. People are willing to help others and give them a chance to excel. They feel a sense of belonging that makes them more amenable to taking direction from others.
- *Initiative.* People feel that what they do matters, that they can make a difference in outcomes, so they offer ideas and suggestions. Expectations of success produce the energy to put in extra effort, to keep going under pressure. People take initiative, and initiative results in improvements and innovations.

These kinds of behaviors are central to confidence. They feed motivation and morale. They create a culture that makes it easier to solve problems. They encourage high performance. People operating in a setting characterized by these winners' behaviors find that the positive climate encourages engaging in more of these behaviors. The cycle of success is reinforced. The next question is how it is perpetuated.

Making Them Concrete: Reinforcing the Cornerstones of Confidence

Leaders of high-performing organizations don't count on impulse or emotions alone to produce the behavior of winners. They establish disciplines and embed them in formal structures.

Some people say that winning organizations are simply able to recruit the best players. End of conversation. There is no question that winning teams are attractive to talented people, and there is also no question that talent matters. That's why the "T" word is on the lips of every corporate executive and leadership developer today. But successful CEOs like Akin Öngör and Ivan Seidenberg want not just talent alone, but talent in a team. Even in sports, talent alone is the starting point, but not the margin of victory. Stars alone do not guarantee winning—just ask the Chicago Cubs if Sammy Sosa's home-run record was enough to end their historic losing tradition in Major League Baseball before a new general manager led a turnaround of the whole team in the 2003 season. Stars can even get in the way of winning, if they do whatever is the equivalent of hogging the ball—that is, focusing on their own careers at the expense of helping others. Distance increases between the stars and the rest of the players, and the stars cannot carry everything alone.

If stars cannot guarantee winning, non-stars operating with accountability, collaboration, and initiative often can. Athletes need to pass a threshold of ability and they need to tap an inner desire to succeed, but both are helped along by training and instruction and data and feedback and teammates who care. Even lesser talents can become perennial winners by the quality of communication, cooperation, and empowerment surrounding them.

That's what Anson Dorrance believed, and he should know. In twenty-four years as head coach of the University of North Carolina women's soccer team, the Tar Heels, Dorrance and his associate Bill Palladino shaped one of the most dominant sports programs in the history of professional or collegiate sports (and were still shaping it, as of this writing). The North Carolina program helped the United States dominate women's soccer globally, winning the inaugural women's world cup in China in 1991, with Dorrance coaching and many Tar Heels on the national team.

The Vision of a Champion

Anson (he likes players to call him by his first name, to reduce the distance between him and the team) told us he felt strongly that having the best team could make up for not having the best talent. He harked back to his own life to illustrate that confidence was essential to victory. His father once told him that he was the most confident person without any talent that he had ever seen.

Dorrance was coaching the North Carolina men's soccer team when he was asked to add a women's team to his coaching responsibilities—the first women's varsity soccer team in the South. He immediately aspired to win championships. The problem was that his entire annual budget for soccer was $5,000, and it would cost $8,500 to take the team to its first tournament. He approached the athletic director (who must have thought Dorrance was out of his mind) and sold him on increasing the budget. The team was on its way.

Dorrance promoted women's soccer, even though attendance was minuscule, by asking whatever small group of fans happened to come to a game to cluster in one bleacher section of a 52,000-seat football stadium behind the players for a photograph that made the stands look crowded. By 1989 women's soccer had become the fastest-growing sport in the NCAA, in no small part thanks to Dorrance. By then, he could drop dual duty with the men's team.

Over the years the Tar Heels included some of the most remarkable athletes in any sport. Mia Hamm, for example, who played on the stellar 1992 team, went professional, was called by *USA Today* in 2003 perhaps America's most famous woman athlete (she married Boston Red Sox shortstop Nomar Garciaparra); Hamm and teammates were among the first women ever to be pictured on Wheaties' famed "Breakfast of Champions" cereal box, in 1999. But Dorrance also fielded winning teams with less-than-stellar talent. In an environment in which women were called "warriors," the Tar Heels' tradition valued tenacity, courage, and resilience even over athletic ability.

But Dorrance was particularly proud of the 2000 championship team, which was characterized by difficult victories involving losing the lead and coming from behind—nine separate comebacks. "For that team, any victory was a success. It just wasn't an overwhelmingly talented team. In fact, that season was a much easier season to celebrate for me, because I think we had no superstars. They won because of their psychological makeup." One of the players on that team, Jordan Walker, had little innate talent. At a soccer camp prior to her coming to North Carolina, Anson told her parents that she was one of the least athletic players he had seen. He went on to say that he could not guarantee that she would play a single minute, but she would be a team captain by her senior year, because of her focus and character. In one of Walker's first starts, she scored the winning goal against Notre Dame on December 1, 2000. And true to Dorrance's prediction, she was team captain for the 2003 season, a team that also won the national championship.

Routines That Activate Talent

A rival coach once said that Dorrance's teams won because he had the best athletes, arguing that "he could attribute his success to eating cream cheese for lunch, and all these parents and coaches would go out and buy cream cheese."

Dorrance argued just the opposite—that there were habits that activated talent and made it more potent. He set out to create structures and routines that would build accountability, collaboration, and initiative.

Disciplines for accountability

There was a yearly cycle of activities to encourage accountability. Every spring, Dorrance met weekly with team members in addition to their practices to explore leadership and values. Then, following the fall season, everyone on the team completed a self-evaluation and peer evaluation covering attitude, character, performance, discipline, leadership, community, and ambition, stemming from a list of core values, each one punctuated by an inspirational quote.

"Let's begin with this," the values statement opened. "We don't whine. We work hard. The truly extraordinary do something every day. We choose to be positive. When we don't play as much as we would like, we are noble and still support the team and its mission. We don't freak out over ridiculous issues or live in fragile states of emotional catharsis or create crises where none should exist. We are well led. We care about each other as teammates and as human beings. We play for each other. And we want our lives (and not just in soccer) to be never-ending ascensions."

The evaluations were shared with everyone, and generally the team captains for next season (voted on by team members) had the best average scores. This was a mini-version of the leadership assessment legendary CEO Jack Welch established at General Electric.

Accountability was drilled into the Tar Heels. Practices were always highly demanding, a "competitive cauldron," Dorrance said, that helped players build confidence in their ability to perform, as they were pushed to beat one another. Players were held accountable for their play and preparation. Each team member was ranked in a "competitive matrix" that recorded data about aerobic and anaerobic fitness as well as soccer-specific skills, modeled after another famous coach's techniques. The matrix was a transparent display of commitment to personal fitness, skills, and team. There were practically no rules otherwise—no curfew, lots of joking, even late arrivals at airports for travel to away games. But players were expected to commit big to the one thing under their control no matter what: their fitness. If someone slacked on her training in the off-season, tests in pre-season practices revealed this, and players could be cut. Jordan Walker, a senior midfielder by 2003, explained that "it's not cool to be lazy. It's not cool to goof off. It's not cool to not do your running or your fitness. And it *is* cool to do it."

Abundant data improved performance by motivating players to ascend to the top of an objective ladder and showing them where they needed to improve. "My environment is very cold-blooded," Dorrance said. "You either win or you lose. We started ranking players and reporting everything in practice. The recording dynamics forced everyone to know that it's important to win at all times. We're pretty good at holding the players accountable because the numbers don't lie." (He sounded like Verizon's Ivan Seidenberg, emphasizing metrics over managing anecdotally.) Senior defender Catherine Reddick declared that she had never participated in a more competitive practice dynamic—a bold statement since she also played on the U.S. Women's National Team.

The chemistry of collaboration

While players competed intensely at practice, they also bonded as a team. "People don't care how much you know until they know how much you care" was a quote in the leadership assessment from a former player, Rakel Karvelsson (Class of 1998). Winning made it easy for people to respect one another, but Dorrance also made sure they had opportunities to like one another. A few seasons after he began coaching, he wondered if his effective but regimented team warm-up was damaging morale. He observed that the women gathered before the warm-up in groups of two or three, then jogged to a place out of his earshot and talked. So he began to let the team start practice without him. It turned out that the first ten to fifteen minutes became more social than warm-up. While stretching and putting on their shoes, the team could catch up on gossip and one another's lives. Dorrance called this a total waste of time in one respect—but critical for team-building.

The Tar Heels always socialized outside of practice. At one point they raised money through a concession stand at a basketball game staffed by absolutely everyone, including Dorrance, who ran the soda machine. Team pizza parties at his house with his wife and children helped the team feel like family, something Mia Hamm noted in her time on the team. In 1995 Senior Goalkeeper Tracy Noonan, who chose North Carolina over Dartmouth, remarked, "What's different here is the chemistry among ourselves. I just fell in love with this place and with the atmosphere here." Catherine Reddick remarked on the strong bonds, the fact that some team members chose to live together.

Leadership for initiative

Players could take a great deal of initiative. Team captains and other seniors set the tone for the team, including attitude, work ethic, and chemistry. Within a general strategy, they could make decisions on the field. Dorrance explained, "We respond to anything the players say. Now, obviously, I have my hand on the tiller, a very gentle hand. By the time they're seniors, they have rarely made a decision I would not agree with, because by then they know the culture. The seniors have huge power. With very few exceptions, I do exactly what they recommend." Creating and preserving this leadership dynamic was crucial to the success of the team. "If you have good leaders, you are going to win; otherwise, the team struggles," he said.

North Carolina's success spiral grew through formal activities producing accountability, collaboration, and initiative. Winners' behaviors were reinforced by processes and principles that were passed on from one generation of players to the next, as though they were part of the organizational DNA of North Carolina women's soccer.

Investments in People: The Winners' Culture

Dorrance's methods for perpetuating winners' habits could have been taken from any standard list of the best corporate human resource practices, the ones associated with high performance in study after study: selective hiring, extensive training, extensive information-sharing and performance feedback, reduced status distinctions, rewards contingent on performance, self-managed teams, and decentralized decision-making. These are all positive investments in people, but not exactly news. Still, these practices are associated with high performance because only high-performance organizations use them. Why doesn't everyone?

Investments in people are much easier to make and justify when teams and organization are already winning. That helps the rich get richer. They can not only attract the best talent but spend money to develop even lesser talents and surround them with an environment of success. General Electric has an impressive corporate university in Crotonville, New York; IBM's state-of-the-art education facility in Palisades, New York, rivals a luxury hotel. Or take the New York Yankees—one of the most formidable winners of the twentieth century. I got a sense of life inside Yankee spring training camp in Florida courtesy of a friend who was a visiting lecturer for six Major League Baseball teams. The Yankees' facilities alone sent powerful signals about their investments in people. Most teams rented a local high school gym, but the Yankees had an elaborate permanent setup, their own closed environment that was protected from external view (except for a gift shop for fans who came to watch games). There were multiple practice fields with spiffy artificial turf instead of the scruffy grass of a high school field.

Motivational posters about winning were mounted on walls of the clubhouse. A sign above the whirlpool declared that "Games are never won in the whirlpool." Of course, it was striking that they even had a whirlpool, which many high schools used by other teams did not. Everything my friend saw had style, including the practice uniforms, and everything sent a message about how much players were valued. There were many more trainers and backup staff than the other teams had. There was a feeling that everyone was part of the family—for example, no talk about minor leaguers versus major leaguers. Everyone was supposed to be competing for the majors, so the farm teams were considered "developmental" stops en route. To make clear how important those on the development track were to the Yankees' future, owner George Steinbrenner kept a locker in their area.

The Yankees certainly had the resources to invest in an environment for winners. They had the resources because they were already long-term winners.

WINNERS' WEALTHY WEBS:
ADVANTAGES OF EXTERNAL CONFIDENCE

Some people say that money is the only thing that's important about winning. They argue that winning streaks are a function of having the resources to attract the best talent, whether that means paying the highest salaries or offering the biggest signing bonuses or providing the best amenities. Winning streaks justify major investments in new technology or state-of-the-art facilities. By 2001, for example, Miami had one of the most advanced football video labs in college football; Garanti Bank's winning streak earned it a luxurious high-rise office building in Istanbul and the best-decorated branch banks in the city.

But the benefits of winning extend beyond simple economic calculations. The ability to recruit top talent is not just about money, especially in situations where there are caps on salaries (such as professional football) or more complicated considerations (such as in health care or education). Winners gain advantages because the whole context is enriched. Top talent wants to join other top talent, and they often play better when surrounded by other high performers rather than being the only one on a team. Connecticut could get players on the bench who could be stars elsewhere. For example, Ann Strother, rated America's number-one women's basketball recruit in 2002, grew up watching the Huskies; she said she wanted to join them even if she had to wait a year or two to play.

Similar multipliers work on the investment side. Large crowds of loyal fans or satisfied customers provide money but also a great deal more. They offer the exhilaration of popularity that reinforces a climate of positive expectations. Although athletes don't always admit it, I've seen that people practice harder so they might perform better when their performance will be visible to a large audience and, hence, seem more consequential.

Winners also gain a variety of non-monetary advantages that propel the success cycle.

Powerful networks

People involved with winning streaks get more access to influence and information. They get board seats or other forms of access to inner circles, such as invitations to the White House (the Miami Hurricanes had many) or to meetings with the prime minister of their country. They get to the championship tournaments, where they not only get the chance to win, but also make contacts, have conversations, pick up information, get advance warning, vet competitors, and make relationships that can be used for future access or intelligence. Winners find that their networks expand as they continue to win, and that loyalty increases, keeping their own alumni in the fold. The Miami Hurricanes of the 2000s drew strength from famous Hurricanes of the 1980s; NFL star quarterback Bernie Kosar, of that championship 1983 team, was known to attend games and encourage quarterback Ken Dorsey from the sidelines. Many collegiate soccer coaches were Anson Dorrance's former players or assistants, giving North Carolina an unusually large network for intelligence gathering or relationship building. Wider networks extending beyond a close circle of friends and family are the best source of referrals, an asset for talent scouts.

Career opportunities

It is easier to hone skills in organizations on winning streaks, because the level of colleagues is higher, the investment in training is likely to be greater, and the competition is tougher. Winning streaks usually result in expansions rather than contractions, so career paths are more numerous, certain, and secure. There is more access to attractive future career opportunities even if people can't stay in the same organization—such as college athletes who graduate. The North Carolina women's soccer program disproportionately staffed the U.S. national teams and professional teams. The Miami Hurricanes were known as a major source of prospects for the National Football League. Between 1984 and 2003, sixty-eight Miami players were picked in the first three rounds of the professional football draft, thirty-six of them in the first round, vastly exceeding the total for any other school. The "afterlife" is better for those who have been involved with winning streaks. The promise of future opportunities makes it easier to recruit talent in the first place, perpetuating the cycle of advantage.

Good deals

Deals come to winners, they don't have to find them. Opportunities come in the door uninvited, such as "walk-ons" in college sports—athletes who show up for the team without athletic scholarships, or "cold calls" suggesting deals—such as GTE chairman Chuck Lee's unexpected call to Ivan Seidenberg in 1998 to congratulate him on becoming Bell Atlantic CEO and then propose the marriage with GTE that created Verizon. Sponsors contribute or discount for the benefits of being associated with a winning team. It is easier to tap volunteers who work just for the pleasure of connection, such as the motivational consultants Anson Dorrance got to work with his team pro bono. The rich pay less because they can afford to buy in volume at a discount—but also because they get more gifts. Winners also tend to get more shelf space for their products, more favorable column inches, more positive broadcast minutes, free. The Connecticut women's basketball team had abundant TV coverage and its own pack of reporters, the Miami Hurricanes their own radio network in English and Spanish.

Network advantages are reinforced by the benefits of association that spill over to the entire network. As the number of people and organizations that want to be associated with winners grows, winners can be more selective. Selectivity further confers a halo on anyone who is invited in, which reinforces the cycle of positive expectations.

Of course, those closest to the team or organization get the largest returns. They share in the tangible assets that come from winning, and experience the positive emotions directly. Their satisfaction reinforces another element of the success spiral: the ability of winners to define their own destiny.

CONFIDENT AND IN CONTROL:
THE POWER OF SUCCESS

Winning streaks are empowering. People feel in control of their game, and, in turn, they are more likely to be handed control. An expectation of continued winning gives decision makers and resource allocators confidence that people can handle responsibility, deserve to know the facts, attract the best talent, benefit from training, pull together as a group without depending excessively on stars—and produce those wins. This confidence means that winners get the power of continuity and self-determination.

Winning streaks feature a great deal of leadership continuity. Winning companies are much less likely than losing companies to get new CEOs. Whether Wal-Mart, Microsoft, General Electric, Southwest Airlines, IBM, or Continental Airlines under Gordon Bethune, organizations on winning streaks tend to retain their leaders and have smooth leadership transitions. In sports, Anson Dorrance and Bill Palladino could ensure that their methods for producing winners endured because they were in charge of North Carolina women's soccer for twenty-four years. Geno Auriemma and Chris Dailey led Connecticut women's basketball for eighteen years. Gail Goestenkors had more than ten years at Duke when we interviewed her. The University of Miami had a succession of head coaches during its twenty years as a football powerhouse, but the last time a coach was fired was in the 1970s. The average tenure of head coaches after that was about five years, and the rest of the coaching staff included long-term veterans who served as the institutional memory. The most recent streak-producing head coach, Larry Coker, moved up from within. The same leadership continuity is true in school systems, hospitals, and other organizations that are winning.

The logic is obvious. *Losing?* Throw the bums out—or control their every move. *Winning?* Thank them and leave them alone. For winners, that logic sets a few more stones in place to support the success spiral that helps winners keep winning.

Winning streaks give people the room and the security to define their own terms and determine their own fate. A history of high performance increases the confidence of authority figures, resource allocators, watchdogs, auditors, regulators, and opinion leaders.

Such confidence on the part of these "controllers" translates into more security for the players and leaders. People are given the luxury of coming and going as they choose, and they often choose to stay. The top person is more likely to be on a longer-term contract. It can even be easier to keep the number-two person, the one whom everyone else wants to steal to take their number-one slot, because some people would rather stick with the secure and growing rewards of a winning team. During the upward cycle of success, everyone experiences more continuity, fewer disruptions, less of the start-over-again turmoil of turnover. That further reinforces the ability to forge close bonds that release the chemistry of success. Instead of always having to adjust to new relationships, winners can enjoy deepening the ones they have. Even on college sports teams that by definition turn over with every graduating class, there are continuity effects. Star college players destined for professional sports are more likely to stay through graduation when their team is winning than when it's losing; the University of Miami's football team had its highest attrition of players before graduation during the only period when the team lost.

Continuity of people is associated with continuity of strategy—that is, smoother, less disruptive improvements rather than vacillation or lurches from one idea to another. The track record of leaders of winning streaks breeds confidence in committing to a plan and sticking with it. Continuity breeds faith during adversity, as it did for Garanti Bank—*there will be time, we'll get through this, the plan is a good one.* At the same time, when people feel secure, they are more likely to improve upon the plan rather than mindlessly follow a script. This is a human pattern that starts soon after birth; it's been found that infants who feel more secure engage in more exploratory behavior. Having a general strategy and not abandoning it in a spate of self-doubt provides steadiness; tinkering with it and adding new twists ensures that competitors can't always predict what will happen.

Success also breeds confidence in the ability of people to manage themselves. Resources and support are provided with fewer strings. Owners, boards of directors, key officials, bosses, parents—whoever is in a position to give or withhold power—are more likely to endorse the organization's direction and less likely to micromanage.

Consider the difference in the management of two American television networks: NBC, owned by General Electric, and ABC, owned by Disney. Why did they diverge in their success for so long?

ABC had begun to slide in ratings, and the losing streak continued after ABC's purchase by entertainment giant Disney. Industry insiders told me that Disney reduced ABC's initiative and constrained its creative output by micromanagement, autocracy, and tight control of budgets, and all this was accompanied by a parade of exiting network heads. The worse ABC did, the more interference there was in its activities, which did not improve performance during the also-ran years. (Disney itself became a takeover target after Comcast's hostile bid in February 2004.)

In contrast, NBC had a long winning streak under General Electric, an industrial conglomerate known for high standards; each GE business was expected to be a "winner" (number one or number two in its industry). As long as NBC's "wins" added up, the network was permitted to control its own destiny and enjoyed continuity of leadership, with Bob Wright as chief executive of NBC since 1986, and Dick Ebersol as head of NBC Sports since 1989. GE held NBC accountable for performance results but otherwise provided autonomy, which allowed NBC people to take more initiative and make creative decisions on their own terms.

As success accumulates, so does freedom from bureaucratic distractions that consume time and energy. Winners can concentrate on polishing their performance, rather than reporting to parades of concerned bosses who keep them on a tight leash.

For all these reasons, winning puts people in control of their circumstances, present and future. Psychologists argue that people who learn to win, who expect to win, tend to be more internally directed and intrinsically motivated anyway. As numerous studies show, optimists tend to believe in their own ability to make a difference and to exert control over circumstances. But what else is going on around people that helps confirm those beliefs? How much control do others in their lives permit them to exercise? Whatever personal confidence people bring to the table is increased by winning, because success makes increased self-determination possible. Of course, even winners don't control everything around them—but they can decide for themselves to put their emphasis on the things they do control. This is what the Connecticut Huskies meant when they said that they define themselves, rather than letting the media define them.

Those enjoying winning streaks thus win twofold. They win not only the game but also the right to greater self-determination. They become masters of their own fate. That feeling of efficacy, of being in charge of circumstances, is the essence of confidence. Winning once or twice is encouraging, but winning continuously is empowering.

JUST DOING THE JOB: THE HARD WORK OF WINNING

As winning streaks gain momentum, winning becomes a habit supported by firm foundations embedded in structures for confidence. Winners are bolstered by a large number of forces that keep them going strong. But the ultimate responsibility for winning is carried by the individuals who must go out onto the field and play the game. Confidence motivates performance, but the people involved must still perform. Confidence produces teamwork, but the team must still do the work. What a tradition of winning should ensure is consummate professionals who do their jobs to the highest possible standards. Veteran *Miami Herald* sportswriter Edwin Pope told us about the 1972 Miami Dolphins, whose undefeated season is still a National Football League record. "It was the lack of excitement that was interesting," he said. "It was all very businesslike. They just kept coming to work and winning games."

On the field, success is a matter of showing up to do the work as a member of a team that can "relax under pressure"—Akin Öngör's principle for Garanti Bank—because they are so well prepared. Calm, steady professionalism is exactly how Larry Kellner and Debbie McCoy described the Continental Airlines team that pulled together during the Great Blackout of 2003 to keep the airline flying: No one was worrying; the people spread around the country knew their jobs and went to work. That impression of professionalism is what the sales team at Target Stores gave their guests from Estée Lauder—that they were well prepared, proud of one another, active and energetic.

At the end of Connecticut's victory over Duke, the Connecticut Huskies did not celebrate on the court, because that would be disrespectful to the losing team. Instead they walked into the visitors' locker room, told one another they'd done a good job, and that was it. They took the next day off, then went back to the grind. They watched film of the game, looking at what they did right and what they did wrong. They still had a job to do.

The Duke women also knew they had a job to do after that game. "In retrospect it was a great learning experience for us. . . . We were embarrassed at home. And now we had to deal with that adversity. That's when your character is revealed," Duke coach Gail Goestenkors said. "We were much more intense post-Connecticut. We changed our lineup and coaching. I said, 'Maybe I'm being too easy on you. We have to put you through adversity every day in practice, so that when you're dealing with it during a game, you're more comfortable.' "

Duke won all but one of its subsequent games that season, and in the next, in January 2004, Duke came back to beat Connecticut on the Huskies' home court. But it was the competition of best against best. In April, Connecticut won the 2004 national Championship.

Success is neither magic nor dumb luck; it stems from a great deal of consistent hard work to perfect each detail. It is even a little mundane. Win, go back to work, win again.

3

Why Winning Streaks End

I F WINNERS ACCUMULATE SO MANY ADVANTAGES, WHY DO CYCLES OF
SUCCESS EVER END?

I'VE ALREADY SAID THAT WINNING IS HARD WORK. IT IS NEVER EASY
or automatic. Winners make mistakes. Winners experience problems and must solve them. Winning streaks are punctuated by
struggles. They contain higher and lower points—some wins are
huge, others barely eked out. Sometimes the entire company does
well, across the board; at other times, surpluses in stronger divisions mask shortfalls in weaker ones. Political campaigns have
their ups and downs; approval ratings of presidents and prime ministers rise and fall. And the history of long-term winners includes
breaks in their streaks. They lose a game or fall short a quarter, then
resume winning.

A loss is a crossroads, not a cliff. Winners make mistakes and encounter troubles all the time without falling off the edge. How
problems are dealt with shapes whether they are just an interruption or a sign of impending doom, whether winners are resilient or
are stuck in increasingly ineffective behavior.

TOIL AND TROUBLES

In some domains, of course, it is hard to win forever because rules
and regulations are designed to encourage competition. In business, antitrust rules prevent winners' advantages from turning into
monopolists' dominance. In politics, campaign finance laws are
(supposedly) designed to dilute incumbents' advantages. In profes-

sional sports, league rules govern player salaries, methods of contracting, and even the sharing of television revenues, to avoid the rich getter too much richer and the poor that much poorer. But for the most part it is not external factors that stop winners, but their own failure to maintain the disciplines and support systems that helped them turn winning into a habit in the first place.

It is also hard to win forever because of the paradox of success. Success creates its own problems that make it hard to sustain. Even without regulation reducing winners' advantages, winners often face circumstances in which their competition gets tougher. "You become the team to beat, and everyone is gunning for you," an athlete on a winning team told me. Paul Dee, the University of Miami athletic director responsible for the successful Hurricanes football dynasty, agreed. "I think it's never easy to win. When you've been successful, you're the target of every opponent," he told us. "We'll get the best of every opponent—their best game, best preparation. There's nothing that would do more for a team or a coaching staff than to beat the best team. It lifts their team. We have to be ready at all times, knowing that we are everybody's target."

Success also produces its own competition. Innovators have the field to themselves until others catch on, jump in, or change the way they play. Success creates attractive markets, encourages imitation, and brings out the toughest competition. In a countercycle to the cycle of success, the game gets harder to win as wins accumulate, because games get tougher. It's a familiar pattern in many industries. The North Carolina soccer program, for example, was formidable but not invincible. As result of its success, women's soccer became more popular, and competition grew stronger. To create a following for his team, Anson Dorrance and his colleagues promoted the sport. Success built a market that encouraged others to enter, and thereby increased the production of high school soccer players. And that resulted in more teams with top talent and more knowledge of methods like Dorrance's, which his books and soccer camps made widely known. Each successive Tar Heels team that walked onto the field had to perform to ever-higher standards.

Winning is a form of toil that can thus breed its own troubles. In sports, the same game is played over and over again. But in other kinds of situations, performances build on one another, and solving one set of problems can create others. For example, a developing country might succeed in saving lives in times of famine, but then the population grows; as more people need more food, food shortages might arise again—a new problem stemming from success at eliminating an old one.

Experiencing troubles is not all bad. Rather than interrupting the cycle of success, responding to adversity might accelerate it. New threats become less threatening when people have successfully solved previous problems. Potential leaders might become stronger when they have successfully resolved crises or weathered adversity. Troubles, in fact, might actually be good for winners. There's a danger of letting down when feeling a goal has been reached. Coaches worry about that moment within a game when the team is ahead, and it stops trying. The same phenomenon occurs across games. Consistent winning can become taken for granted, no longer a source of exhilaration. If it looks too easy, it hardly makes news. The eternally winning football team of De La Salle High School in Concord, California (151 straight victories over twelve years, and counting), hardly had a following on campus by the 2003 season, because there was no drama—but attendance by opposing teams' fans soared when it played on opponents' turf at away games, because for rivals' fans it was exciting to play the undefeated team.

Sometimes high expectations in advance mean that a winning team gets no credit for victory—which is why political candidates try to keep expectations low so they can claim a triumphant upset if they win an election. One athlete wrote on my survey: "You are expected to win but not praised when you do." When winning is taken for granted, members of some winning teams feel unrewarded if they win and punished if they lose: "Every year the expectation to win seems to get higher. I wish some of the fans would not take a loss as if it were a disaster," another said. "When you are known for winning in this city there is a lot of pressure on you to win again, and if you lose they act as if you are the worst team ever, and that sucks," a third said.

The occasional crisis makes winning less boring. "Winning is great, but sometimes it takes a loss to get you motivated again. It humbles you down to reality," was the view of another athlete in my sports survey. Continental Airlines' turnaround CEO Gordon Bethune said, "It's a lot harder to keep things going great than to get them going great in the first place. People who have put in long hours willingly during the crisis can start to relax a little, enjoy the success, and maybe figure that they're good enough, unless they get more motivation to keep getting better." A tight game, a difficult challenge, even a loss, can add drama and excitement, an occasion for renewal.

If renewal occurs. People must rise to that occasion. It's not the things that happen to winners that end a winning streak, it's the things they do to themselves—not their circumstances, but their own responses to those circumstances. What helps a team win repeatedly, what helps a company succeed even in tough times, is the capacity to solve problems, to put troubles in perspective and deal with them.

Every layer of confidence that we saw winners accumulate in the previous chapter helps them get through dangerous or troublesome situations that put winning in jeopardy. A positive emotional climate of high expectations reinforces self-confidence. Winners' behaviors and attitudes—including abundant communication, thorough preparation using detailed metrics, mutual respect and deep knowledge of one another's strengths, the desire to work together and help one another succeed, and an empowering environment of shared leadership—reinforce confidence in one another. Organizational culture and routines supporting accountability, collaboration, and initiative reinforce confidence in the system. Strong networks providing encouragement, resources, and information reinforce external confidence.

But winners get in trouble when confidence turns into complacency and arrogance, when water walkers forget that there are stones holding them up beneath the water and let those underpinnings of confidence crumble. They undervalue their support systems, their disciplines, their obligations to others, and they overestimate their own abilities. The rocks that help high performers succeed provide a buffer against adversity, a resilience that helps them bounce back from troubles. But winning streaks end when those supports crumble, and people fall into the three traps of panic, neglect, and denial.

PANIC: THE RISK OF CHAOS UNDER PRESSURE

Fumbles are execution errors that occur in the normal process of carrying out tasks—dropping the ball, forgetting to reset the production line from test mode to production mode, missing a deadline. Some are innocent, some not so innocent (a few corporate executives misstating earnings, or a few priests crossing the line from affection to child abuse). But mistakes by themselves don't necessarily cause winners to lose.

Potential fumbles lie around every corner. Everyday acts such as stepping off the curb to cross a street without being hit by a car running a red light are miraculous in their own way; why does everyone play his part in making the world orderly? This thought haunted me in the days after the terrorists' destruction of the World Trade Center in New York on September 11, 2001, when Americans became conscious that every aspect of ordinary life could be filled with dangers. I sometimes urge corporate clients to include a "worst-case scenario" activity in launch meetings for major projects, in which small groups brainstorm all possible sources of trouble, routine or unexpected, that could torpedo their plans. I'm always amazed at the length of the lists. It doesn't take a rocket scientist to identify potential dangers (but tragically for two space shuttle crews, even rocket scientists sometimes ignore them).

"Kanter's Law"—*Everything can look like a failure in the middle*— applies even within a single game. Happy endings or wins are often the result of persistence—of not giving up when everything seems to be in jeopardy. Shut-outs are rare, even for the teams on winning streaks. There are often moments when winning teams are behind, and a loss seems imminent. In every walk of life, schedules slip, teams get tired, projects hit dead ends, people burn out and leave, processes fail and need to be adjusted, critics attack, and unanticipated obstacles are discovered. Every victory contains ups and downs en route to success, and it might have been fraught with uncertainty up to the final moments. (Just like football games. Adam Vinatieri helped the New England Patriots defeat the Miami Dolphins, 27–24, on December 29, 2002, when he kicked a thirty-five-yard field goal in the final seconds, after many fans had already left the stadium; this event generated a new slogan: "It's not over until Vinatieri kicks." Sure enough, in the 2004 Super Bowl, Vinatieri kicked the game-winning points for the Pats in the final seconds.)

Faced with problems or overwhelmed by troubles, people can make the situation better if they keep their heads. They can look for root causes (asking *why* questions); dig deeply in their analysis to consider many factors; test numerous hypotheses about what went wrong and what lies ahead; scrutinize their own behavior and modify it as necessary; find numerous possibilities for influence; and remain focused on a well-thought-through course of action. The situation will get worse, however, if people seek overly simple solutions and refuse to question them; leap from one idea to another in ad hoc fashion and become easily distracted; and, when faced with stubborn problems, give up or blame someone else.

It's not mistakes that cause winners to lose, it's panic. Panic is a sudden, anxious feeling of loss of control, and panicking can make a small fumble worse, by causing people to lose their heads and forget to think clearly. Or sometimes threats stop people in their tracks, paralyzing them or causing them to revert to the most familiar actions of the past. Panic is the enemy of good decision making under pressure. Threat triggers a primitive, instinctive fight-flight response even before rational thoughts can kick in. As brain scientists have found, the body is ready to lash out or run away before the mind can figure out what to do.

When a few people panic, a modest crisis escalates. We have already seen how powerful emotional contagion can be in simple situations in the psychological laboratory; imagine it when people are performing consequential tasks under the pressure of high expectations. If they panic, their anxiety can spread in an emotional chain reaction that throws many others off their stride. In short, panic occurs when water walkers lose their balance and fall off the stones into the water.

Bridging Over Troubled Waters

Confidence can be a calming influence. Trusting in the power of the group to do the right thing can prevent a fumble from turning into a loss, when people act on the "relax under pressure" principle of winners.

A dramatic moment in a pivotal University of Miami Hurricanes football game illustrates the virtues of poise under stress. The game was against Florida State at the Orange Bowl on October 7, 2000, and a Miami fumble almost interrupted a significant winning streak. Miami had lost to Florida State for five straight years, and once again Florida State was widely favored to win. The day was hot, the pressure everywhere. The locker rooms at halftime looked like they were full of war casualties—players stretched out with IVs to replace fluids lost in the heat, and doctors everywhere. Linebacker Dan Morgan hadn't realized the second half had started, a coach observed. Morgan ripped out an IV line, put on his helmet, and ran out of the locker room straight onto the field into his position, sending the player standing in for him to the sidelines.

Miami was ahead going into the final minutes of the game. Then the Hurricanes fumbled near their end zone. Florida State recovered and quickly scored a touchdown to take the lead. The coaches on the sidelines talked about what could be done. The team stayed calm. "I remember three of my kids coming to me, putting their

arms on me and telling me, 'Coach, we're gonna get this done,' "
one said. They needed to shift to another strategy, but time was
running out. Offensive coordinator Larry Coker called for a gutsy
move that required steadiness and faith—an unusually long pass
thrown by freshman quarterback Ken Dorsey to receiver Jeremy
Shockey. Shockey caught it, scored, and the Hurricanes won the
game, 27–24.

"I love winning," assistant head coach Art Kehoe declared as he
talked about that Florida State game. "In football if you win five in
a row you're doing a heck of a job. Once you hit double digits, ten
in a row, you're probably in the top 3 or 4 percent of teams in
Division I football. When we hit twenty, I was into it. From a coaching standpoint, it was just another log you can put on the fire because you are always trying to perpetuate winning and consistent
performance and consistent effort. I knew we had overcome a big
hurdle. The momentum would build on that."

Athletic director Paul Dee was impressed by Coker's leadership
in a crisis, how he protected the clock, how he took advantage of
the whole field, his composure under pressure. The players lobbied
Dee to pick Coker as the new coach when Butch Davis moved to the
professional ranks, joining the NFL's Cleveland Browns. They liked
it that Coker didn't get rattled and exercised good judgment under
pressure. Coker became head coach on February 3, 2001. His selection and then his messages to the team stressed continuity. Miami won its fifth national championship that year and continued
its unbroken winning streak to thirty-four games in 2002. Coker,
the first rookie head coach to lead his team to a national championship since 1948, immediately won two national coach-of-the-
year awards. Miami began the 2003 season ranked number two
nationally.

There was an interesting footnote to that 2000 Miami–Florida
State game. After Miami's victory, Florida State personnel kept
complaining publicly that they were robbed, that Miami stole the
victory—a classic blame trap, a victim's mentality. Some of the
Miami coaches couldn't help noticing that in Florida State's next

game, they lost badly to Notre Dame. Was Florida State slipping into losers' behavior? Was their blame-shifting a sign of avoiding responsibility for dealing with pressure? Miami defensive coordinator Randy Shannon explained how Miami's attitude differed from that of teams that found winning more difficult: "When things get rough here, people say, 'Don't worry about it, keep on going.' In other places, when things get rough, people point fingers. When teams struggle, you notice some players going to the media and talking about other players. Then all of a sudden you watch that team go straight down."

The Reality Principle: Don't Lose Sight of It

Overcoming obstacles, leaping over hurdles, and recovering from fumbles can strengthen a team that has the discipline not to panic under pressure. Expectations remain realistic, grounded in knowledge of what people are actually capable of doing, based on detailed metrics and feedback, like the rigorous self-assessments and group assessments of the North Carolina women's soccer team. The deep knowledge teammates have of one another, and their mutual respect and commitment, makes it possible to regroup quickly, to take initiative without throwing out the game plan. It helps to have practices that are tougher than games (as Connecticut did), rehearsals of responses to disasters (one of Nokia's ways of remaining on top), or written scenarios that anticipate alternative futures (a Shell Oil trademark, helping Shell be ready for a variety of situations). Going through the physical or mental discipline of performing under the most difficult circumstances—like finding a solution for each trouble in my "worst-case scenario" exercise—strengthens problem-solving and builds collective skill in how to work through disasters, the way the Continental Airlines team did in the Great Blackout of 2003.

Confidence is based on reasonable expectations; so-called overconfidence is not. The dot-com stock market boom of the late 1990s was dubbed "irrational exuberance" because it involved emotional contagion without a basis in reality—not confidence but wishful thinking. Executives who routinely exaggerate benefits and discount costs in planning major initiatives are said to exhibit "delusional optimism." Spinning tales of possible success without examining the potential for fumbles is foolish.

Cognitive psychologists have defined "overconfidence" as a person's certainty that his or her predictions are correct, exceeding the accuracy of those predictions. This kind of overpromising is sometimes pushed by greedy investors, or it is encouraged by managers who stretch goals well beyond reality. Inaccurate expectations are more likely when people oversimplify and thus fail to see some of the things associated with success or failure. They might say that success is a matter of action A, when it actually results from A plus B, C, D, and E. And, not surprisingly, this kind of overshooting is more likely to occur when there is little prior experience with similar circumstances. (I'm reminded of the famous physicist's saying, "Forecasting is a dangerous occupation, especially about the future.")

Arrogance makes people lose sight of reality as they fly high in their fantasies, and when they are no longer grounded, they are tempted to panic at the first signs of trouble. When winners keep their heads under pressure, they are better equipped to recover from fumbles. But when they become complacent, take winning for granted, begin to believe with little evidence that they can succeed in untested realms, and neglect to maintain the foundations supporting them, then winners begin to lose.

NEGLECT: FORGETTING THE FUNDAMENTALS

One of my favorite movies is a baseball comedy, *Major League*. It is the ultimate come-from-behind story about a ragtag group of players for a fictional Cleveland Indians who pull together to win the championship in defiance of their evil owner, who wants them to lose so she can move the franchise to another city. Charlie Sheen stars as Rick "Wild Thing" Vaughan, a pitcher from the streets, who becomes unbeatable once he gets glasses. The sequel, *Major League II*, is neither as funny nor as inspiring. The make-believe

Indians are no longer winning. The Wild Thing has been tamed. His punk haircut with a pattern of shaved X's has grown in. He has traded leather jackets for three-piece suits, his motorcycle for limousines, and his sweet schoolteacher girlfriend for a hardboiled PR executive. He diversified his pitches—unsuccessfully—and started working on his career rather than on his game. Vaughan is not a baseball player any longer, he's a rock star. This is an archetypal story of being seduced by success into undermining the very things that made victory possible in the first place.

Let the discipline go, forget the routines, feel the rules don't apply—those are all temptations when someone feels on top and invincible. Assuming that walking on water doesn't require the stones can cause neglect of basic maintenance to keep confidence on a solid foundation.

Success means that people or teams or organizations survive long enough to need maintenance and repairs—in other words, reinvestment. Winners undergo natural aging processes, as people get older, slow down, leave. Their facilities, tools, and bags of tricks get older, deteriorate, run down. Winners also face natural limits—the organizational equivalent of "shelf life" and "shelf space." Some winners' advantages reach limits, as all seats in the stadium are filled, or as product markets become saturated.

These normal processes put a brake on momentum. The upward trajectory cannot continue; repeating the pattern brings diminishing returns. A winning streak requires renewal and rebuilding. Chris Wallace, general manager of the Boston Celtics, explained what happened when that once-invincible professional basketball franchise went downhill: "As long as your team still has good health, and your players are still in the prime of their careers, obviously you can have an extremely successful organization. But if your key players are now winding down, your success is going to diminish. We were not winning, we were not building."

As momentum runs down, people and buildings begin to look rundown. Neglect takes on tangible physical manifestations. It might show up in sloppy clothing, out-of-shape bodies, dirty fingernails, peeling paint, or broken windows. Sometimes running down/getting rundown begins with removing just one element, ignoring just one rule, neglecting just one element. *Let's defer those roof repairs for another year . . . Let's cut out one practice; we already have so many . . . Let's save time by eliminating the weekly team meeting . . .*

In the lead-up to the Chernobyl nuclear disaster, experienced reactor operators allegedly violated safety rules because they had done so before, and no disaster had occurred; anyway, it made life easier to have one less process. The operators were well-respected, award-winning experts apparently seduced by overconfidence into ignoring the safety rules, as they started to act automatically rather than reflectively and reinforced one another's conviction that everything was just fine, in a classic example of groupthink. The disaster that resulted wasn't due to the failure of individuals, but to the breakdown of a system. Fundamental pieces of the support for high performance were neglected.

Certainly losing football games is not anywhere nearly as consequential as nuclear disasters, but it is instructive to see how neglect of the cornerstones of confidence can cause failures in every kind of system. That's what happened to the Miami Hurricanes in the mid-1990s, when the team hit major troubles for three years and had its only losing season in two decades. Between the Hurricanes of the 1980s, called one of the greatest college teams ever, and the equally victorious Hurricanes of the 2000s was an object lesson on why winning streaks end. (When he spoke to us about this, Paul Dee preferred to call this "the period of misunderstanding.")

In 1992, Miami weathered Hurricane Andrew, a natural disaster declared a national emergency that forced the team to practice far north in Vero Beach, but that did not interrupt the winning tradition. The real disaster was internal. The 'Canes were full of themselves, and the head coach at that time was not prone to rein them in. They became known as the "bad boys" of college football. They became selfish and self-indulgent. There were lurid tales of abuses within the team.

Others had gotten lax as well. In 1995, Miami's football program was put on probation for three years because of accumulated problems with the administration of financial aid, and the school lost about thirty football scholarships. This combination of wounds hurt the athletic department's reputation, recruitment, and retention, all of which were reflected in poor performance on the field. In 1997 the team lost five top players; three went to the NFL instead of coming back for their senior year, one was out due to injury, and another was declared ineligible by the NCAA. Home game attendance dropped from 361,986 in 1994 (an average of 60,331 people per game) to a low of 173,495 in 1997 (an average of 28,916 people per game). The Hurricanes finished the 1997 season with a won-lost record of 5–6, the team's only losing season since 1979.

A new head coach, Butch Davis, had been appointed in 1995, but the turnaround took several seasons. Davis, who had been an assistant under Jimmy Johnson in the winning years of the late 1980s, was described to us by veteran *Miami Herald* sportswriter Edwin Pope as part Sunday School teacher and part sheriff. He brought back accountability, teamwork, and the feeling of responsibility for behavior on and off the field. When the full complement of scholarships was restored, the Hurricanes were a better-behaved team that started to win again. In 1998 their record was 9–3; in 1999, 9–4. The year 2000 was the takeoff year for another streak, 11–1 overall, 7–0 in the Big East Conference. They won the conference championship with that sweet victory over Florida State that I described earlier, the one that helped make Larry Coker the next coach when Davis left. It was also the year Miami enjoyed the largest attendance increase ever in Division I-A football, increasing by 48.8 percent to hit 350,578, heading for a record of 417,233 in 2002.

Defensive coordinator Randy Shannon stressed the importance of a team that knew how to show respect, even during the "down time" of 1997, and that helped the team avoid slipping further. "Just think of this," he said. "When UM was on probation in the mid-nineties, you never had a player go to the media criticizing another player. When you go 5 and 6 and you still don't have any grumbling, you're fine. The people who are always talking to the paper and criticizing the coaches, players and organization, you have to get rid of them. They may be great players, but they just have to go."

DENIAL: THE HOBGOBLIN OF COMPLACENT MINDS

Life is not benign, but that doesn't mean that winning streaks end because of troubles. Winning ends when threats and problems are denied.

Winners are not immune from problems, and winning streaks are not trouble-free periods. Competitors can get stronger, conditions can become more unfavorable. Winners face adverse conditions that can weaken the ability to play to high standards, and may mean going into the next round of performance burdened by handicaps—injuries of key people, turnover of leaders, suppliers that go out of business, fires that close the factory. Worse than mere handicaps are strategic upheavals that change the nature of the game itself. The game is no longer hardware, it is software; it is no longer music bought in stores, it is music file-swapping online. The competition is no longer domestic, it is international. The most popular game in the West Indies is no longer cricket, it is American basketball. Leagues are no longer segregated, with black players going to black colleges, they are integrated. In short, to continue to be successful, decision-makers need to be tuned into changes in the wider environment in which they play their games.

It is still possible to continue a winning streak throughout a series of handicaps, setbacks, and changes in the business environment, as long as problems are faced head-on, and the discipline of winners' behavior remains in place. Garanti Bank accelerated its success cycle during a series of daunting challenges: Turkish currency crises, market volatility, heightened international competition, earthquakes, death threats against the CEO from union agitators, national political upheavals, and disruptive technologies such as the Internet, which changed the context for retail banking. The Garanti leadership team's ability to face major crises and handle them was a direct function of the open dialogue, widespread accountability, collaboration, and initiative that CEO Akin Öngör built into the organizational culture. Even when Turkey plunged into recession in 2000, Garanti was well-positioned to weather the storms much better than its counterparts, continuing to increase profits (though at a slower rate). A young executive from a rival bank said that everyone looked to Garanti as a model of how to meet the highest internal banking standards, build a cohesive staff, and innovate in technology.

The winning-streak teams in my sports study experienced serious injuries, financial crises, attacks on leaders, natural disasters, and changes in the rules of the game that diluted winners' advantages (for example, rules governing talent mobility in professional sports; regulation of financial aid in college sports). And they continued to win, because the cornerstones of confidence continued to be nurtured by leaders as a central aspect of the culture. The University of North Carolina women's soccer team continued to win even after a shocking problem hit head coach Anson Dorrance: a lawsuit for sexual harassment filed by two former players in 1998. It was a charge Dorrance and the University vehemently denied, but it was not scheduled to be heard in court until 2004.

Sources of Denial

If winning can continue despite fumbles, handicaps, and strategic upheavals, why doesn't it? Why do some decision-makers fail to act on threats? Why are so many organizations and so many people so slow to see and solve problems? Why do people persist in actions that could hurt them? Why do they fail to learn from mistakes, but instead repeat them? One reason that the mighty inevitably fall is a preference for denial. Lapses from efficient, rational, law-abiding, virtuous, or otherwise functional behavior are a constant danger, and when they occur, denial is tempting.

Common explanations for denial boil down to this: Decision-makers make flawed assumptions based on past successes, but the past may be an inadequate guide to a future in which something has changed. In an old team or a mature organization, a way of operating has been built around premises that people no longer bother to examine for their relevance to new situations. (No one points out that all those desktop telephones might not really be necessary in a world of wireless cell phones.) Business strategies and cultures might contain dysfunctional assumptions—products of past successes that "operate as silent filters on what is perceived and thought about." (It doesn't occur to anyone to question a nine-to-five workday, even though new customers are ten time zones away.) People can become so good at one way of doing things that they cannot switch to any other mode—the paradox of "trained incapacity." (Students get better at using calculators for complex math problems and find it harder to do basic arithmetic by hand.) People can get caught in "competence traps," continuing courses of action that have been successful in the past, because they are comforting in their familiarity. (Physicians become so good at conventional surgery that they deny the value of innovations.)

Denial can be a deliberate political act to stop other people from seeing change, or an unconscious tendency to put on one's own blindfolds. People have a stake in maintaining any theory of how the world works that gives them advantages in competing for resources, such as insisting that nothing has changed that would decrease their own department's funding. So they try to manage how the situation is defined, making their own proposals look good by downplaying information that doesn't fit their theory—and thus ignoring the true facts of the situation and hoping others will ignore them, too.

Sometimes the blinders are unintentional. Denial is reinforced by the limitations of human intelligence, such as not being able to keep too many variables in mind all at once, so people are tempted to pick just a few to focus on, denying the importance of the rest— like boiling down the Ten Commandments to the four that are easiest to remember. When companies lag in terms of embracing new waves of technology, for example, denial can stem from a combination of entrenched interests that prefer to ignore change (to preserve their position) and a tendency to oversimplify the world in order to have short reports on crowded agendas at management meetings. Thus, they miss subtle signs of change until changes have become major phenomena.

That's how Seagate, once the world's most successful manufacturer of hard disk drives for personal computers, got into trouble in the mid-1990s. Founded in 1980 by Silicon Valley legend Al Shugart, Seagate grew to a dominant position in the growing market for personal computers. A long winning streak had masked a variety of weaknesses. Lavish employee profit-sharing kept people from rebelling against increasingly punishing work conditions that earned the company the Silicon Valley nickname of "Slavegate." Seagate's winning streak ended when the company made more acquisitions than it could swallow, expanded overhead in an era of shrinking revenues, overspent on R&D that failed to produce new technology because each division jealously guarded its own resources and ideas. Seagate was stuck in assumptions that were no longer appropriate as the industry changed around it. The company's traditional strategy of being a fast follower offering lower costs was not enough to woo increasingly powerful customers who wanted more innovation and faster delivery—important customers such as Dell or Hewlett-Packard that represented a large share of the personal computer business. A weakened Seagate started losing to IBM.

The impulse to hide bad news and instead offer rosy forecasts has a long history and infects every sector of public life, in many countries. Political cover-ups are well known, including sex and spy scandals in the UK in the 1960s, which started with War Minister John Profumo's denials and ended up bringing down the Tory government; the Watergate scandal that eventually caused Richard Nixon to resign the U.S. presidency in the 1970s; bribery scandals involving senior members of government in Japan in the 1970s and 1980s, which were not exactly denied but were recast as "donations"; denial of an affair that led to U.S. President Clinton's impeachment hearings in the 1990s; and the resignations of Japanese prime minister Yoshiro Mori, economic minister Fukushiro

Nukaga, and others over various financial scandals in the early 2000s.

"Creative accounting" to hide bad news from stockholders and creditors while making managers feel better is not an invention of Enron, Tyco, or WorldCom, nor is it confined to business. It was found to be a factor in the bankruptcies of British companies in the 1960s and 1970s. Many currently excellent companies had earlier slid from winning to losing by a failure to communicate and deal with obvious problems masked by overly optimistic projections. For example, a former COO of Continental Airlines was shocked to discover in 1994 that previous finance staff had inflated profit projections by plugging in overly optimistic revenue estimates, keeping hidden the fact that cash was overstated. In the 1970s, public school officials hid data on declining enrollments or on school dropouts. More recently, the Houston school district, once a national model, became mired in scandal when it appeared that test scores were significantly lower and student dropout rates were significantly higher than had been claimed. It was reported that administrators pushed out kids who would skew test scores, then entered codes indicating that those students had transferred somewhere else, reducing the official dropout rate to near zero not by real actions but by false data. Texas state representative Robert Noriego told the *New York Times* that school officials were in denial of the severity of the problem.

See No Trouble, Hear No Trouble, and *Speak No Trouble* are the three monkeys of denial. Some people don't even know there's a problem, others don't want to hear about it, and a third group refuses to talk about it, perhaps because they have something to hide. Whatever its origins—in organizational patterns, politics, or mental limitations—denial can feed on itself. Chris Argyris, an organizational psychologist who became well-known in the business world for his analysis of defensiveness, found that when people wanted to protect themselves from change or their mistakes from exposure, they covered up, making some topics off limits, and then they covered up their cover-up.

Dialogue as Antidote to Denial

Denial is not inevitable, even if it is always a temptation. Dialogue—the capacity to discuss the undiscussable—is the antidote, and confidence makes it possible. Winners who continue to reinforce accountability, collaboration, and initiative are better equipped to both see and want to see mistakes and changes, because they have confidence in their ability to do something about the situation. They are much more likely to respond to troubles or threats by conducting self-examinations and reflecting on their own behavior, while losers shift blame and drown in denial. North Carolina women's soccer coach Anson Dorrance wanted his team to avoid the "victim mentality" he saw on other teams, especially opposing teams that lost to the Tar Heels. He was happy to use the press to feed whatever excuse an opponent used for why it was not their fault that they lost, such as North Carolina's "unfair advantages," like scooping up all the best players. If other teams wanted to feel like victims, let them go right ahead, he thought. Let them deny their own responsibility. Not his team. His team would have the confidence of winners to pick apart their own performance and then improve on it.

The security that accumulates in a winning streak—from longer tenure of leaders to knowledge that people can count on one another—builds confidence. That confidence makes it possible to look at one's own shortcomings rather than shift blame to others, and thus to learn from setbacks. Winners are also more likely than losers to be able to admit mistakes in public, because mistakes are so obviously a rarity, not a defining event. Miami Hurricanes head coach Larry Coker was known for attributing problems in a game to his own calls rather than to the mistakes of players. But of course he spoke from a position of strength—a long-term contract, coach-of-the-year awards, and national championships.

People associated with winning streaks are unlikely to create negative perceptions when they admit flaws before being forced to do it. Indeed, the opposite occurs: Others think more of them for being big enough to assume responsibility. That's what happened in the famous case of Johnson & Johnson's withdrawal of Tylenol from the market when it was discovered that bottles of the medicine had been sabotaged. J&J was applauded for this move. No one opened an investigation of all other J&J products to see if they had been tampered with. Instead, trust increased because of the quick confession.

Problem-solving begins with open dialogue, diagnosis of the situation, facing the facts, and mobilizing to take corrective action. When this occurs, even a loss that ends an unbroken winning streak does not interrupt a longer-term cycle of success.

Dialogue instead of denial was the mode for Geno Auriemma and the University of Connecticut Huskies after they lost the Big East Conference championship to Villanova on March 11, 2003, about six weeks after their big win at Duke, which I described in Chapter 2. Connecticut's loss ended their seventy-game winning streak in regular games as well as a streak of ten Big East championship titles.

The Huskies' first trick in avoiding denial was to reduce defensiveness by redefining the situation so that the winners hadn't suddenly become losers. No one denied that Villanova had played a better game. But the Connecticut party line was that getting beaten was different from losing. The Huskies had played well, but Villanova played even better, and there was something to learn from picking apart the game and scrutinizing themselves. Against a streak of seventy wins, losing one game wasn't a funeral, and there was no law that said that the team should win every single game. Still, they had lost, and they had to look closely at the reasons.

Auriemma told us later that in the locker room after the game, "I had to put it all into perspective for them. Usually after a game is not a good time to do that because of emotions and all. But they're all sitting there, and I felt like 'Geez, I don't want to wait until they get home to do this.' " Auriemma led them to look deeply at themselves. He talked with them about having gotten selfish and stopped caring about one another. That they'd stopped making that extra pass. That they needed to restore the chemistry of collaboration.

"We talked about getting back to where they could feed off of each other, instead of going it alone and getting tired."

Back on campus, Auriemma talked to team members in small clusters, calling on each to examine herself and find the strength to recover. The post-season NCAA tournament was still ahead. First he met with Diana Taurasi and two other upperclassmen. Though Taurasi was injured and struggling with her own game, she was the person everyone needed—"as Diana goes, so goes the team," a player said. Auriemma told Taurasi and the other two leaders about the tournament ahead, "We have either one game or six games left. It's up to you. You have to pull together. You have to fix this. It has to be you leading this team."

Then he called in three of the freshmen, asking them if they were going to roll over and fall back on the freshman excuse. "Now's the time to show why you're here," he recalled telling them. "Last year you watched us on television and said, 'Next year I'm going to be at Connecticut doing the same thing.' Well, it's here. What are you going to do about it? The three of you are going to decide whether we win this tournament, because we can't do it without you. If the three of you play like you played in the Big East tournament, we're going to lose. If the three of you play like you did at other times in the season, like in the Duke game, we'll win. You can either let that scare you, or you can let it give you confidence because all you have to do is go out and play like you are able to play."

During those ten days between games, the Huskies communicated extensively and renewed their chemistry. "The time off after the Villanova game was perfect," Auriemma declared. "We got away from everything. We didn't practice for three or four days; and we talked about a bunch of things. It gave me a chance to reconnect with them, too." Taurasi bounced back, and the team resumed winning, sweeping all six of their tournament games.

The Huskies had avoided denial and restored their confidence. Like natural optimists, they assumed that problems were temporary and solvable. They felt empowered to act, and so they were more likely to examine their own performance and make adjustments. The communication, respect, responsibility, collaboration, and initiative that surrounded them needed to be renewed, and with that renewal came the collective strength to meet any challenge.

Avoiding panic, neglect, and denial helps a team recover. Not panicking gives people the composure to think and to talk. When they talk, they are more likely to identify areas needing improvement, thus avoiding neglect. And open communication makes it impossible to sink into denial.

ERODING CONFIDENCE

Winning streaks don't end because of a fumble, a challenge, a threat, or even a loss, as we've just seen, and they don't end abruptly. Winners' advantages are a buffer against adversity. The network of investors and supporters doesn't want to see winners fail. Winners can enjoy the benefit of the doubt or the luxury of time to recover. They can afford a few losses before they panic because losses are such a small proportion of their total record—there's not so much riding on each game. There's a lag before their sins or mistakes catch up with them. But sometimes winners enjoy the benefits of their advantages, such as a network of devoted fans and a climate of emotional exuberance, without reinvesting in the core—the behavior and disciplines that ultimately produce high performance.

If relatively small sports teams in simple games can take their eyes off the ball, consider how many more traps await larger, more complex organizations that have many balls in the air.

In the mid-1990s, Gillette fumbled and lost its way, ending a decade of extraordinary success. The company had begun a ten-year winning streak after defeating several hostile takeover attempts between 1986 and 1988. At that time it convinced shareholders, many of whom were employees or retirees, that the future was brighter for them if Gillette remained independent. Gillette reorganized, closed factories, and streamlined operations to ward off future takeover attempts. In 1988, legendary investor Warren Buffett bought about $600 million in stock to become the company's largest shareholder. That year, Gillette introduced the first in a series of global blockbuster products, the Sensor Excel shaving system. It was an instant hit.

From the mid-1980s to the mid-1990s, sales tripled, profits increased sixfold, and market capitalization was up tenfold. Growth came from emerging international markets, particularly in China and post-Soviet Eastern Europe. "We were the darlings of Wall Street," recalled Ned Guillet, senior vice-president of human resources. "You worked for Gillette, and you walked with a spring in your step."

But then, just as the company was being lionized for its success, "We started believing our own press," Guillet said. Confidence became detached from its underpinnings and turned into arrogance, especially the false belief that Gillette could manage anything the same way it managed its razor-and-blade business. Strong sales and high profit margins in superstar shaving systems plus a market-leading position in toothbrushes, both stemming from earlier technology and manufacturing innovations, were a cushion against losses and hid the fact that many other parts of the company were deteriorating from neglect. Basic disciplines were ignored; managers could present a total number, but did not have to look at the details of how the total was achieved, and they became accustomed to receiving performance ratings of "exceeds expectations" no matter what they did.

In 1996 Gillette acquired Duracell for $7 billion in stock, declaring that continued high growth in alkaline batteries would offset slowdowns in other categories and create economies of scale in sales and distribution. Was this an example of "overconfidence"? Instead of helping, Duracell added to Gillette's troubles. Gillette denied problems with the acquisition, made rosy projections, and was arrogant enough to eliminate about 1,700 positions, including 80 percent of Duracell's marketing and senior sales management. Duracell's customer-service levels dropped significantly. Glossing over differences between batteries and shaving systems, Gillette attempted to manage Duracell much as it had its razor-and-blade business.

Gillette's winning streak ended in 1997. Sales growth slowed significantly, though profits remained strong. In 1998, sales were flat and profits decreased, and Gillette started losing market share in major product categories. Emerging markets in Asia were no longer a driver of growth, following a major financial crisis. Duracell was particularly hard hit by slow sales in 2000, after retailers and consumers had stockpiled batteries in 1999 in anticipation of Y2K power outages that didn't occur. By the spring of 2001, Duracell had endured twenty-one consecutive months of declining market share in an industry with high fixed costs, excess capacity, and price wars.

Ignoring signs of potential decline, Gillette continued to project high growth and increased infrastructure (and expense) to support the projections, regardless of the facts. Pressure to meet unrealistic targets led the sales force to a form of collective panic. They did anything they could to push inventory on retailers (the "trade") at the end of a quarter—discounts, promotional incentives, everything short of volunteering to work in the stores (though some of the offers of help came close). This panic-driven behavior was called "trade loading," and it only made things worse. It put Gillette in a hole at the start of the next quarter because retail inventories were full and retailers did not need to buy more, which increased desperation in the next round. "We were like a hamster running around on a wheel; it was almost impossible to succeed," declared Peter Hoffman, an executive running Gillette's grooming business.

A reorganization made matters worse. A confusing new structure diluted accountability and collaboration. Roles and responsibilities were hard to sort out, and people were told to focus only on their product category or region or function. Some groups that had been close colleagues in the previous structure were now in separate organizations. They rarely were included in the same top executive meetings, and regular meetings of the top people decreased. Everything about Gillette's complex structure made it hard to put all the facts about the business on the table and made it easier to shift blame than to take responsibility. Poor results were always someone else's fault. Later, after a new CEO came in to lead a successful turnaround—a story I tell in Chapter 7—senior managers claimed they had known all along what the problems were. But at the time, no one felt empowered to open the dialogue or initiate the actions to solve them. The three mischievous monkeys (*See No Trouble, Hear No Trouble,* and *Speak No Trouble*) popped up everywhere to stop them.

Even a great company can slip off the pattern of success. That is always the danger when the foundations of confidence crumble. Confidence is not just putting your best foot forward, it comes from having something solid to stand on. When people let the disciplines go, when they let the support system crumble, when they stop investing in one another, when they stop taking responsibility themselves, that's when they start promising things they cannot deliver. And that is when winning streaks end.

4

Losing Streaks: "Powerlessness Corrupts" and Other Dynamics of Decline

P EOPLE WHO THINK THEY ARE BEING HELD RESPONSIBLE FOR A LOS-
ING STREAK DON'T LIKE TO TALK ABOUT IT. IN THE BEGINNING,
AFTER THE FIRST FEW LOSSES, DENIAL STILL WORKS. IT IS STILL
possible to make excuses and offer upbeat forecasts. But eventually
the evidence is out there for all to see. It's bad enough to live
through those losses, but to discuss the streak adds insult to injury.
That alone is one of the human tendencies that sets in motion the
dynamics of decline.

History is written by the victors—and not just because losers
often disappear into oblivion. To put up a good front, people want
to push problems out of the mind and off the record. People would
rather characterize themselves as successful than unsuccessful.
In some situations, failure is so shameful that Japanese executives have been known to commit suicide over it. Losing certainly
makes people feel powerless, and that is not a feeling they want to
remember.

Low-performing companies, teams, schools, or hospitals do not
want their dirty linen washed in public. Those eager to talk with me
(on the record, instead of just picking my brains for advice) were
overwhelmingly likely to be successful or headed for success. In
business, that group included a disproportionate number of people
in companies that had performed relatively well from 2001 to 2003
despite the economic downturn and who felt fairly optimistic about

the future. In sports, more than three-quarters of the athletes and coaches considered their teams to be winners; only a handful whom I spoke to could be called perennial losers, because they feel punished and defensive enough without being asked how it feels to be a loser. The head of a losing sports team told us, "We may criticize folks amongst ourselves, but not to the outside world."

Later, after a turnaround, leaders are comfortable with recounting—and even exaggerating—how dreadful it was under previous regimes. There are many retrospective accounts of the decline and fall of this or that empire, many Enron–type postmortems dealing with what went wrong. But when a team first begins to accumulate losses, when a person starts feeling like a failure, when a company starts having problems, when panic and chaos reign, it is hard to get them to tell the world about it. That's why the company in the story that follows will remain anonymous. I call it "Static" because of the extra noise in the system when this once-successful enterprise started losing, the sound of a culture that made it harder and harder for Static to recover.

GETTING STATIC: HOW DECLINE BECOMES A HABIT

I made repeat visits to Static over several years. I spent time in executives' offices, on the production floor, and chatting with receptionists behind the security desk at the front entrance of the company's headquarters. The offices were in a former warehouse in a remote location, the result of a recent move to cheaper space, because Static had abandoned its once free-spending ways. (My stint as occasional strategic adviser was after the era when they would send the company plane for visitors and meet it with the white stretch limousine's bar fully stocked.) The CEO hoped he could will the company back to health through the power of speeches; he liked my message about strategy and organizational culture, and he hoped it would reinforce his. But looking at his own behavior as a leader was about the last thing he wanted to do, even though I urged him to do so, and so we parted company. The depressed atmosphere was wearing down even the natural optimists among the "we try harder" types at Static, who were valiantly trying to do their jobs.

Static was once a rapidly growing industry darling involved in Information Age products and services. A new CEO took the helm after it had become a shrinking industry laggard. He did not do too much to improve the situation, despite three or four grand announcements of three or four bold new strategies in less than three years, each of them taking Static in another direction. Some of those years were during the technology bust, it's true, but Static had a few high-quality products and other assets that might have served it better.

A series of lackluster products and expenses too high for a shrinking post-tech-crash market had started Static on a downward path. At the same time, its largest rival went from strength to strength, in the same unforgiving market. It was almost as if they were now two different species. The rival could do no wrong, Static could do no right. One analyst declared that Static was worth more dead than alive. Institutional customers called to ask whether the company would meet service commitments to its products. Each group that questioned Static's viability caused other groups to lose confidence.

Static tried to bounce back with the launch of two innovative products. But neither of those moved Static off the death watch, because everything Static did was now viewed as evidence of weakness. Earlier, when Static was on the rise, its founders were lionized as brilliant strategists, and the praise heaped on Static made its products more desirable, reinforcing a growth spiral. Now everything Static did was interpreted in the least favorable light, giving the company a negative halo. Reviews of Static's hot new products invariably included questions about whether they were good enough. In good times, halo effects hide weaknesses; in bad times, they hide strengths.

Outsiders had lost confidence in Static, and that encouraged Static to lose confidence in itself. Here is how accountability, collaboration, and initiative disappeared at the company, and how the crumbling of the foundations of confidence caused it to sink below water.

Turf: The Enemy of Change

As problems mounted, so did the likelihood that managers would retreat to their own turf and defend it against change. People tended to either blame or avoid one another. Since bad news is never as welcome as good news, and there was more bad than good, Static managers became less communicative. It's not that they were consciously hiding problems, but they found reasons to cancel meetings to avoid having to relay and receive bad news, often invoking workload as the excuse. Managers retreated to their own territory instead of thinking about Static as a whole.

When Static had its first string of consecutive quarters of decline, the company's leadership thought they could push their way out of it by exhorting people to increase their efforts to reduce expenses and launch new products faster. Commands started flowing from the top. Tighter cost controls were greeted with cynicism, as people whispered that none of it mattered if the company collapsed. Some began to do the minimum, showing up at work only long enough to earn their end-of-year bonus; everyone assumed that others would be leaving, so they said it was not worth getting to know them. Managers distanced themselves from company decisions, telling me that they weren't involved, or that they disagreed, or that someone in another department was responsible.

The CEO told managers to focus on improving their own performance, and he put their bonuses at risk. As group heads emphasized meeting current targets, the company virtually eliminated cross-functional or cross-division projects. Groups knew less about what was going on in other parts of the organization and stopped caring—or they fantasized about what others were doing to cut them out of their share of a declining budget. Avoidance of engagement with one another led to duplication of effort because each group felt it was faster and easier to do it themselves than to try to persuade others to join them or to get coordinated action. One example was the variety of methods for ensuring accountability and tracking projects that several large units established on their own. The result was that differences grew greater over time, furthering isolation.

Turf was clearly the enemy of change. Secrecy and isolation, blame and avoidance, accelerated the death spiral. Time and energy were spent on self-protection instead of on joint problem-solving. Invisible walls grew taller. Most senior executives at Static sat within a few feet of one another in offices with glass walls, yet many professed ignorance of the plans of other units to solve Static's problems. The CEO and the finance chief tended to control the information that circulated. Though reporting requirements increased during Static's troubled period, communication outside of formal meetings decreased.

Meetings of top management at Static became less frequent, and it was unusual for all of the senior executives to sit down in one room together. Executives found reasons not to attend meetings, because those few meetings that remained had degenerated into commands by the CEO, followed by uninformative reports. No one wanted to raise questions because that tended to produce angry exchanges as department heads accused one another of putting obstacles in their path. The game became one of blaming others before they could blame you, and when there was no obvious external enemy to attack, there was always another internal group. For example, the head of customer service wrote memos outlining the problems other divisions were causing that his department had to fix. Since good performers did not want to be tainted with the failure of poor performers, those units with strong sales became openly scornful of their colleagues in other units and made sure to communicate their scorn to people outside the company, including customers and investment analysts. Managers bypassed meetings by invoking the need to focus their efforts on improving the performance of their own units.

Isolation and avoidance were both cause and result of lack of mutual respect. Those who had opportunities were leaving, though to companies less prominent than Static, which further reinforced the loser mentality—and the feeling that one should jump ship now before the "loser" label was applied. Not all of the departures were mourned, as some senior managers had not lived up to expectations. But the fact that Static was constantly recruiting to fill holes at the top, and that critical functions were left undone because executives were given double duty (e.g., the CIO taking on operations), further reinforced decline dynamics.

It was whispered that anyone still left at Static must be a loser because they couldn't find another job; people felt it necessary to assure an outside consultant that they did not have to work at Static. There was so little interest in socializing outside of work that the CEO *ordered* his direct reports to show up at a company social event. Executives who tried to comment about broad company issues were shot down if they ventured an opinion outside of their formal responsibilities. The head of technology planning, who had successfully founded and sold a software company, was shut out of conversations about finding new markets; no one respected his views on anything but technology.

The Timidity of Mediocrity

Many people at Static began to feel there was little they could do to make a difference in the fortunes of the company. They were trapped, with no exit in sight. They were mired in "learned helplessness," a state identified by psychologist Martin Seligman, in which repeated failures to get out of a difficult situation teach people not even to try.

The CEO complained that he had to come up with all the good ideas. The more he complained, the worse people felt about their own ideas, since presumably their ideas were not the good ones. Managers set low goals to guarantee that they would achieve them. One group tested a new method to sell company products that doubled sales, but other managers wrote much lower numbers into their plans, in case the new method wouldn't work for them. Think of this as the opposite of the arrogance of success—it is the timidity of mediocrity.

To cope with decline, Static got caught up in trade loading, a common trap in financially troubled companies. By discounting aggressively or offering special delayed-payment deals, Static adopted a tantalizingly simple short-run "solution" to declining sales that only made the situation worse. Price cuts reduced funds for marketing, which increased the company's reliance on promotional deals; and customers knew they could wait until quarter's end to get even better deals. Static's managers felt they had no choice but to continue to discount. Acting from a weak bargaining position reinforced an ever-weakening bargaining position.

Meanwhile, the CEO was overpromising results to the investor community in order to avoid further decline in the stock price, so he put more pressure on executives, especially the finance head, who began to hide bad news as long as he could, which meant keeping certain numbers to himself. A combination of managers with low aspirations and little innovation, a CEO making inflated promises, and numbers that couldn't be relied on was a formula for reducing everyone's confidence. When quarterly results proved lower than forecast, or when the company had to restate figures, outraged analysts and infuriated reporters took revenge by stories discrediting even the positives at Static, causing further decline in the stock price.

Individual choices, in which each person or group tried to exercise whatever power they felt they had, added up to a system that made all of them feel powerless—caught in a system impossible to change.

Doom Loops

Static was caught in a number of "doom loops" in which responses to problems made the problems get worse, not better. Panic leads to a search for quick fixes—something, anything to feel better, to feel that action is being taken, to feel a modicum of control. Quick fixes in the face of a loss can both undermine the long-term strategy and deflect attention from it. The classic business quick fix is to cut costs. After all, costs are something that can be controlled. But by focusing only on costs, the company might create a product no one wants to buy, which reduces revenues and creates losses, which makes it impossible to borrow at reasonable rates, which increases expenses, which means cutting costs further, which means reducing employee compensation, which creates disgruntled employees who take it out on customers with further declines in service. As more customers leave, the company must cut costs further.

Every unhappy organization is unhappy in its own way, to paraphrase Tolstoy's famous conclusion about families. Yet the dynamics of decline are remarkably similar. Underlying the problems of distressed organizations are pathological patterns that are self-perpetuating and mutually reinforcing. Decline is not a state, it is a trajectory. Losing teams, distressed organizations, declining empires, and even depressed people often run downhill at an accelerating pace. Common reactions to failure prevent success and make losing in the future more likely. Unchecked cycles of decline can easily turn into death spirals. Problems are exacerbated by responses that make them ever harder to solve. Secrecy, blame, isolation, avoidance, lack of respect, and feelings of helplessness create a culture that makes the situation worse and makes change seem impossible.

Decline generally does not stem from a single factor, but from an accumulation of decisions, actions, and commitments that become entangled in self-perpetuating system dynamics. Once a cycle of decline is established, it is hard to simply call a halt, put on the brakes, and reverse direction. The system has momentum. Expectations have formed, and they can turn into a culture that perpetuates losing.

SORE LOSERS:
WHY POWERLESSNESS CORRODES AND CORRUPTS

Everyone likes to win. No one likes to lose. You'd think that people would do everything they can to avoid losing. So how does losing become a habit?

If losses mount, pressure goes up—or the perception of pressure. (Losers in my sports research are much more likely than winners to answer "too much" to a question about the amount of pressure facing athletes today.) Stress makes it easier to panic. Panic makes it easier to lose. Losing increases neglect—letting buildings get run down, discipline deteriorate, good manners disappear. Signs of failure cause people to dislike and avoid one another, hide information, and disclaim responsibility—key elements of denial. All this makes the cornerstones of confidence crumble. People doubt themselves, feel they cannot count on others, and do not trust the system around them. The climate of expectations turns negative, and everyone begins to feel powerless to change anything.

Plunk an optimist with a history of winning into a loss-inducing situation, and even the optimist gets dragged down.

Consider the experience of Lou Piniella, who had a lifetime of winning before he took over a losing professional baseball team, the Tampa Bay Devil Rays, and immediately started to lose not only ball games but his confidence. Piniella opened his professional baseball career as a player in 1964 and spent eleven seasons with the New York Yankees, a winning dynasty. Later he became a manager and general manager of the Yankees as well as other teams. In sixteen years as a Major League manager, his teams had eleven winning seasons.

On October 28, 2002, Piniella was given a four-year, $13-million contract to be the Rays' third manager. In his first season, 2003, the Rays finished with a total of 63 wins and 99 losses, just the same as their 1998 record, though marginally better than their 55–106 performance in 2002. "Losing beats you down," he told a *New York Times Magazine* reporter in midseason. "It's not an easy transition for me. I'm win-oriented. I came to the realization a few days ago that I can't be concerned with losses. I should evaluate and develop talent for next year. But that's easier said than done. My ego told me I could win in any situation. Now I've been humbled."

The atmosphere in Tampa Bay was totally different from the positive, energetic climate surrounding winners. The Devil Rays played at Tropicana Field, a domed stadium built in 1990, but despite its modern exterior, it was described as a "barren and dispirited place that often has no more than 6,000 fans sprinkled among the seats." Team employees were cheerful, but "with the gallows humor of the doomed." The team's media representative said to the *Times* writer, "I was gonna wait until we won a game before I introduced you, but, hell, we may never win another game." Silence pervaded the dugout, and players didn't talk about the game, nor did they gather after games. Passivity prevailed. Piniella was said to have "gone berserk, a real meltdown," because he was furious with a player who didn't swing at a pitch that ended the game with a third strike. The player said that he didn't argue with the umpire because it didn't matter. The next day the player wasn't even sure he'd show up at the ballpark.

Temper tantrums, no-show workers, absent fans, and gallows humor—that is a classic description of some of the things associated with being sore losers. Being a sore loser is usually blamed on the person. But when people are sore losers, it is often because they have been wounded; they are sore in the sense of being in pain, covered with aches and bruises. It is often not the fault of individuals that they become sore losers. Instead, that behavior stems from the system surrounding them. An ailing system inflicts wounds.

Losing streaks begin in response to a sense of failure, and failure makes people feel out of control. It is just one more step to a pervasive sense of powerlessness, and powerlessness corrodes confidence. When there are few resources or coping mechanisms for dealing with problems, people fall back on almost primitive, self-protective behavior. Nine pathologies begin to unfold, as an emotional and behavioral chain reaction:

- Communication decreases.
- Criticism and blame increase.
- Respect decreases.
- Isolation increases.
- Focus turns inward.

- Rifts widen and inequities grow.
- Initiative decreases.
- Aspirations diminish.
- Negativity spreads.

These behavioral tendencies are polar opposites of the characteristics that help winners win. Such responses to losing make it harder to recover, harder to solve problems, harder to ever win again. These losers' temptations feed on themselves, each tendency reinforcing the others. Powerlessness corrodes the cornerstones of confidence, reducing accountability, collaboration, and initiative. And at the extreme, it can corrupt, if losers' habits lead to acts of petty tyranny, selfishness, and a desire to harm others.

Understanding each of the losers' temptations makes clear how to recognize the symptoms of decline, and why it is so important to avoid them. If untreated, these responses can turn a few losses into a long losing streak, and modest decline into a death spiral.

Communication Decreases

Conversations about losing are not too much fun, nor are they always productive. Meetings with defensive people on uncomfortable matters are difficult, as anyone knows who has ever tried to talk with a teenager about keeping the house clean or a building contractor about missed deadlines and cost overruns. When the agenda involves problems that provoke anxiety but do not yet have explanations or solutions, discussions tend to wander into uncomfortable territory, digging up old hurts and unrelated issues.

Since meetings are less productive and less enjoyable, people try to avoid them. Losers are twice as likely as winners to report that communication has diminished. In losing companies and losing sports teams, individuals say that others in their work group or on the team are "too busy with their own work" to attend meetings or put in extra time to make improvements. (Maybe they are, or maybe that's an excuse.) They say that they generally don't talk about past successes or past problems, so they are not learning from experience. And the losing companies are twice as likely as the winning companies to have reduced the number of management meetings in the preceding two years. At the very time when communication is most needed, losers are more likely to stop talking.

Decreasing communication begins at the top. Since no one intends to lose (except on rare occasions when there's a political reason for letting someone else win), then when an organization loses, those in charge feel out of control. Executives who are accustomed to controlling everything short of making the earth move are uncomfortable about standing in front of people and in essence admitting that they are not in charge of the universe. It is very hard for many executives to reveal that they do not have answers. They are unable to say the words "I don't know" out loud, fearing that their authority will be undermined. Instead, after bad results, there's a tendency to cut off conversation and shut the doors. Losers, compared with winners, are nearly four times as likely to keep information in the hands of a small group that operates in secrecy behind closed doors, shutting everyone else out.

Sometimes "focus" is invoked as a reason for a decrease in communication—a few people in the "war room" while others go about business as usual. Sometimes silence involves a plot or a cover-up. Sometimes communication decreases because officials think they must make unpopular decisions. Fearing retaliation, they try to sneak those decisions through when they think no one's looking, and say as little as possible about them. That's the rationale some companies use for brutal mass layoffs in which people come to work after a weekend to find their office doors locked and their belongings removed. Stealth moves like this are not confined to the corporate world. The administration of a foundering university canceled its sports program while its sports-loving students were on spring vacation.

Of course, when word leaks, as it inevitably does, or when facts finally must be faced, lack of communication has reduced opportunities for others to offer solutions and has increased the anger floating around the system. Whatever its source, denial leads down the same blind alley. As numerous recent scandals have shown, coverups are often worse than the original mistake. Companies in trouble compound their financial and strategic woes when they keep information secret from their employees and the public. Teams that are left in the dark can't work effectively to improve. And problem-solving is impossible if people do not have all the facts.

Blame Increases

Everyone knows how much finger-pointing accompanies losing. *It was his fault, not mine! Find the weak link! Off with her head!* Blame starts flying in all directions. People make excuses for themselves and pass the blame on to someone else. And the scapegoat, whoever he or she is, is sacrificed in a ritual slaughter that creates the illusion that the problem has been purged. By finding the person or group supposedly at fault, all the others can breathe a sigh of relief that they survived and go back to business as usual. But while the scapegoat is gone, the problems remain. This was a historic pattern in baseball: Losing teams frequently fired their managers, getting a light immediate uptick but failing to improve after that. And watching the treatment of the scapegoat makes people fear for their own security should the group turn on them. Anxiety increases. And as we saw in the last chapter, anxiety can produce panic, which can produce fumbles, which can contribute to losing.

Losing teams and work groups in declining companies are more than twice as likely as winners to indulge in blame and look for scapegoats in response to problems. Anything but self-scrutiny. Anything but admitting one's own need for change. Sometimes a culture of victimization and blame is taken to ridiculous extremes, such as a shoe chain (Just for Feet) suing an advertising agency (Saatchi & Saatchi) for $10 million because its 1999 Super Bowl ad was labeled racist and didn't increase sales; Just for Feet, already in a downward spiral after a growth spurt in earlier years, filed for bankruptcy less than a year later.

Self-doubt, which arises among those on losing teams, is masked by attack: *I'll attack you before you can attack me.* Defensiveness is externalized. Convenient enemies on whom to blame problems can be found even on one's own team—other positions, departments, or divisions; or among people who are different in race, ethnicity, or class. The desire to retaliate against the people or circumstances assumed to be the "cause" of failure can become all-consuming. When getting revenge becomes more important than getting results, losers continue to fall behind. Attack and blame might be temporarily satisfying, but they don't do much to address the reasons the group is losing.

Constant criticism has other pernicious effects. At a New York City financial institution that started slipping badly, a "blame culture" of dressing down people in public was exemplified by the punishing behavior of the chief investment officer (later fired), who was described as having a "big attitude, a Wall Street attitude, and a blame mentality." He attacked people even when they worked hard. So why put in the effort? Everybody left the office at exactly four-thirty; on the dot. Customer complaints piled up until someone felt like getting to them. This losers' culture was pervasive and endemic. Of course, the fact that people put in little effort meant that the chief investment officer got angrier and more irritable, taking it out on his employees by publicly scolding them.

Criticizing performance in unwelcome ways can set people up to fail. Social psychologists distinguish between informational feedback, which can be constructive and useful, and controlling feedback, which is often perceived as punitive and destructive of self-esteem. Constant criticism of people assumed to be low performers reinforces poor performance when it focuses on failures rather than successes, provides too many detailed instructions, offers unsolicited advice, and keeps people on a tight leash. The targets of criticism and blame perceive their bosses' "help" as interference, their bosses' "suggestions" as insulting and inhibiting. As their feelings of defensiveness and powerlessness grow, they put in less effort and came to doubt their own abilities.

Respect Decreases

The sheer amount of criticism surrounding people undermines their confidence in one another and makes them feel that they are surrounded by mediocrity. In a declining insurance company, for example, there was a prevailing view that this was not an "A" company that could attract the best people. Because it was assumed that only people with few options and little talent would work there, a culture of mediocrity reinforced low self-esteem and meant that people rejected one another's ideas because they clearly came from losers. A culture of mediocrity suppresses innovation.

It is certainly possible that winning teams have more talent than losing teams, because the ability to attract talent is one of the advantages that winners accumulate. But to overcome this bias, I included high school sports in my research, since public high schools do not recruit, nor do they even control the population from which they draw athletes. Among the high school groups, people on losing teams have much less respect and admiration for teammates than do those on winning teams, and they report that not only do other people lack talent, but they don't work to improve their individual skill level. And those who do work hard lose respect for the people who don't. An athlete said, "I don't like my team because nobody works as hard as I do. I am the only one that shows a certain amount of drive that makes me successful." Another, responding to what he liked most about the team, said flatly, "Nothing. School sports sucks. If I have to choose one thing, it would only be the bus ride to and from the games. . . . I wish they were more serious about the game and took the time to play year-round to improve their skill level."

People lose not only respect for one another, but confidence in the system. When things start to slip, there is a widespread perception that it is because low performance is tolerated. Losing companies are more than three times as likely as winners to be seen as tolerating deadwood, as having low hiring standards. This perception of company mediocrity carries over to work groups in which people in declining organizations are much more likely to wonder if others in their group pull their weight, lack admiration for the skills and talents of other people on the team and say so, and doubt if trying to improve their own skill level would make much difference.

Loss of respect surrounds the whole organization. A loser culture casts an aura of negativity over everyone. Failing to root out the bad performers taints the good ones.

Isolation Increases

There is a common saying that "Misery loves company," as though Misery were a living character. But Misery loves company only in the sense of wanting to spread the gloom. Otherwise Misery prefers to be alone, thank you very much, sitting in the corner sulking while keeping an eye out for his own interests. Misery certainly doesn't want to be reminded of failure by being in the company of other losers.

While those associated with losing isolate themselves, other people compound withdrawal by in turn isolating them. Other people take guilty pleasure in hearing about losers, they just don't want to sit next to them at dinner parties. Losers are shunned as if losing were contagious. And other people don't want to have it assumed that if they're in the company of losers, they must be losers, too. Consider this indicator of how people in losing situations can distance themselves from one another: Almost half of the people in declining companies told me that they rarely or never socialize together outside work hours, compared with only a quarter of those in successful companies. I find the same gap between losing and winning high school sports teams, which is especially striking given that a high proportion of teenagers play sports to be with their friends. Perhaps this withdrawal from nonessential contact is why the CEO of the company I've dubbed Static had to order executives to show up at a company party.

Focus Turns Inward

Depressed people turn inward and become self-absorbed. As individuals they can indulge themselves in reclusive behavior, withdrawing, staying at home, licking their wounds, or drowning in their sorrows. Depressed organizations have the same tendency to shut off contact with the outside world, to ignore or neglect customers or suppliers while they meet purely internal goals. When its period of decline started in the 1990s, the BBC had lost contact with its audience. Low-performing public schools in my study were out of touch with parents and the community.

An inward focus characterizes people in work groups that have started to lose, but it is muted by outward appearances, because sports teams or work groups require people to at least show up and go out on the field together. Still, going through the motions is not the same as being engaged with other people. People associated with losing streaks are more likely to refrain from telling other people what is on their minds and are much less likely to offer constructive suggestions to help other people improve. In short, they become self-absorbed and look out for themselves first. They become selfish.

Whatever its origin, "self-focus" (the term psychologists use) is likely to perpetuate losing. Studies have shown that self-focused attention is associated with depression and failure experiences. People under stress become more self-focused, and as they pay more attention to themselves in the process of executing a task, the more likely it is that their skills will fail. Basketball novices who were instructed to focus on the mechanics of ball-shooting during practice did more poorly in a stressful test phase than those required only to do their best. Becoming over-aware of every little thing is distracting and can cause mistakes.

Organizations in trouble tell people to improve their own results, as Static did, and that exacerbates self-focus. Concentrating only on one's own numbers or one's own small group avoids the risk of contact with others who might attack, deprive, seize an advantage, or just remind you that you're a loser. In professional baseball, it is well known that players on losing teams focus on their individual statistics, such as home runs or base hits, without regard to whether this helps the team win the game. That is the equivalent of star performers in a declining company doing things for the sake of their résumés, not for their company.

There is less trust among people caught in a losing situation. Why should people have faith in those who let them down—or whom they feel might be thinking that it was the other way around? But trusting only in yourself and yours is profoundly adversarial and can easily lead to animosity, power displays, armed conflicts, and corruption. As people take only for themselves, they deplete reserves rather than contribute to building. Organizational selfishness sets in. Losing raises the specter of deprivation, of a shrinking pie. No one wants to put off feeding if the pie might disappear. It is a primitive instinct. No one wants to be the first to put his or her share of the pie back on the table for fear that others will just grab it and gorge.

Rifts Widen and Inequities Grow

It is apparent how pathologies are perpetuated. If people are self-focused and have little respect for others, they might succumb to the temptation to become autocratic, shutting others out of decisions. This is only one of the many rifts that come between those who start losing and their ability to work effectively as a team.

People in losing situations are over four times as likely as those in winning situations to tell me that their team or work group never or rarely pulls together nor presents a unified image—one of the strongest differences between losers and winners of any of the behaviors I asked about. Athletes on teams that always or generally lost during the most recent season who predict that they will also lose the next season describe more fighting than bonding, more conflict than collaboration. They make comments such as these: "Our team has a lot of ups and downs because we argue a lot. We lose a lot because we fuss and fight." "If everyone would get along better off the court, it would make us a better team." "The thing I wish was different is including the whole team in bonding events."

Not surprisingly, the same divisiveness occurs in declining companies. More than twice as many people associated with decline than with success told me that their company is characterized by internal rivalries and competition between groups. Even more revealing is the fact that company bosses seem to like it that way, because they rarely or never utilize teams that include people from many parts of the company. In business-speak, this divisiveness is likened to staying within separate silos, in reference to figurative grain towers in which people sit to watch their own crops and protect them against thefts by their neighbors (even when neighbors are supposedly on the same big team).

Competition among individuals, cliques, or departments can easily make some feel deprived relative to others. That's why sports teams that rely solely on a few stars do not seem to win as regularly as ones in which the whole team feels important and the stars feel their obligations to the team. Stars can do things that improve their own statistics without contributing to victory. And as stars hog the ball—and attention, glory, and rewards—other people get fewer chances to play, to improve, and to contribute, so they let their skills lapse. When team members feel closer to one another, they are also more likely to work out their differences, although it's hard to tell which is cause and which is effect. Power differentials and social distance make collaboration difficult.

Growing inequality perpetuates decline when it is based on factors other than performance and seems to be unfair. The temptation to hoard for one's own use or to dole out favors and buy loyalty is greater among losers than among winners, because people in authority have fewer of the expanding winners' assets that permit widespread generosity. I see this as one of the seeds of graft and corruption in poor countries or deprived communities. The less there is to go around, the more people fight about it, and the greater the temptation becomes to get more by forming a cabal. Certainly in troubled organizations, managers are thought to play favorites—giving people privileges or promotions for reasons other than objective performance. A similar tendency is reported by disaffected athletes who think that their coaches give unworthy players too many opportunities; some lament that they wish their coaches would play the right people and not their favorites. Favoritism not only widens rifts but also is felt to cause teams to lose.

Minimizing inequality doesn't mean that everyone gets exactly the same treatment; it means that they play by the same rules. Envy arises when people see differential treatment that is perceived to be unfair. Then envy makes the situation worse. If group members are resentful of one another, the result is a great deal of dissatisfaction, very little cohesiveness, and poor performance, as people withhold effort.

Lack of contact and localized decisions—emphasizing only what's good for one's own group—means that stereotypes are perpetuated and the basis for cooperation undermined. Rumors can spread unchecked, and people can come to see others as enemies. Without firsthand contact by Nora in New York or Michael in Miami, Harry in Hawaii can be viewed as hostile, and when he senses that he's viewed negatively, it almost invariably comes true. Knowledge that one is stereotyped depresses performance.

Aspirations Diminish

One way to cope with losing is to reduce aspirations, to look for life satisfactions elsewhere, to say that winning or losing really doesn't matter. Athletes are considered to be competitive people, yet some athletes on losing teams feel that others on their team have given up on wanting to perform to the highest standards of their sport; no one on winning teams says this. The willingness to settle for mediocrity burgeons for work groups in declining companies. People in businesses caught in a downward spiral are likely to report that others do not care about performing to the highest standards for their industry.

The motivation for groups that start to lose often becomes not losing by much. They don't even think about winning; they simply want to hold losses to a minimum. The motivation in declining bureaucracies is often just to keep the job, not to contribute to results. It's enough to get through each period and survive without too much punishment; there's no need to aim higher. Over time, low aspirations produce low performance and justify low aspirations.

Psychologists use the term "defensive pessimism" to describe the way some people set low expectations to cope with anxiety in risky situations. This set of people is not trying to make excuses or deny responsibility, they just prefer to expect failure, so as not to be totally debilitated by anxiety about whether they can meet a lofty goal. By indicating that they expect to fail, they can focus on the task rather than becoming overly self-conscious. But the psychological laboratory is not real life. In real life—as in the sports teams, businesses, schools, and communities in my research—pessimism, whether defensive or not, is associated with excuses for failure, with denial of responsibility, and it serves as a self-fulfilling prophecy, even more than optimism does. Pessimists are proven right so often because losing is easier than winning. And setting low aspirations means losing the will to win.

"Defensive pessimism" seems the safer bet. It is often better to underpromise and overdeliver than to overpromise and underdeliver. But there is a difference between cautious forecasts that stick close to the facts and avoid irrational exuberance, and believing that nothing more is possible or worth aiming for. There is also a difference between manipulating expectations to keep them deliberately lower (as politicians do so they can prevent their supporters from becoming complacent) and not even believing that victory is possible.

For people accustomed to losing, it is too risky to aim higher—to even venture out onto the water, let alone try to walk on it. They do not want to take any risks—and no one associated with them believes that they are capable of success if they do take risks. As aspirations diminish, people begin to feel fatalistic—that they can't do anything to help achieve a win. They give up, they retire on the job.

They are physically present but mentally absent—a state now labeled "presenteeism" to distinguish it from "absenteeism." The body is there, but the spirit is gone.

Initiative Decreases

People can become paralyzed by anxiety—the "learned helplessness" I saw at Static. After a series of failures, decision paralysis can set in. People feel discredited and demoralized, as they don't know which way to turn because there seems no way out. Then bosses swoop in to make decisions with an air of impatience and scorn—like the CEO of Static who complained that his executives were worthless because he had to do all the thinking himself. But having the boss ignore their ideas and then make a big deal out of announcing the solution further paralyzes people.

Even when people know how they should act to get ahead of a problem when losses begin, they don't do it for fear of failure or reprisal. Why speak up if they are likely to be wrong? People on losing teams or in losing companies are much more likely to think that there is little they can do to change their circumstances (helplessness), and that there are too many things stacked against them (hopelessness). If this is how people in losing situations interpret the troubles faced by themselves or their team, they sound exactly like pessimists. Pessimists see problems as stemming from stable and universal causes, thus making them less susceptible to corrective action. Optimists, in contrast, view problems as temporary and resulting from specific factors that will either change or be changed. There is also a slightly greater tendency for pessimists to believe that things that happen are directed by others (technically an "external locus of control"), while optimists believe in their own self-determination (an "internal locus of control"), but any difference is small.

If people think that there's nothing they can do, then why bother doing anything? Losers are much more likely than winners to go passive. Not many people actually withhold all effort for long, because, after all, players, workers, and managers go to work every day and must get involved in meeting the challenges of games or high-profile tasks regardless of the streaks their groups are on. But losers are likely to do just the minimum of following routines; they rarely or never make suggestions that will help their team or organization improve. Winners, on the other hand, are almost universally likely to jump in with their suggestions.

Why is it that losers, who really need those improvement ideas, don't get them, thus perpetuating the cycle of decline? Their helplessness is reinforced by the culture around them. The general work style of losing businesses is nearly twice as likely to include many ingrained policies and routines that are hard to change, and nearly one-third offered zero encouragement to employees to propose new ideas and no support in creating projects. (In contrast, every single person I spoke to on a winning streak said that they never encounter a lack of support for new ideas.)

Because hopelessness, amplified by helplessness, can make people feel that there is no point in trying to improve the situation because there's not much they can do about it, initiative decreases, and hopelessness becomes a self-fulfilling prophecy.

Negativity Spreads

We have already seen that moods are contagious. Emotional contagion works to spread a positive atmosphere for winners, and it does the same thing to sprinkle negativity in the vicinity of losers. People become adept at reading the cues associated with the negative or positive moods. After a Major League Baseball team lost fourteen straight games, their body language when they walked out onto the field exuded defeatism—a little sluggish, a few slumped shoulders. They looked like—well, losers.

Negativity reduces energy. When people feel depressed, their energy decreases; they feel depleted, drained. Carolyn Cohen, a clinical psychologist, told me that in her practice, the major effect of antidepressant drugs is to help people feel more energetic. In work situations, lack of energy is often experienced as burnout, or emotional fatigue. Negativity has a sufficiently strong influence that even when people vow to be positive, they can't be. Athletes know the importance of self-talk; when the loser word enters their minds, it gets in the way of their performance. However small, the effects are stronger for pessimists than optimists and for losers than winners.

Call this a loser mindset in a loser culture. Failure becomes a self-fulfilling prophecy, and poor performance is both cause and effect. Poor performance is the *consequence* of ineffective actions in the past, but it is also the *cause* of actions that further depress performance.

THE UNDERTOW OF DEFEAT:
WHY LOSERS END UP UNDER WATER

This chapter is a cautionary tale. It is not a prescription for a cure—that comes later in the book, when I go inside the turnaround process. But an understanding of the symptoms, and how they work together as a system to start an escalating cycle of decline, illuminates how confidence erodes, and thus is the first step in considering what to do about it.

When losing makes people feel out of control, and when they give in to the temptations associated with defending against feeling powerless, the seeds of systemic pathologies are sown. Powerlessness undermines resilience. It eliminates the accountability, collaboration, and initiative winners use to solve problems and get on with the next game. Instead of believing in positive futures, everyone expects the worst of everyone else—and then acts to make those expectations come true. Self-confidence, confidence in one another, and confidence in the system disappear.

Sometimes powerlessness not only corrodes the foundations, it corrupts the whole system. At the extreme, truly pathological behavior can emerge, the kind that produces cataclysmic social diseases: conspiracies and cover-ups by small cabals or elites acting only for themselves; autocratic bosses and officious managers who exercise total control, whimsically; rampant greed, selfishness, and petty turf battles; resentment, envy, and plots to punish those who escape or succeed; the temptation to cut corners, skirt rules, make excuses, and shift blame to someone else. These pathologies hurt everyone. When such behaviors show up, they are signs that accountability, collaboration, and initiative have not just weakened, but have disappeared entirely. Instead of stones enabling people to walk on water, there are only predators just below the surface, ready to pull them under.

When powerlessness corrupts, the situation gets systematically worse, not systematically better. Healthy coping and healthy problem-solving are undermined. If these tendencies and temptations are carried into the next game, and even into the next generation of players, then the cycle of decline deepens.

That is how losing starts to become a habit. And that is how a few losses can turn into long losing streaks.

5

Why Losing Streaks Persist

"EVERYBODY STARTS OUT AT 0–0 AT THE BEGINNING OF THE GAME. EVERYBODY IS EVEN," PROCLAIMED ONE COACH WHOSE TEAM WAS IN A DECADES-LONG LOSING STREAK. BILLY BEANE, revolutionary general manager of the Oakland Athletics baseball team, made a similar point, that mathematically each game is a new start.

Unfortunately, they are both wrong. The scoreboard on the field might say 0–0, but the scoreboard of history is already filled. Each game does not reset the organizational score to zero, any more than each quarter is a fresh beginning for a business or than each day a new life for a person. Reset an old car's odometer to zero, and it is still an old car. Having performed well or poorly creates a legacy, a record, that is carried into the next rounds. When a few losses turn into a losing streak, forces pile up that burden athletes when they start playing the game, project teams when they start meeting on new tasks, executive groups when they start making strategic decisions, public school teachers when they begin teaching classes in a low-performing school, and presidents and their cabinets when they take office.

It is a common human error to attribute patterns to events that are firmly independent, such as rolls of the dice or turns of the cards. Gamblers talk about their "hot hands," even though the odds are no different in each subsequent round from what they were in previous rounds. But people also make the opposite error—denying that there are patterns underlying events in organizations, ignoring

113

dynamics of the system that make it easier or harder to win the next one.

At first it is not clear whether problems are a trend or a blip. Once losses accumulate, however, a streak takes on the weight of history. A Chicago Cubs pitcher who had been with the perennially losing team for two years told us, "I don't go out there thinking that we've got to find a way to get this ninety-five-year jinx out of the way." But it's hard to believe that the jinx is not in the back of players' minds. Other Cubs told us they are aware that more is riding on every game because of their long residence at the bottom. There's an old parlor trick in which one person instructs others, "Don't think about elephants." The trick is that once the thought of elephants is planted, it's almost impossible to put elephants out of mind. Past performance shifts expectations, and expectations can often turn into self-fulfilling prophecies.

Often, but not always. What else is going on that turns a few losses into a longer losing streak? Once a person, a team, or an organization starts losing, why does it become harder to win? How do a few bad habits on the part of a few people become a culture of losing that is transmitted from one generation to the next? What causes confidence not just to dip but to erode at an accelerating rate? And why does it take so long for anyone to do something about it?

Losing creates pressure. It tempts people to behave in ways that erode their ability to solve problems and causes them to lose confidence in themselves, in one another, and in their leaders. When losses continue, often as a direct result of blame, turf protection, or passivity, something larger occurs. The investment climate surrounding losers changes dramatically—the institutional environment from which they draw their support becomes significantly less nurturing. As investors, suppliers, customers, talent sources, sponsors, traditional allies, opinion-shapers, watchdogs, or rule-enforcers lose confidence, resources stop flowing, talent stops coming, suppliers and customers seek alternatives, and goodwill shuts down—cutting off favors and eliminating benefits of the doubt.

Once the "loser" label is slapped on, those suffering losses are set up to fail. They find it harder to get support, harder to get opportunities. They are targeted, pressured, distracted, punished, second-guessed, shunned, marginalized, ruled against, starved, or tempted to cut corners. The streak hardens, the bust deepens. Despair can cause acts of desperation.

That's what I found across generations of football players in Texas. It is not necessary to understand football, or Texas politics, to identify with the reasons that sometimes even talented people just can't seem to win, no matter what.

PRAIRIE VIEW'S LONG DRY SPELL

Prairie View A&M University is housed in a namesake tiny college town forty-five miles northwest of Houston, on a sprawling, attractive campus of green lawns and low-rise buildings where administrators give tours by golf cart, and the campus police chief meets visitors at the Houston airport.

Prairie View has spunk. I was impressed by the deep well of hope from which it draws—especially the hope that next year could be the one to end a tradition of losing at football. In 2003, Prairie View was holder of the record for the longest unbroken losing streak in National Collegiate Athletic Association football history—eighty straight losses between 1989 and 1998. It had been even longer, more than twenty-five years, since Prairie View had a season in which it won more games than it lost.

The Prairie View Panthers were not playing obscure games that no one cared about. Football is almost a second religion in Texas, and the Panthers often played before crowds of 50,000 in the Houston Astrodome or the Cotton Bowl. The Panthers were famous. They were famous for losing, and this reputation plagued alumni, among them numerous engineers, doctors, dentists, and teachers who felt that Prairie View's reputation for academic strength was overshadowed by its football weakness. Prairie View's engineering school was among the top three producers of African-American engineers, and its biology department had a similar position as a source of talent for medical and dental schools. A new president with stellar academic credentials was appointed in 2003 to further expand academic programs.

Just why did the losing streak persist for so long? In some ways it was simple—each year's football team was failing to win its games, so perhaps the team lacked the talent and the confidence to win. But the Prairie View story was about bigger facets of life than football. A variety of institutional forces perpetuated a tradition of losing and made it increasingly difficult to end the streak. A culture of losing was transmitted across each year's new crop of players, even those with strong athletic ability, because of the context surrounding the Panthers—including a population historically treated like second-class citizens, deprived of their share of resources and set up to fail.

A League of Their Own: The Winning Years

Prairie View had not always lost at football. At one time, from the mid-1940s into the mid-1960s, it was a big winner.

Prairie View A&M was Texas's oldest black college and its second-oldest public university. It was founded in 1876 on the site of an old plantation, in parallel with Texas A&M—separate but definitely unequal. The school joined intercollegiate sports in the 1920s, playing highly competitive Division I-AA football in the Southwestern Athletic Conference (SWAC). Its significant winning streak began after legendary coach Billy Nicks, a former professional football player, arrived in 1945 at age forty and guided the program for the next twenty years. Under segregation, Prairie View was a football powerhouse. In the 1950s the Panthers won four SWAC championships in a row. In the 1950s and 1960s they won five small-college national football championships. The 1964 team was undefeated and was named as the national champion among African-American colleges.

In that era, Prairie View enjoyed abundant winners' advantages that propelled success. The Panthers sent numerous players to the NFL, including Pro Football Hall of Famer Ken Houston (inducted in 1986). Billy Nicks's long tenure ensured numerous relationships in the sports world and gave Prairie View a reputation for being an excellent place to play ball. Prairie View was at the center of a network that helped attract the best talent and reinforced an expectation of winning. Its stature as a premier African-American college made it the site for black interscholastic high school championships, giving it an edge in recruitment because it was familiar to the athletes and its staff could easily befriend them. About 75 percent of the African-American teachers in Texas were Prairie View alumni. Billy Nicks helped place coaches in many high schools throughout the state and could call in favors, such as having those coaches encourage their best players to attend Prairie View. He often had his choice of the cream of the crop, with as many as 100 football stars in an entering freshman class.

So far, so good. But the wider world intervened to change Prairie View's fate. Landmark legislation ended racial segregation. This opened the whole world to African-American students but threatened to leave Prairie View in the dust.

Interference and Fumbles: The Shift to a Losing Streak

Prairie View's winning streak ended soon after the reverberations of the civil rights movement of the 1960s affected the racial composition of college campuses—and their football teams. Racial integration was a major disruptive change that brought new opportunities to large numbers of students once confined to historically black institutions if they wanted to go to college in the South. African-American athletes were suddenly courted not only by Northern schools but also by Texas powerhouses close to home, and they had scholarships to offer potential student-athletes from poor families in Prairie View's traditional recruitment zone. The University of Texas, for example, fielded the last all-white national championship team in 1969.

Coincidentally, Billy Nicks retired in 1965, and stability retired with him. The Panthers' performance and the university's finances started slipping together. The Prairie View family, from administrators to alumni, seemed to be in denial about the implications of the altered market in higher education, and performance on the field reflected inattention to change. In 1976 the Panthers won six games and lost five—its last "winning" season ever. By 1986 the team was losing badly, winning only two games out of eleven. The Panthers finished the 1988 season 5–5 under a new head coach—one of a parade of coaches hired and fired every two to three years. But the 1988 season ended with a strike by most of the sixty-five players against the coach, who was accused of achieving results through brutality. Players complained about six-hour practices, often late at night when they would interfere with study time, and high-risk drills that caused injuries. The 1989 season was catastrophic. The Panthers' last win for nearly a decade was on October 28, 1989.

Other problems were mounting for the university at that time, including the concern that it would lose its independence and become a shrinking satellite campus for Texas A&M. University presidents were turning over almost as fast as football coaches. Auxiliary reserves designated for athletics, dorm renovations, and a student health center were depleted between 1982 and 1987 mostly for athletics, according to a report in the *Houston Chronicle*. A special prosecutor and the Texas Rangers investigated these expenditures; one athletic official settled charges of forging restaurant receipts. Were underpaid staff cutting corners to make ends meet?

By the late 1980s, Prairie View A&M University was an example of what sociologists call "permanently failing organizations." These are systems with low performance but a set of constituencies that won't let them change or, heaven forbid, go out of business. For example, workers fight to keep jobs in companies that owners would prefer to sell, politicians keep social programs alive after they've outlived their usefulness, and communities fight to keep sports franchises with dwindling attendance from leaving town. Despite consensus that performance is low, the argument runs, those constituencies don't do anything to improve it or end the agony—that is, to invest, to spend, or take risks. This leaves the organizations they're trying to protect in a state of perpetual deterioration, losing but not dying.

Prairie View was kept on life support by the memories and loyalty of alumni and the career interests of politicians in Texas who could not afford the symbolism of letting a historically black institution disappear. Nor would alums let the football team shift downward into a less demanding league. So when the Panthers' classic decline cycle turned into a death spiral in 1990, alumni fought to keep football alive without, at first, investing in improvements.

Piling on the Losers: Forces Hardening the Streak

That last winning game in October 1989 would later become a milestone, because it marked the beginning of not just a losing tradition but a streak of unbroken losses, as all the forces around the Panthers converged to reinforce their inability to win football games.

Problems in the university itself, combined with a number of poor decisions, undermined the ability to succeed, and not only in football. Prairie View dropped football and most other intercollegiate sports in March 1990, sneaking this decision into effect while students were on spring break, in the secrecy characteristic of declining organizations. The ostensible reasons were financial. A new president had been appointed just before Christmas of 1989 to replace still another temporary head. The new leader faced a budget crunch yet wanted to invest in upgrading aging campus facilities. The sports suspension was for five years or until the football program and other major sports could become self-supporting. But once out of the SWAC league, football might never come back to Prairie View.

Alumni protested, and two months later the administration succumbed, announcing that football would be reinstated. It was too late for the 1990 football season. Student athletes had already exited, and the school's enrollment dropped. Years later Douglas Fowlkes, an offensive line coach with the team since 1984, still spoke wistfully about what might have been, if not for that year's hiatus. He told us about the winning teams on which the almost-Panthers played after leaving Prairie View, and the big one who got away, who became All-American and then played professionally. "That could have been for us," he sighed.

The next season, 1991, Prairie View started fielding a team again. But the deck was now stacked against the football team in just about every way, especially since its own parent institution had shown utter lack of commitment to the Panthers. Doom loops began to surface. Because of weak organizational support, it was hard to get competent leadership for the Panthers. A new coach, hired in November 1990, quit four months later without having managed a single game, and the golf coach, of all things, became the head football coach. There were no athletic scholarships (most competitors had sixty or more). The team was composed of a small pool of inexperienced players, not all of whom could go on the road to play "away" games because of budget constraints, which further undermined the ability to play the game effectively.

In 1992, Prairie View began to set records, but they were the wrong kind. The combined football and basketball won-lost tally was 0–65; no other school ever had both teams go winless in a season. The football team's worst defeat was to Alabama State, 92–0. The worst moment in that worst game was when the Panthers were down 73–0 at halftime. The cheerleaders reverted to purely defensive cheers about holding the line rather than actually scoring. The head coach was later asked what he told the team at halftime. His reply: "Don't let Alabama score 100 points." This is typical of those caught in a losing streak. Losers often find that their aspirations not only diminish but change; the goal becomes not losing too badly, rather than trying to win.

The national media quickly discovered Prairie View, piling on ridicule for the losers. One writer called it "the worst little sport house in Texas (and everywhere)." Attendance at home games dwindled. The stands were empty at halftime, and Prairie View's own band and cheerleaders left with time remaining in the game.

The players had little basis for confidence. Many comments to the press during this period exuded self-doubt. "It hurts to walk out for the second half and see everybody leaving; we hate it," a player told the *New York Times*. "But we've grown accustomed to it. It happens every home game. At other colleges, football players walk around campus and people respect them. Here, you get more respect being in the band." Another player said, "We work really hard in practice, and everyone wants to win, and then we always seem to do something to shoot ourselves in the foot." A third worried if he was a jinx. At the forty-four-lost-game mark, an athlete said it was too depressing to think about, that if he thought about it he'd want to quit.

Economic and institutional deficiencies were internalized by the athletes. The players on the field were the ones who had to deliver, but surrounding them was not only a climate of doom but a cluster of enormous handicaps, not the least of which was a huge financial disadvantage. There was practically no investment in the team. How could the players have confidence if no one else did? Throughout the first half of the 1990s, Prairie View's athletic budget for all sports was under $850,000 total. Compare that with Texas A&M's $13.5 million, with $3.2 million for football alone—or with the more typical NCAA football budget of that period, about $2 million. Prairie View's budget was the lowest in the Southwestern Athletic Conference by a considerable margin. Lack of funding meant that coaches had to be full-time classroom instructors carrying big teaching loads. The five football coaches taught thirty-one classes one year, pushing meetings with the team to after 10:00 p.m.—and they had to pay their own way on recruiting trips. Players' on-the-road food allowance was raised from $12.50 to $15 per day in 1995, still about half of what other teams received. So much for steaks to feed athletes' muscles.

Going to games underfed was only one of the factors that influenced performance during those years in which the Panthers lost every game. Football practices were held in a lopsided intramural field because the athletic department couldn't afford to get the fields mowed. Wearing Houston Oilers' hand-me-down practice pants, players walked from a dingy basement locker room to practice throwing dirt clumps toward an imaginary sideline. There were no goalposts on that field, and no coaching towers. The kickers practiced extra points against a softball backstop. The water fountain was a garden hose. The stadium showed its age. The weight room was shared with seventeen other sports, and the football players had to vacate it when the women's basketball team wanted to use it. On game days, players put planks around the stadium to make a walkway, which doubled as weightlifting.

Player turnover is natural in college sports, as students pass through the university. But lack of continuity in coaching, management, and the rest of the institution creates uncertainty, insecurity, strategic lurches, and an absence of strong sponsors who can fight for the interests of the players. In the 1990s, head coaches seemed to last about two years and were often replaced by someone with even less relevant experience than the one before. University presidents lasted slightly longer, but numerous interim officials served between presidents.

In 1995 the former golf coach was fired and was replaced by an interim head coach who had last coached football in 1972. Not long into that season, on September 30, 1995, the Panthers set another negative record. They became the team with the longest losing streak in the NCAA, achieving fifty-one straight losses, one more than the previous record-holder, Columbia University in the 1980s. Dissed by the Panthers' own cheerleaders, one player, a talented student with a respectable "B" average, felt that the team was being treated like a bunch of animals, like they wanted to lose. "No one wants to be labeled a loser," he told an observer.

When Prairie View surpassed Columbia's record, unwelcome national attention instantly increased. A student running back became nationally famous as someone who had never won a game in high school or college. (There was a thin silver lining in his cloud of doom; he was a communications major who hoped to be a sports media director, so he was making good media contacts.) Despite athletes' insistence that they were having fun, enjoying the game, and didn't want to be quitters, there were signs of desperation in the locker room. Player superstitions prevailed, as people cast around for the source of their bad luck. Was it the boxed chicken dinners? Food was switched. The bus company? They got another one. Line coach Douglas Fowlkes recalled that the media wrote about the losing streak so much that it was always at the forefront of the players' minds: "When are they going to win? Can they win? How will they win? Those questions were always there, and you have to face that all the time. You're identified as a loser. And that's something you want to end as a coach."

Ironically, because of its losses, Prairie View was a target. Other teams played harder against the Panthers because of the career-destroying humiliation for a coach if his team lost against them. "Each week was a fight because nobody wanted to lose to us," Fowlkes recalled. "Other teams were highly motivated, they weren't going to take any chances because the coach could lose his job by letting someone with nothing beat you."

The loser label had other consequences. All of the Panthers, even good players, were stereotyped as even worse than they were, and even positive steps were interpreted in the most negative light, which often happens to those on losing streaks. Coaches were certain that referees gave opponents the benefit of the doubt on close calls but called penalties for the Panthers, on the assumption that a losing team could do no right.

Engraved on Fowlkes's memory was an example of how Prairie View got treated unfairly: a heartbreaker of a game against traditional rival Texas Southern, which was delayed because of lightning, and then continued with a field that was a mud pit. "We thought we had it, but they ended pulling it out. Then the biggest surprise was when we picked up the interception. And here we go. All of a sudden, they said it was a personal foul and Southern ends up with the ball going the other way. When you get into the losing streak, some folks think we're not good enough to play, and when we did make a play in that game, they look at us and think that maybe we're just holding. We always end up getting the worst [calls]." The Panthers had played well enough to have a player nominated as national Player of the Week for that game, yet they still lost—in their view, because others had no confidence in them.

As the losing streak continued well beyond the record for college sports, the turnover of coaches accelerated. Another new head coach was appointed in 1997, the second in three seasons and the third in the 1990s. He arrived a little late, and the media got in another loser dig, saying it was because the Panthers were always a little late. He tried to book two games against teams he thought the Panthers could beat, but both dropped out—perhaps because they didn't want to be the ones to help the Panthers end the losing streak.

This time, though, the new coach had more resources, because fifteen athletic scholarships (still under a quarter of what others offered) helped him attract talent. He got a bigger office and more staff. He cut off players from the media so they wouldn't be exposed to the inherent negativity. To symbolize burying the past, he had players watch an NBC documentary about Prairie View, then bury the video in a plastic bag in the north end zone of the field. The financial investment and motivational push produced glimmers of hope. On September 19, 1998, the Panthers played the league champions and held their rivals to a low score.

Then, at long last, VICTORY!

On September 26, 1998, the Panthers ended a nine-year and eighty-game losing streak in Oklahoma City, beating Langston University, 14–12. With fourteen seconds left to play, Prairie View stopped a two-point conversion attempt and won the game. There was pandemonium on the field. Players cried. A linebacker said that the only thing that went though his mind was "It's over, it's over." Players felt immortal, that they had made history. A team member told us that they felt like they had just won the Super Bowl.

One person reportedly yelled, "The streak is broken!" Another shouted, "No, the streak has just started!" Neither was right.

One Victory Does Not Make a Turnaround

The cycle had been dented but not broken. Prairie View had spent so many years losing that the people around the school did not know how to win—that is, how to adopt the behavior and demeanor of winners. It takes much more than one victory to unwind a losing streak; a great deal of behavior has to change on the part of many people, well beyond the players themselves. At Prairie View, other people involved with football games were not accustomed to the responsibilities of supporting winners; they still behaved like losers who had nothing left to lose. Troubles continued.

A week before the September 26 victory, Prairie View's marching band had been suspended for brawling during halftime of the Southern game on September 19. But the band had played on. So, less than ten days after the streak-breaking victory, Prairie View's athletic program was suspended indefinitely from SWAC because the school had violated the two-game suspension against its marching band. Prairie View officials protested, and the suspension was reduced. Still, the last thing an organization struggling to turn itself around needed was to deflect time and energy into dealing with additional crises, continuing negative press.

It is more costly to be known as losers than to be known as winners. Identified losers have more problems to solve. Their energy is depleted just keeping things from falling apart. They must overcome biased judgment calls from officials unable to believe in their positive actions.

In 1999, after failing to get a second win, the head coach was fired for NCAA rule violations, an interim coach was appointed, and the Panthers won two more games, finishing the season at 2–8. Three wins in two years were enough to build hope, and players began to lift weights on their own. But years of bad habits, passed on from seniors to freshmen, were ingrained in the culture of the Panthers. In 2000, still another new head coach tried to institute discipline, to ban vulgar language on the field, to get the players to practice on time—that is, if they came at all. The athletes beat one another up in weekday practices so that they were neither fresh nor motivated to show solidarity on Saturdays when the games counted. An athlete on the team that year felt that newer players looked up to the seniors and emulated what they saw, which was an utter lack of discipline. "There was no senior leadership, "a fresh-man athlete said. "Seniors were telling us to miss practice so they could miss it without looking bad and getting punished for it." For 2000 the final won-lost tally was 1–10.

Prairie View attracted some talented athletes, because of aca-demic programs or alumni ties, but many of them felt their high school teams were in better shape than the Panthers. Sammie August, a defensive tackle (six feet, 263 pounds) and engineering major from Missouri City, Texas, whose father (Prairie View '81) en-couraged him to attend, joined the team as a freshman in 2000, the first year under a new coach. August recalled, "I came from a win-ning program to coming here and losing 42–0 at the first game. My first spring practice was way different from my previous coaches. I did more work in high school than in my three years here." Players shrugged off responsibilities, preferring to laugh and joke in the locker room. "But you got used to it. Every week, Monday through Friday, was same thing for practice. Then play on Saturday and lose. I kept hoping that one day it would turn around. Plenty of times, I sat in my room and felt bad after a game."

Individual talent was not enough; the team needed to work to-gether. In 2001, in Charles Washington's first game as a freshman quarterback, he ran sixty yards for a touchdown against Southern, a competitive game that Prairie View came close to winning but lost in the last few minutes—its historical pattern. But then things started to take a turn for the better. The Panthers had their first back-to-back wins since 1986, including three victories in home games, with the big win coming in the symbolic homecoming game in which the Panthers were the underdogs. Sammie August left the field overwhelmed by fans. "Finally, everybody said they were just tired of losing," he said. "Everyone came in focused and ready to play football." Three games in a row was a big boost in confidence:

"After the first victory, players got confident that we could actually win instead of going to the game expecting to lose. That confidence rolled over the next game. We started to get a little respect. Teachers started to give us more respect and students would come and say, 'Yay! We're finally winning. Turn the program around.' "

But then it went away fast. Not losing was good enough for some players. Rather than growing in confidence, they—and the coaches—let up and then gave up. "When [we were] winning, it was mostly because the players wanted it so bad, and when they got what they wanted, we started to lose again," August continued. "I don't know what happened. When we started losing again, Coach got scared. By halftime he gave up on us. You could see it in his face, on the sidelines. You could see he was thinking, 'I don't know what to do and everything I'm trying isn't working.' " It was hard to keep playing when the head coach had already given up.

The team still had the pathologies of losers. Coaches let them flounder rather than leading them to improve. The players were fragmented into subgroups that went their own way. Some players practiced on their own and developed backup strategies for games, but the rest were said not to care, not to want to help the team, not to be interested in learning from mistakes. Second-guessing and blame-shifting abounded. Fowlkes said, "You do something [that doesn't work] in a game, and other kids tell you that's why you can't win."

The Panthers were caught in a classic doom loop that undermined confidence at every level:

- They lacked depth of talent because they had no resources.
- They received no resources because they had weak and constantly changing leadership.
- They had weak and constantly changing leadership because they lost.
- They lost because they had no resources and low aspirations.
- They had low aspirations because they had a poor record.
- They had a poor record because they had low aspirations.

Those are only a few of the universal connections between poverty of resources and impoverished spirits. Economics and psychology reinforced each other in a complex web of self-perpetuating loops. Could anything break the vicious cycles?

The Momentum of Losing Streaks:
Why Turnarounds Are Difficult

The wider world outside the team was again about to change Prairie View's fortunes. The years of starvation for the whole university were ending. In 1997 the U.S. Office of Civil Rights (OCR) undertook a two-year review of public higher education in Texas as part of its enforcement of civil rights laws. In March 1999, OCR officials issued a preliminary conclusion that financial and other disparities traceable to *de jure* segregation (racial segregation under the law) still existed at Prairie View and Texas Southern, Texas's two historically black public universities. A committee of representatives from the two schools, other public universities, and business met from November 1999 through April 2000 to recommend steps to address the disparities. For Prairie View, this meant an infusion of resources everywhere—for academic programs, faculty development, support staff, information technology, new buildings, and scholarships. Dr. George Wright, a distinguished academic who had served on the review committee as provost of the University of Texas at Arlington, was appointed Prairie View's new president. Prairie View had about 7,200 students in 2003, up from a dip to 4,000, and there was talk of doubling its size.

Awakened hope for the athletic program took the form of a capital campaign led by the athletic department to tap alumni to build a $10-million endowment fund and an amazing vote by students (many of whom were on financial aid) to pay an additional $300 each over the course of a year toward an upgraded athletic facility. A revitalized football program was one component of plans to nearly double enrollment to 13,000 students. There were aspirations to upgrade Blackshear Field, the Panther's home stadium, and expand seating from 6,000 to 21,000; and the Panthers could offer sixty-five athletic scholarships (matching the league average). A talented young athletic director, Charles McClelland, was making better choices; the basketball team had already turned around and won a conference championship. The institutional environment was shifting.

Now conditions surrounding the Panthers were much more favorable. But lack of external confidence in the football program, built up over many years, had been internalized in lack of confidence on the part of players and the coaching staff. There had been so many losses over such a long period—and fewer than a dozen wins in fourteen years—that a culture had been ingrained. It would be impossible to leap from loser to winner overnight, but losers sometimes get desperate and try to get there too fast. And, as I've said, more is riding on each game for a loser than for a winner. A single loss does not damage the reputation of a winner, but for a loser, each subsequent loss is another nail in the coffin.

In January 2003, Prairie View tried again with still another new head coach. C. L. Whittington, a former NFL professional athlete and a Prairie View alum, took the helm. Although it was his first head coaching job, many were hopeful that he could bring two of the many things that the Panthers had lacked: professionalism and school spirit. At Coach Whittington's first meeting with the players, he shook everyone's hand at the door and gave them a copy of the school song. When they were assembled, he asked them to sing the "Alma Mater." The players were puzzled at first by this strange request (they didn't even know the song), but then it began to dawn on some of them that things would be different now. Coach Whittington wanted to instill team spirit and a feeling of bigger responsibility, not just to themselves but to their whole school and alumni and fans. He put pictures and trophies in his office from Prairie View's championship teams in the glory years. Players were surprised to learn that the Panthers had been champions forty years previous, but it made them feel proud, and pride walking out onto the field could build confidence.

Whittington required the team to run every morning at 5:30 a.m., followed by weight lifting. Players found it hard at first to get up at five to run; they weren't accustomed to it. But the coach went with them, even though he didn't like the early start any more than they did. They were all in it together, and they all had to work hard. Soon the players enjoyed being back in shape—and those who didn't like it quit. (Good riddance, a dedicated Panther said.) Between early-morning exercise and afternoon practices during spring training, there was so much contact among the players that they bonded as a team, Many went to summer school and started meeting after classes to work out. "We were around each other so much that when we didn't have to practice, we were still around each other," Sammie August observed. "We work out. If there's a game on, we'll meet up at someone's house and watch the game or go to the movies. Or play touch football when we can." Charles Washington said, "The players are starting to believe in themselves more."

The coach's emphasis on discipline was evident from the moment he arrived in his office in June 2003. He was dressing down a player for wearing an earring. The player later said that he appreciated how much Coach Whit cared, how wonderful it was to find a coach who only wanted you to win, who banned the "loser" word. "The coach is accessible. He keeps us out of trouble," a senior on the team said. There was a strict dress code: no bandannas, sleeveless shirts, or backward caps. They had to sit in the front row in classes. A notepad was taped on the back of players' dormitory doors as an accountability device, so that every time they walked out the door, they could assess their actions for the day.

But then the coach pushed too far. Was he trapped in the classic desperation of people who will do anything to get out of a losing mode, but then overshoot and never make it? Was it the inexperience of a novice, or the pressure to leap from losing to winning before the people around him were ready? When classes began in the fall, practices were moved to 4:30 a.m., and players had to arrive much earlier to get their ankles taped. They were sleep-deprived in classes and still had to show up for evening meetings before trying to study. Coaching staff who lived forty-five minutes away in Houston had to get up in the middle of the night. The coach imposed lockdowns the night before games, putting mattresses in the gym so that the players stayed together. He punished them for infractions by making them run, which further wore them out, and turned the joy of sport into practices that felt like punishment. Players felt they couldn't complain, or they wouldn't be allowed to play.

Classic losers' habits were still in play. The coach was an equal-opportunity blamer, finding fault with everyone. He did not forge a cohesive group of coaches or athletes, letting divisions among players fester and getting into heated arguments with some of his assistants, we were told. He appeared to play favorites, not putting the best people on the field. "It is his way or no way at all," a close observer declared.

When things started to go wrong early in the season, "here we go again" was echoed within the team. The four team captains tried to maintain a positive attitude, but the exhausted players had no tradition of winning to propel them to high levels of effort.

The Mississippi Valley State game on November 1, 2003, was another in a string of revealing losses. On the field, players did the minimum to stay in the game. A Prairie View player blocked an opponent from catching a ball, jumped up and down, slapped a few high fives, and walked with a new spring in his cleated step, but without appearing to notice that the football was so close to him that he could have caught it himself. Off the field, small clusters of players were engaged in separate conversations unrelated to the action. At halftime, Coach Whittington tried to get the team to make adjustments, but the locker-room mood was more negative than positive. Whatever confidence he wanted the players to have in one another was undermined by divisiveness on the coaching staff and within the team.

The fourth quarter was a sea of confusion and anger on the Panthers' side. With ten minutes left on the clock, and Prairie View well behind, players were already swearing in frustration, and when the opposing team made another touchdown, the mascot threw herself to the ground, facedown, pretending to cry. Charles Washington and other team leaders approached angry players to try to lift spirits. "I just talk to them, saying we are still in it," Washington said. "But it is hard to get that in their heads when we've already been losing and we haven't came back too many times. It is hard to make them believe." When the game ended with another Panthers loss, the band played the school song, and many in the stands put a single index finger in the air as a symbol of unity, representing the idea of togetherness through thick and thin—a ritual that stemmed from repeated losing.

Failure for Prairie View was still a self-fulfilling prophecy. "I had a feeling they weren't going to perform," a woman said after the game. She was the mother of a talented freshman on the team who hadn't had a chance to play in three or four games, even though he had turned down another school to take Prairie View's athletic scholarship because his parents and siblings were alums. His father complained that they were losing to second-rate schools. "Every week they are getting worse. They have accepted losing and can't overcome that. We knew it wouldn't be overnight, but we need to see improvement somewhere." An insider said, "We have better athletes because of the football scholarships, but they are not playing like they are good athletes."

On November 20, 2003, athletic director Charles McClelland announced the firing of Coach Whittington, not for losing (though the season was 1–10) but for allegedly hitting two players while breaking up a fight during a football practice in mid-August, a charge Whittington disputed.

McClelland was looking for a new coach who could come into a program that did not have a history of winning and turn it around—"a strong motivator with a commitment to building young student athletes to become productive citizens of our great country," he told us in December. There was that trademark Prairie View hope again. One former Prairie View coach's slogan was, "If you don't have hope, you don't have anything." But you can't have hope if you don't have resources and support flowing from investors, administrators, high-level sponsors, cheerleaders, fans, and sympathetic reporters. You can't have hope without rule-makers or enforcers willing to give you the benefit of the doubt. You can't have hope without the support of all the others whose confidence determines investment, and whose investment determines your will to pull together as a team. You can't have hope if no one else believes in you, or if people lack confidence in one another.

It seems glaringly obvious in retrospect that the football losing streak had long historical roots and reflected much more than whether a particular group of young men could block and tackle. Way back in the days of the civil rights movement that ended segregation, Prairie View failed to shift its strategy when the environment changed. Just as in the downward spiral of troubled companies, weak leadership of decades past made poor decisions and remained in denial. But they also had little support from Texas politicians, were the victims of racial inequities, and were given neither the financial nor the academic resources to succeed. (Dr. Wright was one of the first academics in years to head the university.) Lack of confidence started at the top and was carried all the way down to the football field.

That's the thing about losing streaks: Once set in motion, they become harder and harder to stop. People are caught in dynamics that are difficult to see at first, and then when they become apparent, confidence has already eroded.

Despite years of losing, there are many people in the Prairie View network who really want the Panthers to win football games and have finally invested to help make that happen. But wins can't be ordered by shouting at the players and making them run at four-thirty in the morning. Something more needs to be done, with the right kind of leadership. Dr. Wright has an expansion plan for the university. Charles McClelland, the athletic director, has a plan for football. Maybe next year could be the season the Panthers start winning again.

A HUNDRED YEARS OF NEGATIVE THOUGHTS

Behind every losing streak is a story like that of Prairie View A&M. Take away the unique features of college sports, of Texas politics and racial history, of nonprofit or public organizations, of the game of football—and there remain echoes of the same economic, political, organizational, cultural, interpersonal, behavioral, motivational, and emotional problems that surround other people and groups caught in losing streaks. They face the same second-guessing, unwelcome attention, pressure on each action, temptation to cut corners, distractions as other things fall apart, starvation and deprivation, shunning by erstwhile supporters, and bad breaks and bad calls that come from being branded as a loser. Ask politicians who have lost a series of elections. Or ask my friend whose work life took a plunge when he became depressed over an ugly divorce, and everything around him seemed to fall apart.

You'd think this wouldn't happen in professional sports, in a business that can buy talent. You'd imagine that owners would be motivated to make strategic changes once a team fails to perform, season after season. You'd definitely think it wouldn't happen in professional baseball, because a team plays more than 160 games compared with the dozen games in a college football season, providing so many more opportunities to get lucky or make a comeback. Yet consider the sorry record of the Chicago Cubs, a for-profit Major League Baseball team in America's "second city," until Dusty Baker led them to a winning season and the playoffs in 2003.

By the time baseball legend Dusty Baker came from the San Francisco Giants as manager of the Cubs to end "a hundred years of negative thoughts," this was the Cubs' situation: only sixteen seasons at break-even or better since 1945 (that's fifty-seven years); no back-to-back winning seasons since 1972 (thirty-one years). The team's last World Series win was in 1908, its last World Series appearance in 1945. The Cubs had sixteen managers in twenty years—discontinuity and churn to the max. The home stadium, Wrigley Field, was about ninety years old, with outdated, inadequate facilities, equipment, everything. The team had been starved for investment, and in an ironic bit of symbolism, the players were not eating well before the games (despite, of course, orders-of-magnitude bigger food budgets than the Prairie View Panthers). Losing made practice feel like punishment, not like an exciting chance to hone skills.

It all sounds depressingly familiar.

The Cubs had a big confidence problem stemming from almost a century of mostly losing. According to assistant coach Sonny Jackson, the constant focus on history was the media's doing, not the players'. That view was confirmed by pitcher Matt Clement, when he said he thinks about each day's game, not about a ninety-five-year jinx. But Dusty Baker acknowledged that low expectations by the media, fans, and observers shaped a negative motivational context. He was surprised, he said, by the letters he received saying things like "I'm eighty years old, and I want the team to win before I die," or "I'm forty-five years old and my grandfather died twenty years ago and told me I'd never see it in my lifetime." Not only were the Cubs labeled losers, but their ways of losing were hardened into media slogans. "There are still a hundred years' worth of negative thoughts around here," Baker said. "When we lose two or three in a row, which will always happen until we do win regularly and might be here after we win, they'll say, 'Oh yeah, here we go, June swoon,' or 'Same old curse.' These people are used to being disappointed, and I can't really blame them. I think the players get affected, I think everybody's affected. They say the mind can move mountains. So why can't the mind move a ball? A collective positive thought process can do wonders."

The fans were like the tenth player influencing the nine players on the baseball field. Baker mused about how, in Notre Dame football games, everyone expects something miraculous to happen in the last two minutes, so no one leaves—so different from the exodus of fans expecting the Cubs (like Prairie View) to lose the game in the final moments. He thought that the coaches he brought with him from the Giants felt worse about losses than longtime Cubs staff did, because his group knew what it was like to win, and Cubs old-timers did not.

With that century of negativity, Baker knew that a turnaround would take not only time and a motivational shift but many concrete items. He already had investment from the owners (whom he called "Upstairs") in training tables, DVD equipment, and other tangible signs of change. A few stars were not the answer, even though the media put all the focus on a small number of star pitchers and hitters. If the whole team did not function as a unit, with "no musician above any other," as Baker put it, then stars could drive wedges between themselves and other players that could make the situation worse, with envy and inequality undermining performance.

Negative thoughts included second-guessing the Cubs' every move. "There's still people every day, 'Do you have enough to do this?' 'Do you have enough pitching?' Every day we're constantly bombarded by negatives. We're constantly reminded of what we haven't done versus what we have done and what we might do." Even the players pointed fingers. We watched one of those "June swoon" games that brought the Cubs under 50–50 in wins/losses. It was a home game on June 26, 2003. Star pitcher Mark Prior (whom *Sports Illustrated* called a savior of the Cubs) threw sixteen strikeouts through the eighth inning, and star batter Sammy Sosa hit a homer to put the Cubs ahead. Then Baker replaced Prior with a relief pitcher who gave up a three-run homer in the top of the ninth to lose the game. Naturally there was considerable booing in the stands. One fan vehemently argued that Baker should have kept him in. He claimed that from his seat he could see the dugout, and that all the players stayed away from Baker on the opposite side of the bench after he pulled Prior.

Baker took this as more negativity: "When you're losing, boy, people manage to segregate themselves. There are a lot of mini-groups. There's a lot of backstabbing. There's a lot of finger-pointing. There's a lot of anything but looking at yourself. It's usually somebody else's fault." Whoops. There's the culture of losing teams again. And to compound it, there was a question of whether Upstairs would back the manager if he tried to discipline star players. The stars made so much money that it was hard to pull them from games, because then management couldn't justify their high salaries to the board if they didn't play all the time. Relying on a few players was risky anyway; in June 2003 Sammy Sosa was suspended for two weeks for using a nonregulation corked bat.

Baker whipped the Cubs into shape, and they had a winning season and a trip to the playoffs, but they could not go all the way. The Cubs lost the pivotal second-to-last game. Some would say they lost confidence, which cost them the series, because a fan proved the truth of Baker's assertion that fans are the tenth player. The man reached from the stands into the air over the field to catch a foul ball hit by the opposing team, turning that "out" into the home run that cost the Cubs the title. Fans had not yet learned how to help the Cubs win.

As in all losing streaks, negative thoughts pop out from the end of a long pipeline connecting owners, fans, media, managers, players, and more. Negative thoughts—collective pessimism—become embedded in behavior patterns that form a culture of losing. Those thoughts flow from a losers' culture that is both cause and consequence of low investment, poor leadership, weak support networks, bad press, low expectations, and constant turnover.

DEATH SPIRALS AND ECONOMIC BUSTS

We can see the pattern. Coast along for a while, assuming that everything will be all right. Start fumbling, but make up for it in another way. When the losses continue, get a little desperate and try anything. Cut expenses to the bone, but then also cut activities that might make the situation better. And above all, avoid change that disrupts tradition. Institutional forces support the continuation of potentially doomed courses of action.

Sports teams may be relatively simple examples, but the dynamics of losing streaks in sports illuminate issues of failure in more complex systems. Losing streaks in business can go on as long as losing streaks in sports. In one study of fifty-seven bankrupt companies of the 1980s and a set of matched survivors, now-defunct losers such as W.T. Grant and Braniff Airlines showed signs of relative weakness as early as ten years before failing. They were propped up by growth markets and had enough working capital to cover obligations, so they thought they could ride out any storms. But as they started slipping farther behind and faced declining profitability, they began to lurch, vacillating in terms of their strategy and either doing too little—such as cutting spending on new initiatives— or doing too much—such as a frenzy of acquisitions, like the desperate gambler with little left to lose going for broke by betting it all on the next roll of the dice. Just before bankruptcy, the failing companies hit a "perfect storm," as markets became more challenging while their own reserves were depleted. Performance deteriorated so badly that an unhappy ending was inevitable.

The leadership groups of the bankrupt companies made poor decisions because of the stress they faced, and they also made changes in their own ranks that weakened their ability to solve problems. Weakness led to flawed decisions, which increased the weakness. During the downward spiral, the most desirable executives left because they had other options, still other executives were fired as the company searched for scapegoats, and resources shrank. The companies lost expertise; they had fewer experienced people at the table and inferior talent in executive offices. These deficiencies accelerated loss of support from external stakeholders whose confidence in decision-makers decreased.

It is well known that people under stress make flawed choices. Lurching, vacillation, and churn contribute to a death spiral. Sometimes the losing streak is masked during boom times, making it easier to remain in denial. But it is hard to ignore in a bust, when business failures and economic downturns become close to synonymous. In desperation, those in charge cast around for solutions, but the classic quick fixes—cutting expenditures or replacing key managers—sometimes make the situation worse. By the time losing streaks become visible, it looks as though organizations or people have no choice. Expenses are too high, poor decisions have been made, and money and time are running out. But being forced into these corners makes the situation worse. Perhaps those expenses are actually investments in projects that could turn the situation around. Perhaps those fired people are merely scapegoats burned at the stake while deeper problems go unnoticed or unmentioned.

Such moves violate two principles of folk wisdom: *Don't cut off your nose to spite your face,* and *Don't change horses in midstream.* Cut off your nose, and you might stop breathing. Change horses while crossing the river, and you might drown.

Winning streaks are characterized by continuity and continued investment, losing streaks by disruption, churn, lurching, and lack of investment. Winners find it easy to maintain momentum, losers find it difficult to gain traction. While the rich might be getting richer and accumulating resources to solve problems, the poor face a large number of disruptions that make life difficult, without the resources to address or eliminate them.

I asked high school athletes and coaches to identify recent changes that might have influenced their teams' performance. Winners were much more likely than losers to get new equipment, signifying investment in team performance, whereas losers were almost twice as likely as winners to have had a change of coaches, which meant constant disruption. "We have gone through three coaches in the last four years," complained an athlete whose team always lost and who expected they'd lose next year. Lack of investment influenced their performance, as another in a similar losing streak said: "Track is kind of a joke at my school because we don't have our own track to practice on. We have to use a crappy public track."

The actions of American and international businesses during the economic downturn of 2001–2003 reveal an even more dramatic contrast between winners and losers than among sports teams. Losers were much more likely to change horses and cut off their noses, as well as eyes, ears, arms, and legs. They replaced CEOs. They cut expenses. They cut internal investment. They cut people. They cut projects. They cut customer service. They cut communication. Both winners and losers faced similar challenges during the "bust" years, but they responded very differently. Losers were twice as likely as winners to have gotten a new CEO or owner, but only about half as likely to have undertaken positive actions such as producing major new projects or new types of products, reaching out to new collaborators or new partners, or forming strategic alliances. Losers were less than half as likely as winners to convene groups to solve problems, instead defaulting to autocracy.

The wider environment can cut off opportunities for losers to recover, but the problems of a losing streak are compounded when losers start doing it to themselves.

ENDLESS LOOPS

My stories about losing streaks are cautionary tales—the how-*not*-to-do-it guide. We have seen what happens when the cornerstones of confidence crumble. When accountability, collaboration, and initiative are replaced by a culture of anger and blame, fragmentation and conflict, vicious cycles are set in motion. The longer a losing streak is allowed to continue, the more forces accumulate in the external world to reduce the ability to win, and the harder it is to change. The first step in change is understanding. But the doom loops of losing streaks are so entangled that it is difficult to see what is cause, and what is effect.

What is the most powerful factor in losing streaks? Is it individual pessimism—too many negative thoughts? Is it lack of communication, lack of discipline, inability to pull together as a team? Is it ineffective leaders who make poor decisions, blame rather than motivate, and disappear frequently, leaving groups adrift and helpless? Is it lack of financial resources to invest in new initiatives or to just keep current ones going? Is it lack of support from sponsors, customers, fans, opinion leaders, or rule-makers?

By now, my answer should be clear: It is all of those. Economic, organizational, cultural, and psychological factors interact. Confidence deteriorates at every level.

Losing makes it more likely for people to respond in dysfunctional ways (in their own attitudes, aspirations, and treatment of others), and that makes it harder to solve problems or to win, and that causes stakeholders to lose confidence (investment declines; support erodes; customers defect; talent becomes hard to recruit; media attention is negative; rule-makers rule against the group, assuming it must have cheated to get good results), and that perpetuates the crisis of losing, and all that cycles back to reinforce the bad behavior and create disruptions, distractions, reductions, and leadership changes, which harden bad behavior and ensure full loss of both internal and external confidence.

That was a long sentence! And that's how people caught in losing streaks feel—that they have been handed a long sentence with little relief in sight. It could be life imprisonment or a death sentence—unless someone is able to break out and lead a turnaround.

Part II

TURNAROUNDS:
THE ART OF BUILDING CONFIDENCE

6

The Turnaround Challenge

LOSING MONEY? LOSING AUDIENCE? LOSING FRIENDS? LOSING TALENT? LOSING CONTESTS? LOSING OPPORTUNITIES? LOSING SLEEP? LOSING HOPE? TIME FOR A TURNAROUND.

It is possible to slide into a cycle of decline without even knowing it until the pattern of losing becomes visible to everyone. The symptoms get harder to ignore, the underlying weaknesses harder to deny. Time and excuses begin to run out, momentum and appearances begin to run down. Quick fixes and facelifts no longer work. Keeping up a brave front is impossible. Cosmetic change—what I call "putting lipstick on a bulldog"—cannot hide the ugliness nor change the nature of the beast.

Now a deliberate choice needs to be made: whether to let decline turn into death, or to try to restore health. There are many theories about the best thing to do, and all of them contain trade-offs. Medicine is guided by the philosophy that every human life has value, and physicians are expected to try to save every patient—but there are triage situations in which scarce resources must be given to some rather than to others. Economics has a more brutal perspective: Mainstream theories advocate letting distressed organizations die so that their assets can be put to greater use elsewhere. But even in the most draconian views there is room for strategic transformation. Rather than a matter of theory, the choice is often a matter of will. Who thinks that the patient, the business, the team, or the marriage can be saved, and who will put in the effort to do it?

This chapter deals with the tough beginnings of turnarounds, the swing times when things can go either way, depending on whether there is the right kind of committed leadership. Turnarounds are when leadership matters most, because confidence has eroded on all levels. Instead of confidence, there is self-doubt and despair, negativity about others, cynicism about the system, and a deficit of external investment. Moreover, intertwined forces associated with losing streaks have manifested themselves in specific financial or strategic problems, and myriad immediate crises must be resolved before one even tackles the task of restoring confidence in the future.

Turnarounds are not for the impatient or the faint of heart. Yet with the right leadership, attentive to the human as well as the financial, to the long term as well as the short term, the cycle can be shifted. Leaders can stop downward spirals, reverse negative trajectories, unwind doom loops, end bad habits, and lay the foundation for confidence.

First, someone must believe that there is value worth restoring, someone who has the initial confidence to tackle the task.

Jeffrey Lurie had that self-confidence when he bought the losing Philadelphia Eagles National Football League franchise in 1994 and enticed his friend and fellow sports enthusiast Joe Banner to join him. They knew they had to restore the confidence of the players in themselves, in one another, and in management, in order to restore the confidence of fans, partners, and public officials that the Eagles were worth their support.

But en route to the winners' circle in the opening years of the 2000s, Lurie and Banner had to face several tough realities common to all turnarounds:

- Coming off a losing streak, the situation is always worse than anyone thinks.
- Promises of change have been made before. What makes people believe that this time is for real?

- Those hailed as heroes when they arrive can become villains when they make unpopular (though necessary) decisions.
- Beware of false recoveries. If victory is too easy, it might be too temporary.
- Turnarounds run on several clocks that are not always in sync: short-term and long-term, internal and external, quick fixes and long-term shifts of culture.

SPREADING THE EAGLES' WINGS

When entertainment executive Jeffrey Lurie bought the Philadelphia Eagles for $185 million, it was the highest price ever paid for a professional football franchise, especially a mediocre one. Diehard Eagles fans, drawn heavily from blue-collar ranks, did not immediately identify with a Hollywood figure, but Lurie initially enjoyed good press as team rescuer, not because of who he was, but because of who he was not. He was not the previous uninvolved absentee owner, for whom the city had no great affection. During the sale process there had been great speculation that a new owner would move the team, but instead Lurie moved his family from Los Angeles to Haverford, a bucolic suburb of Philadelphia, thereby demonstrating his commitment to the city.

The National Football League was changing from a system in which passive ownership and management could still lead to success on the field, to one in which free agency and a salary cap would require an excellent, proactive, aggressive front office. So Lurie thought that good management could reap rewards. He enlisted Joe Banner to help manage the franchise, with the initial title of "adviser." Banner had recently sold his family's discount clothing business and was doing volunteer work at hospitals. "All he said to me was 'I want to buy the franchise, come help me run it,'" Banner reported. Lurie felt that Banner was ready for this challenge. "It was a gut feeling," Lurie recalled. "Joe was dedicated, smart, a good person, we think alike about sports. We were both newcomers, but we would think outside the box. I didn't want someone just like everyone else; that was not the way to get a great turnaround. I'm sure that a lot of people thought I didn't know what I was doing, and why bring in someone else like that? But I had confidence in myself and Joe that we could turn it around."

The Shock at the Start: It's Even Worse

"The public perception was that the team was in decline on a moderate slope," Banner said. "But when we got into the organization, we saw that it was really in deep trouble." The problems were everywhere: in finances, community relations, management, relationships with player agents, and attitudes. There was a great deal of animosity between management and the players, even more than the usual contractual differences common in professional sports. It had been years since the team had a number-one, -two, or -three draft pick who reported on the first day of training camp. Some athletes negotiated salaries by holdout, missing training and games.

Facilities were particularly bad. Lurie's due diligence before buying the franchise had included everything short of a site visit to the offices, because negotiations had to be kept secret as a condition of the deal. So when he walked into Veterans Stadium in Philadelphia on his first day as owner, all he could think of was "*This* is an NFL franchise? Every image I had was completely put into disarray. The offices were in an old stadium. I saw no windows, lighting that could put you to sleep, rats walking across offices, and a lot of unenergetic expressions." People had become accustomed to getting stuck in elevator breakdowns or finding hot water pouring down from an office ceiling when the heating unit over an office burst.

Even worse, he thought, the people running football operations were completely separated physically and culturally from the people managing the business. How could he get everyone to work in tandem? The football side was three stories below, connected by an elevator, and it felt like a dungeon. With that sub-basement environment and the worst workout facility in the NFL, how could he ask players to stay in great shape? This was not conducive to winning, he thought. And the dual-purpose, city-owned stadium had been built for baseball. There was no place a head football coach could meet with all fifty-three of his players in one room at the same time. There were barriers, walls to walk around and peer around if all the players tried to squeeze in. Furthermore, he saw AstroTurf installed over concrete, a design stemming from the 1960s, which was responsible for a high rate of player injuries, and which the city refused to upgrade.

Lurie had known intellectually that the Eagles would require a major turnaround. He just hadn't quite realized how many things needed to be fixed before he and Banner could even get to the point of attracting the best coaches and players to rebuild the team. It wasn't like Philadelphia was a Paris, to which people would move just because it was Paris. "How can we turn something around if we can't attract people?" he lamented. "If we wanted Jimmy Johnson or Mike Shanahan"—referring to legendary coaches— "they'd walk in, get interviewed, say 'Great intentions, but what have you got here?' Without facilities, we can't get them."

As soon as he was officially the new Eagles owner, he decided to visit Bill Walsh and the San Francisco 49ers, then one of the big winners in the NFL. He observed the complete opposite of the Philadelphia situation, from the modern training facility outside the stadium to the pride and expectations of success everyone conveyed. This made Lurie and Banner vow to bring the same winners' environment to the Eagles.

Signals to Skeptics: This Time Is Real
On the first day, he met all the employees and spoke to them as a group. He told them that his goal was to build an elite franchise. The best. None would be better on or off the field. He would try very hard to create a wonderful place to work and train and would make every possible effort to get a new stadium in Philadelphia. "They probably thought I was pipe-dreaming," he mused, "because at the time I was."

Lurie and Banner got through the 1994 season learning the nitty-gritty of football operations, observing the coaching staff (and deciding that the head coach wasn't championship quality), and wondering how to inject an entrepreneurial spirit into the organization, which just seemed to repeat the same patterns every year. (Lurie made a series of hand circles as he told me about their losers' loop in the summer of 2003.) There had already been a public battle with the coach in the middle of the season when he demanded a new contract and took the issue to the press—which confirmed Lurie's view that the man was more interested in job security than in building winners. The most Lurie could do to boost the players' confidence was to show them that the owner cared, by knowing every player's name, by going into the locker room to "put an arm around them, tell them they're going to have a breakout season, little things to boost them, never criticize them, and appreciate every single one."

Lurie and Banner were aware that everything they did sent a signal. They did trivial things that were important to people, such as making sure every salary review was done by the date of the anniversary. And they also made bigger investments to overcome the perception that the organization was cheap and didn't care about winning. They chartered bigger and better planes, put the team up in better hotels, and upgraded the food at the pre-game table. "We believed we had to do things in a first-class manner. We went overboard in size and quality in the beginning," Banner said.

At the end of that first season, Lurie and Banner cataloged the key ingredients for a turnaround. Lurie kept the shopping list by his bedside:

1. a superb leader/coach
2. a "franchise" quarterback (that is, a leader around whom the team could build)
3. an excellent player personnel department
4. an outstanding practice facility
5. a state-of-the-art stadium

The Clocks Are Running: Quick Fixes,
False Starts, and Long-Term Goals

Lurie and Banner could make progress on some of those five goals much more quickly than on others. In 1995 they took steps to fix immediate problems while recognizing that quick fixes might not be long-term solutions. To help the players win games, they fired the head coach and hired Ray Rhodes, a rising assistant coach with a taskmaster reputation. To help the Eagles win friends and a new stadium, they established a significant philanthropic foundation, the Eagles Youth Partnership, to serve disadvantaged youth in the greater Philadelphia community, and they initiated discussions with city and state politicians about a new stadium. The foundation was an opportunity to overcome the stigma of distance from the community associated with the previous absentee owner and to build goodwill during the turnaround—not to mention public support for stadium dreams. Lurie was proud of the Eagles' community service, which grew as a national model. (I first met Joe Banner in 1996 around community service, and we serve on a national nonprofit board together.)

The move most visible to the Eagles' network when Rhodes became head coach was the signing of running back Ricky Watters, one of a handful of elite players available as a free agent that year. Attracting a star, and investing the dollars this required, was another signal that the Lurie regime was playing to win. Initially, they did. In Rhodes's first two seasons, the Eagles finished with 10–6 won-lost records. Lurie felt that Rhodes vastly improved the culture of the locker room—that he was supportive, gave the players a chance to win, and was totally committed to success. Early momentum, he said, came from players' identification with Rhodes as "one of us, a street fighter."

But Rhodes was also widely viewed as a disciplinarian who thought tactically game to game, rather than as a leader who could build talent and teamwork by thinking strategically. Disciplinarian coaches, like tough corporate bosses brought in to tighten things up, often wear out their welcome relatively quickly, as players begin to just tune them out. The Eagles fell to 6–9 in 1997 and descended further to 3–13 in 1998, leading to Rhodes's firing. "The 1997 season hadn't gone well, but we wanted to give him one more chance. In 1998, we hit rock bottom," Lurie said. "It was only one bad season, but we didn't like the direction of things strategically. At the same time so much frustrating and potentially positive work was going on around a new stadium and training facility. We were under pressure from fans and the media."

Less visible to external audiences was that Lurie and Banner had a strategy to build a winning team, and they were committed to it. They wanted to hire "ascending" talent (players with big potential) and not try to retain "descending" talent (those with their best years behind them), doing this within the salary cap so they could build a war chest to use when the right free agent came on the market. They wanted a head coach who could not only lead the players game by game, but would also understand and execute the strategy. (That is why a top-notch player personnel organization was also on Lurie's bedside shopping list.)

Sticking with the Program: Risking Unpopular Decisions

The hiring of Andy Reid in January of 1999 was initially controversial. He was a largely unknown assistant coach from the Green Bay Packers in Wisconsin, not the big name the fans and media were hoping for. But Lurie and Banner liked his compatibility with their strategy for building the team. They had studied a half-dozen leading coaches, including Bill Walsh, Jimmy Johnson, and Bill Parcells, and had talked to players and agents who knew them. They discovered that this diverse group had leadership ideas in common, not sports ideas. They were detail-oriented people, whose leadership skills were more important than their football knowledge, and they were not afraid to be wrong.

Andy Reid was strong on all counts, Banner later said. "He plans every moment of the next year, every minute of every practice, every agenda of every meeting, and has conviction. He builds leadership in the locker room. He doesn't care how much anyone else second-guesses him." For his part, Reid had to overcome skepticism about the Eagles. "Everyone, including my kids, thought that this was the worst place to go," Reid said. No one believed the story about new facilities; people around the league said it would never happen. But Reid's agent told him it was a great opportunity, because he had checked out Lurie and Banner. "So I had trust that they were shooting straight," Reid recalled.

Thanks to their lousy 1998 season, the Eagles had the second pick in the 1999 NFL player draft. The first pick went as expected (quarterback Tim Couch to the Cleveland Browns), meaning that the Eagles had a number of good players to choose from, among them both quarterback Donovan McNabb from Syracuse and Heisman Trophy–winning running back Ricky Williams from Texas. Lurie recalled the pressure: "Everyone in Philadelphia including the mayor and the city council wanted us to draft Ricky Williams. Mayor Rendell introduced a resolution in city council about it. It got very few votes, but it was a sign of mass hysteria about a quick fix to turn around the Eagles." The mayor's actions incited a call-in campaign that tied up the Eagles' switchboard.

The Eagles selected McNabb instead. "We all felt this was an opportunity to build around a franchise quarterback, and if we could get one good enough, we shouldn't miss the chance," Lurie declared. "Andy Reid's first take was that we'd do what we felt was right to win, regardless of public opinion." Reid thought McNabb had character and could lead the team because of his secure upbringing. "I put him in as many different situations as I could to get to know the real man," Reid said. "I watched him in restaurants; I took him to my home; I watched him with my kids. After a while you get a sense for what kind of guy he is—not just how much he can bench or how far he can throw."

Eagles fans at the draft in Madison Square Garden theater in New York loudly booed McNabb, and the City of Brotherly Love showed him none of it, just bitterness. But this risky selection was one of the key points in the Eagles' turnaround. While Williams became a good player, McNabb was a star at the league's most important position, a talented athlete and a good team leader. Lurie described him also as articulate and mature, someone who treated people with respect rather than acting like a rock star.

In Reid and McNabb's first year, expectations were low for the team in what was clearly a rebuilding year, and the Eagles struggled to a 5–11 record, although many of the losses were by five points or less, heralding a potential turnaround. Banner said that Reid needed a year to teach the team how to win. This was not just about football, it was about the culture.

Culture Change: A Long March to Success

Andy Reid had formed a players' committee soon after his arrival, which included a representative from every position on the team, and he met with them every Wednesday at 8:10 a.m. in his office for a candid discussion of problems—for example, how to get veteran players to take care of rookies who were not accustomed to the rigors of professional play after the comparatively lighter schedules in college football. Such approaches worked, the longer-term strategy kicked into high gear, and the next season was the turnaround year, when the Eagles made it clear they had reversed the losing cycle and were headed into the winners' column.

In August 2000, in training camp just before the season began, Lurie's annual "state of the team" address to the media exuded confidence that the Eagles were going to become a very good football team soon. Evidence from the field proved it. In the first game of the season, against the Dallas Cowboys, Andy Reid called for an onside kick, a risky and aggressive play, and one that sent a message to the team and to opponents. "I called that play to make a statement," Reid told us. "What I was saying was 'We're going after this and we'll have some fun doing it. It's part of the game; you don't hold back in the NFL.' So it was a great statement because it worked." That gutsy call built confidence in Reid. Joe Banner said that onside kick was the first time he was confirmed in his certainty that they had picked the right head coach. Cornerback Troy Vincent said that he had never been on a team in which players had such belief in one another—or for which a coach had done so much with so little. The team went 11–5 and made the playoffs.

That same year, the efforts to get a new practice facility and stadium began to coalesce. Construction was under way for the NovaCare Complex, a state-of-the-art training facility and franchise headquarters that opened in March 2001. Ground-breaking took place in May 2001 for the new stadium, Lincoln Financial Field, across from the old Veterans Stadium, to be completed by 2003 and featuring a roofline with eagle-like wings. Lurie had benefited from fortuitous timing in his quest for stadium funding during the economic boom years. The Eagles received $150 million in loans and grants from a new NFL stadium loan program, as well as a contribution from the state and even more from the city, approximately $200 million in public funding for the $500-million project. The Eagles' CFO, Don Smolenski, was quick to point out that the stadium had the NFL's largest private funding, negotiations had spanned two mayoral administrations, and the team had never threatened to leave Philadelphia (although if the practice facility had moved beyond city limits, most of the payroll subject to the city's wage tax would have departed with it).

Things were going well on every front. In May of 2001, Lurie and Banner increased Reid's front-office responsibilities, giving him the additional title of Executive Vice President of Football Operations. In 2001 and 2002 the Eagles' winning seasons drove them to the playoffs and vindicated the support of all those who had invested time, effort, and loyalty. They won even when Donovan McNabb was sidelined with injuries, and they won even under NFL rules that evened out the competition. "We want to disprove the conventional wisdom that you can't get good and stay good under NFL rules," Banner said.

"We preach team. Team, team, team, team, team," Andy Reid told me on a visit to his office, tapping his fingers on the arms of his leather club chair to emphasize each repetition.

A culture of teamwork was an important part of the Eagles' turnaround. Joe Banner believed that "the skill of an athlete is irrelevant until the right culture surrounds him." Taking "surrounds" literally, the Eagles had designed a physical environment to reinforce the desired culture.

Identical locker rooms at the stadium and in the NovaCare Complex had rich cherry fittings, vaulted ceilings, and no support columns, because Andy Reid wanted an open environment. As reminders of pride, everything carried the Eagles logo, including the wastebaskets. At NovaCare, the cafeteria was in the most central location. The 200-seat auditorium (with oversized seats in front for football-sized bodies) had film nights for families every few months, such as a screening of *Chinatown* in December 2003. The fitness center could be used by anyone when the players didn't need it—employees making $20,000 a year using the same facility as athletes making $6 million. For the players there were many extras, including a unique amenity in the form of their personal assistant, Karen Gerstle, who staffed a desk with fifty-three mail slots and handled messages—sometimes for their wives and girlfriends, too. The players' lounge, off the locker room, had a mini-kitchen, Ping-Pong, dominoes, computers, and cell-phone docking stations.

All these attractions enticed players to converge at NovaCare in their discretionary time, contributing to the sense of Eagles community. Andy Reid often slept in his office on an inflatable mattress; his fifteen-year-old daughter occasionally joined him for a sleepover, and they made milk shakes.

In the front lobby of the NovaCare Complex were tributes to Martin Luther King, Mother Teresa, and Jonas Salk—not the expected role models for an NFL team. Football legends were relegated to inner corridors. Lurie wanted to signal the team's values in a more uplifting way, honoring heroes "whose lives embodied the essence of leadership, vision, determination, conviction, and courage . . . who fought through adversity, defied and subsequently overcame the odds."

Fighting through adversity was the mode for the 2003 season, which was the test of whether the turnaround had taken. The

Eagles lost the first two games, and they were both high-profile losses. The first loss was to Tampa Bay at the grand opening of Lincoln Financial Field on a nationally televised game, a monumental occasion for Philadelphia and the entire Eagles organization. People had been working day and night for months to get ready for the new football-only stadium, especially since the Eagles now controlled operations and had to hire and manage security, ushers, ticket-takers, guest services staff, and seat-fixers. (Andy Reid's request for software for his Avid computer system had to take a backseat to the technology needs of the stadium.) The second loss was to the New England Patriots on a nationally televised Sunday broadcast.

Banner said that the Eagles have been called the only franchise that could start the season with two high-visibility losses and not panic, but stay on an even keel. We asked Andy Reid how he handled those losses. "You travel when the light's not shining, early in the morning and late at night. You don't want to be seen," he laughed. What he actually did was refocus the team on fundamentals. He decided to step back, take out sophisticated plays that the team was not ready for, and return to basics. He told the team, "It's time to take off the tuxedos, put on the blue jeans, and go to work." Then he used his "great locker-room leadership" (including the players' committee) to help him "defeat defeat and turn a negative into a positive." Donovan McNabb was clear about his responsibilities. "Everyone looks to the quarterback to make thing happen on and off the field," he told me. "What really helped was our years of growing together. The way we started in the first few games, confidence was definitely still there. We know how to get our chins up, go to practice, and get things done. Mentally we stay on course. The first two losses helped us because we don't want to go back there."

The team won the next two games but then lost to the Dallas Cowboys. Reid tried another of his famous onside kicks that had won the 2000 Dallas game. This time Dallas recovered and ran it back for a touchdown, resulting in a 23–21 Eagles loss, making them 2–3 in October. Banner said, "Even Andy wondered whether what he did cost us the game. Jeffrey and I walked into the locker room and said that we hoped he wouldn't hesitate to do it again. He said, 'You know me, you don't need to worry about it.' Our philosophy is to be super-aggressive. Don't lose because you're afraid of failure."

On a Monday at the end of October, when the team had recovered to 4–3, I was talking with Joe Banner when he took a call from Andy Reid to coordinate the usual Monday message to the press. Banner wanted credit for the Eagles' phenomenal job against obstacles, such as the large number of starting players who were sidelined with injuries. Banner wanted the message to be "We're determined and rising to the challenge."

And rise they did. From the depths of an 0–2 start, the Eagles soared to the top of their league. In December, when the Eagles were 11–3 and had just enjoyed their ninth consecutive win, Donovan McNabb said, "We were confident, and we were together."

The Eagles took that confidence into the championship game with the Carolina Panthers, but the aggressive Panthers piled on McNabb, and his injuries were a big factor in the Eagles' defeat— their third consecutive loss of the championship. The Panthers, not the widely favored Eagles, made it to the Super Bowl. Throughout Philadelphia, there was considerable anger and anguish about another near-miss. Would this undermine the Eagles' faith in the culture built during the turnaround years?

The Eagles could find comfort in the fact that the New England Patriots, who defeated the Panthers in the Super Bowl on February 1, 2004, had taken the same long march to build a winners' culture, instilling similar values. Patriots' owner Robert Kraft had bought the franchise in the same year Jeffrey Lurie acquired the Eagles, starting with a similarly mediocre team with dreadful facilities and sore-loser fans. Both brought business savvy to the new rules about salary caps, began the process of gaining public support and financing for state-of-the-art stadiums, and created a culture stressing character, teamwork, and responsibility to the community. After false starts with unsatisfactory coaches, both recruited coach-leaders—the Patriots' Bill Belichick and the Eagles' Andy Reid—known not for big egos but for building teams of player-leaders.

"The Eagles are good people," Patriots' vice chairman Jonathon Kraft told me, while insisting that the Patriots had started with less—a poorer record, worse facilities, and fewer fans—and come further. Certainly the Pats' two Super Bowl victories in three years put them in the record books with the best football franchises ever. But their turnaround journey was not all that different from that of the Eagles—first solving operational problems but then emphasizing a culture for sustained excellence that helped the Patriots bounce back from their own early-season defeats. After all, the Eagles had won more regular season games since 2000 than any other NFL team, including the Patriots.

TRIGGERING A TURNAROUND: THE EARLY AGONY
The Patriots and the Eagles soared beyond the early challenges of their turnarounds to build a winners' culture based on accountability, collaboration, and initiative—the cornerstones of confidence, whose construction will be explored in detail in the next three chapters. The lessons from the Eagles' early days make clear why turnaround leaders must have the stamina and persistence to deal with problems worse than they thought, skepticism about whether they will deliver on promises, difficult and unpopular decisions, false recoveries, and a lag between internal changes and actual winning performance.

The Eagles fall in the middle of three types of situations that trigger a turnaround. The Eagles had it tough, but not as tough as groups at the extremes, either in deep crisis or not yet clearly sick.

The first group is the fatally ill. Some of the turnarounds I examined did not start until the ailing system had reached the brink of imminent death. Continental Airlines had emerged from several bankruptcies but was still bleeding cash. Invensys, a large British industrial conglomerate, was a few potential missteps away from defaulting on its financial obligations. Dimock Community Health Center in Boston was a nonprofit organization trying to emerge from court-ordered receivership because of failure to pay debts. The Montreal Expos baseball franchise had been taken over by Major League Baseball in order to close it or move it.

A second batch of organizations begins the turnaround process when loss of external confidence finally compels boards or owners to seek change, but before an overt crisis. Such organizations are in the market for new leadership to end losing streaks and get things back on track, but they are not at death's door. This includes Gillette, Seagate, Washington Hospital Center, and the Eagles.

For a third set, a turnaround is an unanticipated by-product of normal life events, such as succession of regimes. The old CEO retires in a blaze of glory, but leaves behind a set of problems that have started a decline cycle. The BBC (British Broadcasting Corporation) was in that situation—not exactly a losing streak but not in good health, either—when John Birt handed the reins to Greg Dyke in 2000. General Electric has appeared to need a turnaround every time a new CEO was named, a member of the inner executive circle told me; Jack Welch started his tenure by shaking up the company, and the handover from Jack Welch to Jeffrey Immelt in 2000 initiated another turnaround. Normal succession within GE frequently triggered a turnaround, even when the party line was that the new boss had inherited a perfectly healthy system, something I observed when "David Lee" (a GE executive who prefers anonymity) took on a weakening industrial division of a winning company widely assumed to do everything right.

It would seem a lot easier to fix something that is just starting to crack, like Lee's division, than to repair a system so weak that it is on life support or in the bankruptcy courts. But the opposite is often the case. Though it seems that problems can be easier to solve when the losing streak is not so long and the cycle of decline not too advanced, there also can be more resistance to the idea of significant change when the situation is not dire. The truly sick are desperate for any solution, and too helpless to resist. It is more permissible and a great deal easier at extremes of distress (though less humane) to slash, burn, destroy, cut, lay off, and start over again. Under extreme distress, extreme measures can be taken; the truly obese get their jaws wired shut to prevent uncontrolled food intake, while the merely overweight must struggle through diets. But when there is no consensus that the underlying system needs to change, or that losses are anything other than bad breaks or a bad economy, then turnaround leaders have a more difficult task.

The Loneliness of the Long-Distance Change Agent

"David Lee" knew that a case for change was hard when disaster was not imminent. Perhaps that is why he felt so alone for the first year of his ultimately successful turnaround of the division. Like Jeffrey Lurie, he discovered that the situation was indeed worse than anyone knew, but unlike Lurie, he was not the supreme authority, and no one else seemed to think the division needed major change. Not his boss, who had brought him in without a mandate for change, and not the big boss several levels up. Certainly not the people in the division, who were accustomed to being patted on the back and living a good life.

Lee soon discovered a sick system whose weaknesses had been hidden by a near-monopoly position that was about to end. A major competitor in another part of the world was coming on strong, with an innovative process at lower cost. Although stated earnings were still high, return on capital was low and getting lower, and if current trends continued, the competitor would soon overtake the division on every indicator.

Problems were everywhere, as Lee discovered when he toured facilities around the world. A plant in Europe paid excessive overtime because workers often called in sick, leaving their buddies to cover for them at overtime rates—with the roles of out-sick and overtime-earner reversing enough to be suspicious. The office in Japan was elegant and empty. When Lee asked how often customers visited, the receptionist told him maybe one came every week or two—which was the result of a partnership with a Japanese trading company that was now the place customers went to do business with this division. Japanese customers did visit the

United States frequently to see sales staff—not to place orders, but because they were wined, dined, and entertained on golf outings at luxury resorts. Back home, Lee observed a top-heavy staff that would stuff meetings with way too many people for any simple issue—but none of them with the ability to solve the simple problem. The finance director seemed capable of producing any numbers the general manager requested—but not necessarily the real ones.

There were so many bad habits that he felt he needed to replace more than half of the managers. His boss, sensitive to the bad press of layoffs, told him he could cut only 10 percent of the people. Lee felt he had good business reasons to get tough and clean house, so he went ahead and did what he could despite his instructions. He closed the Japanese office. He cut budgets for sales and eliminated the salespeople who only knew how to entertain. He bargained hard with the union to eliminate overtime in Europe, giving the workers an extra 10 percent in their regular paychecks instead—and policing sick days by calling people at home (if they didn't answer their phones, he sent staff on motorcycles to check up on them). Now Lee felt he was unpopular with just about everyone.

Those moves were bold strokes, each commanded by a single decision of the boss. Each bold stroke cut expenses, certainly, but also ran the risk of further alienating workers or customers. And getting good habits in place takes a lot longer than eliminating bad practices; it takes the long march of culture change in which many individuals change their behavior in order to head in the same direction. Once Lee cleaned out a top-heavy organization, he could empower talented people in lower ranks who had been stifled by the bureaucracy, but who could now take on bigger tasks with greater self-confidence. Still, they had to develop confidence in one another, in order to work as a team. Replacing workers' self-indulgent games with productivity targets and rewards for achievements would not be believed or show results immediately. Confidence could not be willed into existence quickly. The noise from layoffs was so loud that at first it drowned out the message of empowerment he was also sending—that if people played to win, they would enjoy the rewards of success.

Lee was miserable for a year. He thought everyone hated him, and they probably did. Gradually, allies surfaced who shared his strategic vision, often from the ranks of the newly promoted. Gradually the workers gained confidence in the system, because the methods they were learning in training classes produced wins in the factory and the field. Finally, about eighteen months after Lee arrived, morale jumped when results started to improve. In less than three years productivity was soaring at higher rates than for the main competitor, and return on capital had tripled. Lee was successful in his turnaround, and later people who had been his worst critics became his admirers. Winning is a good way to attract friends.

Each Turnaround Is Different,
Each Turnaround Is the Same

I can tick off many differences between Lee's division of a giant global corporation and the turnaround of the Philadelphia Eagles—or, for that matter, between any two turnarounds, whether personal, organizational, or national in scope, because each situation has unique elements. Lurie was the owner, Lee a hired hand with bosses to satisfy. Lurie needed to show local commitment; Lee operated on a global stage. Lurie operated in the spotlight of constant press and public scrutiny; Lee was hidden in an obscure corner. Lurie wanted to be popular with the workers; Lee acted as though he could not have cared less. And of course the specific technical problems to be solved were entirely different—although I imagine the Eagles' coaches would resonate with the human problem of instilling discipline in workers who know how to game the system.

All these differences in context and details sometimes make people think that every turnaround is unique, a matter of finding the specific problems and solving them. But every turnaround starts with the same overriding challenge: the need to make unpopular decisions about a situation whose full ugliness has been denied, and yet, at the same time, restore people's confidence that they can start winning again.

Most popular conceptions of turnarounds feature hired guns who come to clean out the town—take-no-prisoners consultants, or an occupying army. "Turnaround consultants" are known (and hated by the people) for reducing head-count and imposing cost controls. The image is "Chainsaw Al" (Dunlap), who turned around Sunbeam by slashing nearly everything, or, farther back, "Neutron Jack" (Welch), who was said to kill all the people but leave the buildings standing in his first few years as CEO of General Electric, before he became a business hero. But more often, turnarounds start by replacing the top people, as the first step in restoring external confidence.

SEARCHING FOR LEADERSHIP: NEW BROOMS OR MAGIC WANDS?

It is hard for leaders who let people down to succeed in pulling them up. That is one of many reasons why turnarounds often start by replacing the people in charge. New leaders at the top untainted by the sins or politics of the past and uninfected by the resentments and negativity of losing streaks can bring a fresh perspective. As the saying goes, it takes a new broom to sweep clean.

How did the previous leadership fail to see what the turnaround leaders find obvious? Were they stupid, or what? That's the kind of thing some of my MBA students might say as they examine a case retrospectively, with all the facts predigested. But, clearly, if some of the smartest managers in one of the most-admired companies in the world (GE) could let losers' habits accumulate, then it is not just a matter of whether people are smart enough. Instead, there are other reasons that people caught in a losing streak may not see the way out. It is often very hard to see a whole system when you are occupying one corner of it. Connecting the dots is difficult if each dot has been possessed by a different person. The situation facing turnaround leaders is often worse than anyone knew because no one has put the whole picture together. Losers, I have shown, avoid dialogue and keep facts off the table.

Former leaders have lost credibility, and new leaders symbolize to everyone that the weight of past losses can be left behind. Even when executives who presided over a period of decline admit mistakes and embrace new ways, it is nearly impossible for them to stir up the organizational energy needed for a turnaround. For one thing, people tend to interpret the old bosses' actions as self-justifying, chosen to rewrite past history. After all, if the old CEO had wrong ideas in the past, why should people believe he or she has the right idea now? Insiders who bring up difficult issues are seen as self-serving, as acting only in their own interest, reflecting the internal distrust of a losing streak. Outsiders, in contrast, are viewed as objective (even when they bring in obvious biases).

The old leadership group is "mired in a puddle of overbrained solutions. They can't see any way out, either," declared Greg Brenneman, former COO of Continental Airlines and partner with Gordon Bethune in its successful turnaround. "Usually they have trouble accepting responsibility for and reversing the poor decisions they made in the past. It's an ego thing. . . . No one in the company trusts them anymore. They got us into this hole, how are they going to have the sense to get us out of it?" As former U.S. Vice President Al Gore observed when he decided not to run for president in 2004, his candidacy undoubtedly would have been dogged by debate over why he lost the race in 2000, at a time when his party needed to focus relentlessly on moving forward.

New leaders are better able to disentangle system dynamics because they were not caught up in them. An important step is putting a name to problems that have long gone unexpressed, even though people individually might have known about them but thought they were the only ones with this awareness—a phenomenon called "pluralistic ignorance." At Gillette, for example, after a successful turnaround was under way in 2001, senior executives claimed, to a person, that they had known for years what the problems were—trade loading; long gaps between new product releases and a proliferation of minor upgrades on existing products; and the inappropriate application of the company's strategy for blades and razors to other categories, especially the Duracell battery business. As a Gillette group director for Europe proclaimed, "I'm absolutely certain there's not one person in the whole company who for one moment thought that we should do anything other than get out of trade loading." Still, it took a new CEO, Jim Kilts, to name the problems and change the habits, as we will see in the next chapter.

Let's assume for a moment that people do know what some of the problems are. That doesn't mean they are in a position to solve them. Just as overweight people know they should not overeat, losing players know they're not pulling together as a team. They might understand the issues in theory, but be unable to do anything in practice—a gap between knowing and doing. In my sports and business research, I asked people to comment about what leaders should do to help produce success and what individuals should do. Losers offered exactly the same kinds of advice as those from winning groups. This is not surprising; they read the same books (including mine), study the same role-model leaders, listen to the same coaches on the motivational speaker circuit.

So why doesn't knowing the theory translate into practice? Consider how many barriers to action are produced by the dynamics of a losing streak. Sometimes the barrier is a lack of imagination about solutions, sometimes it is passivity from a losers' legacy of punishment, sometimes it is lack of power. A senior manager in a company trying to move off a losing streak told me that in his company, "The idea that has grown over time is that taking risks, feeling empowered, and doing what is right . . . is wrong. Therefore, even where people know how they should act or respond to get ahead of a problem, they don't for fear of failure or reprisal." At Invensys, the ailing conglomerate, new CEO Rick Haythornthwaite reported, "Everyone knew the problems, but the structure inhibited them from doing anything about it. People could only take shots across the silos. Some people knew the issues technically and could prevent obviously bad decisions, but they lacked the power to act outside their own fields of concentration. They knew change was needed, but they were not sure how to make it happen." New leaders can more easily remove barriers erected by previous bosses and provide a fresh perspective—even fresher if they come from outside the company and the industry.

So far, these are all good arguments in favor of new leaders. There is just one problem. A new leader does not wave a magic wand and automatically transform everything. Moreover, changing the CEO or removing the head coach is a very familiar feature of long losing streaks. So why should it suddenly be such a good idea to start a turnaround this way?

As we have seen, decline cycles are known for a rapid turnover of people in the top positions. Their suitcases are barely unpacked before they are out the door again. Each new CEO makes an introductory speech saying that this time things will be different, that this time the group will resume winning. But if there are so many people coming to the microphone one after another saying the same thing, how do we know that this time a turnaround will take? What makes skeptics who have watched the big guys come and go suspend their negativity and let hope revive?

In his influential book *Searching for a Corporate Savior*, my colleague Rakesh Khurana issued a powerful warning about the dangers of pinning the hopes of an entire institution on one charismatic individual and presented compelling data showing that changing the CEO of a corporation does not necessarily improve performance. Nor does changing the coach or manager of a sports team by itself automatically convert the team from perennial losers to continuous winners.

Continental Airlines had ten CEOs in as many years before Gordon Bethune's turnaround took hold. The Prairie View Panthers had a new coach almost every two years during their long dry spell, before C. L. Whittington was fired in less than a year. Add to the Continental/Prairie View record the experience of the Anaheim

Mighty Ducks—six head coaches in ten years, as I describe later in this chapter—and we could easily conclude that new chiefs fail at least five times as often as they succeed.

Clearly, it cannot be just the fact of a new CEO per se that produces a successful turnaround; something else must be going on. Just what makes the difference?

NEW MONEY, NEW MEANING: TANGIBLE SIGNS OF CONFIDENCE

The clue to beginning the process of renewing confidence is the confidence leaders show in the people who must work to deliver winning performance. That confidence does not come from empty pep talks, but from tangible indications that someone cares enough to invest in those people and to empower them to take new actions. Leaders show confidence in the people by finding resources to invest. Building confidence in advance of victory requires a leap of faith—a belief that the sick system can recover, even when the situation is most dire.

Although sick systems might need surgeons who cut out dead-wood and unnecessary expenditures, if that's all that happens, losses are temporarily stemmed but the system has not been led to a winning path. The art of turnaround leadership is knowing how to shed deadwood without killing the tree, to dig down to find root causes and make systemic changes, and to help the tree blossom. That takes a healer.

Healing a Community Health Center

The real start of the turnaround of the Dimock Community Health Center in inner-city Boston was not when the court-ordered receiver reduced expenses, but when Jackie Jenkins-Scott, a social worker and administrator, agreed to work beside the receiver as Dimock's new CEO and brought hope that renewed confidence in its future.

Dimock had gone into bankruptcy a few years earlier, one of the first nonprofits to take that route. Debts included back taxes, heating oil, and electricity—the kind of bills that should not be ignored. The health center had spent its small endowment, and the receiver had cut expenses to bare bones by the time Jenkins-Scott first visited in 1983. There was nothing left to cut except the minimum needed to run the facility. She was sent to either pull the Center out of bankruptcy or tidy up the affairs after its death.

"There was just something about the spirit, the environment" that attracted her, she said. "The buildings were old and tumbling, but they were places that made history, and it all clicked: the women and African-Americans who built it, its longevity. I thought, 'Boy, we can't let this place just wither away.' " The staff was committed and hard-working, hanging in despite no pay increases and poor facilities, wondering when the administration would make improvements for the people that they served. The board was small and dispirited. But Jenkins-Scott could not let Dimock disappear because of despair: "I just couldn't see allowing it to go. How awful it would be to have this place boarded up in the inner city. They were beautiful buildings, just in bad shape."

We were talking from the vantage point of twenty years later, well after a successful turnaround that brought Dimock recognition as the best community health center in America, designation as a national historical landmark, a set of innovative programs that were national models, visits from U.S. presidential candidates, partnerships with state governors, and a diverse board of some of Massachusetts' best-known corporate leaders. In 2004, Jenkins-Scott was getting ready to hand a healthy organization to a new CEO as she assumed the presidency of Wheelock College.

Back then, survival was a toss-up. But where the receiver saw costs to cut, Jenkins-Scott saw potential to grow. She saw that there were costs associated with the receivership—the receiver's salary, for one thing. And she saw that people needed hope. Dimock provided primary health care (adult medicine, dental and eye care, pediatrics, OB/gyn) and offered entry-level job training for low-income people in health professions (dental technicians, nurses' aides). At the time, all primary care was on one big floor lined with chairs on either side of a dark, drab hall, with no air conditioning. Buckets caught the water from leaking roofs. People blamed one another: The clinicians weren't bringing in enough revenue, the administration was wasteful. And the receivership created dependency; people could not take responsibility for the future of their organization.

"Our receiver was good at the business side but not at the people side," Jenkins-Scott observed. "He could look at a balance sheet and say, 'Cut 20 percent here.' That led to a lot of fear. The receiver becomes God Almighty, Big Brother, and what he says goes. No one felt they could build a team to create Dimock's future."

She vowed to end the receivership. Her first move was to ask the judge to appoint her as co-receiver, so that she could participate in the financial decisions. "The judge was pretty reasonable, pretty cool, a good liberal person who wanted this to work," she said. "I became co-receiver about six months after I got there. I took the position that the court needed two reports. The receiver was reporting on the financial side. I wanted to be looking toward the future. People need to feel leadership could do something." The person whose power she wanted to share was very different from her in every respect. "I was thirty-three and African-American, he was fifty-three and a white male. I suspected this would end with one of us in or out."

Jenkins-Scott's messages of hope attracted new resources. She rejuvenated and re-energized the board by adding new members who would bring external support. As long as people felt the place was closing, it would continue to go nowhere. So, persuading just a few visible leaders to join the board sent a big message of confidence to the staff, turned around external PR, and provided a base to attract new resources. She worked on strengthening and expanding current services, because those were the players whose actions would win games. And she tackled the physical environment. "It takes on symbolism for everything," she said. "When people want the organization to be better, they express it as 'Can't we get the leak fixed?'" It turned out that only about one-third of the

200,000 square feet of space was being used. Generating revenue by renting space would provide funds for renovations everywhere.

These plans resonated with the board, who helped find external partners to invest in the revitalization of Dimock. "We only put forward issues that we could win," said Joseph Feaster, a lawyer and long-term Dimock board chair.

"Jackie brought a can-do attitude. She has a very high energy level, and her enthusiasm is infectious. She was willing to knock on doors that others wouldn't," recalled longtime board member Richard Karoff, director of investments for CIBC World Markets. "She cemented those relationships into hard dollars."

Ending Poverty of the Spirit

Jackie Jenkins-Scott and the Jeffrey Lurie/Joe Banner team took on rundown organizations of similar size (though highly dissimilar financial prospects). They invested in physical facilities, in order to back the people delivering the service. This encourages a more positive emotional climate and gives people both hope and resources for success. That's why the early stages of many turnarounds involve painting walls and redecorating the facilities, to lift spirits. Big visions are just words, but the equipment and decor are in sight every minute and make a difference in carrying out tasks every day.

What matters in restoring individual confidence is not the source of the new investment but the fact that new leaders are willing and able to find ways to invest in people and their work environment. Lurie used his own money; Jenkins-Scott had to find new board members and donors; Prairie View A&M University got reparations money from the State of Texas to correct past inequities, funds that could be reinvested to rebuild multiple programs. In his turnaround of the BBC, new director-general Greg Dyke found new money to invest by cutting bureaucracy and reallocating existing funds to the people who produced BBC programs. The new general manager of the Montreal Expos shifted money to player services, even though funds were scarce.

New leaders coming from outside can sometimes bargain for new resources from owners or bosses. Drs. Craig Feied and Mark Smith made new investment a part of the deal when they took on the turnaround of the emergency department at Washington Hospital Center, then considered one of the worst in Washington, D.C. They insisted on replacing contract physicians with full-time staff, and they received seed money for the creation of a pioneering digital information system that ended up transforming not just the ER, but the whole hospital. Of course, Feied and Smith had to resuscitate the ER before they could build confidence to reclaim the trauma unit (which had been operating in a separate silo) and get the rest of the system on their digital network. Not only did their emergency department rise to become the city's best, but when its new all-risks-ready disaster preparedness capability was tested in the terrorist attack on the Pentagon on September 11, 2001, it caught the attention of U.S. Secretary of Health and Human Services Tommy Thompson, who helped the Feied/Smith vision to grow.

New leaders can attract support from the external network. A new CEO may already have personal connections with customers, fans, investors, suppliers, opinion shapers, or rule makers and certainly may have more credibility in representing their views. This also helps reverse the losers' inward focus. In his first week at Gillette, Jims Kilts visited a major retailer with a sales executive, signaling his emphasis on customer relationships; and as a former CEO of several food companies, Kilts was already well-acquainted with key trade customers. When he arrived to turn around Invensys, Rick Haythornthwaite spoke passionately about what he learned from customer interviews and used that perspective to unify a company divided by narrow views.

An infusion of resources, however small, applied to things that show people their value and their potential, is the first step in creating a more positive emotional climate even while layoffs or cost reductions are necessary to fix financial problems. Investment in the work environment for the people who play the game indicates the leaders' faith in the future, and that helps restore everyone's confidence. But fix-it plans must be accompanied by a mission and values larger than repair work, to help guide the work of problem-solving—a positive vision of the future and a game plan, like the ones Jackie Jenkins-Scott and Jeffrey Lurie had in mind. Then, even difficult and unpopular decisions can be based on the desire to build the future. Need to cut expenses? Cut first the areas that do not directly contribute to performance on the playing field, and invest more in the players who deliver it. Need to reduce staff? Replace people who indulge in losers' habits, and replace them with people already embodying the behavior of winners.

In short, turnaround leaders must stop the bleeding so as to get back into the game but also build the confidence to win it. That does not happen overnight.

FIRST STEPS ON A LONG MARCH: THE DANGERS OF FALSE RECOVERY

The turnaround leaders' agenda is daunting: endless problems to fix, unpopular decisions to make, skeptics to convert, and the need to secure investment before investors see any wins to attract them. My law about failure in the middle applies especially well to turnarounds. There are so many things that can go wrong. Turnarounds often proceed unevenly, in fits and starts, and are fraught with the danger of false recoveries that cannot be sustained because fundamentals have not been fixed.

If a new leader does not automatically walk on water, maybe that's because he is skating on thin ice. At least, that was the situation for the first five coaches of the Anaheim Mighty Ducks. Then the situation turned around in the 2002–3 season. But well into the following season, it seemed that the ice was still thin, and the cornerstones of confidence had not yet been firmed up.

Skating on Thin Ice

The Mighty Ducks were long the laughingstocks of the National Hockey League. Named after a junior hockey team in a series of

Disney movies, and playing in Orange County, California, where "ice" is more likely to signify diamonds than frozen water, the Ducks were perennial losers since their creation as an NHL expansion team in 1993.

"The reason we got into the business to begin with was solely our desire to be supportive of the Anaheim community. The city had built a facility—the Pond—and didn't have a tenant," a former Disney executive told us. The community embraced the Ducks. For the first two or three years, merchandise sales were at the top of the league, and the team made the first round of the playoffs. But it was downhill after that. Until a turnaround in 2002–3, the Disney-owned team barely eked out a winning season in 1996–97 (36 wins, 33 losses, and 13 ties), had not won a playoff game since 1997, and missed getting into the playoffs every season between 1999 and 2002.

Management appeared divided from the beginning, and that was only one factor in high coach turnover. The first head coach, Ron Wilson (1993–97), was fired due to "philosophical differences" with the team's management, which was criticized for his termination. Wilson was reported to rub people the wrong way, blame others for game losses, and be critical and negative in his dealings with players—typical of losing streaks. The next coach, Pierre Page, was fired after one year because of "differences of opinion" with the then–general manager; Page declared that negative attitudes were dragging the team down. There were two more short-lived coaches and several management shuffles during the next four years, including the firing of a general manager who was too tight-fisted to spend to recruit good players.

The Ducks hit bottom in the 2001–2 season, finishing in the basement of the Western Division with a 29–42 won-loss record. The situation seemed to call for a coroner instead of a new coach, a sportswriter proclaimed. "Disney owned us, and they owned ESPN. But at that time, we couldn't even get our games covered on ESPN," exclaimed Mike Babcock (who later became the winning head coach).

"Who's laughing now?" could have been the Ducks' refrain in the 2002–3 season, as victories mounted. That season, their win-loss record was 40–27 in league play, and they came close to winning the Stanley Cup championship, losing to the New Jersey Devils in the seventh game of the best-of-seven final series. It was a huge reversal of fortune for a team that nearly everyone thought Disney wanted to sell.

The turnaround started with an injection of new investment. In 2000, Paul Pressler became chairman of Disney Parks and Resorts, and in late 2001 he stepped in to head Anaheim sports, determined to improve the Disney-owned Anaheim sports franchises. He knew he needed a new type of executive in hockey (but he was cautious about this when he talked to us, because it was Disney policy not to talk about why executives left). Bryan Murray, a highly successful coach, had been hired as head coach in the spring of 2001. Pressler promoted him in 2002, after Murray's first season, to senior vice-president and general manager. With Disney CEO Michael Eisner's agreement, Pressler increased resources for the team so that Murray could do what he felt was required for a turnaround, especially with respect to strategy and player selection. "Bryan had a very clear vision of what he needed to make the team stronger, a turn away from the European style to a more North American style," Pressler recalled. ("You mean from finesse to brute force?" my researcher Scott Hildula asked. Pressler laughed. "We refer to the difference as European versus North American," he said.)

Murray brought Mike Babcock up from the Ducks' affiliate team in Cincinnati as head coach. It was considered a risky move to hire a minor-league coach. Murray also used the newly won cash from Disney to attract a few new top players and add scouts and marketing staff. Babcock then hired new assistant coaches, a strength coach, and a video coach. A weight room was added, the dressing room was renovated. "We took it from being a 1980s program to on the cutting edge," Babcock said. By the time Pressler left Disney to become CEO of apparel retailer Gap Inc. in the fall of 2002, the Ducks were on their way.

The changes had a big impact on players who had been part of several years of losing. "All the players ever want to see is that you're trying to get better and trying to upgrade," Murray said. "There were guys who had been here for eight or nine years, and they needed that little boost. When they saw that we were really making radical changes, they knew that there was a commitment here to be better, and they played better accordingly. You can tell them that you're going to get better but you have to show them that you're doing things to make it happen. I made player changes, but I did other things around the facility to get that message across. Even coming into training camp there was a new look and new attitude—more positive than it had been."

Babcock explained how he converted the skeptics: "You go into training camp and they are evaluating you and you are evaluating them. And they're not 100 percent sure. So you gotta get them onside. You do that by being who you are and doing what you do and being professional. And showing them your work ethic, your preparation, your attention to detail. I think it's not about what you say, it's about what you do." Veteran player Keith Carney recalled the impact of increased investment in the team: "It gave the rest of the team the attitude that we were trying to get better, and it will be better. You go into training camp with a better outlook. Everybody was more excited, of course, because of the people we brought in, and it begins to snowball."

Murray, who had never been around a losing group before, had found the Ducks' negativity depressing—which made the reversal that much more satisfying. "The winning helped stimulate an unbelievable feeling of confidence and pride. We lost game seven, but we walked away feeling, 'Wow, this franchise is on the right road.' "

"Winning is not all about money but also about putting together the right chemistry," Pressler observed. Murray and Babcock tried to reverse the hypercritical divisiveness that marred the Ducks' earlier years. Their presence and actions were made possible in the first place because an infusion of new resources from a boss at Disney renewed team confidence. Paul Pressler never put on skates, but his fingers were on the hockey stick that drove the puck into the goal to win in the turnaround season.

But despite that impressive season made possible by new leadership and new investment, the Ducks also prove the point that turnaround leaders should not assume that a few bold strokes will change the situation forever, and then the work is done. In the next season, 2003–4, the Ducks reverted to losing more than winning. By Christmas 2003, they had a poor record (11–14–4) that put them at the bottom of their division. One season is not enough to make a turnaround stick.

The Time Lags of Confidence

Destroying confidence can take minutes, while restoring confidence can take millennia (or so it seems to impatient investors). Building the foundation for sustained success—setting the stones under the water—is a laudable goal, but how long will impatient investors and supporters wait for walks on the water? Better not promise too much too soon, some turnaround leaders conclude.

Dusty Baker was the latest in a parade of managers imported to fix the Chicago Cubs. He sat behind his slightly cluttered desk in his office in the bowels of Wrigley Field about two hours before a midseason home game in 2003, carefully filling in the lineup card for that day's game while talking about the importance of keeping expectations in check. "In the beginning I'm not going to create any expectations. I'm not one to go sell some bill of goods," he said. I thought his desire to avoid hype and keep it low-key was wise. After all, fans get tired of declarations that this time things are different, that mistakes are a thing of the past, that victory is ahead.

A few months later, after a strong winning season in Baker's first year, he took the Cubs all the way to the National League championship series and to within five outs of advancing to the World Series. Yet, despite a strong start, Baker also knew that restoring confidence in the Cubs would take years. "They haven't had back-to-back winning seasons in almost forty years. I mean, just a winning season. Not playoffs, championships. Winning eighty-two victories, you know what I'm saying? So if we win this year, people are still going to think we won't win next year. My goal here is to have continued years of excellence." He knew the importance of going beyond quick wins ("plucking the low-hanging fruit" is the popular business phrase) to showing continuous progress.

Baker also knew that the honeymoon period could end the minute he made unpopular decisions. "Your first year is easy because everybody is posturing for position. Everybody is on their best behavior. Everybody buys your program," he said. Whether or not his first year was easy, it worked; the Cubs won steadily and almost made it to the World Series. Still, he felt it would be impossible to know if he had full support until there was a crisis and a choice of whether to back him or not. "The real test is years two or three, when they've heard your speeches over and over, they've seen you manage, they've seen you rant and rave, and nothing comes out of it."

Various turnaround tasks operate on different clocks. Bold strokes are fast and can be done by one powerful person; long marches to change culture and behavior take more time and the commitment of many people. Execution is play by play, game by game, while strategy is season by season, as the Eagles concluded in 1998, when they replaced a purely tactical coach with one who understood the balance between execution and strategy. Some things can be done immediately, like bringing on new players or announcing a new direction, but the results of those actions might not show up for years. "You can start cross-functional teams meeting in a day. But to get new products benefiting from cross-functional teams takes two to three iterations of a product development cycle," declared Steve Luczo, Seagate's turnaround CEO. Renewed internal confidence produces improvements, but skeptical external investors can take longer to be convinced. Gillette was widely praised as headed in the right direction two years into its turnaround, but its stock price had barely budged.

Restoring confidence involves demonstrating the absence of problems as well as the presence of wins, and the former takes longer to do. An event such as a fistfight in a public school is immediate; but how does one prove a non-event, such as an end to fistfights? (If Chicken Little of the old children's story reversed his stance and said, "The sky isn't falling," no newspaper would cover it.) A small number of corrupt or criminal accounting tricks in companies in the United States (WorldCom), the Netherlands (Ahold), or Italy (Parmalat) weaken confidence in the entire capitalist system; but then, how long does it take to provide convincing evidence of the non-event of no accounting tricks in most companies? It took one hour on September 11, 2001, to destroy Americans' faith in the safety of their shores; how many years without terrorism does it take to feel safe again? Turnaround leaders contend with a legacy of mistrust that is easier to break than repair.

In the early stages of a turnaround, various components of a system move at their own speed. Economists know this, as they search for the meaning of indicators that don't all move in the same direction. In May 2003, for example, American consumer spending had increased, but American consumer confidence—an index of intention to spend—had decreased; American businesses were raising productivity and profits, but not adding jobs. Which are the best bases for confidence in the economy? Within organizations, people examine similar sets of inconsistent formal and informal indicators (job security down, widespread communication up) in making judgments about the likely success of a turnaround, and therefore how much confidence they have to make emotional and behavioral investments in change.

There are false negatives in the early stages of turnarounds—when actions taken with long-term objectives in mind seem to exacerbate short-term losses. Do sports fans understand a "rebuilding year" such as the first season under the Eagles' Andy Reid, which involves a promising new team, low on the learning curve, that is destined to win next season but cannot win this season? If people become confused or scared by the actions of turnaround leaders, if they are made insecure by the sacrifices required today in order to build a brighter tomorrow, then they fail to invest, and their lack of confidence becomes a self-fulfilling prophecy that undermines the turnaround.

There are also false positives—early signs of recovery that bring so much relief that effort decreases, or rewards are taken prematurely. Dieters lose a few pounds and feel so good that they celebrate with chocolate cake or other indulgences, gaining back the weight. When the Prairie View Panthers won their first game in nearly ten years, players felt that they had achieved a lifelong dream, and the team lost subsequent games. My clinical psychologist friends tell me that the time their depressed patients are most suicide-prone is not in the depths of despair, but when they start to feel just enough better to have the energy to act on plans for self-destruction. People stop taking their antibiotics when they begin to feel better, despite doctors' orders to finish out the prescription, and then their infections return with a vengeance.

False recoveries can also provoke selfishness if they occur before leaders have restored team spirit. For this reason, early successes can sometimes be the most dangerous points in a turnaround, if easy problems are solved but a new team culture has not yet been built. The losers' legacy of selfishness compels some people to take the money and run at the first sign of victory, rather than compound their investment—which, of course, has the perverse effect of withdrawing resources and ending the recovery. An upturn in a depressed stock market might be followed by a defensive sell-off— a reaction that delays a sustained recovery. As a turnaround begins but its longevity is doubted, it is tempting to take personal advantage. A dicey time in marriage counseling is when communication first starts to open, and one partner uses that new climate of disclosure to deliberately hurt the other. A dangerous time in peace negotiations is when arms are first put aside and defenses are down, tempting one of the parties to use that opening to strike.

Turnaround leaders are trying to push a heavy object out of the mud, and it can start rolling back the minute the pressure is off. That's why it is important to combine bold strokes with long marches. Some immediate problems of decline—financial, strategic, or operational—can be tackled with decisive actions to stop losing *(Cut expenses! Off with their heads!),* but leaders must also start the long march of culture change, to create winners' behavior as a basis for long-term success. So how the bold strokes are carried out, humanely or brutally, putting people first or putting them last, defines whether there is sufficient confidence even to begin the long march. Early steps signal later goals and shape the potential to restore confidence.

THE LONG WALK AHEAD

People must stop drowning before they can even think about walking on water. In this chapter I have examined the early stages of ending a losing streak. But that does not necessarily start a winning streak. Stopping losses is not the same thing as gaining the confidence to create wins.

All I have done in this chapter is get us started. Now the long march begins. The next three chapters take a look deep inside many teams and organizations, to see how leaders shift the cycle away from the sins of losers to restore accountability, collaboration, and initiative—the three cornerstones of confidence.

7

The First Stone: Facing Facts and Reinforcing Responsibility

ACCOUNTABILITY IS THE FIRST CORNERSTONE OF CONFIDENCE, A PILLAR OF WINNING STREAKS. WHEN ACCOUNTABILITY CRUMBLES—WHEN TROUBLES PROVOKE DENIAL, OR PEOPLE COVER UP THEIR own mistakes or find an enemy to blame—winning streaks end. Accountability is missing in losing streaks, when people stop talking, stop practicing, and stop trying, or become more accustomed to finding fault than facing facts. To shift the cycle from losing to winning, leaders must develop accountability—the discipline and responsibility of the best athletes and the best teams.

Gillette, a global consumer products company and a household name in 200 countries, has experienced this pillar of confidence from the perspective of both winning and losing. Over the course of two decades, Gillette moved through each of the cycles and turns: a near-death experience in the early 1980s; a dramatic comeback later in the decade producing a significant long winning streak; another slide onto a downhill path in the last third of the 1990s; and another turnaround beginning in 2001, leading back into the winners' circle. It went from poor to good to great to okay to vulnerable to heading for sustained excellence again.

That history is what made victory so delicious in 2003, when turnaround CEO Jim Kilts and his leadership team paused to celebrate Gillette at a football game.

GILLETTE'S CLOSE SHAVE

On a sunny September Sunday afternoon in 2003, Gillette's top leadership team gathered with their spouses and a few guests, including my husband and me, to watch the New England Patriots beat the New York Jets in a National Football League game in Gillette Stadium. It was a nice conjunction of winners. The Patriots were embarking on a series of dramatic victories, and Gillette was about to announce record earnings.

At the start of the previous season, Gillette had acquired naming rights to the Patriots' home field in Foxboro, Massachusetts (midway between Boston and Providence). The numerous signs for "Gillette Stadium" picked up by television cameras represented shrewd marketing for a company with so many grooming products appealing to the millions of fans who watched professional football religiously. They were also signposts of a new culture for Gillette— the bigger splash the company was making with its corporate name and the fun it wanted to inject into its own organization as everyone at Gillette played more competitively.

The energy, camaraderie, and optimism in the Gillette corporate suite, a sky box above the fifty-yard line, seemed to match that on the playing field. Unlike the troubled recent past, Gillette executives worked closely together as a team, and the team had a younger, livelier cast, including the company's first woman among the top dozen leaders, Kathy Lane, who was at the game with her husband, an artist. Gillette even had its own cheerleaders, a trio of svelte young women in bright red wigs touting Gillette's superstar product, the red-label Mach3Turbo, part of a public-relations road show that was also an innovation for Gillette. They came to the suite for photos but spent most of their time engaging with the fans.

Jim Kilts, Gillette's CEO since 2001, sat with his wife in the first row of seats. He looked just as pleasant, calm, and steady as he appeared in the office. For the first half of the game, the Patriots had a small lead with little scoring—just basic blocking and tackling. I remarked to Kilts that it seemed to be a game in which good defense was the key to victory, and was that how he saw Gillette? He smiled and said that you could practice and perfect defense by paying attention to details of execution, but offense meant taking risks and seizing the moment. As if he had ordered it, that moment to seize occurred in the second half of the game, when Patriots' rookie Asante Samuel intercepted the ball and ran fifty-five-yards for a touchdown that was the margin of victory. Lay the foundation, do the basics well, and then an occasional flash of brilliance moves the ball to score. Gillette's recent flash of brilliance was called Venus— an innovative shaving system for women launched in 2001 that beat competitors six to one in blind tests, Gillette's best performance, and was the most successful women's shaving system ever, capturing 10 percent of all U.S. blade sales (male and female).

The Patriots went on to a record winning season. And Gillette, after a close brush with disaster, was back to winning ways. That football afternoon was one small reflection of how many things had changed under Jim Kilts's leadership. This was no longer the club-like, complacent company of "good old boys" that had started to slip into losers' mode. This was now a confident competitor.

Good Old Gillette

In Chapter 3, I enumerated reasons why Gillette had slipped from winning streak to decline cycle around 1996 or 1997: the troubled Duracell acquisition, uneven performance of product categories outside of shaving systems, unrealistic sales targets that led to costly end-of-quarter discounts, sloppy internal practices, a confusing organization structure that made it easy to duck responsibility. Some of the company's historic strengths had become weaknesses, and the foundation for high performance had crumbled.

Pre-turnaround Gillette was a kind and benevolent company nearing its hundredth birthday, and it was showing its age. Gillette rewarded its loyal employees with lifetime careers—which is why Gillette could mobilize retirees to fend off hostile takeover bids between 1986 and 1988. On my first visit to the company in 1994, I felt like I was in a time warp—that the aging men in nearly identical suits on Gillette's executive floors must be clones of the Organization Man made famous in books about the 1950s. I admired their strategic savvy and product innovations, which had produced Gillette's stunning successes of the early 1990s. But cutting-edge products and lively, exciting advertising contrasted with the faceless anonymity and homogeneity of the top people. Executives were pleasant, helpful, and low-key. Corporate headquarters was tucked away on upper floors of an office tower in Boston bearing another company's name.

"It was a good-old-boy organization valuing seniority over competence," a senior manager recalled. "At the top, they were all white males with gray hair and thirty years at Gillette."

Corporate loyalty was traditionally strong, turnover traditionally low. A typical career path included assignments in many countries. Consider two examples from the class of 1977: Eric Adams joined Gillette in 1977 as a trainee in Puerto Rico, transferred several times between Puerto Rico, Colombia, Buenos Aires, and Boston, went to Poland in 1993 as general manager and then regional manager for Eastern Europe and parts of the Mediterranean, and in 2000 became vice-president for marketing and sales for the Latin America region. William Yeoh joined Gillette in 1977 as a trainee in Singapore, moved to Australia and Thailand for long tours of duty before leaving Gillette briefly, then rejoined in Singapore in 1992, eventually becoming regional general manager for China, Hong Kong, and Taiwan in 1999.

Many managers moved around the world in a Gillette multinational bubble, barely connecting with the communities in which they lived, which were just way stations on a global career. Gillette was a generous corporation, but its philanthropy was quiet, and its executives were generally not the up-front, out-there community leaders celebrated at charity banquets. In Boston, some leaders even forgot Gillette's generosity when itemizing the companies on which civic life depended.

Gillette had some brilliant technologists and product designers. The SensorExcel and then Mach3 shaving systems were the premier products in their categories, sometimes reaching a whopping 80-percent market share. An enormous amount of technology went into designing and making a high-performance, multi-bladed razor, and Gillette factories featured highly advanced computer-controlled systems. But no one would confuse this for a high-tech company.

Products were the stars, not people. While this emphasis helped guard against the emergence of executives with big egos, it had a pernicious effect on self-confidence. Most of Gillette's key people had never tested their specific individual skills outside the company or in difficult contests; rather, their identity melted into the company, and the company coasted with a few blockbuster products that were so good that they hid weaknesses in other domains. It was like letting a few stars play the game while everyone on the back bench shared reflected glory without knowing whether their own abilities could measure up. On yearly performance reviews, so many managers received the same "exceeds expectations" score that entitled them to a bonus that it was almost a joke. I was reminded of the fictional town of Lake Wobegon, Wisconsin, invented by radio humorist Garrison Keillor, which was known for the remarkable and impossible fact that "all the children are above average." This was grade inflation of the worst kind, because it didn't distinguish between actions that made a difference and those that did not.

"When you're on the upward slope, in terms of growth, no one asks you, 'Hey, I want to know how you grew by 15 percent.' They just pat you on the back and say, 'Great job!' " recalled Ed Shirley, president of Gillette's commercial operations in Europe. He said that this was a symptom of an insular culture. "We were blinded by our past successes. We weren't spending much time with our customers. We weren't benchmarking ourselves against our competitors." It was the business equivalent of a sports team that comes to believe it can win without practicing or even watching what happens in particular games—so it starts to lose. "A level of conservatism built up in our culture," observed Ed DeGraan, a widely respected Gillette leader. "Because we had been so successful, everything we were doing was seen as being good. There was a group mentality to not only support the status quo, but to work hard to sustain it."

The Bunny and Other Inconvenient International Details

During the 1990s, Gillette got caught up in grand generalizations and neglected attention to details. The globalization theory under which Gillette had operated since the late 1980s had made Sensor razors one of the world's truly global products, with manufacturing efficiencies resulting from making it in just a few factories for world shipment, and with a common marketing message. But some executives conveyed the feeling that the whole world could be controlled from the top, in big chunks. Gillette had tried to group Europe and North America into one big "North Atlantic region," as though all differences between the continents had been erased.

A bright pink stuffed bunny crystallized for me the flaws when local specifics were swept under the rug of global generalizations. I spotted it on a bookshelf in David Bashaw's office at Gillette Europe headquarters in London. As an American, I enjoyed the entertaining bunny that starred in TV commercials for Energizer batteries, a direct competitor of Gillette-owned Duracell. I asked Bashaw, who was a group marketing director for Europe, why he had a competitor's symbol on his shelf. He told me that Energizer owned the bunny image only for America; in Europe, the bunny was Duracell's spokescreature. This was a sign that the "North Atlantic region" still contained many national differences important for a consumer products company to take into account, whether symbols or structures. Europe's small appliance stores had few U.S. counterparts. France had small trade margins, Germany had big margins, Italy was slow to pay. Differences affected strategy. In Latin America, disposable razors dominated the market, unlike the emphasis on premium-priced shaving systems in North America and Europe.

Evidence that Gillette was overdoing global homogeneity was

there if people wanted to see it, but it tended to be brushed aside. People at the corporate center labored mightily to get everything to happen the same way everywhere, regardless of differences in what it took to win any particular game. On a visit to Gillette Singapore in 1996, I heard about the struggles of this country group to manage all the demands imposed by corporate staff (such as conversion to new software) while trying to integrate new staff, move to new facilities, and carry out a marketing campaign that the corporate requirements derailed.

When things stopped breaking Gillette's way in the latter half of the 1990s, it was easy for external investors as well as internal people to lose confidence. Gillette's downward spiral included stagnant sales, declining profits, declining market share in a number of product categories, and a declining stock price (despite the U.S. stock market boom). Behavior slipped into a losing-streak pattern of decreasing communication, blame-shifting, and denial of responsibility for poor performance. Quick fixes made the situation worse. In an attempt to cut costs, because earnings were declining, Gillette began reducing advertising expenditures while keeping sales targets high, an impossible combination that led to the doom loop of having to discount to meet targets because there was too little advertising to drive demand, which kept sales and profits low. Everyone said they knew what the problems were, but those problems were always someone else's fault. "People were working incredibly hard and yet were very frustrated because we didn't feel like winners," Ed Shirley said.

Time for a Change: Finding New Leadership
Then longtime CEO Al Zeien retired in 1999 after thirty-one years with Gillette. He was replaced by a thirty-eight-year veteran, Michael Hawley, continuing the pattern of Good Old Gillette. Hawley endured a difficult eighteen months that saw sales remain flat and the stock price lose one-third of its value, while communication and accountability further deteriorated. The company was

neither setting realistic goals nor encouraging responsibility for meeting them. A long-term senior vice-president observed, "Targets were so unrealistic that missing commitments was commonplace, so we didn't spend a lot of time worrying about responsibility for meeting them."

The Gillette board accepted Hawley's resignation in mid-2000 and appointed Ed DeGraan as acting CEO while conducting a search. I was one of a number of experts quoted in *Business Week* magazine as urging Gillette to look for an outsider to lead a turnaround.

In February 2001, James M. Kilts was named chairman and CEO—the company's first chief from outside the company in seventy years. He was a food-industry executive who had most recently led a successful turnaround of Nabisco. Though he was generally unknown within Gillette, the selection of an outsider was applauded. Several executives declared that they would have left if Gillette had chosen an insider, because the company needed major change. "Medicine wasn't going to cure our disease. We needed surgery," exclaimed Pradeep Pant, then general manager for Russia. A North American executive added, "We were so inbred that we didn't know what we didn't know."

For his part, Kilts knew a few things immediately. Before accepting, Kilts, with his longtime associate Peter Klein, had researched public documents and spoken with friends working for Gillette customers. He knew that Gillette was about to close the books on one of its worst quarters in a decade—the fifteenth consecutive quarter in which Gillette failed to hit earnings estimates. "A repeated theme was that Gillette lacked accountability and didn't deliver on its promises," Kilts later recalled over dinner in a traditional Boston club a few blocks from Gillette headquarters. "Even the trade had figured this out. One retail buyer told me that he waits until the last week of the quarter to place an order because he knows he can get an extra buck off a case." He had seen this problem in other companies that set unrealistically high growth targets and then undercut their long-term prospects by scrambling to meet quarterly projections. Kilts' term for this vicious cycle was the Circle of Doom.

Gillette executives around the world told me later that they hadn't heard of Jim Kilts before his appointment. They got to know him really quickly. Kilts did not look very different from the Gillette mode—tall, white-haired, pleasant, and low-key. But he quickly set in motion a series of changes that transformed behavior while solving business problems. His actions illuminate the elements of unwinding denial, getting people to face facts, and restoring responsibility to set accountability in place:

- straight talk about problems and expectations
- the courage to admit responsibility for problems
- open dialogue and widespread communication
- clear priorities and attention to details
- performance feedback—the mirror of accountability

GROOMING A NEW CULTURE

For new presidents and prime ministers, the first hundred days are often considered the critical period in which an agenda is set and leadership established. For Jim Kilts, it was more like his first hundred minutes.

Kilts took charge on February 12, 2001, a frigid winter day in Boston when the temperature was well below freezing. (Anxious Gillette managers were not feeling much warmer.) He reached his new office on the forty-eighth floor of the Prudential Tower around the same time that all Gillette employees received a letter from him outlining some of his preferences and expectations, and inviting dialogue.

His coat was barely off before he convened his first meeting in the boardroom with the dozen men holding the top executive positions. But if anyone thought the meeting would consist of little more than polite introductions around the table, they were immediately proved wrong.

Straight Talk: Naming the Problem,
Establishing Expectations

Kilts had a cordial and gracious manner, but he wasn't there to schmooze. He got right to the question of how Gillette played the game and how that behavior would change. He turned on the overhead projector and displayed a set of slides that detailed his style, management philosophy, and expectations, and his analysis of Gillette strengths and weaknesses from his month-long external review.

The first shock was that he put the facts on the table—right out there, with no spin and no ways for people around the room to pretend he was talking about someone else. His own thorough and detailed advance preparation was the first sign of the new behavior he found essential to restoring responsibility and thus building internal and external confidence. He presented his initial perspective on Gillette from his month-long external review, including strengths, weaknesses, and key issues—a fact-based analysis he would also present in three days at his first board of directors meeting. Gillette had championship assets, he said, but people were caught in bad habits, especially trade loading, and had stopped taking responsibility for performance. He showed them a drawing of the Circle of Doom and explained that Gillette was caught in a self-perpetuating cycle that made losing inevitable.

The Circle of Doom slide caused a ripple of recognition. The new CEO had given a name to the problem that everyone was experiencing but didn't fully understand. He had discussed the previously undiscussable. He had pointed out that the emperor had no clothes.

The second shock was that he told people exactly what he expected of them in terms of new behavior. He laid out a regimen of meetings, measurements, reports, and methods for working together. He showed slides labeled "My Style" and "My Expectations of You" and spoke about how to behave.

Kilts described himself as open and straightforward—what you see is what you get. He said he was action-oriented—fair but somewhat impatient. He wanted outstanding performance. He wanted integrity. He didn't want competition between functions. Some of his words could become slogans:

- *Expect excellence; reward the same.*
- *Often wrong, never uncertain.*
- *Contribute before decisions are made; support decisions once made.*
- *Don't make dumb mistakes, don't punish smart mistakes, don't make smart mistakes twice.*
- *Never overpromise, always overdeliver.*
- *A promise made is a promise kept.*

"If something bothers you, I want open dialogue," he said. "And I hate anyone saying: 'Jim said' or 'Jim wants' as the reason for doing or not doing something. Things are done—or not—based on rigorous assessments and considered deliberation."

He expressed his determination to set and achieve realistic targets. He outlined a disciplined process for setting annual and quarterly objectives and providing structured feedback, through weekly operating committee meetings, quarterly two-day meetings away from the office, and weekly e-mail postings from the next layers of management around the world. Meetings, he said, would feature fact-based management, open communication, simplicity, and collaboration. Attendance was required, meetings would start on time, there would be no gossip, he wanted full attention and active listening, he strove for consensus, and he expected preparation.

Kilts made clear that he had neither preconceived notions about people nor any plans to make sweeping changes in management. Ed DeGraan would remain president and COO, his positions before he became acting CEO for the six months before Kilts arrived. While everyone would be evaluated, and many people would see their roles change, people would not be cut unless they did not perform.

He also told the new operating committee that jokes were acceptable. But it was highly unlikely that anyone was in a mood for humor that day. Gillette executives hadn't heard quite that kind of speech before. The company had been a little like a gentlemen's club in which everyone knows the secret handshake and silently agrees to pretend not to notice poor performance. Still, Kilts's presentation was just a bunch of words. The proof that he meant what he said came over the following weeks and months.

True Confessions: The Courage to Admit Responsibility

Rebuilding confidence requires acts of courage. To break with the past often involves admitting the errors of the past. It takes courage to face facts that have long been covered up, to voice truths that have been unspoken, or to apologize for past wrongs. It takes courage to face people who have come to expect something and tell them that the game has changed.

Within a few days of joining the company, Kilts went on the road with the sales force to visit retail stores. Doing this so soon showed the emphasis he placed on customer relationships, and it reflected his interest in dialogue with the people who were in the field representing Gillette. Kilts found one conversation with a young sales representative particularly troubling and revealing. "He told me about the trade loading at the end of every quarter, so I asked him why he did that," Kilts recalled. "I'll never forget his response. He pointed his finger at me and said rather harshly, 'It's you guys up in Boston who make us do it.' I saw right away that we had people in the field who knew what they were doing was wrong, but were being told to do it anyway."

Kilts knew that there was more to ending this practice than just shouting "Stop!" The pressure from the top that perpetuated bad habits stemmed from the collision of overly optimistic earnings forecasts and unrealistic sales targets. This false front was causing everyone to lose confidence in Gillette.

As CEO, Kilts reinforced a giant step in saying, "We were wrong." He reiterated the board's earlier decision to stop issuing earnings advisories before the end of a quarter, one of the first U.S. companies to do so. And he told investment analysts that Gillette would lower its quarterly targets to make them more realistic.

This was the shot heard round the world. Everyone talked about it. I was told about Kilts's action in London, Singapore, Boston, and Shanghai. Seeing Kilts stand up to Wall Street was the moment that made Gillette managers and employees feel a turnaround was possible. "I began to believe that Kilts had the courage to make the needed changes when he told us to forget Wall Street, we were going to deal with the trade loading," David Bashaw recalled from his office at European headquarters.

I think of trade loading as the business equivalent of eating fast food: loading retail customers with empty calories in the form of product they don't yet need. Fast food is a constant temptation on every street corner. It's quick, it's easy, no preparation necessary. It's filling and addictive. And it's terrible for you. Many people know that, yet they still flock to fast-food restaurants, just as the Gillette sales force flocked to trade loading despite knowing it was bad for the corporate body. "We hated trade loading," a European executive declared flatly. "How can you talk category management with a customer and then three weeks later come in on your hands and knees and say to them, 'Oh please, here is 15 percent to buy more.' But we'd been loading for six years," he said. A European colleague made a similar declaration. "I'm absolutely certain there's not one person in the whole company who for one moment thought that we should do anything other than get out of trade loading," Chris Adcock said.

Like most bad habits, vowing to stop was easier than stopping. Expectations had to be changed. Salespeople had to be reeducated. Customers had to be told. New ways to stimulate market demand had to substitute for the lazy habit of discounting. "It was a very tense time because people were pounding on other people to meet their earlier (unrealistic) promises, and they were starting to get into bad habits again," Kilts recalled. "You could tell they wanted to load; they were rationalizing why the trade really did need more inventory. Watching them helped me evaluate how effective I was in changing things. There was still a bit of the old culture in them saying, 'This too will pass.' They did not believe I would follow through with the discipline."

Relationships with customers had settled into a routine that some people found easier to live with than to confront. Trade loading had been going on for so long that customers had come to expect it. Some even built it into their budgets, assuming that Gillette would somehow provide extra resources. And few believed that Gillette would have the courage to stop, or that sales personnel would be able to face their customers and tell them the truth. "We had an issue of credibility," a sales manager said. "We'd get into the last month of a quarter, and they'd stop buying from us because they would say, 'Well, we know you're going to show up on the twenty-eighth of the month with a deal.' And we would say, 'No, no, no, we're not.' They didn't believe us. And when the twenty-eighth would come, they'd say, 'Come on, where's the deal?' And again we would explain we were not doing that anymore. This would also happen on the twenty-ninth and thirtieth of the month. Eventually they would realize we were serious."

It took Gillette nine months—three rounds of quarterly performance—to back away from trade loading sufficiently to make people feel confident that they could succeed without falling back on it—that customers would still buy Gillette products, that the business would be healthier, and that the money freed by ending discounting could be invested in creative ways to grow the market.

One of the side effects of trade loading had been a proliferation of product and packaging variations—colors, languages, sizes, seasonal promotions, or special bundles created as a deal for a particular retail customer in order to make sales targets. These variations added costs and consumed attention. They were like extra calories that accumulated to create an overweight corporation whose warehouses were stuffed with inventory, adding to the pressure to discount or make deals to move it. There were 25,000 of these variations, each a separate stock-keeping unit (SKU). Just 20 percent of them accounted for 99 percent of Gillette's sales. The rest were extra fat. Kilts asked for the elimination of all obsolete SKUs, a cut of 20 percent of the remainder, and for each new one added, an old one would have to be removed. But for each proposed cut, there was a salesperson claiming business would be lost. Should the Oral B group keep making a toothbrush for people with braces on their teeth, in order to please orthodontists who could influence the sales of other Oral B toothbrushes? And what about all the numerous package variations in obscure local languages in small countries? What made it tricky was that each excuse had a grain of truth. But Kilts kept putting the requirement in front of people and coming back to it. The discipline eventually led to innovations. Told they could not have so many different packages, the Duracell group invented flexible packs that could be used many different ways. By the end of Kilts's first year, 17,000 SKUs had been eliminated—a whopping number, yet they represented less than 1 percent of sales.

Hundreds of initiatives like these to improve performance were cataloged in piles of loose-leaf binders in Peter Klein's office, each several feet high.

Dialogue and Widespread Communication

Kilts wanted a new kind of conversation about how to win. The mode was the give-and-take of dialogue. "Before Kilts, you went to a meeting, you said your piece, and you went away. I felt I was not growing enough," a manager said. "Kilts asks questions—did you do this, did you try this, has it been modeled, did you do research, did you run tests? He brought a whole new lexicon."

In his first weeks, Kilts met individually with each of his twelve reports, then with their reports, and, within a month, with each of the top 100 managers, both in Boston and at European headquarters in London. Luis Gigliani, senior vice-president of commercial operations in Europe, noted that Kilts worked hard to understand the business, visiting retail stores in France and Germany to look at products on the shelves. Kilts used these visits to learn and assess. He observed that talented people were stifled by an insular culture in which people did not always follow up on what they promised. He recalled, "The things I looked for most when making my initial judgments were their ability and willingness to understand and explain what was going on."

It was not surprising that the first quarterly off-site meeting of the new top management in March of 2001 was tension-ridden. As facts were put on the table and difficult issues surfaced, there were some angry outbursts and sequences of attack-and-defend. Having all key executives at the table helped Kilts end the finger-pointing that had gone on in the past. If, for example, Manager X said he had not reached a certain target because Manager Y did not do his part, Kilts would turn to Manager Y and ask him what had happened. It was hard to deny facts, make excuses, or shift blame when the leader wanted everything discussed openly or, better yet, resolved in advance by each person accepting his own piece of responsibility and getting together with teammates to seek a new course of action. Gradually, as people became accustomed to the new openness, they seemed to understand that their goal was to solve problems, not to hurl accusations, and a focus on positive actions reduced negativity.

Kilts's calm, matter-of-fact manner helped create the positive emotional climate. He expressed confidence in people's ability to rise to the occasion and use the talent he believed they had. "We have a very good cadre of people who want to do the right thing," he repeated. "When you look at their résumés, they are from excellent schools with great backgrounds and good experience bases." The problem was in the weak system for accountability. "A lot of people did not know what their specific job was, other than to show up and do some things and not necessarily have accountability for anything," he said. "They wanted to be told how to do the right things and helped to accomplish this." Kilts blamed the culture, not the people: "Unfortunately, this was one of the more insular cultures I had seen, and one where people did not always follow up on what they promised." Kilts's message was that it was no one's fault, but that they each had to commit to their own share of responsibility for winning performance going forward and communicate with everyone else on the team.

Gillette was not just a single team, of course, but a web of many overlapping teams—a complex global system in which people controlled only a portion of the actions required for them to succeed. People heading each line of business—shaving, oral care, Braun appliances, Duracell—were dependent on others in the technology and manufacturing organizations to design and make the products, and on still others in marketing and sales throughout the world to sell them. Each had different priorities and was measured on different things; manufacturing might want to keep inventory low, while sales might want to keep it high so they could ship immediately to new customer orders. Accepting personal responsibility meant working harder to influence other people to develop joint plans. Kilts no longer allowed his key managers to use other people as an excuse; he expected them all to work together to work it out, and, if priorities conflicted, to find a compromise. An Italian executive told me he was learning to do whatever it took to persuade his peers: "You explain, you present, you have meetings, you beg, or you cry!"

Communication increased dramatically. Now people wanted to see one another's priorities and numbers, and to help them achieve goals so they could all win. Every week, managers around the world circulated a summary of significant facts that it became imperative for everyone to read. Kim Fa Loo, group business director for the Asia-Pacific region, provided an example: "We might say in the weekly posting that 'Advertising approval for Duracell has yet to be received from Global Business Management. This is two weeks behind schedule.' Everyone knows Jim sees this. So the moment the global business head reads this, he goes to a subordinate to make something happen." Others convened weekly or monthly meetings of people from across different areas to anticipate and solve problems. Peter Hoffman, president of the Grooming business unit, invited representatives of all the geographic regions and the people in technology and manufacturing concerned with razors and blades.

The agenda would involve specific problems in one area—such as currency crises in Latin America or weak performance in Australia—but the rest of the group pitched in.

Kilts traveled everywhere he could, and key managers worldwide gathered in Boston about six times a year. For Europeans, getting to Boston was an easy trip with a manageable five-to-seven-hour time difference. For Asia-Pacific executives halfway around the world, travel took about thirty hours door to door, consuming two to three extra days. Even conference calls meant being in the office in the middle of the night. Yet the Asia-Pacific leadership team was among the strongest performers, an energetic group willing to put in the effort to hold up their end of Gillette's constant communication. The day I met with the top people in their Singapore offices, we broke for lunch in the hotel next door, where I was mesmerized by a rain-forest garden outside the window, but their attention was focused on the stream of Gillette people in town for a regional information technology conference, with whom they were eager to talk. They took initiative not just to implement but to improve on corporate requirements, especially involving the people side (motivational contests, recognition, coaching for leaders). Such innovations got the human resources director promoted to a corporate position.

Priorities: Clear Focus and Attention to Details

"With Jim, what you see is what you get," Ed DeGraan observed. "He does not attempt to wrap himself or the company in any mystical qualities. He tries to keep it as simple as possible." This was clear in the company's straightforward new vision: "To build Total Brand Value by innovating to deliver consumer value and customer leadership faster, better, and more completely than our competitors." Kilts was not looking for drama, he was looking for delivery. Delivery required attention to details. He spent much of his first eight months acting as "assistant to the chief financial officer" to bolster financial disciplines and to guide strategy with real numbers.

Many executives felt that one of Kilts's most important turn-around moves was to set quarterly priorities (new behavior for Gillette) and to hold people accountable by measuring and report-ing very specific aspects of their group's performance. Individual managers developed objectives that were much more detailed than in the past, based on a new strategic planning process spearheaded by Kilts's trusted sidekick, Peter Klein. Management groups from each line of business were asked to focus on a few broad priorities for future growth, but then dig into the details of implementation. The process forced a deep review of each business, its market, and its competition.

In the past, people had been able to achieve their overall targets by doing well in one area while neglecting others. Kilts contrasted the old way with his way: "Take the guy running North America. Maybe he was supposed to go from $3 billion to $3.2 billion in sales. If sales hit $3.2 billion, he made his numbers. But if you looked underneath, maybe he sold blades and nothing else. Now he has to make five numbers. He has to grow blades, of course, but personal care, oral care, Braun, and batteries all have to grow, too. Now he will be measured on how well balanced the delivery is. You can't just run for glory in one product line or in one geography anymore."

Instead of letting people hide behind grand generalizations ("great results—who cares how we achieved them?"), Kilts wanted them to analyze all the details that accumulated to produce win-ning performance. The analogy to the best athletes and the best teams was clear: paying attention to discrete actions—a turn of the shoulder here, a difference in the stance there—that could provide the margin of victory. This was also Ivan Seidenberg's emphasis at Verizon, as we saw in Chapter 2.

Gillette managers were asked to break down performance into specific elements, look at many details, chart statistics, and analyze the patterns. People responsible for each line of business in each re-gion around the world completed a "business health chart" track-ing a variety of indicators. For example, shipments to retail stores were compared with actual sales to consumers, which would help people spot red flags, such as whether there was any end-of-quarter trade loading (indicated by a spike in shipments in the last two weeks without accompanying consumer purchases). It was a challenge to get people to look at so much data and use the facts to guide actions. European managers tried to make this more fun by emphasizing the similarity to sports scores. They created League Tables for performance, mirroring those used in European professional football, to show where each national "team" stood in the Gillette "league." For example, the table might show that 90 percent of Italy's sales were in growth segments while Germany's were 50 percent. This provoked friendly competition to improve relative standing.

Looking in the Mirror: Performance Feedback

Confidence requires a close look in the mirror. Before Kilts arrived, Gillette managers showed bravado—a false front based on limited data, memories of past successes, and unrealistic promises made to be broken. Pretending that things are all right when they are not is a recipe for everyone's loss of confidence.

Kilts's mirrors came in the form of performance reviews based on objectives that people set for themselves, in dialogue with him. Issuing of report cards started at the top. Prior to each quarterly meeting of his top executives, Kilts met individually with each of the people on the operating committee to review the completed quarter and develop a report card. Each executive graded his or her own performance on agreed-to items on a scale of 1 to 100 and compared that with Kilts's review of the executive's performance to determine a final rating. Then, at the meeting, Kilts presented a list of the grades, anonymously, so that every person knew where he stood in relation to his peers. Imagine the feelings they had the first few times at seeing their grades displayed openly, even without names, wondering whether they'd be exposed, nervous about how to make excuses. After that, presenting priorities for the quarter had to seem easy.

Gillette's next step was to reduce grade inflation throughout the company. A new performance appraisal system introduced in the fall of 2001 changed the process from merely rewarding effort to differentiating employees on the basis of results. Kilts insisted that doing a job well should be considered "effective," with "highly effective" and "exceptional" reserved for extraordinary accomplishments. This was a threatening change, because performance ratings affected raises for more than 9,000 people in the salaried ranks, 3,000 of whom also could get bonuses and stock options. Some of them were upset about what felt to them like a downgrade in their ratings, especially when they were being asked to work much harder. Some managers initially refused to use the new ratings. Others argued for exceptions, such as higher ratings for their own people, based on hard work. Kilts and other executives had to explain over and over that the ratings were for performance, not for effort, and that the numbers did not justify an upgrade, though occasional settlements were negotiated because of market conditions outside of the company's control. When bonuses were paid in March 2002, and people with lower nominal ratings received higher bonuses than previously, they could see that the company had merely recalibrated.

Eventually the noise subsided. High performers were especially happy with the new system because they were no longer lumped in with everyone else. Conversations shifted in character. Objectives had never been top-of-mind; now often the first thing people talked about was the progress on quarterly numbers and the weightings that would determine their bonuses. There was also a sigh of relief that the process was fairer than in the Good Old Gillette club of the past; one did not have to be Kilts's best friend, or to have worked for Gillette for thirty years, to do well. "The performance culture is clear," a senior vice-president said. "You make a commitment and you keep it. If you deliver, then he's happy, and if you don't, he isn't. It's as simple as that."

Another set of mirrors reflected external comparisons—how Gillette practices stacked up against world-class companies. About

25 percent of Gillette's 2001 sales came from products that competed directly with offerings from the three top consumer products companies—Unilever, Procter & Gamble, and Colgate-Palmolive. Gillette's players had to feel confident that their practices reached the standards necessary to win the toughest games. Under the umbrella of "functional excellence," every group started gathering facts to identify gaps between their performance and the best teams', and then to develop plans to close relevant gaps. In 2002, Gillette added an employee survey that rated the environment for performance in each work unit, with scores compared with those of other companies. Interviews were videotaped with heads of departments that had high scores, to use as sources of ideas for those with lower scores. The top executive team looked at their own scores together. Bosses throughout Gillette were held accountable for their leadership and work culture.

External and internal comparisons made it hard to hide behind excuses or to duck responsibility. "There has been huge improvement. Why? Focus and measurement," a European executive said. "Jim Kilts said we needed real data. When you see that we're out of line with six different companies, you say, 'I guess he's right.'"

To many, Kilts's disciplines were a breath of fresh air, but others felt threatened by having their performance picked over and exposed. Performance metrics were not meant to "name and shame," but some people took them that way because of the legacy of the losing-streak years. They felt that identifying best practices meant exposing the worst. "Some people can't take constructive criticism," a boss complained. Another manager observing life outside of headquarters felt that some people had not really changed, that they were merely going through the motions so they wouldn't lose their jobs—but were secretly hoping that the new regimen wouldn't work. I sensed residual fear even in upper ranks. At one casual meeting I attended, a manager anticipating low numbers on the employee survey kept referring to "being killed," with a big smile on his face as if to pretend he was joking.

The soft human issues are sometimes the hard ones. Trouble

spots remained, especially in some support functions, but managers felt that the company was on the right path, as problems were recognized, even though all the solutions were not yet in place.

"A Promise Made Is a Promise Kept"

Gillette had picked up the pace to look like a winner again. There was improved communication and coordination across the corporation. Energy had increased, as the positive climate became contagious. Many people said that they had never before worked this hard, or for so many hours.

For nine of the next ten quarters, since Kilts's arrival, Gillette met or exceeded analyst consensus EPS forecasts. Trade loading had been virtually eliminated. Market shares were increasing for key products, and quarterly financial targets were being met. The stock price, while still well below its mid 1990s historic highs, had rebounded and steadily increased.

About 80 percent of Kilts's direct reports were new to the company or to their jobs, as were about 70 percent of the top sixty executives. An Asia-Pacific manager praised Kilts for the fresh talent: "He has eliminated or moved some old Gillette stalwarts, put in new people. Some people say there is too much change, but a few years ago we were complaining that nothing ever changed. You can't have it both ways. To me, it is for the better."

Innovation had increased beyond the visible blockbuster products such as the Mach3 and Venus shaving systems. A new battery-powered toothbrush built on capabilities of three businesses, Oral B, Braun, and Duracell, that had never previously collaborated. Gillette as a corporation was stepping out from the shadows and exuding confidence, not only putting its name on the Patriots' stadium, but also branding its community philanthropy in the United States and Brazil under the label "Gillette Face Forward"—a tag line that worked across brands while signaling Gillette's desire to favor the future over preservation of the past. Kilts announced a thrust toward Total Innovation, with an innovation fair to showcase product and process ideas scheduled for March 2004.

Gillette was in better shape to win financially (it was leaner, more disciplined), strategically (it was focused on growth segments), and operationally (there was abundant communication, measurement, and teamwork). The company's renewed confidence was critical, because in 2003 its battery rival, Energizer, bought a razor and blade company, Schick, which was touting a new four-bladed razor. Gillette sued Energizer Holdings for infringements of four Gillette patents, with the matter still pending.

A senior Gillette executive summed up the feeling of renewed confidence: "I have twenty-seven years of emotional and actual equity in the company. I want to be part of a winning team."

HOW LEADERS TEACH

It is a long distance and a big leap of imagination from global giant Gillette to a small inner-city elementary school in a poor neighborhood in the American South. But Marty Pettigrew, the principal of Peabody Elementary School in Memphis, Tennessee, tackled the task of restoring the first cornerstone of confidence with the same energetic leadership shown by international business executive Jim Kilts. I was struck by the similarities in actions and style. Both men established widespread dialogue, relied on objective data and performance metrics, and taught people to use feedback to guide improvements. By surfacing problems and discussing them openly, they encouraged teamwork and development of innovative solutions.

Pettigrew got started as quickly as Kilts. He was described by teachers and parents in terms that could have applied to Kilts. They said Pettigrew was "very direct." He "lets you know what he needs." "He wants your input." "He is sure of himself and his expectations." Even his words reminded me of Kilts's messages. Pettigrew told a teacher unnerved by rapid changes, "If you think this has been fast, I haven't begun yet." He informed a parent who had asked about his emphasis on data and frequent measurement that "it's not about the numbers, it's about the consistency."

Unlike Gillette, of course, report cards and testing are part of the requirements of a school, especially important under American state and federal legislation trying to make K-12 schools more accountable for children's achievement. But that didn't mean the people working in the Peabody school automatically embraced accountability. Pettigrew had taken on a rundown school with many of the characteristics of a losing streak.

Pettigrew was appointed in December, just before the holidays. Although the school year was more than half over, nearly 50 percent of the teachers had not yet undergone the regular staff evaluations that the Memphis City School board required. Peabody had also ducked accountability because test scores and dropout rates were improved by the addition of an optional magnet program in international studies, which attracted good students from other parts of the city, thus hiding the fact that the school was failing the generally poor neighborhood kids.

Pettigrew walked into a school with dingy brown walls and run-down attitudes. The walls were papered with posters explaining the school's discipline guidelines and students' discipline options. But, in reality, discipline standards were inconsistent. This was an organization in which no one seemed to take responsibility for the overall performance of the school, or even for achieving educational results themselves. There was no shared structure to the school week, nor was time set aside for planning. Everyone was on his or her own. Teachers had not been required to submit lesson plans, and they often reorganized their own class schedules when they felt like it, without concern for any impact on others. Monthly faculty meetings had been merely rote recitals of routine logistics. Teachers had rarely visited the former principal's office during the day; anyway, she had been seen as uncommunicative and as someone who played favorites.

In his opening week, Pettigrew started to open dialogue and increase accountability for common objectives. First he tore down the sign on the principal's office that said DO NOT ENTER WITHOUT PERMISSION. Next he sent home a letter to parents inviting them to get involved. And he convened teachers to discuss a new vision and mission statement that became the basis for a new set of goals. Each teacher and administrator was expected to take responsibility for these goals.

Monthly faculty meetings became dialogues in which everyone could propose ideas to improve the school. Daily class schedules were revised and standardized, to permit regular weekly time slots for groups of teachers within each grade to meet with Pettigrew to report on activities and share best practices. To facilitate review and communication, teachers were required to submit lessons plans for the following week before they left on Friday afternoon, and they were expected to use e-mail to keep the communication going between meetings. Collaboration increased within the school, and that led to ideas for new ways to reach out to parents, who were not only "customers," but also vital partners in their children's education. After establishing a parents' resource center, Pettigrew and his team convened a meeting of 150 fathers at the school to open dialogue about the problem of security in a tough neighborhood. The fathers formed a group called DOGS (Dads Of Great Students) to deploy a volunteer security team of men who committed to being at Peabody at the beginning and end of the school day.

Pettigrew set higher standards for teachers in their classrooms and backed up the standards with extensive data analysis and performance reviews, including purchasing a commercial evaluation tool. This was a big shock. But soon data analysis had a big impact on them, opening their eyes to new ways to work with their students. In the past, some of them thought their students were achieving good results, but once they looked at more data, they could see which students had not progressed since the previous year. Mr. Pettigrew also met regularly with teachers to show them how to use Tennessee state test results to help individual students raise their performance.

Less than six months later, Peabody School hummed with dialogue. Teachers seemed more energetic, emulating Pettigrew's exuberance. "If there were any divisions among the staff before, we just don't have time for that anymore," a teacher said. "He's making us realize that to be successful we have to take responsibility as a team." Teachers felt more confidence in themselves and one another, and parents felt more involved. Confidence on the part of teachers and parents encouraged greater engagement with students, which meant more attention to school and school work, which made it more likely to get results that justified feeling confident.

SHIFTING THE CYCLE:
LEADING TOWARD ACCOUNTABILITY

Marty Pettigrew could put the entire Peabody School population in one small auditorium. He could see, touch, and influence every person in the school directly—even if he himself was just one principal of many in the Memphis City Schools, subject to rules and requirements from a hierarchy of bosses, union contracts, politicians, and school boards. Jim Kilts might be able to fit all 30,000 Gillette employees into Gillette Stadium, but he probably wouldn't. He had to work through complex systems and reporting channels for products in five lines of business sold in over 200 countries. But the challenge of leading people to embrace accountability in these and other turnarounds I examined involved dealing with similar fundamentals and similar fears.

Open dialogue tends to be well received. People like to get a seat at the boardroom table or see an open door into the principal's office. Report cards, in contrast, are not the fun side of leadership. Evaluating details of performance can sound a little cold-blooded and technocratic—the stuff of impersonal accountants rather than inspirational leaders. Exposing people's ratings to one another can seem harsh and punitive, and some think that this kind of action actually destroys confidence, because it produces anxiety and fear. The very word *accountability* conjures up bad memories of bureaucracies run by bean-counters who create excessive rules, measure everything, and stifle innovation.

But those fears are the fears of losers. Ducking the facts about performance for fear of being judged, criticized, humiliated, and punished characterizes losing streaks, not winning streaks. In a losing streak, facts are used for blame, not improvement; they are turned into weapons to persecute, not tools to find solutions. Under such circumstances it's no wonder people get defensive and want to hide. Contrast that with winning streaks and the ways perpetually winning teams such as the Connecticut Huskies or the North Carolina Tar Heels use detailed tracking of individual actions and discussions of performance details, dissecting tapes of games or charting players' progress. In winning streaks, players get and use abundant feedback about their performance.

Before people can shift to the habits of winners, turnaround leaders must overcome the anxieties that stem from the experience of losing cycles: the fear that people can't handle negative information because it is too depressing; the fear that open discussions of performance problems are humiliating; and the fear that metrics and data turn people into robots, crushing their initiative.

In her turnaround of SBLI, an insurance company in New York, new CEO Vikki Pryor felt that she needed to increase respect and empowerment before she could hold people accountable. Her message that "I believe in you" helped almost everyone make the transition successfully to higher standards and more responsibility. Pryor initiated a management meeting once a week, an all-employee meeting once a month, ad hoc meetings to address issues, and frequent e-mail communications. She tried to keep people focused on the problems and challenges and not on tearing down one another. It was her deft touch with people that helped them accept standards and measurements and evaluations and larger, more demanding jobs.

Leaders can send messages about new expectations, model new behavior, introduce methods for learning and practicing new disciplines, and ensure that measurements ultimately empower rather than punish people.

Leaders Show the Way

"I don't believe as a leader you can ever expect anybody to do things you are not willing to do yourself," said Mike Babcock, head coach of the Anaheim Mighty Ducks. He was talking about the work ethic, preparation, and attention to detail he brought to the team's 2002 turnaround. "I think it's not about what you say, it's about what you do. We are not who we say we are, we are what we do."

It builds confidence in leaders when they name problems that everyone knows are there and put facts on the table for everyone to see, as Jim Kilts did, and when they refuse to shift responsibility to some nameless "them." It also helps other people get over their fear of exposure and humiliation to see leaders providing examples of accepting responsibility. Early in the Continental Airlines turn-around, the executive team divided angry letters from customers among themselves so that each could call them to apologize personally for past problems. Each executive also took on one city to offer apologies to travel agents and corporate customers. Then they could describe solutions with greater credibility. "It was a humbling experience," executives recalled, but one that generally ended with appreciation for the gesture. Confession is good for the soul, but in this case at least, it also seemed to be good for business.

Confidence is real only when it is grounded in reality. The positive outlook that optimists project does not come from ignoring or denying problems. Optimists simply assume that problems are temporary and can be solved, so optimists naturally want more information about problems, because then they can get to work and do something. Pessimists are more likely to believe that there is nothing they can do anyway, so what's the point of even thinking about it? Indeed, psychologists have proven that optimists are more likely than pessimists to pay attention to negative information. For example, when people were given information about possible health-related dangers, optimists read, remembered, and could elaborate more of the details than pessimists did.

Optimism is associated with proactive coping—that is, getting better information about incipient problems and tackling them before they get worse. Because they pay attention to problems and take corrective action, optimists have been shown to master difficult situations, including recovering from coronary bypass surgery, adjusting to college life, or dealing with a diagnosis of breast cancer. Optimists are also more likely than pessimists to elicit and use feedback to improve. The one kind of negative information optimists find threatening is a personal attack on their sense of self-worth.

It is said that truth sets us free; it also helps us win. Duke men's basketball coach Mike Krzyzewski felt that telling the truth was essential to the success of his legendary winning teams. "We have a rule on our team that we always look each other in the eye and tell the truth," he told us. "Bonding is not just about hugging one another, it is about being truthful with one another at a moment's notice. And that can change the course of a game. Absolutely."

Openness without Humiliation
Leaders can also provide safe havens in which dialogue with peers can take place without making any one of them feel on the spot. This principle works across national cultures. Akin Öngör, of Garanti Bank in Turkey, had to order his executives to attend seminars on change when he was first building a winner's culture. But after it was clear that it was safe to speak up and that even the CEO could be challenged, his top executive group could openly discuss his performance and one another's—an amazing feat in a country where lesser-performing institutions still featured the stilted silence of hierarchy.

Rick Haythornthwaite created safe spaces for dialogue. Invensys was a troubled UK conglomerate created largely through acquisitions when Haythornthwaite became CEO, with more than 50,000 people working in industrial and energy services around the world. The company was close to defaulting on its financial obligations, and some managers felt it was also bankrupt in terms of ideas. There were few common meetings of the top group; divisional rivalries existed despite their isolation from one another; and the company had an inward focus. Perpetual reorganization had created a culture of fear. Haythornthwaite faced complex restructuring challenges that would plague him for years, as assets bought at high prices in boom years would be divested during the bust (leading to huge losses and write-offs even when the turnaround was well under way). But if he could build confidence internally as well as externally, he had a shot at restoring the company to health. He wanted to expose all the facts so that people could see the system as a whole and get everyone thinking about their contribution to problem solving.

To act on his belief, Haythornthwaite met with groups around the world in town hall–type meetings in the largest of the company's 400 sites. In a company where there had been perceived distance between the leadership and the workforce, he made a point of standing before his people with no podium between himself and them. Haythornthwaite picked up the phone to call people who raised an interesting point or a note of dissent on the company's "Ask Rick" help line and stayed personally involved in the drafting of responses to employee questions. "If you drop the ball, people know about it very quickly," he said. "And even though it creates an incredible amount of pressure, you've got to be thinking every day, 'Is there someone I cut short? Is there something that someone said in a meeting that I haven't followed up?' Because those things just undermine the effort."

Haythornthwaite was conscious of walking a fine line. "You've got to speak to where the organization stands. And you've got to do it in a way that doesn't make people wrong, but at the same time doesn't leave them in denial," he observed. He wanted to avoid punishing anyone for past mistakes, and he wanted to build mutual respect among colleagues. "You've got to create some space to make a mistake or two," he said. "We are but a collection of human beings."

At one town hall meeting at an American facility, he spoke about company issues in front of what felt like a factory floor of humanity. When it was time for questions, the first person asked him why the company had trimmed the health plan. "It was one of those moments where you could see everything was hanging on my answer," Haythornthwaite recalled. "I hadn't even been responsible for the decision, so I could have said that it wasn't me, that it was the previous guys." Instead he said that the decision wasn't his—but that he was accountable for the fallout. He presented the facts about the costs of the health plan. Faced with those facts, the crowd could see that cutting from the health plan was the only sensible course of action. "The only way I could give you a different answer is by fundamentally shifting the U.S. health-care system," he told the group, and at that point the audience was back on his side. "People just hadn't been treated to the facts in the past. That's just so consciously condescending. If you're all in the same game, then you share those facts."

Using Data to Empower

Data, details, metrics, measurement, analyses, charts, tests, assessments, performance evaluations, report cards, grades—these are the tools of accountability, but they are neutral tools. They do not restore confidence by themselves. What matters is the culture that surrounds them. For losers, they are another sign that they are watched too closely, not trusted, about to be punished. For winners, they are useful, even vital, tools for understanding and improving performance. People embrace tools of accountability when they are in control, when the information empowers them and helps them succeed.

Drs. Mark Smith and Craig Feied took three basic steps and one highly innovative step to turn around the emergency department of Washington Hospital Center from the worst in the nation's capital to the best. The pair of physician-leaders, whom I introduced in Chapter 6, were hired to revive the department, familiarly known as the ER. Accountability for outcomes was a big piece of their problem-solving.

First, for people to be accountable for patient outcomes, they had to know they were responsible for particular patients along with a set of colleagues with whom they could work out details of specific tasks. That meant health-care professionals connected to one another in teams, rather than drifting in and out individually along with a floating cast of fellow medical workers.

Second, for health-care teams to be accountable, the ER could no longer rely on contract physicians who presumably cared about individual patients but certainly didn't care about the success of the department. That meant shifting to full-time physicians with a commitment to Washington Hospital Center.

Third, for the whole process to work, more information needed to be available to everyone about who was doing what to which patients, and where. Amazingly enough, one of the sources of confusion and inefficiency in emergency departments came from doctors not being able to find patients they had started to treat when those patients were moved to new beds, a common occurrence in a fast-paced ER. Making the facts available and dialogue possible began with the simple addition of a large, visible white board onto which information was entered as it became known. Those three basic steps by themselves reversed an organizational losing streak and raised performance to the winners' column—which in this case meant winning struggles to save lives. Higher performance meant they could treat more patients with better outcomes, which brought more patients to the hospital as a whole, since the ER is increasingly the entry route into hospitals. Winning also meant financial security.

The basics made a difference, but it was the innovative action involving data and data analysis that put them over the top and made the Washington Hospital Center a national role model. Dr. Feied was a multitalented whiz kid. In addition to his MD in emergency medicine, he had a background in biophysics and had started several software companies. He convened a "stealth team" of developers to create a digital information network that enabled doctors and nurses to access enormous amounts of information about their patients quickly, and perform nearly any analysis to track any pattern. The system, called Insight, was not only user-friendly but user-directed and user-controlled. Speed alone was useful in saving lives, as test results in digital form could arrive in minutes instead of taking hours. But Insight also increased accountability. Suddenly people were clamoring to see information bearing on their performance; it could improve what they did for patients. The tool proved just as useful in uncovering ways for the whole hospital to improve, including discovering lost billing records.

Insight brought healthier prospects to everyone—patients, medical staff, and the hospital system itself. Confidence in the ER permitted implementation of a new all-risks-ready model that proved critical in two major emergencies in 2001, the terrorist attack on the Pentagon and the anthrax scare.

This chapter has focused on accountability, but one stone leads to another. In every case, from Gillette to Garanti, from Memphis schools to Washington hospitals, accountability is intertwined with collaboration and initiative. People become more accountable when they feel responsible to others, when they know how to connect their own and others' contributions to produce a victory for the team. And accepting responsibility implies moving from passive to active mode, taking initiative to tackle problems and create new solutions.

Whether resuscitating the ER, transforming a school, leading a company back to greatness, or coaching a team to victory, leaders must encourage people to face facts honestly and to embrace responsibility for their own performance, commiting to take it to the highest levels. That builds self-confidence, confidence in others, and confidence that the whole system can deliver on its promises.

8

The Second Stone:
Cultivating Collaboration

*I used to believe in biology, not chemistry. Give me big
and strong and fast. But after twenty years, I'm a big be-
liever now in club chemistry. . . . You almost always have
it when you win; and oftentimes it is team chemistry that
leads to winning. But it's hard to say which comes first.
Still, make no mistake: when we build teams, we build
them with an eye on chemistry, because we know how
destructive the opposite can be.*

—*Larry Lucchino, President and CEO, Boston Red Sox*

THE MONTREAL EXPOS' TURNAROUND WAS ALL ABOUT MAKING
TEAMWORK APPEAR OUT OF NOWHERE. THE EXPOS HAD EKED OUT
ONLY 68 WINS TO 94 LOSSES IN 1999, THEY WERE 67–95 IN 2000,
and 68–94 in 2001. By 2002 the club was in Major League Baseball's
equivalent of receivership. The league had bought the losing franchise as a holding action and was threatening to eliminate the team
at the end of the season or move it to exile in Puerto Rico. Yet, despite one of the smallest payrolls in baseball, the Expos had star-
quality athletes, including ascending talents such as a quartet of
younger players from the same winning minor-league team.
Everyone viewed the Expos as just a temporary assignment, hoping
to be traded later in the year. So they believed that their best bet
was to focus on their individual statistics, even if swinging at

pitches with home-run hopes didn't help win games for the team. It was every man for himself.

This was hardly a promising start for a new set of managers and coaches. But on Frank Robinson's first day as manager, he signaled a focus on collaboration, which led to new rituals for the team. Some seemed corny, but they worked. At the beginning of the season, the players stood in a line, held hands, and said whatever was on their minds. They wanted to clear the air of feelings about being branded as losers and, by implication, being surrounded by losers on their own team. Catcher Michael Barrett remembered it as a powerful turning point. "We got everything off our chests," he told us, "and at the end of it we felt that we were one." The players learned to do "the small things that mattered to sacrifice themselves so the team could be successful," hitting coach Tom McCraw observed. To everyone's surprise, the Expos began to win. When Robinson tried to quit partway through the summer of 2002, the team wouldn't let him. That season was their most successful in many years, at 83–79.

Collaboration is the second major cornerstone of confidence, and it is equally necessary for small sports teams or complex organizations containing many teams. In order to solve strategic and operational problems, anti-teamwork sins of decline must be eliminated, and people's confidence in one another must be restored.

Like the Expos, pre-turnaround Seagate Technologies and Continental Airlines had been playing badly. Both companies were in decline spirals, losing money and touching bottom on indicators such as productivity, costs, and on-time delivery. Their ability to solve their problems was hampered by losers' pathologies. Seagate, as I indicated in chapter 3, had reached an abrupt end to its winning streak in the mid-1990s and was struggling with a serious losing streak, even before the technology crash in the economic bust of the early 2000s. Around the same time, Continental was barely clinging to life, during that ten-year bad patch before Gordon Bethune took the helm. It is pure coincidence that Continental's Houston headquarters is not far from Prairie View A&M University, and that Continental's losing streak was just as bad as Prairie View's. But unlike sports, where at least everyone is nominally on the same team and must show up at the same field, the competing factions in the pre-turnaround silos at Seagate and the far-flung migrant workforce staffing Continental's flights did not even have to see one another unless someone made them do it. They were not even in the same game, let alone pulling together as a team.

How these companies found their way back to a positive path illustrates the challenges, the methods, and the rewards of collaboration. In some ways it sounds so simple, like Teambuilding 101. *Problem:* People have been isolated or withdrawn, avoiding or attacking one another, showing no respect. *Solution:* Get them to engage in positive ways. (Work together! Be nice!) *Problem:* People have become accustomed to organized selfishness, to looking out for themselves. *Solution:* Find reasons to identify with everyone's fate. (Help others! Be generous!)

But of course it takes much more than slogans or exhortations to shift human behavior to achieve these goals—as anyone knows who has dealt with warring factions, abused children, resentful have-nots, or simply people with no confidence in those around them. It takes a consistent message, the model of leaders' personal conduct, and productive conversations across positions. In many ways an organization is just a vast series of conversations; the structure of who talks to whom, and how, determines the likelihood of success. Seagate's leaders enforced and reinforced teamwork until it became common practice, raising productivity and unleashing innovation. The turnaround leaders at Continental built a collective definition of success that included everyone in producing higher performance and stimulated collaboration across functions. Each company had unique problems to solve, but both showed the power of teamwork.

SEAGATE: *THOU SHALT FORM TEAMS*

Fumbles on the football field or errors on a baseball diamond are one thing. But imagine making a $10-million mistake, and your teammates rally to help win anyway.

Shortly before the end of the first quarter of 2003, Seagate, the world's largest manufacturer of computer hard-disk drives and a Silicon Valley mainstay, had recovered from an emergency that demonstrated the essence of its turnaround. An engineer, running tests of a new process to improve the quality of disk-drive recording heads, had forgotten to reset a chemical bath from test mode to production mode, inadvertently leaving it in the worst possible place for ongoing yields. Several weeks later he discovered the problem, but only after many days' worth of inventory had been destroyed, potentially jeopardizing as much as $10 million in revenue. Although the engineer could have said nothing and perhaps have escaped unnoticed, he reported the problem. An ad hoc group flew into action, working through weekends to figure out how to replace all the damaged parts. In just two weeks they scraped together the extra capacity, moved orders around, and achieved the quarter's numerical targets.

CEO Steve Luczo felt that this incident reflected a new culture of open communication, mutual respect, and teamwork. Soon every Seagate employee knew about it. At the quarterly employee satellite broadcast, COO Bill Watkins told the story of the engineer's courage and the excellent cross-functional teamwork, adding a personal example—the time he accidentally dropped his wallet in a plating bath and messed up production—to reinforce his message that mistakes happen, especially when people try new things, but that the mark of a great company is how the members of teams support one another in dealing with problems quickly, effectively, and collaboratively.

Prior to the Luczo-Watkins turnaround, Seagate was in big trouble. At one point in the mid-1990s, 30 percent of its products required rework, and scrap levels reached $200 million in one quarter, representing a loss of one dollar per share. When IBM introduced a series of new high-end products in 1997, superior to Seagate's in performance and cost, Seagate lost $1 billion in high-end revenues in nine months—a huge chunk of an $8-billion revenue base. Market share dropped from 65 percent to 40 percent while Seagate blinked. Factories built what they wanted, with little regard for market demand. Division heads focused on getting the best results for their divisions, even if that lowered someone else's. People tried to optimize the performance of individual components, and not the product overall—like baseball players trying to make their own statistics look good even if that doesn't win games. The conflicts and complexity of seven design centers with their own tool sets, software, and component designs contributed to a disappointing return on investment from the highest R&D budget in the industry.

True to California style, the signs of a loser's culture were big and dramatic, including the nickname "Slavegate" because people were expected to follow orders, work sixteen-hour days, and give up personal time; the live hand grenade on a particularly intimidating senior executive's desk; or the jokes about which managers would be missing from next year's annual picture, given a high "executive execution rate."

"People didn't talk across the organization," an insider said. When people did talk, it was sometimes with angry voices. People in operations blamed people in sales, and vice versa. Senior staff showed little respect for one another and seemed to think they were mediocre, at best. Managers were known to shout at one another. At management meetings, each department sat as a group in assigned seats. A new senior executive who took the wrong seat at his first meeting recalled being yelled at and humiliated. Meetings rarely ended in consensus. "They even rewarded people for being the biggest jerk," an executive recalled. A "Dog Head" award was given to the manager who had been the most argumentative in the meeting—and people were actually proud to get it.

Dog Head awards, hand grenades, competitive silos, and "Slavegate" were why it was so remarkable that five years into the Luczo-Watkins era, an engineer could confess to a $10-million mistake, and a Seagate all-star team could act quickly to win that game anyway.

Ground Rules for Team Behavior

In late 1997, Luczo, a former investment banker who had joined the company a few years earlier to head corporate strategy, was named president, and in July 1998, when the board "retired" founder Al Shugart, he became CEO, with Bill Watkins as president and COO. Luczo and Watkins were convinced that Seagate needed a new strategy and business model, involving technology leadership, investment in innovation, and operating efficiencies to free up capital. They knew that none of this could be implemented without teamwork across the company. But teamwork required mutual confidence that Seagate people just didn't have.

The new imperative was to act as "One Seagate," not as protectors of separate silos. The new ground rule was a united front. One of Luczo's first moves was to establish a corporate management council of about a dozen top executives to focus on company-wide issues. He told them that once a decision was reached, members were expected to support it fully. Some managers said Luczo's ideas about collaboration were crazy. Those dissenters (and screamers and intimidators) were soon replaced or reassigned to positions where they could be coached in appropriate behavior. Watkins recalled, "We said, 'We will work as a team.' We had to find out fast who was with us who was not," Watkins declared. In the first few months, he got rid of two of the top people in a components group, three of the top people in materials, and the top person in Asia. During the next two years, over 70 percent of management changed.

Luczo and Watkins opened dialogue with senior management about vision and mission. Everyone had the opportunity to voice criticisms, but then the top team committed to a vision and values, providing notes to the vice-presidents under them to help spread the word. Luczo started a regular satellite broadcast to employees, with detailed financial data. He required monthly management meetings at each facility.

Seagate turned to sports to support learning about teamwork.

Watkins began the Seagate EcoChallenge. Once a year, a cross-section of employees was invited to attend a four-day retreat in Hawaii, New Zealand, Nevada, or some other appealing place. Groups of six competed in individual sports such as swimming or biking, and then, as the grand finale, in a multi-event race with one big requirement: The team must work together and cross the finish line as one unit. That teamwork was what Luczo and Watkins wanted for the whole company, but many people learned how hard it was to do. "We were lousy, a motley crew," a female manager said. "We didn't pull together. But I saw what I could have done better to support the team."

Confidence in the Team: Stretching for Important Work

Collaboration wasn't just fun and games or a fuzzy leadership slogan, it was vital to solving business problems. In 1998 Seagate launched the first wave of what would become numerous projects, many more than anyone could have imagined. One way Luczo and Watkins got people in warring factions to forget their battles was to put them in a room together, preferably with a round table, give them incredibly hard and important work to do, and not let them go until they did it.

An early effort to develop a cross-functional product development process was followed by an even bigger initiative to develop a new production strategy, known as "Factory of the Future." A group was charged with figuring out how to coordinate production and design to get the right products with the right speed, quality, and cost. After benchmarking competitors, and even exchanging factory visits with one of them (Fujitsu), leaders decided Seagate should adopt a fully automated system that produced high volume at a medium level of complexity. The goal was to start fresh and differentiate themselves from the pack of commodity producers by leading the industry in performance. To accomplish its task, the group would need teamwork within and without, as it would have to connect with many functions and other initiatives.

Engineers and managers had seen previous automation projects get scrapped for lack of support. So Luczo and Watkins communicated early and often that these new initiatives *would* work, setting positive expectations. On every possible occasion they talked about supply chain changes and factories of the future, increasing the confidence of team leaders. Doug DeHaan, senior vice-president of product and process development, recalled his desperate phone call to Watkins after a series of meetings that had featured endless arguments against Factory of the Future. "I told Bill I needed him in Minnesota, to talk to these guys about what we're trying to do. The next day, he was on a plane. He gave them a speech saying that we are going to do this, everybody's going to fall in line, and if you don't want to do it, don't be part of the company."

The performance target was a true stretch for a company then producing 1,500 to 2,000 disk drives per line per day: a whopping 20,000 drives a day off one line, a drive every 3.5 seconds. It was like asking a soccer team to score on every move in soccer, or every baseball player to hit a home run every time at bat.

Leaders said *Do it*, and the engineers said *We can't*. There was no confidence. The group assigned to this said that loading heads on a disk in 3.5 seconds was virtually impossible. But DeHaan felt that stretch goals spurred innovation, and he believed in the engineers. He told them, "We have to do it, and if we have to throw away a couple of machines, we'll throw away a couple of machines." Permission to fail created psychological safety and helped the team bond. They supported one another in going further than anyone had imagined. "Once the guys understood that they could take chances and wouldn't get blamed if it didn't quite work, they started trying some pretty risky things," DeHaan recalled. "The next thing we knew, an engineer found a very innovative solution for swinging these heads on a disk really quickly."

With collaboration rock-solid, the team walked on water. Based on that innovation alone, Seagate's productivity improved dramatically, and by 2003 the company was producing one drive every 3.8 seconds, or 16,000 per line per day, and sometimes more. This accomplishment gave Seagate a big advantage, because competitors were saddled with facilities and equipment that produced, on average, 3,000 per line. The Factory of the Future project also brought a side benefit that helped Seagate people shift to a winners' path: respect for internal talent and an increase in confidence in one another.

New Conversations: A Structure for Playing as a Team

Seeing that collaboration could accomplish important tasks helped spread the teamwork idea. Convening cross-functional groups from many locations became a more common mode for solving problems. These groups were empowered to tackle big issues, which increased people's interest in joining them. "Getting together like this gave us a common language and helped us see a common need for change," a middle manager said. "It created bonds between people. Steve and Bill wanted a culture where you could pick up the phone and call someone across the company. It worked! You felt like you could work with anyone."

The most significant vehicles for collaboration were called "core teams." Many people credited technology chief Tom Porter with the concept, when he launched the first core team in May 1998. The term was used for any cross-boundary group that took a leadership role on an issue or product. Product core teams, for example, featured a representative from each of the divisions of the company (design, materials, production, business development, etc.). While members of the team still officially reported to the head of their division, they were mainly responsible to one another for the duration of the project.

A methodology soon grew up around core teams. These groups were given special resources and training in teamwork. There was an effort to create equality. Members of a core team were co-located in one large office with a central meeting space featuring a round table and chairs, and a white board. Every member of the team had an equally sized cubicle within the office, in order to break down the siloed and hierarchical thinking that plagued the organization. When core teams were composed of members from more than one location, they would rotate the place for meetings, so that no one site would dominate. Core teams could make many decisions on their own, without constant input from officers. They started to propose their own follow-on initiatives. This took a huge weight off upper-level leaders, freeing time for them to focus on longer-term strategic issues. Of course, a great deal of time was also saved by multilateral disarmament, as each fortress no longer had to be defended.

Membership on a core team gave people in the rank and file a way to shine, a way to demonstrate leadership. A virtuous cycle of confidence developed: The more top managers trusted the people below, the more work could be delegated and done, the more respect there was for people in lower ranks, and the more confidence there was that they could take on still more of the responsibility.

Joan Motsinger's experience typified the best of core teams. Based in Minnesota, she headed the core team for a new high-performing product line. The goal: Make more of these components more quickly. Motsinger was not an expert on the technology, but she knew about people. She conducted many interviews to pick people whose personal dynamics would work well together, e.g., a strong collaborator over an intellect. Her core team used standard practices from any corporate or sports teamwork tool kit, from team-building to speaking the lingo of "forming, storming, norming, and performing"—standard phases of team development. They wrote contracts to make expectations clear. Coaches helped team members do their best. A key vice-president dropped by to ask what he could do to remove bottlenecks. "I was the leader, but really I was just a member, and we all took seats," Motsinger said. "I was better at spreadsheets, so I was the queen spreadsheet person. Others had other gifts."

The group bonded and worked through serious illnesses and personal crises. Her team reminded me of the Philadelphia Eagles or New England Patriots, choosing players for character, letting natural leaders emerge, and winning despite injuries. Seagate declared victory (selling three times as many of the components as originally hoped), and the players who had exceeded expectations received big career rewards.

The impossible-to-imagine of a few years earlier, that Seagate could ever work collaboratively, became the impossible-to-resist. "Senior executives really force collaboration," a manager reported. "I sent out a communication a week ago, and my boss said, 'This is great, can you make sure you're connecting up with these other people on that?' This approach has improved decision-making at lower ranks by pushing cross-functional leadership. It's not perfect yet. It might be foreign for a person sitting in Minnesota to get a call from Singapore from an engineer doing a similar job. But that was totally impossible two years ago."

Another losers' habit that became unacceptable was for people to poach on one another's territories. For example, a rogue group decided that they were going to work on a problem assigned to another team because they felt they could do it better. Working in secret, they appeared at a meeting to show off their solution. It was certainly well done, but the manager said, "Sorry, guys. You might as well throw it away. The other team is responsible for doing that. You're not allowed to go off and spend company resources on a non-authorized project." They were given the choice of trashing their solution or persuading the official group to use the idea. The official team was confident enough to incorporate some of the rogue group's solution in their design.

To collaborate effectively and avoid unproductive duplication, people had to be aware of one another's goals, an action that also reinforced accountability. Employees could use an online tool called MAP to see how their personal objectives tied to those of their bosses, peers, and subordinates, and how all those fit with the top corporate goals. Employees were rated on how well they demonstrated six behaviors stemming from Seagate's official values, and this rating accounted for 30 percent of their performance review. By 2003, 91 percent of employees reported that they "clearly understood how my job supports Seagate's corporate objectives."

Winning Performance: The Contagion of Confidence

Consider this impressive before-and-after comparison: In 1997, Seagate had 111,000 people producing 6 million drives per quarter in twenty-seven plants worldwide. By the spring of 2003, the company produced three times as many drives with fewer than half the people—45,000 employees making 18 million drives per quarter in fourteen plants.

Seagate had gone private in 2000, becoming publicly traded again in November 2002 in one of the few successful public offerings of that year—which Glenn Hutchins, general partner of SilverLake, the buyout firm that helped with the financing, attributed to management and teamwork. Over the preceding two years, Seagate's share of the personal storage market improved from 20 percent to 30 percent. Customers who had called Seagate arrogant in the past now praised the company for responding quickly. "We used to be the last company customers would ask for extra supply. Not anymore," the head of sales reported. Luczo took pride in Seagate's numbers and also in how the team achieved them—by being "best in class *and* making thirty times the changes anyone said was possible."

The difference in culture and behavior was credited to the Luczo-Watkins model. "Steve and Bill are honest and engaged. I'm blown away by how much they care," an employee enthused. "When they don't meet their metrics, they show them and explain why. That's a big deal to us. They're just like you and me, pimples and all—humble leadership with a focused set of goals."

Executives spoke with one voice in public and never made disparaging remarks in private. They were engaged. They asked questions, connected organizations, encouraged teamwork, and invested time in one another, always having a good time and joking together. People pitched in and helped when needed. "At that level, the silos are gone," a manager declared. At a spring 2003 meeting of the top hundred managers, Kathy Snouffer, vice-president of strategic projects, noted a dramatic difference. Instead of functions presenting their own goals and accomplishments, each focused on what it could contribute to the whole company. She thought to herself, "Everyone's effort is having an impact! I have connected and collaborated with my brethren."

Respect among managers and employees blossomed. Despite large layoffs and plant closings, the vitriol of e-mails directed at management decisions declined. Respect for people had made its way down the chain, and people acted to deserve respect by taking responsibility. Employees were proud of victories large and small, such as the world record set by the Shakopee plant for quarter after quarter of high performance—and that this was done not in Japan but in Minnesota, and not at IBM but at Seagate.

Because of renewed confidence, initiative increased. Joan Motsinger credited an engineer in Longmont, Colorado, with a great idea for recovering lost data, called SuperECC. He approached the quality and sales organizations, the design centers, and a member of Motsinger's team, who told her about it, knowing her fondness for collecting business cards and putting people in touch. She invited the engineer to present to her group of fifty. They were impressed with his innovative solution and also with his initiative and fortitude. It was a sign of a new culture. "He was given enough leeway to assess the problem and a solution, then he had enough guts to sell it company-wide," she said. "If you've got a good idea, you don't have to run it up the chain and 'mother may I' all the way up. It's now easy for a person who's got an innovative idea to get some play time."

There was no guarantee that the company wouldn't slip in the future, especially as a challenging technology environment required Seagate to reexamine its business model. There were still pockets of people trapped in silos, and in mid-2003, Seagate employees still scored low on a survey item about feeling free to speak. But the "Slavegate" reputation had faded, and winners' habits were back in place. Top people—including Jeff Allen, a vice-president—confessed to us that they had never intended to stay at Seagate, they just wanted to get some skills before leaving, but now they were committed for the long haul, turning down attractive offers because Seagate was so exciting and fulfilling. A manager expressed amazement that the shift in work environment Luczo had promised when he became CEO had actually occurred: "People today will say Seagate is a good place to work. The hours are still long and the pressure high, but that's balanced by a sense of mission and progress—and by sunny spirits."

Sunny spirits were everywhere, and they were contagious, just as they are in any winning streak. Positive expectations were transmitted person by person, group by group, reinforcing confidence in self and others. Collaboration was embodied in behavior and embedded in the structures for teamwork. Greater accountability and initiative further reinforced confidence. And renewed confidence showed up in high performance.

CONTINENTAL AIRLINES:
A COLLECTIVE DEFINITION OF SUCCESS

Seagate proved the value of collaboration as a cornerstone of confidence when the team recovered from a $10-million fumble. Continental got even greater benefits from its teamwork during the power blackout in August 2003, as I related at the beginning of this book. How Continental reversed a losing streak to get on that winner's path adds other important lessons about teamwork.

Continental's Nosedive: The
Years of Missed Connections

U.S. airline deregulation in 1978 set the stage for the near-death spiral of what had once been a model airline, led for forty years by one aviation pioneer, the legendary Bob Six. In October 1982, Frank Lorenzo's Texas International Air bought Continental, then based in Denver, and moved its headquarters to Houston. Lorenzo's acquisition started a long cycle of decline.

In September 1983, less than a year after Lorenzo's takeover, Continental filed for bankruptcy. This was widely seen as a move to break union contracts, enabling Continental to replace unionized workers with lower-wage non-union workers and require longer hours and shorter breaks. Lorenzo's reputation for harsh business practices continued through Continental's emergence from bankruptcy in the middle of 1986, and the consolidation of other Texas Air acquisitions, such as Frontier, People Express, and New York Air, under the Continental name. In 1986 Lorenzo bought Eastern Airlines, which collapsed in 1991. (In 1993 the U.S. Department of Transportation denied Lorenzo permission to form a new airline.) In the summer of 1990 Lorenzo sold most of his holdings in Continental. A few months later, in the fall of 1990, Iraq invaded Kuwait, the Gulf War began, and Continental again filed for bankruptcy, citing rising fuel costs due to the loss of Middle Eastern oil.

Airline employees are the ultimate migrant workers, always mobile, often remote, and unsupervised at critical moments in the air. They can easily feel disenfranchised. Running an airline might be a big team sport, as Gordon Bethune wrote in his book *From Worst to First* and repeated to me, but before the turnaround people were playing individual games.

When Roosevelt Nesbitt, a director of internal audit, joined the company in 1988, it was "rude and crude," an "embarrassment" to the industry. "Morale was very bad, the product was very bad. We were treating our customers very poorly, and we were treating each other very poorly," he recalled. Mechanics and ramp agents would take off their badges as soon as they got on the employee bus to leave the airport. "If someone asked me what my job was, I would say, 'I work for an airline.' I did not want to say Continental Airlines," Karen Radabaugh, a manager of airport training, confessed.

Lack of information made employees feel stupid. More than merely emotional, the problem that stemmed from that feeling contributed to Continental's high cost structure. Customers would call reservation lines with questions involving news reports about airlines or airports, and the embarrassed staff had no idea what the customers were talking about. They were the last to know. They had to refer even small questions or issues to supervisors, at a cost of about six dollars per transferred call. With millions of transactions, that extra six dollars because employees weren't trusted added up to real money.

The atmosphere across departments was poisonous. "Prior to Gordon's arrival, there were silos built up all over the company. Nobody talked to anybody, and if there was something wrong, everybody blamed it on the other person," said Mary Matatall, director of global recruiting. It was even hard to get other departments to give up their trash. At one point Matatall was asked to create the belly of an aircraft for cabin service training, but to do it cheaply, so she tried to get seats from old aircraft that were going to be thrown out anyway, and remnants of carpet that no one could use. "You could not get someone above your rank to call you back unless you name-dropped," she declared.

No one wanted to see anyone else after work, either, reported Danny Watson, manager of aircraft support (which included cleaning the planes), who joined in 1987. "They wanted to get the blazes out of here, go home, ignore—just forget about Continental. I mean, it was too painful!" He explained the pain: "You would have senior management in offices screaming for people that would be rows away. It was so disrespectful. People would be crying in their cubicles. It was horrible. It was nasty. You lost your self-worth."

By mid-1994 it was uncertain that Continental would live to 1995, and there was concern among employees that the company would not be able to meet its payroll. Losses had mounted, cash was running out. It was later learned that finance staff had inflated profit projections by plugging in overly optimistic revenue estimates, keeping the discrepancy hidden. There was no leadership, no game plan, and no focus, as Continental swallowed acquisitions and shifted strategies. "The airline was so messed up," Watson said. "You had the old Eastern, New York Air, People Express, Old Continental, New Continental, In-between Continental, and you didn't know if you were on home base or in the dugout. We were called the 'presidential sweepstakes airline' because you didn't know who was president in a given month or year."

No one had confidence in Continental—not investors, customers, regulators, or employees. Employees had lost confidence in one another and doubted themselves. In those years the company's response to industry changes was to tighten the screws on employees or go to court. The authoritarian mode fed on itself. Abused by bosses, people abused one another. Years of feeling like failures made failure seem inevitable.

The airline industry has seen many self-perpetuating cycles of lost confidence that accelerate decline and lead to bankruptcy or death. The pattern is usually like this: As passengers decline, tickets are discounted, and the airline loses money. The stock price drops. Flights are canceled. Because they are afraid that tickets won't be honored, customers defect. The airline cuts costs. Food deteriorates in quantity and quality. Customers take out their displeasure on agents and crews. Agents and crews, defending themselves in advance of expected punishment, are surly to customers, who then become even more agitated and try to avoid that airline. Demoralized employees refuse to take pay cuts. Defensive managers are tempted to cover up problems rather than solve them. Analysts begin a deathwatch.

That was the essence of Continental in its bust years—in a nosedive heading for a crash landing. Then Gordon Bethune arrived and shifted the cycle.

Becoming a Team: New Goals, New Conversations, New Respect

Bethune was appointed chief operating officer in February 1994, and in October, when the CEO resigned, he had a chance to become acting CEO and decided to act like one. He created a vision for Continental's future, the "Go Forward" plan, that focused on finance, product, customers, and employees. As soon as he was named the actual CEO a few weeks later, he got moving. Bethune replaced autocratic bosses with team players and began spreading information early and often to everyone.

"When Gordon came, there wasn't anything different at first. We all thought, 'Here is another new one, okay, he's going to be a year here also,'" Karen Radabaugh said. "Then we started getting a daily news bulletin, and that was every day, and it's been every day. There was a lot of consistency."

Bethune wanted to get the potential team to play like a real one. So he made an impressive and unusual decision: to spend $2.5 million on employees to save $5 million, the amount Continental lost because of failure to land on time. Shortly after he became CEO, he offered each employee an equal $65 of that $2.5 million if Continental scored in one of the top four positions for on-time arrivals for a quarter. (They had been at the bottom.) This small bonus applied to well over 30,000 employees, absolutely everyone except director-level managers and those above them.

The work was important and the goal inclusive. Everyone cared about it and had room to contribute. On-time performance mattered to customers. It mattered to employees, because late flights made their work harder in nearly every respect and reverberated throughout the system, as delays in one place were felt in other places. Customer and employee dissatisfaction reinforced each other, anger provoking anger.

Deborah McCoy, then running flight training, was asked to head a task force about on-time performance. Many people controlled a piece of the goal, so working across groups could create new relationships and build mutual respect. Flight crews and ground crews were empowered to make decisions on the spot, such as whether to push off before extra meals were loaded, or whether to fly faster, and they weren't second-guessed. The scheduling group (which sometimes set schedules without input and marked them "confidential") and flight operations (which had to execute on schedules handed to them sometimes at the last minute) got together to establish better schedules.

Between January and March 1995, the first quarter for the bonus, Continental's on-time performance went from seventh to first, and about 38,000 checks for sixty-five dollars went out. Buzz about found money was an immediate confidence-booster.

Management had promised, management had delivered. Customers could regain confidence in Continental's reliability. And since on-time performance was reported by the U.S. Department of Transportation, everyone knew Continental people were winners. The goal and the offer continued through subsequent years, though the bar was raised, and occasionally Continental didn't make it. More often it did. In the first and fourth quarters of 2003, employees received $100 on-time bonuses.

This was the most visible manifestation of a big collaboration-enabler, a collective definition of success. Bethune's message: "You get paid when we all get paid. All get nothing if any of you work against each other." He called this "bait to appeal to the fish. If you're the operations people, you won't get paid if sales doesn't deliver."

Other gestures of respect helped restore employees' confidence. Early in 1995 at a parking-lot ceremony, Bethune burned a nine-inch-thick rule book he had inherited, known as "The Thou Shalt Not Book." In 1996, Bethune made a video with comedian Rodney Dangerfield of "can't get no respect" fame, to exhort people to treat one another with dignity. Planes were painted and spruced up. These things mattered to people, and as they saw their work environment improve, they felt valued. Debbie McCoy, who became senior vice-president of flight operations in 1999, decided that people spending up to fourteen hours together in a cabin could help determine who was hired, so she established rotating panels of pilots and flight attendants to select their peers. She added a speed-dial hotline to on-board phones to get problems solved quickly, such as a catering issue (cereals but no spoons) or a mechanical problem (a broken seat on a full flight).

The turnaround powered a success cycle. More sensible schedules and better equipment helped employees do a better job, which got them on-time bonuses, which made them cheerful, which spread to customers, which improved financial results, which made it easier to keep doing a better job. Between 1995 and 2000, Continental had an impressive winning streak of twenty-four profitable quarters, reliable on-time performance, numerous awards for customer satisfaction, low turnover, increased safety, and performance ahead of its competition (the other major U.S. carriers with international flights). The company shared over $500 million of profit with employees.

Teamwork through Troubled Times

The new culture of communication and collaboration helped Continental weather the worst storm the industry had ever known, the terrorist attacks of September 11, 2001. Within two hours after the first plane hit the north tower of the World Trade Center in New York, and just an hour after the Federal Aviation Administration closed U.S. airspace, Continental broadcast a system-wide voice mail to its employees, telling them that co-workers at the World Trade Center were safe. Continental employees at airports around the world reported that people from other airlines came to Continental for news, because they weren't getting any from their own bosses. Continental was the first airline to put its CEO on national television, the first to help displaced employees, the first to fly into Washington's Reagan National Airport when it reopened. Those kinds of firsts were bittersweet, of course. But there were other awards for more positive accomplishments.

After 9/11, when the entire industry was losing passengers and money, Bethune defined winning to employees as "beating the competition, being the best at what we do." Continental adapted quickly to new security requirements because of innovations created through collaboration, such as having among the largest numbers of e-ticket machines of U.S. airlines. Employees found ways to save money without cutting service or people, by being alert to opportunities and getting the teamwork going. One day Debbie McCoy was in Newark, making sure jetways were pulling up in time. She noticed that a dozen or so aircraft auxiliary power units (APUs, the source of electricity when the engines were off) were still running, even though the planes could have plugged into ground units much more cheaply. This was one of those opportunities. A cross-functional team set up a procedure to get electricity as soon as the plane docked, and then they measured performance daily. They trusted people on the ground to decide when it made sense to run a plane's APU, like hot weather in Houston or ice in Cleveland. Without passengers noticing any differences, Continental saved many millions of dollars.

"The post-9/11 environment could wear you down," Debbie McCoy said in May of 2003. "We didn't want employees to have a hopeless feeling. We tried to be supportive of them." To support people, Continental had established some of the most flexible work arrangements in the industry. By contract, its work rules were less restrictive than those of other airlines. Sick leave for flight attendants was the lowest in the industry; they didn't have to call in sick because they could take a month's leave, a half-month's leave, share a job with someone else, or trade trips via an online system. (One flight attendant traded a reserve day off numerous times in an hour.) All divisions could trade work schedules—a reason Continental made *Fortune*'s list of the 100 best places to work every year since 1999.

Playing to Win the Game: The Team in Action

If confidence was strong, the reason was that everyone faced the future as one team, one enterprise. On a typical weekday in October 2003, I joined McCoy as she walked into a narrow conference room at 8:30 a.m. in Houston, Texas, ready to lead the morning operations meeting, as she had done every weekday for years. This was a daily gathering of about thirty-five people, twenty in person and another fifteen or so by phone, representing departments and groups across Continental.

The meeting took place on the nineteenth floor of the Continental building in downtown Houston. Everyone could get to the meeting quickly, because Continental's floors lacked security checks or controlled access, in order to make it easy for people to dash between floors and to cross departmental territories to work with one another. (Continental employees liked to point out that this was dramatically different from the closed Enron building nearby, where the public couldn't even get access to the Starbuck's coffee shop in the lobby.) Continental's open building reflected a preference for open communication. LED displays above entrances to hallways and on monitors flashed headlines from the airline's daily news update and that day's up-to-the-minute percentage of on-time flights, one of the main goals for everyone at the airline.

McCoy sat at the head of the table. She certainly had plenty of self-confidence—from childhood, when she had dreamed of flying before more than a token number of women had ever even made it into the cockpit; and in her career, as a Continental pilot since 1979, a captain on wide-body jets, and the first woman to head the flight operations of a major airline. But it was the confidence of the team that was most striking. Around her were people from maintenance, material services, in-flight services, dining services, pilot scheduling, airport services, purchasing, technology, and marketing, with speakerphones so that various key airports could dial in. Her boss, Larry Kellner (Continental's president), sat near her along one side of the table. Everyone had a one-page color-coded set of statistics, highlighting all the metrics Continental tracked to assess the daily performance of each part of the system.

The meeting got started. Not a second was wasted, and everyone knew what to do. The team started passing the ball so fast that I found it hard to follow the action.

Debbie to Tim to report on the weather. Then a series of passes around the room: *". . . the Houston-Richmond-Newark flight . . . sick-outs . . . door openings . . . red zones . . . missed connects . . . weather . . . aircraft . . . load planning out of Frankfurt . . . thirteen straight days with no baggage delays . . ."* A telephone voice picked up the ball, as it started to move around the Continental airports: *". . . this is Randy . . . no events . . . over to Diane . . . the Tampa flight . . . two flight attendants injured in turbulence . . . met by paramedics . . . they're okay, we're tracking them . . . over to Bill . . . this is Cleveland . . . four red-zone opportunities, made three . . . tech operations . . . over to Jane . . . Los Angeles has good visibility . . . the convention in Philadelphia is not a problem, but we're watching weekend traffic . . . a VIP to Waco . . . solar activity in Seattle . . . watching the Tokyo flight . . .*" Bounce back to the room: "*. . . the fleet . . . one seat out of commission, two flights on the watch list . . . working with Dan's group on Newark to Boston . . . engineering project with GE and Boeing, new prototype reducing engine stress . . . three minutes delay to Newark, dropped meals in the aft galley . . . watching Hong Kong . . . Tuesday a great day for web sales . . .*" Larry Kellner got the ball: "*Southwest is coming into Philadelphia and will impact Newark . . .*" McCoy summarized, flagged issues, and expressed thanks.

Click-click-click-click seamlessly through their routine, with an occasional pause to discuss a problem area—the meeting had the spirit of the drills and disciplines of a winning sports team in its daily practices.

Small huddles had begun the day, so problems could be worked out before the meeting. Afterwards, others would duplicate the drill at their own staff meetings. Throughout the day, people could listen to five voice-mail updates. On Fridays they could call in for Gordon Bethune's weekly voice mail, and depending on their location, they could attend a CEO Exchange, a dialogue about the airline open to any employee.

All this communication created an informed, accountable workforce, able to exercise judgment—the kind of judgment and teamwork that served Continental so well during the August 2003 power outage, or in solving other problems with the style of winners. An operations meeting earlier that year, in March 2003, considered data showing a falling-off of on-time performance toward the end of the day. Initially there was some finger-pointing and blaming of the people doing the scheduling. McCoy said that was not an acceptable response, that the scheduling group should be invited to describe its challenges. She reminded them that everyone wins or loses together. Then, at a brainstorming session that month, the operations group came up with the idea of focusing on the most difficult flights to get in on time, even with schedule changes. These "focus flights" were given special resources, such as additional ground agents or baggage handlers; pilots were given advance information on flight plans; agents could query the system to see if the flight would be late without an early push-back (if all passengers had boarded); and local stations could try their own creative solutions. In April, 203 of about 2,304 flights were focus flights. The attention paid off, as 88.4 percent of Continental's flights that month were on time, the third-best performance since 1995.

Some wins were small, such as becoming the first U.S. airline to be approved under the United Kingdom's pet-travel scheme, which eliminated the usual six-month quarantine for cats and dogs traveling to London. But the new Continental seized any initiative, knowing that low-cost competition was changing the nature of the game.

Team sports were more than metaphors. "We are always doing something as a group," Danny Watson said. "We've got volleyball teams going on after work, departments challenging other departments. We have fishing tournaments. I was talking with Debbie Larza—her son plays soccer, and she said, 'Let's get a soccer team going!' Somebody takes the baton and runs with it, the next thing you know, it is an event."

Consider the T-shirt barometer. If Continental employee confidence were charted the way economists chart consumer confidence, using consumer spending to predict future economic performance, a boom cycle was under way at Continental. People were now proud to wear the logo. From 1994 to 1998, sales of Continental-logo merchandise at company stores had increased by more than 400 percent. In 2003, sales steadily increased to reach over a million dollars for the year. A Continental shirt introduction had spawned "Hawaiian-shirt Fridays" in several departments.

Continental's culture now reinforced self-confidence, confidence in one another, and confidence in the system. Everyone felt like a winner. That's what Gordon Bethune conveyed in his weekly messages, like the voice mail in mid-October 2003:

Hello, this is Gordon, and it's Friday, October 17. I hope you had a chance to listen to our conference call on our third-quarter earnings, which we completed yesterday. If not, you can still call in. We reported a net income of $133 million, but $100 million of that was an after-tax gain from our disposition of ExpressJet stock. You really made $33 million, which is a heck of an achievement. It was a tough quarter. We had really heavy load factors with very low ticket prices. So we worked extra hard for that. Once again, your efforts make a difference....

The Tony Jannus award is a prestigious award, and I have been nominated. I will accept it in Tampa on Tuesday and Wednesday. I am proud to be joining a list of people like Bob Six and others who have been honored. And, I know that I am being honored because you guys do all the work and I am getting all the credit, but I will make sure that they know the truth.

I will be doing a CEO Exchange in Tampa at the Airport Marriott in the ballroom on Tuesday at 1:00 p.m., and I hope to see many of you there. I am also going to meet with AAA, the agency and managers and headquarters staff while I'm in Tampa. So I will kiss a few butts over there for all of us. They are a good business partner, and it is good to pay attention to them while I am in the territory.

That's it for this week. It's been a good one. It is beautiful weather across the system. We have great performance. I'll talk to you again on Friday.

On January 16, 2004, Gordon Bethune announced plans to retire at the end of the year, after more than ten years as CEO. Larry Kellner was named his successor, ensuring a seamless transition that signaled Continental's continuing pride in the team behind its winning streak.

GETTING TO WE: ACTIONS THAT
BUILD CONFIDENCE IN TEAMS

Cultivating collaboration would have been easy if Continental, Seagate, or the Montreal Expos had started from scratch. Then there would be no bad habits to reverse, no legacy of sins of decline to overcome. People embodying the pathologies of the past can always be replaced, but eliminating the bad does not automatically produce the good. It takes a major effort on the part of leaders to foster confidence that a demoralized company or group is capable of working together and succeeding at it. Restoring people's confidence in one another requires four kinds of actions:

- getting connected in new ways through new conversations
- carrying out important work jointly
- communicating respect
- demonstrating inclusion (that everyone is part of the picture)

New Connections: Structuring the Conversations
"Engage!" That's the famous command issued by Captain Jean-Luc Picard of the starship *Enterprise* that gets everything going in the *Star Trek: The Next Generation* television and movie adventures, and it is the essence of the invitation that leaders issue when they convene people and tell them to join hands (figuratively, though the Expos did it literally).

It sounds dangerously close to an oxymoron to talk about ordering collaboration. But for those trying to move off a losing streak, relationships do not come naturally. During economic downturns, just when one would think people could get benefits from conferences and associations, attendance and membership drop off. Depressed people could benefit most from other people's company at the very time they seek it least. People in losing situations have gotten out of the habit of engaging with one another. So leaders use their convening power to get people to the table and get them talking. Garanti Bank's senior managers were "invited" by CEO Akin Öngör to attend leadership development seminars at the beginning of the bank's transformation; those who didn't show up after three invitations were asked to leave the company. Or recall Jim Kilts's first day as Gillette CEO, when he laid out a schedule of mandatory executive team meetings, larger management meetings, and off-site retreats.

Rather than continually reorganize, which is highly disruptive, turnaround leaders augment the organization chart with flexible, sometimes temporary, groups that open relationships in multiple directions. Steve Luczo formed numerous new groups, starting at the top. Invensys's turnaround CEO, Rick Haythornthwaite, referred to this process as structuring the organization to get the right conversations. "The only thing I really do is lead conversations," he says. "Any group is a network of conversations. I continuously thrust people into situations that force them to challenge the current conversation they're holding, to get beyond that conversation to one that's more productive."

Invensys's leadership team acted on this theory by adding new groups and new roles, slicing through the organization chart vertically, diagonally, and horizontally. In his first months at the company, Haythornthwaite formed nine strategy teams comprising people from across the divisions, with each team focused on one of nine customer segments. When the company launched this strategy, it involved the top 300 people in rank at the organization and 100 additional participants called "ambassadors for change," ensuring that people below the managerial ranks would be part of the strategy conversation. Haythornthwaite also recruited experts to lead in four areas cutting across the business—supply chain (procurement), customer development, service delivery, and project management. They had very small staffs and no P&L responsibility. Their charter was to set standards and to work with others to bring about necessary improvements.

To ensure cooperation, leaders promote the natural connectors, the people who instinctively reach across divides to form relationships. On the North Carolina women's soccer team, Jordan Walker was a team leader because she was a connector, even though coach Anson Dorrance called her one of the least athletic players he had ever seen. Joan Motsinger at Seagate was also a connector; asked to head a technical area without being a technical expert, she was known for her business-card collection. Dusty Baker felt that conversations across positions helped the Chicago Cubs win baseball games. "I want my pitching coach talking to my hitters about things and my batting coach talking to the pitchers about things, because if the pitcher doesn't know how the hitters think, he's not going to get them out. It really helps, the more communication you have," he said.

Important Work

The reason people are having new conversations is that there are critical problems to be solved. The game can't be turned into Trivial Pursuits. When people are given tasks with big consequences, they are more likely to forget their differences and bury the slights of the past, real or imaginary. There's nothing like a huge responsibility and a deadline to focus the mind.

At Seagate, Steve Luczo never singled out "culture change" as a goal in itself; he and Bill Watkins wanted a new culture because collaboration could raise productivity. Performance was the goal, culture was a tool, and initiatives assigned to cross-functional core teams were real and important. What sold collaboration to hard-nosed engineers was that it was a practical way to get bigger wins. Task commitment, not people's social attraction to one another, is what creates high team performance. Group cohesiveness is the result of success as much as the cause of it.

Important work has a clear strategic focus and significance, so that it matters to everyone's fate; and it offers the opportunity for everyone in the system to see where their efforts might make a difference. Both of those elements made Continental's on-time-arrivals goal such a good choice for an initial turnaround activity. The airline not only achieved the performance targets, it showed everyone that it could do something to win the game, and that winning the game benefited everyone.

Important work makes people proud that they can stretch to meet impossible goals (the work is important because it's difficult), like the Seagate team that leaped beyond the possible to find a way to dramatically raise productivity. Even getting the assignment in the first place is a confidence-booster, the way people at Invensys reacted to being given the chance to contribute to strategy after the previous regime felt they were worthless functionaries. Accomplishing an important task together brings immediate tangible results—shipments tripled, airplanes painted, classrooms wired for the Internet—which reinforce the intangible future benefit of greater confidence in one another.

Every turnaround leader, every coach or CEO, has to ask people to put in more effort—more practices, longer hours, more sacrifices, all the stuff of saving a sick group and moving it to better health. When people know that the work is important, they are more likely to show up to do it. When they see how small aspects of their behavior can help accomplish important tasks, they are more likely to put in the effort. An important part of Billy Beane's strategy in turning around the Oakland Athletics baseball team was to find small behaviors with large impact, such as getting on base.

It's doesn't take very much in the way of incentives to focus effort. Continental paid only sixty-five dollars a quarter at first and later didn't raise it much. When he coached in Houston, the Expos' Tom McCraw offered fifty- and hundred-dollar rewards to the player who drove in the winning run. "Guys making millions chased me around after the game for that money," he said. It couldn't have been the money, it was the recognition of an important contribution.

"Chemistry"—confidence in one another—builds one win at a time: game by game, project by project, flight by flight. The Montreal Expos' 2002 goal was simply to win two additional games each month. Each win helps people learn what to expect from one another and share the experience of success. Small victories build pride in the group and accumulate to become big victories, such as Seagate's Factory of the Future innovations. "I think the real team building, the real bonds, come from going through the battles together on a nightly basis and finding out who is there for you and who is not," observed Mike Babcock, head coach of the Anaheim Mighty Ducks.

Rituals of Respect

Shifting a culture of mediocrity, in which everyone doubts everyone else's abilities, to a culture of confidence is a challenge in troubled companies. When Rick Haythornthwaite arrived at Invensys, he asked executives individually to identify three people in the company for whom they had the greatest respect. Most, he told me, could barely name one person. By making only one change in the senior-management ranks in his first months, Haythornthwaite signaled that there was talent among the people already in the company. He told the 100 people on the nine strategy teams that he trusted them and believed in them. At a three-day reporting session after their forty-five-day intensive effort to plot a new direction for Invensys, he said, "The mood was extraordinary. People we didn't know existed offered high-quality presentations of strategic thinking. The overall level of respect for one another in the room rose."

Respect is signaled by leaders in how they treat people, and how they expect them to treat others. Post-Enron codes of conduct are fashionable in major companies, though generally they don't cover appreciation and interpersonal etiquette, and they do not go deeply. Leaders can set ground rules for discussion and decision-making, as Luczo and Watkins did at Seagate. They can foster the language of contribution rather than blame, insisting that people seek solutions and value one another's potential to contribute, as Debbie McCoy did in Continental operations meetings. Teams that produce innovations encourage people to speak up but to express their concerns without rancor or contentiousness.

Leaders can shape how people talk by insisting on respect— Gordon Bethune made a video about it. Of course, dissent or cynicism might go underground while people fake politeness in public, and some rituals seem artificial at first (my own reaction when I learned that big, powerful athletes on the Expos team were being ordered to hold hands and tell all). But soon the consistency principle kicks in—if people hear themselves say certain things often enough, they start to feel the associated feelings.

Inclusion: Investing in Everyone

To get people to invest in one another, leaders need to show people that they are worth investing in. That's the symbolic benefit of renovating rundown buildings, refurbishing dingy aircraft, or getting the latest technology and equipment, as I indicated in Chapter 6. A collective facelift changes demeanor. Improvements in something tangible that people see every day when they come to work keep reinforcing the message. The other virtue is that these investments are by nature inclusive; everyone shares them, just as Continental's collective definition of success stemmed from the inclusive symbolism of the same sixty-five-dollar reward to everyone. To treat everyone on the Expos team like winners, despite limited cash, the new general manager somehow found the money to invest in services for the players, such as trainers and fitness tools. The new director-general of the BBC had to cut expenses, but he did it by shifting priorities so that more money went to local programming and new local facilities, as we will see in the next chapter.

When Thomas Highton began the nationally recognized turnaround of the failing Union City, New Jersey, schools, he immediately invested in repairing the buildings, and he added a second big sign of inclusion: opening dialogue with all the teachers in the form of a needs assessment, asking them about what changes they most desired and acting on their responses. Debbie McCoy at Continental reinforced both respect and inclusion by letting pilots hire pilots and flight attendants hire flight attendants.

Such actions help reverse patterns characteristic of losing streaks—that decisions are made in secret behind closed doors, that inequalities reflect favoritism, not fairness, and that people are being left out. Jim Kilts of Gillette was lauded for not playing favorites, for giving everyone the same objective measures and holding them to the same standards. Seagate removed assigned seats from top executive meetings and added new meeting rooms with round tables to major facilities. The symbolism of the round table seemed to work at Seagate. (It also passed the try-it-at-home commonsense test: When my husband and I replaced a long dining room table with a round one, the first twenty-five people to see the new dining room all exclaimed spontaneously that round tables produce better conversations.) When people feel understood and heard, their commitment grows.

To lead a turnaround of the Chicago Cubs, manager Dusty Baker began with inclusion. He said to us that he knew who the stars were, but he didn't tell them that. Starting in spring training, reported Sonny Jackson, Baker's special assistant, "The first thing you do is make sure that players understand that everybody's in this thing together: coaches, players, the minor-league people. Dusty has us call some of the minor league players so they get a chance to play and show their stuff. And that starts everything rolling. He lets them know that he's here to help them." After his second year with the Cubs and his fifth in the major leagues, pitcher Matt Clement said about Baker: "He goes that extra mile to make you feel that he's in your corner. For a team to do well, you need a lot of positive energy, and he exudes it more than the normal manager. It's not just rah-rah. He's behind you, he cheers for you. Maybe somebody's having a tough game, everybody else is having a big game, he'll say, 'Let's get him a hit here. Let's pick this guy up.' He truly wants to see everybody succeed."

All four of the things leaders can do to promote collaboration— new connections, important work with shared goals, rituals of respect, and investments that include everyone—help unleash positive energy and aspirations. This can occur even in unexpected places and under the most challenging circumstances, as we are about to see.

MAKING THE GRADE IN MEMPHIS

Basketball superstar Jerry West came to Memphis, Tennessee, to turn around the Grizzlies, a losing National Basketball Association professional franchise just moved from Vancouver. We followed him to Memphis to interview the Grizzlies. But when I think about Memphis, my mind returns to another leader we met there: Elsie Bailey, principal of Booker T. Washington High School. Her turnaround challenge was infinitely harder than West's (though many of her students aspired to play for the Grizzlies) and, for that matter, harder than any business turnaround I know.

Elsie Bailey was a high school English teacher in 1989 when then-superintendent Willie Herenton began a move to turn around the seven deteriorating schools in the economically devastated south-central Memphis neighborhood in which she had grown up. Herenton declared the schools "void," and all employees had to reapply for their jobs. He offered salary incentives—a $3,000 pay supplement—to help draw the best teachers and administrators into the schools. Bailey was hired as assistant principal of Booker T. Washington High School and became principal in 1991.

Most students in Booker T. Washington's nearly 100-percent African-American enrollment were drawn from four low-income housing complexes in the area. Mondays were always days to dread. Disruptive and sometimes serious fights spilled into the school from weekend tensions in the projects outside, or from rival groups who wouldn't let others cross certain roads on the way to school. "It wasn't as bad as in some cities, but it was bad enough," Bailey said. "People lived in super-crowded conditions, and tempers flared." The police ward surrounding the school led the city in aggravated assaults (184), nonresidential burglaries (278), and homicides (12) in 1991; and police blamed drug trafficking for much of the crime. In light of a downtown poverty rate of 97 percent and with a school dropout rate of 49 percent, many students had little confidence in their ability to change their futures. Attendance hovered around 84 percent, and student achievement was well below the fiftieth percentile on state tests. Some Memphis officials wanted the school to close or move.

Teachers had become more discouraged each year, and students more hopeless. Bailey set about to create a culture that would foster self-confidence in the students and confidence in the school. She instituted a practice of daily walk-throughs in each classroom, to show both students and teachers that she cared about what they were doing. She encouraged teachers to know all students by name, whether or not a teacher had them in class. When Bailey told teachers she wanted to see student work displayed in the hallways to build pride (an unusual action for a high school), some teachers protested that the students would tear the work down or destroy it. Bailey persisted, and though some of the work was displayed in Plexiglas showcases, even the work that was accessible was left alone.

After observing some of the school's young men who struggled with schooling sit through separate "special ed" classes with their heads down, ridiculed by other students who walked by, Bailey changed to inclusion teaching, which brought all of the students into the same classrooms and offered extra tutoring, without labeling and stigmatizing special-ed students. They were more likely to stay in school if they didn't face daily embarrassment. She also treated the teachers as colleagues, not as subordinates. "If Ms. Bailey knows something, she makes sure we know right away, too, so there are no surprises," social studies teacher Judith Nahlen commented.

Investment by the school district in upgraded facilities was part of restoring confidence. Superintendent Herenton's battle for funds to upgrade B.T. Washington resulted in construction of a new, light-filled, atrium-style lobby connecting the older wings of the school with two new hallways of classrooms. Finished in 1993, the courtyard atrium became the heart of the school, with a curving staircase to the second floor and open walkways upstairs around the lobby. All the students crossed through it several times during the day, and a teacher or administrator standing in the middle of the lower level had a good view of what was happening on both levels.

The turnaround was accelerated and collaboration enhanced when a new school superintendent for Memphis, Dr. Naomi Geraldine "Gerry" House, was appointed in 1992. House, who later won national awards for her leadership in Memphis, empowered the schools to choose their own improvement model from a set of twelve alternatives that had worked elsewhere. At Washington High, Bailey and a teacher-selected committee chose a model called

ATLAS, implemented in 1994. The educational core of ATLAS involved interdisciplinary projects, often in teams, to reinforce knowledge through real-life applications with concrete achievements. For example, physics students built cars to run to specifications on a wooden track crafted by the carpentry students. Some projects became school-wide in scope, such as one in which students created multimedia presentations based on research into the Memphis sanitation strikes of 1968, using funds from a National Endowment for the Humanities grant, or the student effort to write and produce their own opera, funded by another government grant.

Interdisciplinary teacher teams called study groups began to play a role in running the school. Each team became thoroughly familiar with a single issue, provided recommendations, and sometimes managed the whole planning process. This might sound like business-as-usual for business, but it was revolutionary for a public school, in which teachers traditionally worked in isolation in individual classrooms and had little responsibility for the performance of the school. A team calling itself the Chiefs was responsible for the athletic program. The Warrior group was responsible for building the activity calendar for the entire year, scheduling events such as the National Honor Society induction. The Wired team worked with the school's technology coordinator; Membrane with the guidance department on testing, career, and college activities. Though the school was too poor to have a teachers' lounge for relaxing, there was a work room with tables where teams could meet, and Bailey used faculty meetings for training and development.

Teachers were proud of their collaboration, and they enjoyed thinking about education in a multidisciplinary way. The faculty was close-knit and comfortable helping one another with classroom planning or special activities. To select teachers, Bailey looked for commitment, intelligence, fresh ideas, and, above all, confidence in the students' potential. "You have to want to be here," she said. "You've got to have some energy. And you can't come in here half-thinking 'those *poor* little children, they can't do it.' You can't have that attitude with me! You've got to believe in them." One man interviewing for a position as football coach wanted to start a chess club, to develop thinking skills. Bailey liked his broad interests and faith that inner-city youth could learn.

Sports played a role in confidence. Beginning in 1995 and 1996, respectively, Washington High fielded tennis and golf teams, sports that kids in the neighborhood would not normally play. Because there were no public tennis courts in the immediate area of the school, the school had to pay tennis fees for practices and make a deal with a municipal golf course for access; and because the school couldn't run buses, administrators had to find people willing to drive the students to practices and matches. But Bailey believed the effort built confidence. "You've got to let them know 'you can play tennis, too,'" she said. "'No, there are no courts around here, but you can play.' We want them to do nontraditional things. Our students excel in basketball—they all want to be Michael Jordan. But we need to show them that they can be a Venus or a Serena or a Tiger, too," referring to the champion tennis-player sisters and the golf star.

The new environment at Washington High attracted unexpected teacher talent. Dr. Bruce Walker walked into the office one afternoon to inquire about teaching mathematics at his alma mater after retiring from a twenty-year career at Federal Express and a post in the Memphis State University School of Education. Now in his sixties, he wanted to give back to his own community. He volunteered to work with the freshmen, because he felt he could make the most difference when kids were young and angry and didn't know what to do with themselves, and there was still time to teach them. "You have to get them to focus on their own behavior, not someone else's. You have to show them that their behavior creates problems or creates good things," he said.

Walker helped students change into winners. At one point, he took aside a student troublemaker who had a group of loyal followers and told him, "You take that same savvy you use to be a bully, and put it into school! You're a natural leader." The boy didn't believe him at first, but he started trying a little bit every now and then. By eleventh grade he won the school's Most Improved Student award. "He had a different kind of swagger coming down from the stage after receiving that award," Walker observed. His new demeanor influenced his followers to change. In his senior year that student was voted "Mr. Booker T. Washington High," the school's highest honor.

When technology took off at the school around 1996, faculty recognized that few of the students had computers at home or parents who used them. The school organized workshops in the technology lab for students to help teach their parents. By 2001 the high school was ready for a course and support system for students aspiring to college. They were given extra help with essay writing, test taking, and systems for studying. This was intended as an extra push toward confidence. "You have to grab them by the hand and move them to action," Walker said.

A few modest advantages began to accrue to Washington High as its turnaround proceeded: winning competitive foundation grants, becoming a site for IBM's Reinventing Education project to bring technology to the school, even being singled out by the superintendent's office as a great example of turnaround leadership for a Harvard Business School case (mine). But Washington High was punished for doing a good job. It became known as a "school of last resort," dealing with the kids who couldn't get into one of the new "optional" schools—specialized magnets for higher achievers. Its teacher turnover was high because its good teachers were promoted to other jobs in the district—or they wanted to move to the first resorts, not the last resort. Memphis had a teacher shortage anyway, with salaries well below the national average. When good teachers left, students' rising test scores fell again. But Bailey controlled no incentives to attract teachers other than the collaborative culture of the school; she had no bonuses to offer for test improvements, not even a modest sixty-five dollars per teacher, Continental Airlines–style.

There were so many things that Bailey and her staff at Washington High did not control, including sudden changes in orders from the top. In 2000, Gerry House resigned as superintendent, and her successor reversed her reforms, replacing the schools' choice of their own models with a centralized approach. Bailey scrambled to preserve her collaborative processes for teaching, learning, and school management while addressing the new orders. The city of Memphis decided to rehabilitate the neighborhood, closing three of the four housing projects that sent students to Washington High and thereby putting a closing of the school on the agenda once again, but meanwhile reducing the school's enrollment, which drastically reduced its funding.

All that on top of increasingly cumbersome testing. Tennessee was phasing in three tests for younger students, while older ones still took two previous graduation tests and optional college entrance exams. Schools were graded on all these test results. The 2001 federal "No Child Left Behind Act" imposed harsh sanctions on low-performing schools, using metrics such as attendance, dropout rates, and suspensions as well as test scores, but offered scanty funds, unlike its original intention. The $745 million promised to Memphis had been reduced to $50 million. (It was starting to look like the "Every Urban Child Left Behind Act.") "All those scores are floating out there," a teacher said. "We've got to help so-and-so come up x points on this, and so-and-so on that. Whether or not we teach that subject, we all work together to prepare students for testing."

Despite the success of particular students, despite the great new programs that had been developed over ten years, and despite the positive atmosphere that pervaded the hallways of the school—especially when compared with the pre-turnaround gang fights—average student test scores below the state minimum put Booker T. Washington on the state's list of low-performing schools. Bailey summed up the problem by saying, "There are more ways of assessing kids than tests. Of course, it's kind of strange to say that, because that's the way we *are* assessed—by state tests." But rather than making excuses, the principal stayed true to her own convictions about putting faith in the students. "So we keep working. You've got to keep the morale up—that's what I believe. You don't want people believing your kids can't do it. If we say our kids can learn, then we have to *teach* them like they can learn." Collaboration among teachers and staffs at the school provided energy to continue the turnaround at its darkest moments.

Elsie Bailey and her teachers were frustrated by all the things that kept test scores down, and wondered why they weren't credited or supported for putting in place the foundations for better future performance. Business executives, who can exercise so much more control than a school principal, get just as frustrated in the middle.

Seagate CEO Steve Luczo's lament echoed Bailey's. He wondered why the stock market didn't seem to value Seagate's operational improvements—the new culture of collaboration giving Seagate winners' momentum for the future. He knew that Seagate's industry sector was considered a shrinking commodity market. But he didn't think that was a reason to write off his company, any more than Elsie Bailey thought that anyone should write off the children attending Booker T. Washington High School.

TEAM CHEMISTRY AND CONFIDENCE

Though every sports team, airline, technology company, or public school is unique, their leadership challenges are similar, and so are the facts of life for their turnarounds. Turnaround fact of life number 1: Leaders don't always control everything that contributes to results. Fact of life number 2: There are lags between internal changes and internal or external confidence. Fact of life number 3: Turnarounds can be a very slow and long-term process. But there's also positive fact of life number 4: A structure for collaboration is like an insurance policy for keeping hope alive, as people with confidence in one another reinforce perseverance. Winning coaches cultivate that will to keep going.

Maintaining confidence when the external environment is supportive is easy. Winners' advantages automatically click in and fuel momentum. But to keep nurturing confidence when everything is stacked against you, and to maintain winners' habits of collaboration even in the most challenging times, is difficult and admirable. That is when leadership is put to the test.

Teams that withstand adversity and go on to win are known for their chemistry (and I don't mean the artificial kind). "Chemistry" is what we call it when people bond, when they seem especially attuned to one another, when their mutual trust and respect makes them feel they can rise, together, to confront any challenge—like the confident crews at Continental.

The brain connections behind that chemistry of collaboration may still be a mystery, but the feelings are real, and the results are powerful. Confidence in one another produces the collective will and determination, the shared knowledge of everyone's potential contribution, the generosity and the reciprocity that convert individual effort into joint success.

9

The Third Stone: Inspiring
Initiative and Innovation

O F ALL THE PATHOLOGIES THAT ACCUMULATE IN A LOSING STREAK, ONE OF THE MOST DAMAGING TO INDIVIDUALS, AND EVENTUALLY TO THE PLACES THEY WORK AND LIVE, IS PASSIVITY AND LEARNED helplessness. When people become resigned to their fate, nothing ever changes. Self-direction is supposedly a basic human desire, but under some circumstances it can wither with neglect. People who find themselves in losing situations are more easily fatigued; they also are more often injured or call in sick. When people are surrounded by pessimism—that feeling that they are the victims of uncontrollable forces around them—they drag others down with them, finding the worst in everything, or resisting other people's ideas but offering none of their own. With diminished initiative, innovation disappears, problems go unsolved, opportunities go unseized. The cycle gets harder to break.

To turn around the Anaheim Mighty Ducks for their one big winning season in 2002–2003, general manager Bryan Murray first had to turn around hockey player Steve Rucchin. "He was not a very confident guy," Murray said. "He would hardly look you in the eye, and he bitched about practice. He had been hurt in games for two years. (When you're losing, you can hardly find enough players to play. When you're winning, they're never hurt.) He was reluctant to take chances, to do things that could make him successful. I just pointed out that I thought he was a big, strong, very creative, hard-nosed kind of guy who could get more physically involved. I told him he could be more of a dominant player on his line, to make more demands on his teammates and to show the leadership we thought he had. Then the spending on our practice facility and adding some new players turned it from a real negative situation to one where the guys felt pretty good about themselves, and we started winning. The winning made him believe he could become a leader. He was outstanding over the balance of the year. Now you talk to him and he's upbeat. He's our captain, a very strong leader, and rated as one of the top twenty centers in the National Hockey League."

What if the turnaround challenge is not just one high-potential Steve Rucchin who needs to be moved from lethargy to initiative, but thousands? Then personal pep talks by themselves are not enough, spending on people becomes even more essential, and gigantic extravaganzas might be necessary to show people how to win. That's what showed up in the culture change effort at the British Broadcasting Corporation (BBC). How the BBC approached its own Steve Rucchin Syndrome had as much drama and flair as any program on BBC television. Consider the episode in "BBC, the Mini-Series" in October 2003 that preceded a surprising season finale in January 2004, when the BBC's people took to the streets in a dramatic show of support for their chief, who had just resigned over an editorial and political miscalculation.

REPROGRAMMING THE BBC

Up a long, wide flight of stairs at New Connaught Rooms, a historic building in central London, the ballroom was adorned with klieg lights, multiple television monitors, a movie screen on the stage set, and people packed everywhere, nearly 400 of them, seated at thirty-six round tables heaped high with boxes, puzzles, papers, black sleep masks, one tall magician's hat per table, and keypads for digital polling devices labeled with each person's name. It was October 15, the first day of a two-day conference of the top managers of the BBC, the third such "Leading the Way" event since Greg Dyke had become director-general in 2000 and had started a turnaround of the culture of the world's largest public broadcaster.

Dyke pointed out in his welcoming speech that this was the site where the rules for British football were hammered out about a century ago. Now rules for broadcasting were changing, and the BBC wanted to play the new game to win.

As the day proceeded, a few sacred cows were attacked. In table-based and then open discussion of the impending government review in 2006 of the BBC's funding through a license fee paid by households with television sets, the question was raised about whether a public broadcaster should compete with commercial broadcasters in providing entertainment programming. But entertainment attracted a large audience. What was the role of a public broadcaster in the multimedia, multichannel digital age? Fingers tapped keypads for instant poll responses.

The purpose of other table paraphernalia became clear as the day proceeded. After lunch, a disembodied female voice instructed everyone to put on his or her black eyeshades and listen to a journey in imagination to the year 2012, with suitable time-travel music. Shades off, eyes focused on-screen for a prime-time-quality video dramatization—three alternative scenarios for 2012. In each, a well-known actor playing the director-general awoke on the same day to watch the morning news and then received a personal phone call about the day ahead. In the final variation—presumably the most frightening—he learned that News Corp's BSkyB, a commercial rival, had acquired the remains of the old BBC; the phone summoned him to Rupert Murdoch's office.

If competition didn't shake up the BBC, technology would. Another video featured interviews with edgy young people who swapped television programs over the Internet, with TiVo-users who created their own broadcast schedules, with digital film festival producers, and with a grandmother addicted to interactive role-playing games who said that regular television was not mentally stimulating.

Then the people just viewed on-screen, and others, paraded into the room with great fanfare and applause. One "expert" sat at each table and explained how he or she used emerging technology and where the BBC fit in their lives, or, it turned out, didn't. This was the defecting audience instructing the stodgy broadcaster. At the table where I was a guest, a twenty-something single woman dressed in black recounted how she surfed the Web for programs from any-where in the world. Both the *British* and the *Broadcasting* in the BBC's name were clearly irrelevant to her—dying relics of the past.

This was the conversation that could have shattered confidence. Instead, it was actually the sign of how much confidence had risen in the BBC during the four years of the Dyke era. It took high levels of confidence for BBC leaders to listen to customers tell them, how-ever politely, that they were obsolete and out-of-touch fogies, and then to immediately huddle with a set of teammates from other parts of the organization to generate (in forty-five minutes) three big ideas for innovations that would totally destroy the BBC of today.

That display of energy, enthusiasm, teamwork, respect for one an-other's ideas, and can-do optimism would have been inconceivable in the BBC of the recent past. This confidence would prove neces-sary to help BBC leaders weather an unexpected political storm that had begun to form in the summer and would do considerable dam-age a few months later. But first, a flashback to the BBC's past.

A Royal Charter

After receiving a Royal Charter in 1926 to "educate, entertain, and inform," the BBC took its public mandate so seriously that early radio announcers (called "readers") were required to wear dinner jackets when they spoke on the air. At home, it was nicknamed "the Beeb." Worldwide, it was praised and admired for high quality pro-grams. (And not just high culture. My family was addicted to BBC sitcoms we received on digital cable channel 241 in Boston, which carried BBC America.) High standards combined with the scope of its activities to make it a prestigious place to work. "You can write, make films, produce and report on radio and the Internet, working in many different countries, with huge responsibility and freedom to create output. You can't do that anywhere else," a manager boasted. Polls of graduating university students consistently ranked it as one of the most desirable employers. Each open position attracted hundreds of applicants. "My parents were more excited to hear I had been selected for the BBC than for Cambridge University," a program maker exclaimed.

The BBC was a mammoth organization, employing more than 24,000 people, with thousands more working as independent contractors and program makers. Over 12,000 people produced entertainment, drama, news, sports, children's, and educational programs. The results were syndicated internationally, winning numerous awards and sometimes breaking stories before the print media—such as the BBC's early documentary on AIDS in Africa. BBC News, considered by some to be the company's crown jewel, was praised for impartiality, accuracy, and a global perspective. About 2,000 journalists gathered and analyzed news in thirteen UK newsrooms and about fifty international bureaus. BBC News provided material for six BBC television channels (two traditional and four digital), BBC Radio, BBC interactive, the new media division, and BBC World Service. World Service reached over 150 million people in 43 languages and 121 countries. Unlike the rest of the BBC, it received its funding directly from the UK Foreign Office, as broadcasting news internationally was considered an element of foreign policy.

BBC journalists were known for their aggressive tenacity. Periodically, questions were raised in the print press about whether the BBC was biased; as far as I could see, the only consistent bias was skepticism about establishments, whatever their stripe. BBC journalists routinely pierced curtains of silence to get the real story beneath official pronouncements. Disclosure was not reciprocated. Although the BBC was under constant scrutiny in the United Kingdom as the country's leading broadcaster and as a publicly funded corporation, that very scrutiny made the BBC cautious about letting anyone peek underneath its own veil to see how the company worked.

I had come to know BBC officials through the years, as a consultant as well as an interview subject for a variety of radio and television programs. In the latter half of the 1990s, I gave a seminar on innovation to a few dozen top executives at the invitation of the training department, which was then engaged in a Sysiphian effort to stop the rock of management from crushing the employees beneath. Shortly after, a BBC producer, at Harvard on a Neiman Fellowship, audited my course, and in occasional chats after class, she shared (unsolicited) tales about BBC layoffs, claiming that only the staff's professional pride stood between the BBC and ruin. When she returned to London, she too was laid off.

So when Greg Dyke undertook the mission of converting the BBC's recent losing streak to a winning streak, I flew to London to visit him in his sleek, modern office. Dyke was open and receptive. But I soon learned that it wasn't just the rank and file who had lost their feeling of efficacy under the previous administration. Managers exuded a similar level of concern about risk-taking and disclosure, and seemed nervous about letting me look. Several years of negative conditioning had created a touch of fear, cynicism, learned helplessness, and perhaps some paranoia.

The Beeb and the Boss
The BBC's slip in confidence in the 1990s started with a crisis that at first seemed positively resolved. In 1991, as its Royal Charter was due to expire, the BBC was threatened with extinction. Earlier, under Prime Minister Margaret Thatcher, nearly every other public enterprise had been privatized, including British Airways and British Telecom. Conservative Party governments attacked the BBC for being bloated, inefficient, and out of touch. In 1992, John Birt was appointed director-general. His background as an electrical engineer helped him drive efficiencies to make the BBC more accountable. Birt's focus on management process helped him negotiate a new Charter and license-fee settlement that ensured the BBC's

continued existence as a public entity with secure funding through 2006. Longtime BBC financial executive John Smith credited Birt with the BBC's survival: "The BBC had been perceived as left-wing, out of control, profligate. The place was medieval in management discipline. We needed to focus on efficiencies."

Birt saved the BBC, but his top-down methods—reengineering, outsourcing, and other anti-people management buzzwords of the 1990s implemented by armies of highly paid consultants—undermined internal confidence and threatened a cycle of decline. People felt they came last. "Instead of being referred to by name, we were referred to by our titles, and frequently just the initials of our titles. It was very militaristic," an executive recalled.

One big sticking point was a reorganization that gave new powers to "channel commissioners" (the people who decided what went on the air on each BBC radio or TV channel) to buy shows from program makers (producers), in essence controlling BBC producers' budgets and forcing them to compete with independent external producers. This "market" generated large savings, but some felt it brought complexity and delays, took focus away from creativity and audiences, and pitted people against one another, especially since more than half of new program ideas were rejected. Then, when a whole division, BBC Resources, was outsourced seemingly overnight, more than 8,000 members of the BBC found themselves no longer part of it. "This was very debilitating. The organization became afraid, lost its ability to take risks, some lost their sense of loyalty. We also lost a huge amount of production talent. It wasn't a rewarding place to work," a manager said.

The grandeur and glamour of the organization's mission contrasted with the frustrations of bureaucracy and the shabbiness of some work environments. Many people felt undervalued and under attack. A pecking order put "high culture" activities such as drama and major news at the top and London in the center. "People who stayed more than five years in local broadcasting were thought defective because otherwise they would have moved to London," a manager reported. The BBC radio division felt it didn't get the same respect as TV. "In the midlands, BBC Radio workers pay five pounds apiece for the Christmas party. Television thinks nothing of spending £120,000 on a launch party at the zoo for a TV program on animals," a Radio executive complained, using an example of a disparity that lasted even well into the Dyke era. BBC Sport felt like a poor relation, unable to afford quality coverage as costs skyrocketed for marquee sporting events. Without broadcast rights to the Ryder Cup or Formula One racing, ratings for sports programs declined, making it that much more difficult to persuade channel controllers to put sports in their schedules, which reduced sports funding. Caught in a vicious cycle like this, Sport staff could easily lower their aspirations and stop trying.

Fees to consulting firms grew to an estimated £20 million a year, while people who put programs on the air felt starved for resources. Extensive use of consultants reinforced another doom loop, sending a message that internal people were not capable, which reinforced passive resistance to top management directives, which induced them to hire more consultants to ram their directives through. The mentality of scarcity in the program ranks led to dynamics akin to that of impoverished communities or Third World countries: hoping that other divisions didn't do well, because that might jeopardize one's own budget, or hoarding funds rather than committing them to new ventures, which further reduced initiative and creativity. "The BBC had a pie problem. They couldn't grow the pie, so people could only get more if they stole from others," an executive observed.

Feeling helpless within the organization, employees aired grievances in the external press. About 70 percent of BBC employees revealed on a survey that they expected to hear internal news from the outside press before they heard it from their managers. The BBC was typically the subject of nearly 1,800 articles a year, an average of five per day. Disaffected employees knew that they could find a sympathetic ear in the print media, since many newspapers were owned by BBC competitors, and their articles carried an anti-BBC editorial slant. External attacks succeeded often enough to reinforce this tactic. When the former controller of Radio 4 wanted to split *Today,* a popular two-hour interview show, into shorter segments bracketing other programs, outraged producers took their battle to the newspapers and won.

Staff valiantly maintained pockets of excellence while pathologies of losing streaks accumulated: growing autocracy at the top; internal rivalries and infighting; a culture of anger and blame; and feelings of cynicism or resignation, a belief that no one could do anything to change the system. The BBC was still powerful and was still churning out good programs, but many people felt that was happening despite the organization. The proof was in declining results.

By 1999 the BBC was losing to commercial competitors. Ratings were declining, especially in the growing number of households with multichannel digital systems; with hundreds and hundreds of digital channels, mass audiences were a thing of the past. The BBC was "arrogant, aloof, self-indulgent, and out of touch with the audience," bemoaned an insider. In spite of impressive reach—at least one of the BBC's TV channels was viewed in 93 percent of UK households—the BBC found it increasingly difficult to satisfy diverse audiences. The BBC was criticized for focusing on the population around London, even though about 6,200 people worked in Scotland, Wales, Northern Ireland, and the English regions. The creation of independent parliaments in Scotland, Wales, and Northern Ireland made it clear that people there felt little in common with London.

Nearly 90 percent of the BBC's funding came from an annual license fee of about £100 collected by the government from individual households. In most households the Beeb was a fixture, a member of the family. But support for the license fee was jeopardized by shrinking audiences. Politicians were not the only ones to ask the dangerous question about the BBC's future: Why should the public pay for programming that fewer and fewer watched?

Confidence was draining from the organization, at every level. Was the BBC losing its winner's advantages? The external network of loyal fans, media, and public officials was shrinking. Had the BBC overemphasized a narrow kind of technocratic accountability and lost collaboration and initiative? Employees were sinking into losers' behavior. The emotional climate was increasingly negative.

The BBC needed a cultural turnaround. It was up to a new leader to shift the cycle.

FROM MANAGERIAL CONTROL TO INSPIRATIONAL LEADERSHIP

In November 1999, Greg Dyke was appointed deputy director-general and heir apparent. "I thought the governors would not appoint him. He is too aggressive, too dangerous. When they did, I said this would be a very interesting place," said an executive who later joined the BBC.

Originally a journalist, and most recently the CEO of Pearson Television from 1995 to 1999, Dyke had grown Pearson into the world's largest independent production company. He had sterling credentials. But he was immediately attacked from the right for his Labor Party ties (how could he be impartial, with Tony Blair's Labor Party in power and Dyke a "Tony's crony"?) and from the left for his for-profit experience (how could he lead *public* broadcasting?). "There were times early on when my mom would call me crying because she had read something about me in the press," he recalled.

Dyke initially had little to do in London, so he left to tour local radio, television, and production facilities. This was a startling departure from the top-down, London-centric style of former BBC executives. Previous chief executives had rarely, if ever, visited the Beeb's grassroots.

Already there were signs that he would shift the emotional climate of the Beeb. Dyke was a natural optimist with infectious enthusiasm who believed in people. His confident manner made a big impression on Pat Loughrey, then the controller (general manager) for Northern Ireland: "When I collected him in the car, I saw immediately he was serious about the BBC. He could have retired,

gone to the House of Lords. But he was full of enthusiasm and exuded commitment—even though the press was giving him hell."

Dyke took the reins as director-general on January 29, 2000. Two
days later he made his first inspirational announcement in an internal television broadcast to the whole organization. He promised
to support those who created and delivered the BBC's products, indicating that the BBC would spend at least £100 million more on
programming and related services in the coming year, directed at
becoming audience-focused and winning the competition for audience loyalty. He set a five-year goal of reducing overhead from 24
percent of income to 15 percent, to free an additional £200 million
a year for programs while meeting the government's savings target.

To eliminate infighting at budget time, Dyke set budgets for five
years and locked them in. To encourage managers to take responsibility, he reduced spending on consultants by a factor of forty—
from £20 million pounds a year to £500,000. To increase audience
responsiveness, he increased funding for local radio by £15 million
pounds, arresting a decades-long decline. He authorized an upgrade in facilities for local production and broadcasting units,
which were housed in dingy buildings outside of center cities—
facilities that looked about as appealing as dentists' offices, as an
executive put it. Moving to newer quarters in city centers would en-
able more contact with audience members who could come inside
the BBC to converse with staff.

In April 2000 he announced a reorganization under the name
"One BBC." This was a clever play on words; BBC1 was the company's flagship television channel. It was also a signal that everyone
would be involved as collaborators for change. The One BBC reorganization empowered those responsible for the BBC's creative
core by removing a layer of the organization that had stood between them and top management. Suddenly nine out of eighteen
members of the executive committee (familiarly known as the
ExCo) represented broadcasters and show producers, more than
double their previous proportion. The organization was simplified
from 190 to 40 business units, which reduced bureaucratic clutter.

For Sport and other divisions, program commissioning and program making, which had been separated in the previous era, were rejoined.

Peter Salmon, director of BBC Sport, described Dyke's One BBC speech as "like *Das Kapital*—the start of a movement."

Power to the People: Permission to "Cut the Crap and Make It Happen"

Dyke's early actions began to rebuild confidence. His messages and his demeanor consistently reinforced his belief and trust in people. He put his money where his mouth was. Shifting resources from control functions to the groups that were out on the playing field connecting with BBC audiences, and increasing their representation on the ExCo, made the message real. "Instead of Managing by Rhetoric, he got the organization right behind him by asking how the organization gets in the way and how can we help," an executive said. Dyke enhanced people's self-confidence by first enhancing self-worth—showing people that they were worthy of investment by investing in them. I was reminded of the tagline on L'Oréal cosmetic commercials: "Because you're worth it."

By style and temperament, and like the best coaches, Dyke showed people they were valued and made himself accessible. "Greg cares about people. He establishes a connection and makes time for people. He touches them on the shoulder and arm, a contrast from the behavior of most standoffish Brits," declared Pat Loughrey, who was Irish. Loughrey was one of the players newly empowered to sit on the ExCo. Dyke had moved Loughrey from Belfast to London, promoting him to the head of "Nations and Regions," the division responsible for local broadcast. It would have been impossible to awaken initiative throughout the BBC without that emotional connection.

Dyke favored open and direct communication. In addition to broadcasts to the whole of the BBC, he was known for personal e-mails to individual employees. The BBC's finance director noted, "He writes the messages himself, to everyone, from the heart, telling the truth, telling people what he wants them to do, and communicating instantaneously."

Restoring organizational confidence started at the top. Top management had to unlearn defensiveness and become an active set of collaborators. Before they could give others the permission to innovate, they had to feel it themselves.

One BBC needed one united team at the top. Dyke wanted the ExCo to meet more frequently but also more informally, and without the turf-protecting politicking of the past. He added playful team-building events away from the office, and changed the agenda in the office. Reducing the divisions' formal reporting requirements—for example, condensing BBC News's status updates from six three-inch binders to a compact ten pages—freed time for big issues that concerned everyone. Discussion of themes that cut across divisions helped executives discover areas in which they could combine forces to tackle new initiatives.

The tone of ExCo meetings changed dramatically. "In the past, managers would lobby the director-general privately, so you would go into a meeting and not know where you stood," John Smith explained. "With Greg, if you have any issue, it needs to be put on the table. Meetings are more chatty, less formal, more sociable. We have away days. We do fun team-building events. We see each other socially." Roger Flynn, head of BBC Ventures, called the give-and-take "passionate," saying that "Greg encourages people to express their views, challenge each other. There is freedom of speech. Is it perfect? No. Is it engaging? Yes, absolutely."

The idea that fun could be a part of the job of managing something as sacred as the BBC was vintage Dyke. He was consistently positive and upbeat, sparkling with energy. He didn't want to focus on why things could not be done, he wanted to people to find what they could do and get on with it.

One ExCo meeting was particularly revealing. A trivial matter was on the table: how to put the One BBC message in front of everyone every day. Dyke wanted to put up some posters on the wall. He was told by a member of the executive committee that "they won't allow that." Dyke said, "Wait a moment—who won't allow it? We *are* them." There was a moment of stunned silence as the implications sunk in—that powerlessness had infected even the top, that they had allowed themselves to act like helpless victims of other people's decisions, when it was in their hands all along. "We had to break out of this infantilizing past," recalled Jane Root, head of BBC2. "It took Greg to show us that we were in charge, that we could change things if we liked."

To drive this idea home in a dramatic and memorable way, Dyke created yellow cards, resembling those used by referees to signal penalties in soccer matches, labeled CUT THE CRAP: MAKE IT HAPPEN. Dyke held up the cards when he heard ideas getting trampled. (Such an irreverent move on the part of the director-general made news in the *Financial Times* and elsewhere.) He encouraged employees to write him for their own supply of "Cut the Crap" cards, so they too could avoid paralysis and be decisive. The cards became a symbol for shifting from losers' passivity to winners' initiative.

With renewed confidence in one another, ExCo members hatched ideas for collaborative projects. They took the message back to their own organizations that initiative was now valued, ideas of all kinds welcomed. They encouraged employees to step forward with ideas, and they gave permission for risks. Dyke had begun with a vision—an audience-focused "One BBC" alive with creativity—but the vision would not truly be shared, or believed, until people themselves tested its possibilities and its limits.

Many employee concerns revolved around physical facilities, which was not surprising, since the condition of their workplace was in their face every day, and felt like a reflection of their value to the organization. Tangible changes in facilities could be accomplished easily and represented "small wins" that made people feel they could seek bigger wins. One early employee suggestion was to reopen the interior courtyard at White City, one of the BBC's largest television production centers. The courtyard had been closed for ten years owing to ill-defined safety concerns. It turned out that all it took to make it usable was installation of a ramp and a second door. Ten years of helplessness were eliminated in a few days' work. "We said, 'Just make it happen!'" Dyke recalled. "We threw an opening party. It was a symbolic moment."

There were numerous examples of innovation in programs, the issue most important to the BBC's audiences:

- *Departures from tradition.* A successful Scottish soap opera was produced locally rather than in London (the source of most programs in the past). Instead of waiting for people to come to BBC offices, BBC buses took learning resources to small, scattered communities.
- *Innovations through collaboration.* Interactive features appeared on the BBC website through combined efforts of the News, Sport, Drama, and Children's Program divisions, guided by the New Media division. The BBC was considered a leader in interactivity because it was incorporated into every department.
- *Fast, decisive actions.* Nightly TV news was moved to a new 10:00 p.m. time slot that reversed a multi-year decline in viewership. It took "cut the crap, make it happen" guidance to overcome fears of retaliation from commercial TV because of noncompetition agreements under the BBC's charter. In the past, new schedules could take up to two years, because of the implications for other programs. This time, after Dyke gave his go-ahead to "just do it," the schedule shuffle took two weeks.
- *Surprising successes.* In a big early win, a new trainee used funds intended for a training video to create a ten-minute pilot for a comedy about life in a dead-end, white-collar job. Soon in production, *The Office* quickly became the UK's top-rated comedy series, compared by critics to the BBC's most popular comedy in history, *Fawlty Towers*, with actor John Cleese.

Dyke boasted that these types of success "give people the confidence to see they can make a difference." Innovation blossomed.

By November of 2001, just over eighteen months since its announcement, One BBC had generated tangible results. The Beeb had reduced overhead from 24 percent to 17 percent of revenues (ahead of schedule), and £270 million had been channeled into new broadcast programs. Ratings were up for both BBC1 and BBC2, and polls of the BBC's acceptance by the public were improving. Audience satisfaction with the BBC overall increased from 6 on a 10-point scale, just before Dyke came, to 6.8. Radio reached record audiences. In July, ratings for flagship station BBC1 surpassed those of its prime competitor, ITV, for the first time in many years. "One BBC freed the organization," Roger Flynn said. "It was a catalyst to spin out more ideas and opportunities."

Improvisation: Taking Initiative to the Next Level

A pivotal moment in the BBC's turnaround was toward the end of the second day of the ExCo's quarterly off-site meeting on November 14, 2001, at the Stokes Park Club in London. The traditional British stuffiness of the meeting room—dark hardwood walls, large old paintings, and ornate medieval tapestries—reminded Greg Dyke of the attitudes he was trying to change at the BBC. The question was whether the BBC needed to do more to shape a new culture. Dyke sat back and listened as the discussion proceeded.

Most of the objectives for One BBC had been met, there was no immediate crisis that compelled further change, and leaders could pat themselves on the back for the success of their teamwork. But self-congratulations were premature. Most of the change had taken place at the top and was directed top-down. ExCo members felt empowered, but employees still felt disenfranchised. On a recent survey, employees rated management efforts to communicate with them at four-year highs, placing the BBC in the top ten companies reviewed by the external research firm, but only 28 percent of employees felt that there was a trusting atmosphere within the organization, only 27 percent reported that teams in different parts of the BBC collaborated, only 25 percent of respondents felt that different parts of the BBC communicated well, and only 22 percent of employees reported feeling valued. These were dreadful numbers.

"The BBC is powerful and successful in the marketplace, but people are still quite miserable," Jane Root observed. Michael Stevenson, director of the Factual and Learning division, said, "People have noticed that the ExCo is working together much more collaboratively, but they haven't seen the change happen at their own level."

The ExCo devoted a portion of the meeting to a trip report from three of its members who had just visited U.S. companies with innovative cultures: Cisco Systems, Southwest Airlines, SRI, The Container Store, Ritz Carlton, and IDEO. It was not just a trip, it was like a religious conversion. "We felt they were a bit naive," recalled Jenny Abramsky, director for Radio and Music. "However, it was clear that they had 'seen the light.' They convinced us that we should be more ambitious."

"Greg is cunning and astute," another executive commented. "He wasn't going to go forward until the whole ExCo was there. People came aboard at different rates and speeds." Ultimately, the ExCo committed to go forward without knowing exactly where "forward" was. This was improvisational theater, not a scripted program. It was an act of courage. How would they explain the benefits of a fuzzy idea like "culture" to a skeptical public that carefully scrutinized BBC expenditures, let alone to those inside the BBC who were cynical about management fads?

One certainty: no consultants. Susan Spindler, a respected senior program maker who understood BBC politics, was appointed project leader (though many people thought she was crazy to do it), working with human resources director Stephen Dando. Spindler and a small team identified seven themes characterizing areas where lasting change would make a real and positive difference: *Just Do It. Inspire Creativity Everywhere. Connecting with All Audiences. Valuing People. We are the BBC. Great Spaces. Lead More, Manage Less.* The ExCo chose leaders for each theme, who would report to an ExCo sponsor, and appointed divisional leaders who would be responsible for implementation in their division, on top of their regular job. Because these were highly visible assignments, and the atmosphere at the BBC was still so political, some well-qualified people felt passed over, arousing jealousy and even a little paranoia about the process.

Dyke introduced Spindler and made the case for change at his third annual broadcast on February 7, 2002. He described the program (now dubbed "One BBC: Making It Happen") as an effort to make the BBC "the world's most creative organization." He exhorted BBC people to "Imagine. Imagine how good the BBC could be for the people who work here, for all of us, but also for the services we provide, if actually we could use all the creative endeavor that's here and not stop it with the bureaucracy that we've got. . . . Just imagine how good it could be. . . . In short, how do we cut the crap and just make it happen?"

A manager recalled, "Greg told them, 'You have a voice, and everyone will participate.' At the time, he had no idea what that meant."

Toward "The World's Most Creative Organization"

In May 2002 the top 350 managers—nearly ten times the number John Birt convened for leadership pep talks when I had come to the BBC in the 1990s—gathered for an unprecedented conference. Many had never met one another, and they were hungry for contact. They sat at round tables of ten, listened to speeches, discussed issues, and reported to the whole group. "Crap cutting" took place on the spot.

One junior manager confessed to her table that she was out-of-pocket about £3,000 for a project, because of archaic reimbursement rules. She was encouraged to speak up in the large group. After hearing her problem, her boss jumped up to declare that he would write her a personal check immediately. BBC finance director John Smith intervened, saying that not only would he provide the check, but he would change the policy. The next day the BBC introduced a cash advance system to allow people to self-authorize £100 of expenses.

Later, the "instant checkbook" idea took hold as a way to support innovation. Andy Davies, the Making It Happen (MIH) representative for BBC Ventures, created a checkbook for the group. In brainstorming sessions, if someone said "If only we did x," Davies would ask how much to make this happen? If the person would take on the responsibility, he would write a check on the spot for up to £500.

Discretionary MIH budgets funded other quick wins. At BBC Wales, the controller made £100,000 available to pay for projects suggested by staff, who then voted for their top seven ideas. About 70 percent of 900 staff voted; installation of bilingual ATM machines was a winner. BBC Radio Northampton used £3,000 to convert a storage room into a staff lounge; ten employees surprised their manager by spending the weekend redoing the space themselves. In the spirit of OneBBC, the first-ever BBC-wide orientation program for new hires was pilot-tested, to show people the whole of the organization before they scattered to the parts.

Throughout the BBC, including in foreign locations, "Just Imagine" workshops were convened for forty to 300 people per session, led by a cadre of 200 facilitators. Over about six months an amazing total of 10,000 people attended the workshops. Their tone was unremittingly positive. The workshops used "appreciative inquiry" techniques to "unlock the energy from positive shared experiences in the past to create a vision of an ideal organization," leaders said. Employees were invited to recall the times when they had been most successful in the BBC. Getting into sensitive areas of feelings in the workplace was risky for a skeptical organization; to the project team's relief, the sessions proved popular.

After workshop data were sorted into topics, divisional MIH teams reconvened Just Imagine participants for a one-day session called "Making Sense," to turn their ideas into recommendations for action in their divisions. The BBC Television group included a flowery bit of verse with their recommendations for the "Valuing People" theme:

Let a thousand ideas blossom
Let a thousand talents emerge
Let a thousand mistakes be made
Let a thousand lessons be learned
Let a thousand voices be heard
Let a thousand stories be told
Let a thousand eyes be opened
One BBC—More than a thousand success stories

Saying they wanted to support all lifestyles, reward motivated people, trust people to do well, meet the audience, and encourage risk-taking, they suggested actions such as flextime, public thanks to employees, and granting everyone one week a year to develop a bold idea of value to the BBC.

Though all these possibilities hadn't yet materialized, 2,100 ideas had been submitted through the Making It Happen website by November 2002, a year after the ExCo decided to go forward, with 700 implemented—an employee discount on digital television boxes for use at home, tea bars or libraries in the office, awards ceremonies and parties. An electronic version of Greg Dyke's infamous "Cut the Crap" card went on the company intranet, with encouragement to use the cards to submit suggestions. Dyke and Spindler personally responded to many of them.

"He opens up ideas, he expands opportunity, instead of keeping innovation in a small community," a colleague said about Dyke's leadership. "People are getting comfortable with taking a bold step."

As steps got bolder, wins got bigger. Speed increased. In Northern Ireland, the length of time required for show proposals to be commissioned for production was reduced from eighteen months to three and a half. Quality increased. Collaboration between BBC News, radio and TV channels, and BBC Interactive helped Sport dramatically improve its soccer World Cup coverage, by producing documentaries about heroes behind the World Cup.

BBC Technology created a first-ever high-definition television broadcast of the England-Brazil match for BBC staff.

Internally at least, confidence was growing.

GRIZZLIES, CANARIES, AND SACRED COWS: THE ZOO OF CHANGE

"It's like dancing with a grizzly bear. You can't stop when you want to, you have to keep dancing," an executive said about Making It Happen.

Susan Spindler had a different image. "In the old coal mines, the miners used to send a canary in a cage to the limits of the excavation to test for explosive gas. If the canary died from the fumes, they knew they had to get back. Sometimes I wonder if I am Greg's canary," she mused.

She would soon be handing over project leadership to Katharine Everett, but meanwhile she worried constantly. She worried that the proportion of BBC employees who believed the program would change the BBC for good still hovered around 40 percent or fewer. She worried that too many of the changes were superficial, even cosmetic; people would soon adjust to prettier workplaces, and such changes would lose their motivational power. She worried about justifying the huge program expenditures and investment of 20–50 percent of the ExCo's time. One employee had stormed into an executive's office and exclaimed, "People are being made redundant, and some cretin comes in and wants to know what color to paint the walls to make us more creative!" Press coverage treated Making It Happen derisively, sometimes characterizing it as a waste of taxpayer money, spent to fund luxuries and treats. Spindler worried about reaching the whole organization. Middle managers had low attendance at Just Imagine sessions, yet this set of 2,000 managers, which included politically astute veterans of earlier eras who protected the BBC's sacred cows of tradition, could sabotage new top-management initiatives.

It was time to move from initial push to momentum building, from artificial program to routine practice, from special event to daily expectation embedded in both formal policies and leaders' daily behaviors. A second top managers' conference featured a new set of One BBC values; Making It Happen theme leaders rolled out plans for changes in policies and practices in their divisions. The Big Conversation involved 17,000 people in an interactive session; hundreds attended live in London, others by webcast. But the heart of the effort shifted from fun workshops and sporadic volunteer activities to systemic change. New policies for flexible work arrangements, family leave, and other employee benefits were announced. Training programs were developed to increase leadership skills throughout the management ranks. Managers below the ExCo went on the road to visit exemplary companies; three of them had visited Continental Airlines headquarters in Houston two days before I was there.

The BBC was on track, but the tests of renewed confidence were still ahead. At the October 2003 leadership conference at the New Connaught Rooms, video testimonials about Making It Happen reflected rising internal confidence—all with the flavor of "once I was cynical, now I believe." That evening, over drinks at the Salvador Dali Museum (a fitting venue for an organization starting to tilt at windmills as it rode to the frontiers of creativity), a few longtime BBC executives told me not to exaggerate the contrast with the old days, that it was not so bad before Dyke came and not so perfect after. The BBC was never exactly losing, they said, and there were always pockets of excellence in terms of the stars on the field, even though many people on the bench and in the locker room had been miserable before the Dyke era. Still, the BBC had been running down, and now it was heading up—at least in terms of employee confidence as well as indicators of viewer and public approval.

Attacking the Wrong Sacred Cow

Although internal confidence had risen dramatically, external confidence was shaken by a dramatic chain of events in which sacred cows and grizzly bears became more than charming metaphors—they were extremely dangerous beasts. These events started with a

BBC News report that gored the most powerful sacred cow in the nation.

On May 29, 2003, BBC reporter Andrew Gilligan included in his early morning broadcast an allegation that Prime Minister Tony Blair's government had "sexed up" intelligence reports about weapons of mass destruction in Iraq. The government protested, and investigations were mounted of nearly everyone on all sides of the story. Greg Dyke and Gavyn Davies, chairman of the BBC board of governors, were quick to stand by the journalist and his story, even when it was later revealed that Gilligan had exaggerated the nature of his evidence. British government scientist David Kelly was exposed as the source for Gilligan's story, and in mid-July, Kelly was found dead in the woods near his country house, an apparent suicide.

Within hours of identification of Kelly's body, the government announced that Lord Brian Hutton, a senior judge, would oversee an independent judicial inquiry, with the BBC broadcast as a centerpiece. Inside the BBC, there was considerable soul-searching and self-criticism, moves to revise editorial guidelines, and the appointment in December of Mark Byford as deputy director-general with a mandate to revise the handling of complaints. But Dyke was slow to investigate, and although Gavyn Davies acknowledged mistakes, no full apology was issued. On January 22, 2004, the BBC program *Panorama* broadcast a 90-minute investigative report on the Kelly affair that was not seen in advance by Greg Dyke, to ensure independence.

It was too little, too late. The Hutton Report was issued on Wednesday, January 28. It exonerated the Blair government of any embellishment of intelligence about WMD in Iraq, but it was devastating in its critique of BBC governance, management, and editorial processes. Many found it one-sided in giving the benefit of the doubt to everyone in government and none to the BBC. Yet even Dyke's biggest supporters felt that he could have exercised stronger editorial control—that he should have investigated Gilligan's story immediately and apologized more quickly once inaccuracies were uncovered.

A small group of BBC executives read the report together, and the whole executive committee gathered to watch television coverage. BBC chairman Davies resigned almost immediately. Then, at the Board of Governors' meeting on January 29, Dyke tendered his resignation, and it was accepted. At 1:38 p.m., Dyke sent an email to all staff, calling it the hardest he had ever written: He acknowledged that the BBC made errors of judgment, and that his leaving was necessary "to draw a line under this whole affair." He said he did not want to go and would miss everyone "hugely" but hoped that the fundamental changes to make the BBC more human "will last beyond me."

Later that afternoon, an estimated 3,000 people mobbed the streets outside BBC studios throughout the UK in an unprecedented display of support for a chief executive. They were crying openly, carrying signs ("Cut the Crap, Bring Greg Back") or shouting their desire for Dyke to return. Dyke went out to talk to the demonstrators outside his office. "He was leaderly through it all," Pat Loughrey told me. Loughrey had stayed by Dyke's side into the evening, until he left the building for the last time.

The Confidence to Carry On

The next day, two of the BBC's most senior executives, Peter Horrocks, head of Current Affairs, and John Willis, head of Factual and Learning, chaired a meeting of hundreds of executives, where people could share their dismay and grief at Dyke's departure while committing to continue his signature programs, Leading the Way and Making It Happen. Following the meeting, Horrocks sent an e-mail to staff inviting them to sign an ad celebrating Dyke's leadership and the BBC's independence. Thousands of names of people (who had dipped into their own pockets to pay five pounds apiece for the ad) appeared in tiny type in a full page of the *Daily Telegraph* on Saturday, January 31. "We are diminished by Greg's departure," the text read, "but we are determined to maintain his achievements and his vision for an independent organization that serves the public above all else."

BBC staff were not the only ones with strong feelings. In opinion polls, a strong majority of the British public said that they respected the BBC to tell the truth; more than twice as many as said they trusted the government to tell the truth. Demonstrators outside the Prime Minister's residence burned the Hutton Report, some carrying signs reading BLIAR. Rumors and accusations flew in all directions—for example, that BBC enemies or political connivers hoping to land the top BBC jobs were behind the "Hutton whitewash." An editorial in the *Guardian* proposed that "this was a fight to the death between the government and the BBC, and no one currently or recently in Downing Street was going to rest until the [BBC] had been decapitated." A post-Hutton inquiry was announced, this one headed by Lord Burton and this time aimed at government intelligence about Iraqi weapons of mass destruction.

"It was a gut-wrenching week," one senior leader at the BBC told me. "We are all still in shock," another said. Although BBC executives were aware that Dyke had not planned to stay at the helm that much longer anyway, they were not expecting to lose him so suddenly. Now they pledged to rise to the challenge of becoming even more forceful advocates for spreading his culture of confidence. "We are determined to build on all of our Making It Happen achievements. Fortunately we had already built strong ownership across the team," Human Resources director Stephen Dando e-mailed me. "We will undoubtedly now learn a great deal about how to sustain culture change following the departure of such a charismatic and inspirational leader."

On February 2, the Monday after Dyke's resignation, Mark Byford, now acting director-general, sent an all-staff email at 3:38 p.m.: "All of us, every member of the BBC, now need to play a part to help lead the BBC through this period. Let's all recognise WE are the BBC. The Hutton Report has been published. We made some mistakes. We have accepted that we are going to learn from them. . . .

So much of what we have achieved in the BBC today has come from Making It Happen. I can tell you that the 2003 staff survey shows that two-thirds of you are now behind the changes. That's fantastic. Let me be clear, the momentum of Making It Happen is unstoppable and we must all ensure during this period we do not take the foot off the accelerator. . . . [We must] do what we do best—making great programmes and delivering great services for all our audience—our ambition remains: to be the most creative organisation in the world."

As a demonstration of success at achieving that Dyke ambition, the BBC had just received more nominations in more categories than any other organization for the Royal Television Society journalism awards.

Events in the final months of the Dyke era are a reminder that people and teams cannot look merely inward for the confidence to win, they must also seek external confidence from all of their audiences, especially from their grizzly-bear-sized stakeholders protective of the sacred cows. They must always be held accountable. The entire flap was about only one inaccuracy, not a series of them, but the nature of the allegation was significant, as it impugned the integrity of the prime minister. Then a single journalistic mistake was followed by political and managerial miscalculations.

Although Dyke did not exercise good editorial judgment, a supporter indicated that he did act on one of the BBC's new core values: trust in people. Perhaps Dyke's successful emphasis on two of the three cornerstones of confidence that had been lost in the previous era—initiative and collaboration—blinded him to the need for the third cornerstone—accountability—to produce a firm foundation for external as well as internal confidence. Without accountability to set boundaries, initiative can sometimes wander into danger zones.

Clearly, Dyke's four years inspired a team ready and eager to take initiative to innovate and to win. The confidence I saw in the New Connaught Rooms in October 2003 was activated in February 2004 to make other leaders rise to the challenge of not letting one big fumble interrupt a winning streak nor eliminate the culture that had produced it. As one top leader put it, "The changes Greg Dyke set in place are already owned by the leadership group of the organization, and it's my view that this tragedy will burn them into the DNA of the entire BBC."

The test of a culture of confidence is whether it is possible for everyone to take initiative, for everyone to be trusted to perform when the pressure is on, even the people on the bench. That was the real change Dyke brought to the BBC.

GETTING INTO THE RHYTHM

To shift behavior from losing to winning modes, turnaround leaders change the context. They teach people to see the world differently because they give them new opportunities and experiences; it's like handing them a kaleidoscope that they can shake to shift the pattern. Then, to overcome inertia, they move organizational and environmental impediments out of the way. Resources must be shifted to support small wins that build confidence and then join with other wins to produce major victories. All the messages surrounding people must reinforce their initiative, from the unified way that top leaders support them to the symbols and signals in the organization. At the BBC, the internal changes began with new behavior on the part of the team at the top, and then they helped model and spread the culture.

The rhythm of culture change at the BBC started with symbols and messages (inspiring speeches, personal touches, "Cut the Crap" cards). Next the top team worked on changing their own behavior, so they could model and spread a new culture. Then formal programs both broadened and deepened the change—a broad swath through the organization with 10,000 people in brainstorming sessions, accompanied by funding of in-depth demonstration projects (small, quick wins) that showed concretely what change could mean. That's almost a textbook formula for how to turn around a culture. The final challenge—and the one that solidifies success—is to build so much momentum that change is unstoppable, that everything reinforces the new behavior, that even the resistors get on board—exactly the momentum that develops in winning streaks. That's the virtuous cycle of initiative and performance: Effort increases, problems are solved, receptivity to change increases, and innovations surface—so winning is easier, and winning reinforces initiative.

The BBC is a company with creativity at its core and a long tradition of excellence. But people can be stifled even in nominally "creative" settings, and people can be creative and innovate even in places where creativity is not the essence of the task. No one would confuse an engineering services and industrial supply company like Invensys for a BBC, where creativity is at the heart of success. Yet Rick Haythornthwaite's message was that all 53,000 employees were now *expected* to show initiative. "The days of autocracy are over. You have it do it yourself," Haythornthwaite told them. Invensys mounted a culture-change program as ambitious, though not as colorful, as the BBC's Making It Happen. The company used thirty-three master facilitators to train a thousand team leaders to seek and find improvement projects, supported by a set of project management tools and a Web-based tracking system.

The same principles work even in places where it seems as though "power to the people" is totally impossible. The tactics might change, but the principles hold.

ACHTUNG!: CHANGING THE IMAGE FROM LOSER TO WINNER

The scene in Hanover, Germany, in late November 1994, had the spirit and style of a football rally. The leader strode around the room in shirtsleeves, speaking in English without notes or a podium, pointing to the game plan on the screen. Nearly 400 young men, and a few women, shouted enthusiastically, "We will make it happen!"

That this was a German company, Siemens-Nixdorf Informations-Systems AG, would have startled most Europeans, especially a decade ago. I was constantly being told by Europeans that

American-style cheerleading and pep rallies would not work in their countries. But that was exactly the spirit CEO Gerhard Schulmeyer wanted to inspire. Schulmeyer had recently come from European engineering giant Asea Brown Boveri (ABB) to lead a turnaround.

Siemens-Nixdorf, formed from a merger in 1990, was then Europe's largest information technology company, with 39,000 people who had never quite come together, as giant Siemens overwhelmed tiny, entrepreneurial Nixdorf. Since the merger, Siemens-Nixdorf had been on a steady losing streak that was getting worse. Among its problems: The company had been slow to shift from mainframes to personal computers; over 65 percent of its sales were only in Germany; and it barely had a presence in high-growth areas such as Asia and North America.

Schulmeyer undertook classic restructuring to stem losses. About 4,300 jobs were cut in a year, and soon twenty-eight businesses were divested, ten new ones added. With a new strategy in mind, the company reorganized into twelve global lines of business and 250 business units, which also reduced several layers of management. But Schulmeyer was convinced that the radical change necessary to turn Siemens-Nixdorf around could only occur if there was an even more radical change in corporate culture to shift behavior from the slow-moving, hierarchical, and excessively formal style of the past, in which people followed their bosses' orders rather than taking initiative. Schulmeyer sought innovation.

It was one thing to theorize about a new kind of behavior, but quite another to get anyone to embrace it emotionally and believe they could do it. To boost confidence, Schulmeyer needed some big demonstrations, fast. That's why he decided on a very new approach: Identify and empower young talent with ideas. Pick people who were still fresh enough that their enthusiasm and optimism had not yet been conditioned out of them. Get them out from under the thumbs of oppressive middle managers. Give them a visible assignment and let them show everyone else what is possible. And in the process, build confidence outside the company by signaling to potential recruits that there is room and reward for initiative at Siemens-Nixdorf.

The 400 potential revolutionaries who gathered for the first of four big conferences in Hanover were picked because they had submitted innovative ideas, not because they were the most senior—not German-business-as-usual. Schulmeyer's informality was another form of permission to test limits. Small groups discussed sixty action ideas under nineteen themes. Some were abstract, such as "learning from successes and mistakes—quickly"; others were more concrete, such as "stopping the brain drain." Under the theme "changing Siemens-Nixdorf's image from loser to winner" was the suggestion to give employees a discount on the company's personal computers so they could develop pride in their own products.

As the conference ended, Schulmeyer sprung a surprise. Attendees could apply for twenty-one special assignments as officially designated "change agents." Change agents would spend thirteen weeks in the United States in a well-funded and interesting educational program, returning to lead significant projects that could make a difference to the business. The catch: Applications were due the next day. Schulmeyer wanted only decisive risk-takers. This program was designed to find and reward initiative.

Andreas Meyer Knonow was among the 100 applicants. Married just five weeks earlier, he had yet to take a honeymoon. Now he would have to defer it. He volunteered because his year as an exchange student in the United States, where he'd earned a high school diploma, had left a profound impression on him, and he felt that the American entrepreneurial spirit should infuse Siemens-Nixdorf. He had joined the company as an apprentice, in the German tradition, eventually becoming a sales manager.

The eighteen men and three women in their early thirties selected as change agents became known as *Schulmeyers Kinder* (Schulmeyer's children). The label hinted at some of the threat their very selection posed to older managers who had enjoyed the privileges of rank and deference to elders. Thirteen weeks of intense education and tours of Silicon Valley in California and the high-tech corridor in Massachusetts built not only skills but also bonds among the group that helped them persevere in the trials ahead. I met them in Boston and found their energy infectious, though I wondered if their hopes were too high.

The change agents identified a big project each would tackle on their return, with the sponsorship of a member of the executive committee. Projects had to involve their peers, so that the change agents would share their learning and inspire peers to take initiative. In Ulrike von Manteuffel's case, peer support proved essential. Upon her return to Germany, she received a warm welcome home from her colleagues. Then she discovered that a major activity vital to her assignment had been killed in her absence. This not only threatened to derail the bigger effort, but demoralized the whole staff. A co-worker, emboldened by what he heard from von Manteuffel about Schulmeyer's support for initiative, decided to write a letter to Schulmeyer protesting the loss, gathering 100 signatures for a petition. Schulmeyer intervened, and the project was back on track.

The change agents' projects were complex and required cross-functional cooperation, which meant that they had to blaze new trails across barriers (and span oceans). Meyer Knonow's project involved better targeting of the North American market, involving complex negotiations with the Toronto office, a small group that felt threatened by the larger U.S. offices. Andy Chew, who was British, took on the task of reducing the time to market for midrange computers.

These projects combined with the general restructuring to convert Siemens-Nixdorf from loser to winner. At the end of the next fiscal year the company made its first profit ever. The abundant personal time and money Schulmeyer had lavished on the change agents had made his point—that initiative was a cornerstone of winning. He had shown his confidence in people by investing in the change agents even while cutting other expenses. In turn, their achievements helped restore confidence in the company.

Now the effort could be replicated at lower cost. The change-agent program was shortened in duration and expanded to encompass many more people, while the pep rallies—known as Hanovers II, III, and IV—reached still more people. "Results Fairs," to show off projects and possibilities, were held in Munich, Paderborn, Brussels, and Augsburg at six- or eight-month intervals.

Over the next few years, productivity and earnings improved dramatically. The company attracted strong, talented recruits. About 43 percent of the original workforce (16,900 people) left the company (not always willingly), and there were 12,400 new hires. Communication increased; the number of e-mail/intranet users jumped from 600 to 25,000. Ratings on employee satisfaction surveys doubled. Siemens-Nixdorf's image score on a public survey went from number ninety-four among German companies to number twenty-three.

Schulmeyer and his team had a range of winning businesses and could take the next steps to position them for future growth. SNI's Services and Solutions business became the core of Siemens Business Services. Siemens Fujitsu Computers was formed as a joint venture with the Japanese giant to take the now-growing and profitable PC business to international markets. The retail and banking systems unit was sold to Kohlberg, Kravis & Roberts and Goldman Sachs to become the highly profitable Wincor Nixdorf. And both Schulmeyer and his *Kinder* received winners' opportunities. Schulmeyer was named president of Siemens-USA, and the young change agents moved quickly up the Siemens corporate ladder. Everyone enjoyed an aura of success.

EMPOWERING INNOVATION

Much later, when I started my study of sports streaks, I thought that maybe the first Hanover conference was a football rally after all. I learned that Coach Carl Franks was using similar principles to turn around Duke University's football team after a particularly long losing streak: finding the natural leaders (Franks created a small leadership council of change agents, to help show their eighty-plus peers what initiative meant); appealing to their hearts as well as their heads, to their innate desire to succeed, and expecting them to encourage others; assigning senior mentors to help novices learn their way through the system; listening to their ideas (it was a just a first step, but the team took the initiative to get involved in decisions about new uniforms).

In a small team playing a simple, bounded, repetitive game, leaders do not have to worry about all the organizational layers and complex, shifting tasks of a giant corporation. In complex situations, leaders must make choices about where to start, whether top-down (more BBC–like) or middle-up (in Siemens-Nixdorf fashion), and whether to begin with a broad call for initiative (Greg Dyke's method) or with a focused set of projects (Gerhard Schulmeyer's choice). The decision rests on judgments about where there is the greatest receptivity, readiness, and prospect for success—and how much risk leaders want to take. In large organizations, initiative depends not just on culture but on formal mechanisms to make creativity, enterprise, and innovation a permanent practice: budgets and seed funds, channels for soliciting and endorsing proposals, methods for reporting and communicating results.

Lessons about reinforcing the third cornerstone of confidence resonate across levels. Leaders energize depressed people, passive teams, or sluggish organizations when they act on four guiding principles:

1. Believe in people and their power to make a difference. Show them they are worth it by investing in things that matter to them.
2. Direct the energy tied up in negativity (resentment, rivalry, or disrespect) into positive actions. If people seem petty, make them more noble by focusing them on a bigger cause and giving them a chance to contribute to it.
3. Make initiative possible and desirable. Awaken enterprise by opening real opportunities to contribute new ideas. Seek them, fund them, praise them, and provide a support system.

4. Start with small wins—things that people can control. Let them taste victory, and further victory will be in their sights.

These principles, commonsensible as they are, are accompanied by deeper paradoxes. The paradoxes of empowerment will be familiar not only to coaches of teams and leaders of organizations, but also to every parent who has tried to urge a child to show greater initiative.

The goal is self-direction, so that initiative emanates from the person herself (that's what makes it initiative, and not simply following orders), but someone in authority first gives permission. This can make empowerment seem like manipulation—like getting someone else to do what the adult or the boss wants him to do, while pretending he is being put in control. Susan Spindler at the BBC and Rick Haythornthwaite were both concerned about how it sounded when I talked about the actions they had taken to get people to think for themselves. Wouldn't that mean people weren't thinking for themselves? If action stops with permission, if it is too dependent on the parent or coach or friend or executive sponsor or CEO saying, "You can," then the cycle has not really shifted.

The goal is to generate significant success, but initiative often has to start with small, even superficial actions—those small wins that sometimes have big symbolic value, although they might otherwise not appear to make much difference. But small wins can too often look like cosmetic change, doing easy things while glossing over bigger issues. BBC skeptics said that too many people were encouraged to paint walls (or don black eyeshades before watching groovy videos about the future), while the rest of the organization had to run the business of putting dozens of programs on the air every hour. If people become content with small wins, they might not go for the bigger ones.

When the cycle finally shifts from losers' passivity to winners' initiative, these paradoxes are easier to resolve. As players stretch to meet greater demands, as people come to know what to do before being told what to do, as they improvise in response to new challenges, the balance of power can tilt naturally and subtly from leaders to players. Geno Auriemma, head coach of the Connecticut Huskies, remembered a game during his team's long winning streak in which the team was struggling with its defense against a tough opponent. "But it seemed like whenever we needed something to happen, somebody did it," he said. "There was this wonderful understanding that we needed something to happen, so somebody would act, without even having said anything."

That is the ultimate sign of confidence: a virtually self-organizing system in which people feel empowered to seize initiative, to solve problems, and to seed innovations without even being told to do it. They just do it.

10

A Culture of Confidence: Leading a Nation from Despair to Hope

THE EUPHORIC SPORTS FANS IN AN OVERFLOWING STADIUM CHEER-ING LOUDLY FOR THEIR TEAM IN WORLD COMPETITION WERE ALSO CHEERING PASSIONATELY FOR THEIR COUNTRY. THAT GAME REPRE-sented one more milestone in the ultimate feat of turnaround leadership: shifting an entire nation from the negativity of decline to the confidence to win.

The country was South Africa, the stadium was in Johannesburg, the game was the 1995 Rugby World Cup against New Zealand, and the most significant moment for the country occurred not during the game but just after it, when President Nelson Mandela walked onto the field.

In 1995 South Africa's rugby team, known as the Springboks, triumphed in their reentry into world sports by winning the Rugby World Cup against New Zealand. The victory was a dream for South African rugby fans. The Springboks had been regarded as pariahs by the world, because of previous segregation of sports in South Africa. To millions of black South Africans, rugby was a symbol of white arrogance and the recently ended apartheid state that had oppressed them for many decades. The Springboks in 1995 were still dominated by white Afrikaners, except for one player whom the old regime would have designated as "colored." Rumor had it that a cabinet minister of the African National Congress (ANC), now the majority party representing the aspirations of black South Africans, cheered when New Zealand scored against the

Springboks. But perhaps it was fortuitous that the Springboks would win, because the whole country was now beginning to embrace a winners' culture.

President Mandela, leader of the ANC, had taken office just over a year earlier, in May 1994, as the country's first democratically elected president. When he arrived on the field on that sunny Saturday in June to hand the trophy to François Pienaar, the captain of the Springboks, the crowd was astonished. Mandela was sporting a green and gold Springboks jersey. Seeing the black president, once a revolutionary opposing the Afrikaner-led regime, wearing their colors brought tears to the eyes of many Afrikaners, as a young white Afrikaner leader who was there that day said later, when I was getting to know her. The crowded stadium, mainly Afrikaner, euphorically chanted Mandela's name and his affectionate nickname, "Madiba." Later, when South Africa's soccer team won a victory in the Africa Nations Cup (Africa's premier soccer event), my young Afrikaner friend found herself dancing down the street in celebration with black South Africans. Mandela's support of the rugby team stimulated her desire to honor the sport that most black South Africans engaged in.

Such personal gestures by Mandela were known as "Madiba magic"—his ability to seize a moment to bring people together and spread hope against difficult odds.

A LONG MARCH

Earlier in this book, I distinguished between bold strokes that a leader can accomplish by a decision at the top and the long march of getting many people to adopt new habits. Changing the behavior of many millions of people and shifting the emotional and the investment climate surrounding a nation involve a very long march. It might take a season or two to turn around a team, a year or two to set an airline or a technology business or a media company on the road to winning, still longer to untangle political complexities to turn around a public school or a health-care system. But the culture of a country? That is a long march indeed.

Yet, across levels, many of the human and social dynamics reflect the same principles. The cultures of oppressive regimes and failed states show striking similarities to the destructive dynamics of decline in troubled businesses, schools, or teams. Like the apartheid regime in South Africa, they are characterized by suppression of information, "tribal" rivalries and antagonisms, isolation and self-protection, passivity and helplessness. A negative climate produces low expectations but also envy toward those in better circumstances. Institutions for accountability, collaboration, and initiative are absent or weak. Misallocated or squandered resources, low productivity, and declining external investment combine to produce financial as well as political crises.

Turnaround leaders of societies in decline must begin the long march with new messages of optimism and hope, new behavior at the top, new investment that shows confidence in people, and new institutions that create more open communication and accountability. They must set the stage for collaboration across social divides and empower people to take initiative to improve their life circumstances.

If anyone should know about long marches with long time horizons, it is Nelson Mandela; he titled his autobiography *A Long Walk to Freedom*. Born in 1918 in a tribal village in the Eastern Cape and educated as a lawyer, Mandela joined the African National Congress (ANC), the movement for black rights, beginning a long struggle against apartheid, the system that fostered separation of the races in South Africa. In 1944, with close friends Oliver Tambo and Walter Sisulu, Mandela formed the ANC Youth League (ANCYL), becoming its president in 1950. In 1953, banned by the apartheid regime from speaking in public for two years, he was forced to officially resign from the ANC. He concentrated on the law practice he had started with Tambo—the first black law firm in South Africa.

After the two-year ban ended, Mandela resumed his public role opposing apartheid. The state's relentless crackdown on the ANC, including widespread arrests, killing of demonstrators, and ban-ning of meetings, eventually led Mandela to conclude that the ANC's policy of nonviolence was not working. He formed and led Umkhonto we Sizwe (MK), or "Spear of the Nation," to move the struggle from peaceful resistance to armed reaction. Operating underground, on the run from the police, Mandela was eventually captured and sentenced to life imprisonment on Robben Island off the coast of Cape Town in 1964. Despite imprisonment, he continued to exercise leadership and helped turn the prison into what became known as the "University," because of the education Mandela provided young activists as they passed through on shorter sentences.

By the late 1980s, South Africa faced a changed post-cold-war global environment and a faltering domestic economy. The apartheid regime became a pariah around the world, with international pressure and sanctions exacerbating the economic slump—a losing streak writ large. Responding to international pressure, F. W. de Klerk, then head of the apartheid government, was ready to free Mandela—after twenty-seven years in prison. To many in South Africa, and to conservatives outside the country, however, Mandela was still a revolutionary. In 1987, British prime minister Margaret Thatcher called the ANC "a typical terrorist organization," adding, "Anyone who thinks it is going to run the government in South Africa is living in cloud-cuckoo land."

Mandela negotiated the timing of his release on his own terms: following the unbanning of the ANC and other anti-apartheid organizations on February 11, 1990. After he left custody, Mandela quoted his well-known statement from the trial that resulted in his confinement almost twenty-seven years earlier: "I have fought against white domination and I have fought against black domination. I have cherished the idea of a democratic and free society in which all persons live together in harmony and with equal opportunities." Opposition leaders echoed this hope. Pik Botha, long-standing Minister of Foreign Affairs under apartheid, drew an interesting analogy to describe the country's condition: "We [South Africans] are like the zebra. It does not matter whether you put the bullet through the white stripe or the black stripe. If you hit the animal, it will die." Three weeks later, on March 2, 1990, Mandela was elected deputy president of the ANC's National Executive Committee.

I met Nelson Mandela in Davos, Switzerland, at the 1992 World Economic Forum. His pitch for foreign capital was one of many that national political leaders made to the business leaders assembled in Davos: *Invest in my country.* Mandela's was different in one respect: He asked the audience to wait for a year or two, until South Africa had a chance to overhaul its entire political structure. Clearly, regime change would be peaceful and smooth if it could be predicted with such confidence by a former imprisoned revolutionary now wearing the mantle of respectable opposition party leader, speaking in front of some of the world's most influential business leaders. And change indeed proved to be peaceful.

Prior to South Africa's first-ever democratic elections in 1994, Mandela led the ANC in multiparty negotiations that created an interim constitution ratified by participants. The ANC was victorious in the 1994 elections, and Mandela was inaugurated in May as the country's first democratically elected president. Doubters were converted everywhere. That year, Thatcher's successor as British prime minister, John Major, made it official that the revolutionary was now a statesman. After visiting South Africa, he remarked that he had spoken to a parliament freely elected by all South Africans, which was "a tribute to the statesmanship and the vision of Nelson Mandela."

I followed subsequent events from a distance but never found reason to go to South Africa; it had not been on my list of destinations during apartheid. The country returned to mind in September 2000, in Istanbul, Turkey, at a conference at which I met Christophe Kopke, the head of Daimler-Chrysler South Africa. Kopke told an inspiring story about his return to the country of his birth in 1989 and how he'd built bridges to a hostile, unproductive black workforce by engaging them in their dream of building a Mercedes for Mandela—a major step in a successful organizational turnaround that eventually made his factories "on the southern tip of Africa," as he put it, a production site for world export. I was intrigued by the unusual way national leadership influenced business performance—it had everything to do with culture and psychology, and nothing to do with taxes or monetary policy.

Then, in March of 2001, the implications of Nelson Mandela's leadership entered my life in a more direct and personal way. Former president Mandela asked former U.S. president Bill Clinton to speak at a conference on civil society. President Clinton, in turn, invited a delegation from City Year, his model for Americorps, the national service program he'd initiated, to accompany him. As a member of City Year's national board of trustees, I was urged to go on the April trip, but my primary responsibility to my classes at Harvard Business School meant that I could contribute to visions for South Africa only from the American side of the Atlantic. Mandela encouraged City Year to play a role in "doing for South Africa what you have done for America" by creating a youth corps and national service movement.

Less than a year later, I had a chance to test the Mandela legacy when I did a lecture tour in Johannesburg, Pretoria, and Cape Town as the guest of CSIR, South Africa's leading science and technology research council, and made a series of visits to poor black townships in Soweto (Kliptown) and Alexandra with City Year colleagues establishing a program in South Africa. I was impressed by the world-class ideas and technology at CSIR, which has customers for its satellite tracking services in high-tech California—and that CSIR is playing a major role in economic development, not just in basic science and technology. Its new CEO was a black South African with a PhD in math and physics from Cambridge University in England, a clear demonstration of the latent talent that post-apartheid South Africa had tapped.

I spoke to audiences of thousands of people, interviewed executives and community activists, visited companies such as Old Mutual (insurance) and SABC (the BBC of South Africa), had e-mail dialogues stimulated by an appearance on national television's largest morning show, and came to know young leaders of all races. I left convinced that "Madiba"—as absolutely everyone called Nelson Mandela—was one of the greatest leaders of our era, a true "water walker" who seemed to cross even turbulent waters without needing much support, but who then set in place numerous stones for the people who followed.

In the summers of 2002 and 2003, several multiracial groups of young leaders of the new South Africa came to the United States as "Clinton Democracy Fellows" under City Year auspices, to learn about citizen service and democracy. They gathered in my living room for meals and seminars, together with South Africans studying at Harvard, including my chief collaborator and tireless researcher, Euvin Naidoo.

The story of Mandela's presidency takes the challenge of turnarounds to a higher level, one that can offer hope for turning around other countries that need to be lifted out of decline and despair to renewed confidence. It also holds lessons for leaders in countries that have long been winners, but are in danger of letting losers' habits take hold.

SOUTH AFRICA, 1994: REVERSING A CYCLE OF DECLINE

South Africa had always been rich in natural resources—in addition to gold and diamonds, it produced more than one-third of Africa's goods and services and nearly 40 percent of Africa's manufacturing output with only about 7 percent of the continent's population and 4 percent of its total land area. But it had been torn by centuries of racial conflict. Despite the official ending of apartheid, its legacy remained. Apartheid—literally "apartness"—had been established in 1948 by Afrikaner nationalists with the goal of securing white supremacy and ensuring Afrikaner control of political power. Under apartheid, South Africa was divided into ersatz Bantu nations, or "locations"—Africans-only settlements for a rural labor force working in gold and diamond mines. Ostensibly established as communities within which "nonwhites" could achieve economic and political autonomy, in fact Bantu nations were a pretense for restricting the movement and autonomy of the black African labor force.

South Africa's first five years as a fledgling democracy were inextricably linked to Mandela's larger-than-life persona. Mandela had to walk a tightrope between addressing the pain and suffering that millions had experienced under decades of brutally enforced segregation, while fostering a spirit of reconciliation aimed at moving the country forward. South Africa's black majority, having finally achieved civil rights after years of struggle, was impatient for economic advancement and the associated delivery of services. But many whites were now living in great fear as to how the past was going to be dealt with and what their future in the new South Africa would be.

Mandela's task was to shift the cycle of decline that had characterized South Africa, despite its impressive natural resources and "first world" enclaves of wealth and prosperity in the cities. Significant challenges stemmed from the legacy of apartheid, including economic inequality, suppression of information, and suspicion and anger of racial groups toward one another. A 1994 report by ANC and government economists detailed the extreme poverty of at least 17 million South Africans who lived below internationally acceptable base standards, including 12 million citizens who lacked access to clean drinking water, 4.6 million adults who were illiterate, 4.3 million families without adequate housing, and a majority of schools without electricity.

Perhaps even more daunting was that the losing streak was manifested in people's attitudes and beliefs as much as in their economic circumstances. Mandela had to change behavior and move the culture of South Africa from denial and secrecy to dialogue and open communication, from anger and blame to respect and accountability, from isolation and turf protection to connection and collaboration, and from helplessness and hopelessness to initiative and enterprise. He had to restore confidence even before he could show results.

All levels of confidence were depressed. Investor confidence had eroded, and although the events leading up to Mandela's election had ended international economic sanctions against South Africa (which were intended to protest apartheid), there was the risk that continuing political tensions (including the threat of retaliation against the white population by an enraged and now politically enfranchised black majority) could create economic and social instability. Within South Africa, many people lacked confidence in leaders. Past decisions had largely stemmed from a tightly controlled regime that operated behind closed doors with a small group of cronies holding the power. The media had been tightly regulated, limiting the public's access to information. Various groups lacked confidence in one another, especially groups identified by race. After all, they had been forcibly isolated from one another, and fear and hostilities remained. Many people at the bottom of the economic scale lacked confidence in their ability to improve their circumstances, especially those living at a subsistence level in settlements with no electricity or running water, let alone schoolbooks and computer access.

Mandela had only five years to shift the cycle—that is, until the next election. He had announced that he would serve only one term—a remarkable gesture not only in Africa, a continent known for corrupt leaders who refuse to cede power, but also remarkable for someone who had waited so long and given so much to reach this position of power.

In a mere five years Mandela could not transform everything. But he could start programs and create institutions that would shift other people's behavior toward a more productive path; and he could serve as a role model, conveying messages through his personal actions and his words about what kind of behavior, what kind of culture, would characterize democratic South Africa. And that is exactly what he did.

ENDING DENIAL, OPENING DIALOGUE

Under apartheid, a vast array of legislation had restricted the flow of information. For example, the government exercised control over the media through the South African Press Council, which fined editors for defying state regulations, such as covering banned political rallies. In the 1980s, reporters were not allowed to report on banned people or organizations, which barred Nelson Mandela's words from ever appearing in any official South African newspaper. While the thought of Mandela was in the hearts of millions, a new generation had neither seen Mandela's writings in official print nor heard his full name spoken aloud in public. The story was told about a young boy who, when asked on the day of Mandela's release whom he was waiting to see, replied, "Free Mandela." This slogan had appeared in the press, on posters, on T-shirts, and on walls so often during the months leading up to Mandela's release that the young boy believed this to be Mandela's full name.

Many of the laws that restricted the flow of information had already been removed soon after Mandela was released from prison. In 1993 the public selection of a new twenty-five-member board for the South African Broadcasting Corporation (SABC), the country's public broadcaster, helped emphasize the move toward transparency within the media. Although nineteen of the twenty-five members of the SABC board were believed to be either members or supporters of the ANC, leading to complaints of a possible new bias, the public still viewed the board as legitimate and reflective of the new South Africa. The SABC increased programs in indigenous languages (e.g., Xhosa and Zulu), to reflect the diversity of South Africa.

Despite some progress, Mandela criticized the press establishment for not changing quickly enough to reflect the makeup of South Africa's population. He was dismayed by what he perceived to be a lack of change, and was vocal in his criticism of a predominantly white-owned media industry. Even when South Africa's leading black businessmen, members of a new generation of black tycoons, Nthato Motlana and Cyril Ramaphosa, gained control of the Times Media Limited (TML) group, owner of the widely read *Sunday Times*, Mandela was not entirely satisfied. He wanted more than just cosmetic change, more than just a few faces of a different color.

Mandela was deeply committed to a free press and access to information by all South Africans. "It was the press that never forgot us," he said upon his release from prison. As president, Mandela continued to champion freedom of the press, which he saw as part and parcel of the liberation of the minds of South Africans: "I don't want a mouthpiece of the ANC or government. . . . The press would be totally useless then. I want a mirror through which we can see ourselves," he said in 1996.

A freer press was just one way to open dialogue. The electoral process for the first democratic election was designed to ensure widespread input. In April 1994, voters could vote for nineteen political parties, highlighting the country's various constituencies (voting was for parties rather than for individual candidates). Voters could cast two votes, one for national representation and another for either the same or a different party at a provincial level. This split system addressed the demand by minority parties during the negotiations leading up to the elections for local voices to be loudly heard despite a strong central government. Of the estimated 21.7 million voters, 16 million had never voted before. Despite an electorate that needed large-scale voter education in a short space of time, 19,726,579 ballots were counted, with only 193,081 rejections. Independent observers from the European Union, the United Nations, and the British Commonwealth declared that the elections were free and fair, and that the outcome of the elections reflected the will of the people of South Africa.

Beyond voting, the public was given a direct voice in other significant issues. For Mandela to govern a democratic South Africa, a new constitution was needed, and the public was encouraged to participate in discussions about its content. This action was virtually unprecedented for any country in the twentieth century, let alone one that had just been characterized by separation of the races and restrictions on information flow. Mandela's desire for input from as many voices as possible hearkened back to the days when the Freedom Charter for a democratic South Africa was being put together by the ANC in 1954. That process involved many meetings and planning sessions with organizations representing all races and many types of civic institutions, including large conferences of people at the grass roots.

The first phase of public dialogue about the constitution began at the end of 1994. Advertisements were placed in numerous major newspapers with the slogan, "You've made your mark [a reference to having voted], now have your say." People could call a talk-line set up specifically to gather responses, submit written statements, or speak at countrywide town hall meetings. A "face to face" outreach program worked toward accessing communities in remote areas, especially areas with low literacy rates and limited print and electronic media. In total, nearly 1.7 million submissions were received.

After integrating the public submissions, over 4 million copies of the draft constitution, accompanied by explanatory material, were distributed. The constitution was regarded as one of the most progressive in the world. Discrimination in terms of race, gender, sexual orientation, religion, culture, or language was outlawed. Protection of freedom of religion, movement, expression, and artistic creativity was enshrined. Torture, slavery, detention without trial, forced labor, servitude, and cruel punishment were outlawed.

The process that led to the creation of the constitution was not perfect. Submissions from the public tended to be mainly from well-educated, middle-class South Africans (including activists, politicians, and academics). Critics questioned whether submissions were representative of public opinion at large, especially in a country with such class and race disparity. In addition, in the late stages of negotiations among political parties on the final content of the constitution, many meetings were not open to the public, leading to accusations of compromises and last-minute deals. Despite these concerns, surveys revealed that the majority of South Africans from all walks of life felt involved in the process, and that a quarter of all adults had discussed the Constitutional Assembly and related issues with friends or family members. The government had imparted a sense of transparency as well as ownership by the people, and in the process had won the hearts and minds of South Africans and made major strides toward restoring confidence at all levels.

RESPECT AND ACCOUNTABILITY

Even before he became president, Mandela used his skill as a communicator to try to heal the country. On April 10, 1993, a year before Mandela's election, Chris Hani was shot dead in the driveway of his home in Boksburg, a town near Johannesburg. Hani was viewed by many as the most popular leader in South Africa after Mandela, especially among black youth. An Afrikaner woman wrote down the license number of the assassin's getaway car and reported it to police. They soon captured the perpetrator, a Polish immigrant. The National Party, still officially in power, feared that all whites would be blamed, and that widespread violence would erupt, paralyzing the country.

Upon hearing the news, Mandela flew to SABC television studios in Johannesburg to broadcast a message—one that some recalled as the speech that saved South Africa from chaos. Aware that factions wanted to stall the democratic election, Mandela addressed an emotional country in a calm, deliberate manner: "A white man full of prejudice and hate came to our country and committed a deed so foul that our whole nation now teeters on the brink of disaster. A white woman, of Afrikaner origin, risked her life so that we may know, and bring to justice this assassin." These words were aired repeatedly. Mandela had provided crucial direction to South Africans on how to react to the tragic loss of Hani in a way that would not undermine the very thing Hani had also fought for—liberation and democratic elections.

Mandela conveyed a sense of respect for each person as well as an expectation for individual accountability, and the people rose to the occasion. Although minor outbursts of rioting did break out, and whites expressed plans to leave the country, the storm never arrived. Two years later, recalling that tense time, Mandela said that the political maturity of his nation had disproved the predictors of doom.

Mandela was effective in that situation and others because he was able to use the power of the media to spread his message—and use it as the mirror of accountability that would help people face uncomfortable facts. John Battersby, a South African journalist and political editor of the Independent Group, told us why the press was mesmerized by Mandela: "For somebody who'd been jailed for twenty-seven years, he came out with an extraordinary understanding of the media. He speaks from the heart. He has a direct connection."

When he became president, Mandela knew that before he could move the country forward as a new South Africa, he would have to reverse the victim culture of anger and blame that stemmed from the legacy of the past. By 1994, when he took office, apartheid was widely acknowledged internationally as a "crime against humanity," per a United Nations resolution. The South African government needed to ensure accountability—that people must take responsibility for their own actions and confess their mistakes, without provoking acts of revenge and hatred that would tear the country apart.

Mandela's administration shepherded a controversial program of accountability without rancor, in the form of the Truth and Reconciliation Commission (TRC). The new minister of justice, Dullah Omar, described the TRC as fostering "the need for understanding, not vengeance; the need for reparation, not retaliation; and the need for *ubuntu* [humanity], not victimization." Parliament passed the Promotion of National Unity and Reconciliation Act in 1995, and later that year, President Mandela appointed 17 TRC commissioners, with Nobel Peace Prize Laureate Archbishop Desmond Tutu as chair. The TRC was asked to examine acts committed only between March 1960, the time of the Sharpeville Massacre, and May 10, 1994, the day of Mandela's inauguration.

The commission began its first sitting in April 1996, and was open to the public. South Africans, whether they were victims or perpetrators, were provided with a forum where emotions could be freely expressed. Rather than pursuing a formal Nuremberg Trial–like approach, the TRC encouraged an atmosphere of openness, aimed at getting participants to reveal all details, no matter how gruesome. This structure permitted details of past atrocities to emerge, including accounts that might have been denied or obfuscated in a trial-like atmosphere. When South Africa and the world tuned in to hear the sessions, the horrific stories of torture, murder, and assassination were worse than most had imagined.

The work of the commission had critics from all sides. Members of the apartheid regime, such as former apartheid defense minister Magnus Malan, declined to apply for amnesty. P. W. Botha, prime minister of apartheid South Africa for most of the 1980s, denounced the TRC process. Many family members of victims criticized the process, feeling it was too lenient on perpetrators. Joe Slovo, an ANC member whose wife, Ruth First, had been killed by a letter bomb, said bitterly, "Now I know that my wife's killers will go free." The process also revealed deeds committed by the ANC that were viewed as human rights violations. In response, Mandela did not play double standards. He accepted the findings and agreed, without any objections, that the ANC had also committed its share of violations. At the end of the process, more than 21,000 people delivered testimonies, either in person or in writing. Many were stories from parents, siblings, and friends of those who had disappeared. After two and a half years of hearings across the country, a 3,500-page report was released on October 29, 1998.

Mandela reemphasized his support of the TRC findings to all South Africans: "We must regard the healing of the South African Nation as a process, not an event. . . . [The TRC] helped us move away from the past to concentrate on the present and the future."

Whatever critics said about the TRC, Nelson Mandela had begun a process of accountability, forgiveness, and reconciliation. Graca Machel (widow of the late Mozambican leader Samora Machel), who married Mandela in 1998, commented to his authorized biographer, Anthony Sampson, "[Nelson Mandela] symbolizes a much broader forgiveness . . . and reaching out. If he had come out of prison and sent a different message . . . this country [South Africa] could be up in flames. . . . The way he addressed the people from the beginning, sending the message of what he thought was the best way to save lives in this country, to bring reconciliation. . . . Some people criticize that he went too far. There is no such thing as going too far if you are trying to save this country from this kind of tragedy."

CONNECTIONS AND COLLABORATION

The message that all races should work together for the good of the whole nation started at the top and was embodied in Mandela's choice of colleagues. Indeed, Mandela demonstrated this belief soon after his release from prison. On May 2, 1990, Mandela met President de Klerk at de Klerk's residence near Cape Town, each accompanied by an eleven-person delegation. While de Klerk brought an all-male, all-Afrikaner team, Mandela's group included two whites, one Indian, one colored, and seven Africans, with two women among them. Later, the structure of the Mandela government also signaled inclusiveness and collaboration across political parties. Of the nineteen parties participating in the first democratic election, seven won seats in the National Assembly. The executive branch had members not only from the winning ANC, but also from the opposition National Party (NP) and Inkatha Freedom Party (IFP), both of which became a part of the Government of National Unity (GNU).

Mandela's personal history and style favored inclusiveness and collaboration. He frequently acknowledged and highlighted the efforts of those around him, including his close allies Walter Sisulu and Oliver Tambo. When Tambo stepped down as president of the ANC, Mandela praised him for a democratic spirit and tolerance that "in the end outwitted the racists in this country." Mandela was known to be an active listener who paid special attention "to those that did not push themselves forward," that is, to the people at the back of the room who were quiet. A biographer noted that Mandela was "enormously patient, and part of that comes from his upbringing as a boy and seeing how the chief listened to what everyone had to say."

Beginning at a press conference soon after his release, and continuing throughout his presidency, Mandela emphasized that "whites are fellow South Africans and we want them to feel safe and to know that we appreciate the contribution that they have made towards the development of this country." He urged whites to stay in South Africa and pointed out that they, too, were a part of the nation. He told a crowd in the shantytown of Khayalitsha, "Those that do not know how useful whites are know nothing about their own country." He delivered speeches in Afrikaans, highlighting his commitment to reach out to all groups.

Mandela realized the influence his actions would have on helping to build bridges between white and black communities that had been artificially separated for decades. In a series of small yet symbolic acts, he met with the widows and loved ones of both white and black leaders who had been bitter enemies during the apartheid years. In 1995 he had tea with the widow of Hendrik Verwoerd, who had been prime minister of South Africa from 1959 to 1966 and an active supporter of apartheid. Mrs. Verwoerd, ninety-four years old, pleaded with Mandela to let the Afrikaners form an independent state, or *Volkstat*, so that they could practice their cultural beliefs in peace. Always a good listener, Mandela patiently sipped his tea. On the flight back home, a companion commented that the Afrikaners would never accept a new South Africa, but Mandela had faith in the process of change that had already begun. He insisted, "They'll come right in the end."

Racial integration of schools proved difficult, capturing a great deal of media attention. Some white schools in conservative areas of South Africa resisted opening their doors to black children, citing "cultural differences" and the right of communities to pursue their own "cultural interests." In the midst of this conflict that often saw parents verbally and even physically engaging one another, Mandela pushed for a spirit of collaboration. A young South African leader, one of City Year's Clinton Democracy Fellows, recalled that Mandela's personal actions helped persuade people to reconcile their differences. Mandela took time from state affairs to personally visit the families of a black student and a white student who had been involved in a school stabbing that was allegedly racially motivated. His actions, highlighting the importance of seeking racial harmony, influenced children who would make up the first generation of South Africans not to grow up under legislated segregation; some of those children were among the new generation of leaders I met who were shaping a multi-racial nation.

OPPORTUNITY AND ENTERPRISE

Mandela understood that a strong economy involved active initiative to build new enterprises and upgrade community infrastructure, including initiative at the grass roots. At the opening of the South African Parliament in February 1996, he issued a call to action: "We can neither heal nor build with the victims of past injustices merely forgiving and the beneficiaries merely content in gratitude."

Soon after his release, Mandela and the ANC leadership spoke to many white business leaders, such as Harry Oppenheimer, to discuss black economic empowerment. In these conversations, Mandela was keenly aware of the impact his words could have on the reaction of big business and foreign investors, whose investment in South Africa he courted through personal visits and phone calls. Yet he knew discussion alone would not be sufficient; he also had to create programs that would open economic opportunity for more people.

So, in May 1994, Mandela announced a Reconstruction and Development Plan (RDP) that aimed to tackle the issues at the very heart of poverty and economic opportunity, such as health, housing, and education. He reassured international investors and big business that the plan would be financed via cuts and adjustments in the government's existing budget, thus addressing investor confidence. As a symbol of commitment to the process, and setting a personal example of sacrifice, Mandela, together with senior government officials, accepted salary cuts of between 10 percent and 20 percent to contribute to social reconstruction.

In line with the proposal to redirect government spending, from 1995 to 1999 annual percentage growth in budgets allocated to health, education, and housing increased by 11.3 percent, 10.6 percent, and 23.8 percent, respectively, while spending on defense dropped by 1.8 percent on average. The previously fragmented public health sector in South Africa faced many challenges at the time of democratic transition, ranging from infectious diseases such as tuberculosis, malaria, and the HIV/AIDS epidemic to an urban-rural imbalance of access to services. Mandela legislated free prenatal care and free health care for all children under six years of age. A program was launched to train nurses as primary health-care workers enabling basic services to be provided in rural areas.

Moving poor people from helplessness to hope and enabling them to take the initiative to improve their circumstances was impossible without education. Under the RDP, free compulsory education was phased in for all children, along with a school lunch program aimed at providing at least one full meal per day to children whose families lived below the poverty level.

Opening opportunity meant addressing the racial basis of economic disparities. Psychological consequences were emphasized by African Black Consciousness leader Dr. Mamphele Ramphele, former vice-chancellor of the University of Cape Town and later a director of the World Bank: "Spare a thought for a black child growing up in a political environment in which there is no formal racial and gender discrimination, yet where most successful people happen to be white and male! What deduction would such a child make about the innate ability of black people and women?"

In October 1998, Mandela signed into law the Employment Equity Act (EEA), the goal of which was to eliminate historic race- and gender-based discrimination and facilitate a move toward achieving a workplace representative of the country's demographics. Businesses with more than fifty employees and revenues above a government-defined amount were required to draw up one- to five-year employment equity plans. Employers were mandated to spend 1 percent of wages on education and training, with fines for failure to comply, but 80 percent of this could be reimbursed if the training was done via registered trainers.

Critics complained that the new act was reverse discrimination against white South Africans, and some argued that it provided a disincentive for smaller businesses to increase hiring. It was further pointed out that the earlier Labor Relations Act, which specifically prohibited any form of workplace discrimination, seemed at odds with the new legislation that now appeared to discriminate against whites. But the EEA described the changes as necessary to redress disparities created under apartheid. Supporters saw it as an essential part of delivering on promises of change in the workplace for the majority of South Africans.

Although it did not happen overnight, gradually a new black middle class began to emerge. A new generation of black business leaders, male and female, became captains of industry, serving as role models for many young South Africans hoping to gain access through doors that were previously closed to them. From 1991 to 1996, the highest earners among blacks had an increase in household income, slowly closing the gap with their white counterparts. (I had dinner with one of these families of black business and professional leaders in a suburban mixed-race development with big houses, swimming pools, and large lawns that could have been any affluent American neighborhood. Similar to many first-generation suburbanites recently escaped from urban poverty, they were careful to distinguish themselves from the poor blacks stuck in the townships.) Black firms listed on the Johannesburg Stock Exchange (JSE) inched up slowly, from eleven to thirty-six. From 1995 to 1999 the percentage market capitalization of black-controlled firms increased from 1 percent to 3.1 percent. Great inroads were made in the delivery of essential services, such as clean water, electric lighting, and telephone access (especially by the advent of mobile phones). Progress was also occurring in education, with literacy levels increasing across all age and gender groups.

However, some considered the RDP a set of failed promises. The gap between the highest and lowest earners among blacks increased. The white population still dominated the higher-paying job segment, while the majority of the African population had lower-paying jobs. Approximately 87 percent of all senior management positions were still occupied by whites. Despite an average percentage increase of over 23 percent in the housing budget between 1995 and 1999, and a goal of 2.5 million houses to be built within a decade, by the end of 1997 only 350,000 houses had been built. While people overall had greater access to health care than before, perceptions of high costs and difficult access persisted. Murder rates were still high, although "political murders" (stemming from racial violence) were down significantly. Houses in and around Johannesburg were barricaded, and there were signs warning intruders that occupants had guns.

The painful pace of progress was apparent when I visited Kliptown, a poor section of the black township of Soweto. Soweto was not too far across the superhighway from Sandton, an affluent suburb of Johannesburg that reminded me of Beverly Hills. Kliptown was just across the railroad tracks and electrical wires from the only school the children could attend, perhaps a daily reminder of deprivation for a settlement that used car batteries for electrical power. A set of community workers, mostly unpaid, was leading my family through the village, with a trail of young children following. As I walked by his side on the dirt paths, a program assistant, called Brother Bob, waved his arm toward the faucet outside a cluster of tiny houses that was the only source of running water and around to the lines of people in front of a half-dozen portable toilets. He asked, "Tell me as you look at this what democracy has brought to South Africa." Clearly Brother Bob did not think a new political culture had done much for the people.

But there were others on my Kliptown walk who had greater

confidence. Sara, volunteer head of Soweto Kliptown Youth, and Grace, an advocate for the elderly from nearby Alexandra Township, also a black settlement, were excited by the children who were gathering in a warehouse-like open hall to perform the play they had written. They were full of stories about how young people were going on to university and making plans for their futures. Every turnaround has its doubters, but the goal is to create confidence, so that more people are willing to grasp opportunities and take action.

Slow as the pace of problem-solving was, there was greater opportunity, greater hope, and greater initiative. The HIV/AIDS epidemic threatened the future of the young people at the high school in Soweto; a group of them became leaders of a new project to paint murals and posters warning their peers about the dangers of unprotected sex and promoting abstinence. With the help of an activated group of citizens taking initiative, the community center in Alexandra Township was enlarging its health clinic and working toward finding more university scholarships for talented high school students (including those having difficulties because their births were undocumented, a significant issue for South Africans from rural areas).

Overall, large numbers of people who previously enjoyed no control over their economic circumstances and had to struggle for survival found more opportunities and tools to improve their life situations. Mandela did not guarantee jobs or higher incomes, but his administration tried to create the circumstances to give people at the low end of the economic scale more capacity to move out of poverty, and to give the more affluent the confidence to invest in growing the South African economy as entrepreneurs or business leaders.

As with all his actions, Mandela was inclusive—and practical. He did not want black empowerment to be accompanied by white flight, which would drain the country of capital and talent. While many white South Africans had left the country to find careers abroad, feeling that they were being displaced by blacks or that they would not be promoted in their current companies, some were inspired by Mandela's message and actions to return to what they saw as a country with greater opportunity and hope.

David Munro, deputy managing director of Standard Corporate and Merchant Bank, a division of an international bank headquartered in Johannesburg, exemplified a generation of white South Africans with world-class skills and the ability to settle and work outside the country if desired. Indeed, I met him in 2003 at the elite Advanced Management Program at Harvard Business School, a program restricted to those with CEO potential. Munro had left South Africa in the 1980s to work in London in a global management consulting firm and later in banking. Then he experienced the Madiba-magic.

In July 1996, during his official state visit to the United Kingdom, President Mandela made a stop at a packed Trafalgar Square. Munro joined a large group of children and adults, Londoners and South African expatriates, many sporting Mandela T-shirts, all packed elbow to elbow in the square, which had been sealed off to traffic. From the balcony of South Africa House, Mandela told the crowd that "I would like to put each and every one of you in my pocket," referring to his desire to take everyone back home to South Africa with him. David Munro recalled the strong impact that these words made on him, influencing his decision to accept a senior position back home in Johannesburg.

Foreign investment also returned to South Africa. Inward direct investment by nonresidents in South Africa was negative from 1985 to 1987, as more capital left the country than entered. Foreign investment was positive every year from 1991 to 1999, rising to a peak of $3.8 billion in 1997, a strong sign of improved investor confidence.

THE PEDESTAL OF HOPE

At his inauguration in 1994, Mandela indicated that he would serve only one term, later joking that it was not right to have an octogenarian president. On June 16, 1999, nearly 50,000 people, including more than 4,000 invited dignitaries from around the world, gathered on the lawns of the Union Buildings in Pretoria to witness a historic occasion: the first transition of power in a democratic South Africa. Millions more watched on television.

Less than a decade earlier, it would have been almost unimaginable for such a mix of people—black and white, men and women, children and adults, local and international—to gather in safety and solidarity near the former headquarters of apartheid South Africa. Historically, very few revolutionaries have voluntarily handed over power, and Mandela's act was unique for Africa—a peaceful transition of power in a continent torn by violence, and in a country surrounded by neighbors with entrenched and corrupt leadership.

When the incoming president, Thabo Mbeki, stepped forward to take the oath of office, he offered a poignant tribute to his predecessor. Mbeki clasped Mandela's hand and raised it, commenting that the day was a "salute for a generation that pulled . . . [the] country out of the abyss and placed it on the pedestal of hope on which it rests today."

A pedestal is a platform, not a pinnacle. Much had been accomplished, and much was still to be done. From the vantage point of four years later, President Mbeki was no Mandela—among other things, he was slow to recognize the magnitude of the HIV/AIDS epidemic sweeping the nation and take action—and many people were disappointed that democracy had not yet solved deep-rooted economic problems.

Mandela's philosophy was that change takes place one person at a time, one community at a time, and eventually across an entire nation. A long march requires patience and a clear vision of the destination. Observers praised Mandela for not losing sight of the big picture despite day-to-day challenges. Reverend Charles Stith, former U.S. ambassador to Tanzania, commented on Mandela's ability to step above his personal plight, whether it was being separated from his family for twenty-seven years or the treatment he received while in prison, to keep in mind his goal for all South Africans. It was this determination and focus that made him a leader with a "big L," according to Stith. James Joseph, the first United States ambassador to democratic South Africa and now my colleague on the City Year board, described Mandela's leadership ability as based on "soft power." Hard power often comes from military might or force, soft power from social and moral messages or acts of generosity. For Ambassador Joseph, Mandela sought power in order to distribute it rather than to use it to dominate others. He was, according to Joseph, "the kind of leader who not only transforms, but elevates all those with whom he is involved."

Earlier in this chapter, I referred to Nelson Mandela as one of the few people who deserve to be called a "water walker." Yet he said of himself, "I was not a messiah, but an ordinary man who had become a leader because of extraordinary circumstances." BBC commentator Brian Walden argued that Mandela, "perhaps the most generally admired figure of our age, [still] falls short of the giants of the past." Asked to comment about this unflattering verdict on his performance as a leader, Mandela simply smiled and replied, "It helps to make you human."

NATIONAL LEADERS AND THE CULTURE OF CONFIDENCE

Imagine getting this list of actions taken by a turnaround CEO:

- a shift in resources from bureaucracy to investment in improving rundown facilities and developing people
- a cut in the leaders' own salaries as a model of reducing waste
- an open flow of information and more means of communication, putting all the facts in front of people
- widespread dialogue in the form of town meetings to solicit everyone's input about important choices for the future
- forums to make it easy for people to speak about past hurts, to admit past errors, and to take responsibility for their own actions, without fearing punishment
- gestures of respect and appreciation for everyone, to show that everyone is part of the team

- inclusion of representatives of key constituencies in the leadership group
- policies that open opportunity to more people, to ensure a wider talent pool
- resources and support for local initiative and innovation

Nelson Mandela's and his team's actions are classic examples of leadership that display all the basics of turnarounds—they deal with both symptoms of decline and the losers' culture underlying it. As prescriptions, they could have been taken from the to-do lists of numerous leaders throughout this book, whether in charge of large or small, complex or simple systems: Jim Kilts of Gillette; Jeffrey Lurie and Joe Banner of the Philadelphia Eagles; Elsie Bailey of Booker T. Washington High School; Steve Luczo and Bill Watkins of Seagate; Gerhard Schulmeyer of Siemens-Nixdorf; Jackie Jenkins-Scott of Dimock Community Health Center; Greg Dyke of the BBC; Dusty Baker of the Chicago Cubs; Geno Auriemma of the Connecticut women's basketball team; Anson Dorrance of the North Carolina women's soccer team; or Akin Öngör of Garanti Bank.

Leaders who guide their teams toward success espouse the value of accountability, collaboration, and initiative in their messages to others, model those qualities in their own behavior, and create formal programs and structural mechanisms to embed them in institutions. Of course, in a small team, leaders can influence people directly, and can even change members to ensure the right mix and the right dispositions. Changing a whole country with a tragic past is much harder, but the difference is one of magnitude, complexity, and means for influence, not one of principles.

Now imagine a leader taking these positive actions to restore and maintain confidence in an entire country after spending twenty-seven years in prison. Mandela did all this while himself a victim, yet he avoided a victim mentality; that is the other remarkable fact of Mandela's life and example. How could he emerge with so little visible bitterness? He had a support system of other leaders of his movement and a network of international advocates, but how could he avoid sinking into despair as change stalled for years, then proceeded slowly?

Mandela clearly had inner reserves of self-confidence, as well as the confidence of his long-term colleagues, who counted on him and whom he could not let down. During his presidency he held firm in his resolve to shift to a positive cycle, while facing critics and naysayers on both sides—some saying he didn't go far enough to elevate the black majority and compensate them for past abuses, others worrying that he was going too far in the direction of reverse discrimination. He reminded people of long-term values even while progress was slow and uneven, the way it inevitably is in turning around a very complex social system.

Mandela's confidence in himself and other people helps account for the remarkable and historically unique transitions he was able to make. A prisoner forgiving his jailers. An activist turned states-man. A revolutionary turned healer. An ambitious man who put the interests of the nation above his own feelings—reflected in such small but highly meaningful gestures as wearing the colors of the former enemy onto the rugby field in a crowded stadium in Johannesburg to celebrate a rugby victory.

Mandela's natural supporters during his imprisonment were na-tive Africans, but most African countries are known for being poorly led. A political scientist pointed to the level of risk in holding office in troubled countries, which can encourage leaders to pursue short-term, economically destructive policies. In countries within the region where leaders face less risk, there are more-open eco-nomic regimes and lower levels of perceived political corruption. But risk is also a self-fulfilling prophecy. Because Mandela chose to exude confidence, his confidence was rewarded. Although difficult problems of poverty could not be solved quickly—it would take generations—a culture of confidence in South Africa increased fi-nancial investment, talent retention, entrepreneurship, and citi-zens' service to their communities.

A culture of confidence at the national level works through all the intertwined levels of confidence of a winning cycle. In South Africa, helping people feel more connected and empowered was a step toward confidence that the institutions of government and law would function effectively, since they rely on public trust and cooperation. Confidence in institutions was essential for earning external confidence from international investors, just as in the early years of another new democracy, the United States of America. George Washington, like Mandela his country's first democratically elected president, needed to attract European financial investment after the Revolutionary War so that the economy could grow. But first, Washington had to build the confidence of the people that they could govern themselves on a national scale, with sufficient trust in one another and in the institutions of government to form a stable, solvent platform that would protect rights of property and contract. Public confidence was bolstered by messages about progress, especially the belief that education could help people improve their prospects. Washington conveyed the optimistic idea that there was no limit to the improvement of human abilities and circumstances.

Leaders must convey confidence at all levels, from the big signs that the government is trustworthy to the small signals that shape an emotional climate. Mandela was particularly adept at the emotional dimension of leadership. After the Hani murder in 1993, he helped his country avoid panic—a reaction that turns fumbles into disasters and exacerbates the possibility of a losing streak. A related example of emotional management by another renowned leader was visible in the actions of Mayor Rudolph Guiliani after the terrorist attacks on September 11, 2001, and the weeks that followed. Forgotten were his sex scandals, questions about his accomplishments in office, and a reputation for meanness. He walked into the crisis rather than walking away from it. He healed, soothed, expressed outrage, rallied people, held hands, kept spirits up, made sales pitches, and said thank you. He focused attention not on the attackers but on the grassroots heroes responsible for delivering safety—police officers, firefighters, rescue workers. Though a more profound example, this is similar to the acts of team managers and coaches that make the players central and shift scarce resources to services to support them.

Optimistic leadership creating positive expectations is necessary but not sufficient for turnarounds. Leaders' choices—their message, example, and programs—determine their success. Guiliani became and remained a hero because of a single episode, but turnarounds require more than immediate crisis-management skills. No controversy dogged Guiliani because his actions provoked no challenges, required no tough choices, and were completed shortly after the crisis event, when he left office. He sent no troops into battle, solved no problems, developed no policies, seeded no innovations. New York City's disaster relief response was effective because teams had already prepared and could spring into action, freeing him to be their cheerleader-in-chief.

Mayor Guiliani rose to the occasion and became a celebrated icon in a crisis, his sexual missteps forgotten, while President Bill Clinton fell from grace despite presiding over a period of peace and prosperity—or, perhaps, because of that. It is harder to seem heroic during a winning streak, when success is taken for granted. President Clinton once commented, midway through his presidency and before his own sex scandals, that he would not be remembered by history as one of the great presidents because there were no threats to peace and prosperity during his presidency. Without a national crisis to resolve, he would not have a chance to demonstrate exemplary leadership. Clinton was a public-purpose president in a private-interest cycle, to use Arthur Schlesinger Jr.'s phrase. The effectiveness attributed to leaders is a function of the situation they inherit, as revealed in a study of "accidental chiefs"— U.S. vice-presidents who unexpectedly became president. Harry Truman is remembered as effective because he modeled accountability ("the buck stops here") while leading the nation through turbulent times; Gerald Ford, who took over after Richard Nixon's resignation, did not have the same opportunity to rise to major challenges.

National leaders influence public confidence by their messages and models, which shape an emotional climate and help determine whether expectations are positive or negative, and by their actions—whether they increase or decrease accountability, collaboration, and initiative. In boom times, just as in winning streaks, confidence is carried by the momentum of success. But times of distress are the true test of whether leaders meet the challenge of shaping a culture of confidence.

Fearmongering and scapegoating are tempting in difficult times, as demagogues (and opposition parties) know, because it is faster and easier to rally people around what they are against than to find common interests, which takes hard work. But turnaround leaders who focus on cutting rather than on building, who emphasize fighting external enemies through shows of power (litigation is the business equivalent of war) rather than improving constituents' conditions and culture, do not last long. Fostering the attitudes and behaviors associated with decline makes further deterioration more likely. When national leaders tilt toward secret decisions, protected information, intergroup antagonisms, and policies that favor elites over people at the grass roots, they are fueling the symptoms of a losing streak.

Optimism helps politicians win elections, while dwelling too long on negative events does not. In eighteen of twenty-two U.S. presidential elections from 1900 to 1984, the optimistic candidate won. In 1988, optimism, as reflected in candidates' speeches, predicted the nominations and elections to a range of public offices. Like Gordon Bethune, President Clinton was known for spreading optimism. Despite turbulence around him—impeachment hearings, for example—he focused on the specific tasks ahead, in the manner of athletes on winning teams methodically focused on improving their skills for the next game. In 2003, when he was out of office and members of his Democratic Party were still angry over their losses in the 2002 congressional elections, he demonstrated the spirit characteristic of Mandela, saying, " I don't blame the Republicans for defeating us. They were just doing their job. Their job is to beat us. I blame us for not doing our job. It was our job to beat them." In short, he urged action, not whining.

Nelson Mandela made positive choices that set a new model and led people down a new path. He let go of anger and blame. He rejected victimhood. He promoted accountability, collaboration, and initiative, and this produced renewed confidence on the part of many, inside and outside of the country. The hope he delivered set a culture of positive expectations that was manifested at so many levels, in so many teams. Perhaps that is why the players on South Africa's rugby team in 1995 knew that winning the world championship meant more to their fans than just a victory in sports. That game celebrated renewed confidence in the nation.

Part III

IMPLICATIONS AND LIFE LESSONS

11

Delivering Confidence: The Work of Leaders

ALL OF US WANT CONFIDENCE THAT OUR INVESTMENTS OF MONEY, TIME, EFFORT, OR LOYALTY WILL LEAD TO POSITIVE RESULTS. WE LOOK TO LEADERS TO DELIVER THAT CONFIDENCE, WHETHER WE are thinking of coaches of professional sports teams, chiefs of major corporations, directors of hospitals and schools, community officials, or presidents and prime ministers of our countries.

Leadership is not about the leader, it is about how he or she builds the confidence of everyone else. Leaders are responsible for both the big structures that serve as the cornerstones of confidence, and for the human touches that shape a positive emotional climate to inspire and motivate people.

Throughout this book are numerous examples of leadership that combines structure and soul—the hard and the soft, the big decision and the small gesture—in order to build or restore confidence. Akin Öngör led Garanti Bank's investments in huge technology programs and financial strategies, but he also led his 500 top people and their spouses onto the dance floor at an annual dinner dance, personally thanking the spouses for their support. At the BBC, Greg Dyke restructured the organization chart, shifted the budget, and, together with the executive committee, created formal channels for proposing innovations, and he also treated people with personal warmth and genuine interest in their ideas. The Philadelphia Eagles' Jeffrey Lurie and Joe Banner went after a $500-million new stadium and also invited players to backyard cookouts. Billy Beane, general manager of the Oakland Athletics, became famous for his reliance on software programs and statistical analysis to manage performance on the baseball field, but he told us that he also devoted time to learning about the players' personal lives, talking with one player about music, and with another about his college, and then mentioned these interests to make them feel better when they were struggling with the game. "Their self-esteem is part of the equation," he said.

Leaders deliver confidence by espousing high standards in their messages, exemplifying these standards in the conduct they model, and establishing formal mechanisms to provide a structure for acting on those standards.

Espouse: the power of message

Leaders articulate standards, values, and visions. They give pep talks. Their messages can incite to action when that is appropriate, or they can calm and soothe people to prevent them from panicking. We saw in Chapter 2 that pep talks are empty without evidence, so let's call this "grounded optimism"—positive expectations based on specific facts that justify the optimism. In the strong cultures that develop in winning streaks, leaders' messages are internalized and echo throughout the system. This can happen in nations—as with Nelson Mandela's healing words in South Africa—or in teams. Players on the North Carolina women's soccer team seemed to have Anson Dorrance's voice in their heads. At Continental Airlines, numerous people in a variety of jobs quoted Gordon Bethune's favorite sayings. From the Go Forward Plan to Bethune's weekly voice mails, people learned from what Continental leaders espoused. The messages provided practical information, inspiration, and a feeling of inclusion, as everyone knew that everyone else heard the same message.

Exemplify: the power of models

Leaders serve as role models, leading through the power of personal example. "I don't believe as a leader you can ever expect anybody to do things you are not willing to do yourself," said Mike Babcock of the Mighty Ducks. The leaders I saw in winning streaks and turnarounds worked to exemplify the kinds of accountable, collaborative behavior they sought in others. Certainly the personal example of truth and reconciliation, inclusion, and empowerment set by Nelson Mandela reflected one of the most remarkable and admirable personal journeys of the twentieth century. In a different country and different way, Akin Öngör of Garanti Bank was an inspiring business role model with courage and compassion— offering to resign when he discovered that the bank had lost $14 million due to a junior manager's mistake that control systems had not caught, because Öngör said he "shared the mistake," or mobilizing the bank's employees to help in the aftermath of an earthquake in Turkey.

Establish: the power of formal mechanisms

Leaders develop processes, routines, and structures. They embed winners' behavior in the culture not just through person-to-person and generation-to-generation transfers of norms, but also through the formal mechanisms that embed positive behavior in team and organizational routines. North Carolina women's soccer coach Anson Dorrance or Connecticut women's basketball coach Geno Auriemma had many systematic ways to forge their players into a victory machine that just kept winning—a yearly calendar of activities including off-season events, routines for practices, metrics and assessment tools, leadership seminars, a schedule of meetings. The teams changed composition, as players turned over, but the structures and processes remained. The winning teams that resulted were not a force of nature, but a product of professional disciplines and structures. Nelson Mandela's leadership in South Africa was manifested not just through his inspiring message and model, but through institutions: the structure of a new government, legislation, formal events such as town meetings on a new constitution, and hearings by the Truth and Reconciliation Commission.

Leaders must deliver confidence at every level: self-confidence,

confidence in one another, confidence in the system, and the confidence of external investors and the public that their support is warranted.

"LEADERSHIP IS PLURAL": HOW CONFIDENCE REPRODUCES

Leaders certainly need self-confidence. ("Often wrong, never uncertain," Jim Kilts cheerfully described himself.) Self-confidence helps leaders persist through problems and triumph over troubles. Remember some of the lessons of turnarounds:

- Leaders do not always control everything that contributes to results.
- There are lags between internal changes and external confidence.
- Turnarounds can be very slow and long-term processes.
- Change can be a zoo. That is, leaders might be dancing with grizzly bears that won't let them stop; they can sometimes feel like a canary in a coal mine, sent to sniff out danger even if it expires in the process; and they must be wary of being trampled by a herd of sacred cows.

But self-confidence is not the real secret of leadership. The more essential ingredient is confidence in other people. Leadership involves motivating others to their finest efforts and channeling those efforts in a coherent direction. Leaders must believe that they can count on other people to come through—like Elsie Bailey's faith as a high school principal that inner-city children can learn and that her teachers can teach them. If the people in charge rely only on themselves as heroes who can rescue any situation, while focusing on other people's inadequacies, they undermine confidence and reinforce losing streaks. In contrast, when leaders believe in other people, confidence grows, and winning becomes more attainable.

Leaders of organizations in success cycles are a little like rabbits, constantly reproducing. In losing streaks, the rabbits seem barren; there is a leadership deficit. In winning streaks, the number of leaders multiplies along with the momentum of the streak. Winning teams and successful organizations become increasingly less dependent on the person called the commander-in-chief—even though, ironically, the same top managers are more likely to stay in place during winning streaks. As a pattern of success continues, many people at many levels take on leadership roles. Some of them are appointed to positions with leadership titles, some of them are self-appointed; and roles are passed around as the nature of the play changes. Larry Kellner and Debbie McCoy had official responsibility for Continental Airlines' decision to keep flying during the power blackout in August 2003, but that decision was foreordained by the actions of all the other people who claimed leadership on the ground and knew they did not need to ask permission.

"Leadership is plural," Mike Krzyzewski, Duke's men's basketball coach, liked to repeat. Winning streaks are associated with not just one but many leaders—a nested series of leaders, like the Russian dolls in which each doll opens to reveal another identical but smaller doll inside. Who was the leader of the turnaround of the Anaheim Mighty Ducks in the 2002–3 season? Was it Paul Pressler as head of Disney Sports, because he got investment funds from Disney CEO Michael Eisner and then hired Bryan Murray? Was it Bryan Murray as the general manager, who spent the money on new facilities and players? Was it Mike Babcock, as head coach? Or was it sub-coaches and player-leaders who made the judgment calls at critical moments? The answer, of course, is all of the above.

Even at the top, leaders often come in pairs, trios, and quartets, operating as a unit in spirit even if one of them has final authority in law. Consider the numerous leaders we have met. Former South African president Nelson Mandela referred constantly to his partners in leadership through the years, Walter Sisulu and Oliver Tambo. Steve Luczo and Bill Watkins guided Seagate's turnaround together. Drs. Mark Smith and Craig Feied came to Washington Hospital Center as a pair. Jeffrey Lurie enticed Joe Banner to join him at the Philadelphia Eagles. Dusty Baker brought a cadre of coaches with him from the San Francisco Giants to the Chicago Cubs.

One person may have the top title and the official authority, but his or her effectiveness is often a function of the quality of all the other people who stand beside them to exercise leadership. At Continental Airlines, Gordon Bethune gave the speeches and appeared in the Rodney Dangerfield "respect" videos, but he had a strong set of leaders with him: Greg Brenneman, Larry Kellner (soon to succeed Bethune as CEO), Deborah McCoy, and others. Akin Öngör had Saide Kuzeyli, executive vice-president of human resources, as his sidekick-in-chief; she shared the duties of coaching the people of Garanti Bank to victory, along with seven other key officers. At the BBC, Greg Dyke encouraged his whole executive team to become leaders, and it was that large cadre that vowed to continue Dyke's programs after he left.

The reproduction process involves finding and empowering natural leaders, regardless of their titles or levels. Elsie Bailey, the principal of Booker T. Washington High School, formed teacher teams to take on leadership responsibilities for the school, something that was relatively new in public education. The 40 or so BBC leaders to whom I spoke under Dyke's predecessor multiplied into the 400 designated leaders to whom I spoke a few years later. Gerhard Schulmeyer sought the natural leaders to be Siemens-Nixdorf's change agents, and gave them responsibilities that cut across existing hierarchical titles. At Invensys, Rick Haythornthwaite put ninety people on strategy teams to find a new direction for the troubled company, and he anointed 400 ambassadors for change, which included the 300 top executives plus another hundred natural leaders from the ranks without fancy titles. The 1,350 South Koreans I met at the Shinhan Financial Group Summit outside of Seoul in the fall of 2003 were all designated leaders for the merger of the two banks that formed the new group.

And in the largest show of confidence in other people demonstrated by anyone mentioned in this book, Nelson Mandela opened discussion of a new constitution for South Africa to thousands of people in town meetings all over his country. He led the first truly democratic elections, which gave every adult a voice, regardless of race. Democracy is the ultimate act of confidence, because democracy implies willingness to share power with other people who might have different views or speak in a different voice.

The more leaders reproduce themselves, the more likely it is that they do emerge, paradoxically, with heroic accomplishments. Mandela claimed he was just an ordinary man who had to rise to extraordinary circumstances, and his speeches are filled with praise for others. Gordon Bethune said that he was getting an award because of everyone else's hard work. Ivan Seidenberg could share the CEO role twice in the mergers that produced Verizon because he put the needs of the institution first, over his own ego. The reward for sharing was an even bigger winning company.

Sports certainly produces a very high number of prima donnas and big egos, yet I was struck by how many of the winning teams were led by unpretentious people who boosted others. Larry Coker, who had one of the best records ever for a rookie coach in his first three years as head coach of the Miami Hurricanes, was well known for crediting the players and assistant coaches for victories, for not promoting himself, and for staying "smaller than his program," it was said. The players' confidence in Coker—that he gave them the support they needed to do their jobs—was a big part of the reason he was given the top coaching job.

Losing streaks are associated with autocrats who cling to control even as events spin out of control—one consequence of my principle that "powerlessness corrupts." But in winning streaks, leadership can come from anywhere, and it might not correspond to the official hierarchy of titles, whether chief executive, head coach, manager, or lord-high-anything-else. Dusty Baker was firm on this point: "Your coaches may not be the leaders. They're in charge of their department; that doesn't necessarily make them into leaders. Just because that person's in charge, who says anybody else is going to follow?"

Baker, like Anson Dorrance at North Carolina, Geno Auriemma at Connecticut, Andy Reid at the Philadelphia Eagles, and Billy

Beane at the Oakland Athletics, looked for the natural leaders on the field. Beane said that this was necessary because "I don't think the general manager or manager can designate leaders. The club-house is *Lord of the Flies*," referring to the novel about a group of children stranded in the jungle. "Social structures evolve, and the ability to manipulate those from the top is probably limited." For baseball, Baker looked for leaders in the bullpen and on the bench, someone from the infield and someone from the outfield, and counted on them to rally their teammates, making his job easier, he said. Dorrance led seminars on leadership for his women soccer players, ran leadership self-assessments and team ratings, and then let teams choose their own captains.

Leaders find the best people they can, ensure their preparation, put them in the right positions, and give them a game plan. After that, winning is up to the players on the field. It is their leadership that matters. The actions of many leaders seizing the moment create the margin of victory.

When people have confidence in one another, they are willing to lead and be led by the team. They do not have to second-guess, double back, or duplicate other people's work. They catch problems more quickly or take bolder steps because they do not worry about embarrassment or punishment. Energy is freed and focus is possible when people have confidence in one another. When they can count on other people's support, they don't have to fear their attacks or monitor their every move. When people give one another the benefit of the doubt and, better yet, believe in one another, more projects are launched, more innovations get seeded, and more work gets done. That's how Seagate could quadruple productivity, how Continental could click-click-click through operations meetings as quickly as a Connecticut-Duke women's basketball game and make money on the Northeast blackout, and how the Miami Hurricanes could recover from fumbles to win that pivotal Florida State game, the one in which the players told the coaches not to worry, the team would take care of it.

Although the charisma of leadership tends to be associated with larger-than-life individuals who weave inspirational spells, charisma can become a property of a whole group of people who believe in one another and the power of their teamwork. That's what the BBC executive committee discovered in themselves when their charismatic chief departed. And that's the real magic—to make leadership appear from many unexpected places, just when it is needed.

LEADERS SUPPORTING LEADERSHIP: THE CORNERSTONES OF CONFIDENCE

Leaders can multiply on the field when leaders at the top establish the support structure to make further leadership possible. Leaders construct and reinforce the cornerstones of confidence, as shown so vividly in the turnarounds I have described. The mission statement for leaders has three imperatives, one for each stone: to ensure accountability, cultivate collaboration, and encourage initiative.

Individual and System Accountability

Jim Kilts said it best: "A promise made is a promise kept." As we have seen, confidence is enhanced when people are held accountable and accept responsibility for performing to high standards. Confidence requires an honest and thorough assessment of the situation and the courage to accept responsibility for dealing with it, even if that means owning up to past mistakes. Confidence and the high self-esteem associated with it rest on real accomplishments, not self-delusion. Leaders remind people of the yin and yang of obligations and opportunities associated with being a member of their team. Leaders keep the mirror of accountability polished and clear.

The job of leaders in every sector and system level involves:

Fostering straight talk

Open discussion, without obfuscation or coverups, enables facts to be squarely faced and promises to be based on reality. "Humiliation-free zones" support objective discussion of strengths and weaknesses without fear of embarrassment. Winning teams are data-rich, as we have seen at Gillette and Verizon, in Continental Airlines' daily operations meetings and multiple-voice-mail updates, or the North Carolina women's soccer team. With many facts on the table and many communication channels open, denial is difficult if not impossible.

Communicating expectations clearly

Constantly repeating the standards to everyone and clearly articulating goals and priorities directs attention both to grand visions and to the details of execution, which ground visions in daily tasks. While holding other people accountable for living up to expectations, leaders also hold themselves accountable for whether people are in a position to meet expectations. That is, leaders should set people up to succeed. "If a guy's a fastball hitter, I'm not going to put him up there against a guy throwing curveballs, because I'd be setting him up to fail," the Chicago Cub's Dusty Baker said. "When bosses want to get rid of someone, they give them assignments that they know they can't handle, and then, like, 'Hey man, you didn't do the job.' Well, you can set a guy up to succeed just as well." Art Kehoe of the Miami Hurricanes put it this way: "If we recruited you, and you're going to class, lifting weights, are on time, giving your best, and you're still not good enough to play, then it's our fault, and we'll live with you because you're part of our team. If you're not doing what we ask of you, then we'll figure out a way to rid ourselves of you."

Making information transparent and accessible

Widespread access to abundant performance data helps ensure that people get the information they need to guide their own performance and hold others—and the system—to high standards. Leaders use diverse tools to produce accountability, chosen to fit the particular game: small caucuses or mass meetings; quasiconfessionals or virtual mirrors; videotapes of games or voice mails of daily operational performance; data warehouses or computer tracking of game statistics; quarterly priorities or quarterly report cards; daily exercise logs or yearly performance appraisals. Regardless of the assortment of tools used in specific situations, the same strong principle is at work: People cannot hide information or duck responsibility.

The chance to be part of a winning team is a powerful motivator, and only those who meet all the standards—for character and commitment as well as skills and abilities—should be allowed to play. Sanctions add teeth to accountability. But the work should be a motivating opportunity for success rather than a weapon for punishment. Leaders of successful teams and organizations have high standards and punish infractions, but they rarely use the work itself as a punishment. Bob Ladouceur, head coach of De La Salle, never forced an athlete who broke a rule to spend more time on the practice field or in the weight room; instead, a violator was sidelined. Similarly, people at Continental or Garanti Bank who did not live up to corporate standards after being given a second chance were not given more work, they were removed. At the BBC, Greg Dyke even removed himself, saying, "If you screw up, you've got to go."

Mutual Respect, Communication, and Collaboration
Confidence blossoms when people feel connected rather than isolated, when they are willing to engage and commit to one another, when they can act together to solve problems and produce results, ignoring boundaries between them. A culture of pride stems from respect for the talents and potential of other people in the system. Mutual confidence begins with firsthand knowledge of one another and the chance to discover human connections. "Chemistry" is not a mysterious factor dependent on whether people happen to hit it off; bonds grow from working together on real and important tasks that achieve success.

Items that leaders should place on their agenda to foster collaboration include:

Structuring collaborative conversations
Dialogue across positions, departments, or groups is a common theme in every winning streak, and it is often an early step in a turnaround from losing to winning cycles. Steve Luczo and Bill Watkins's goal was to eliminate the competitive silos at Seagate that depressed performance. Greg Dyke sought "One BBC." Debbie McCoy's daily operations meetings at Continental were determinedly cross-functional, including every area that had anything to do with flying passengers from one place to another. Forming teams within teams to carry out strategically important tasks, including cross-representatives from all affected positions, builds critical connections that produce team or organizational "chemistry."

In sports, leaders worked to bridge the divides between pitchers and hitters, offensive lines and defensive lines, front benches and back benches, locker rooms and business offices. Dusty Baker encouraged pitching coaches to talk to batters, batting coaches to talk to pitchers, and he was especially conscious of helping a diverse "rainbow coalition" of nationalities to get along. At the Philadelphia Eagles, owner Jeffrey Lurie, president Joe Banner, head coach Andy Reid, and player personnel director Tom Heckert were in constant communication. Reid formed a players' committee of representatives from every position on the field to meet weekly about team issues, which was an innovative step in professional football. As part of the turnaround of a losing basketball team, Jerry West at the Memphis Grizzlies encouraged high levels of communication between the player side and the business side.

Reinforcing respect and inclusion
Publicizing achievements of individuals and teams reinforces pride in one another. To ensure collaboration, it is important to invest not

just in stars but to lift everyone's level of play; too much inequality of attention drives a wedge between people and groups. It is interesting to see that organizations with great disparities in compensation (consider the Philadelphia Eagles or any professional sports franchise) can still create a sense of an inclusive community by stressing the dignity in everyone's work, that everyone deserves respect, and that everyone's voice should be heard. Of course, collaboration is not voting, although Luczo and Watkins asked Seagate top executives to strive for consensus. Consensus cannot be built on suppression of dissent, and it is often improved by argument, even if the final authority rests with the bosses. Art Kehoe reported that the Miami Hurricanes' coaching staff had fierce arguments, usually about recruiting or practice time. Head coach Larry Coker would let the group spout off; he would listen carefully, and then announce a decision. End of discussion. "Once it's decided, whether it's against your wishes or not, we are all going to do it together," Kehoe said. "Whether that is what your firmest convictions are, we go in and sell it to our players as the best strategy. That's why we have to believe it before we bring it to them. That why we have to hash it out beforehand." The principle is to argue, and then to speak with one voice.

Defining joint goals and collective definitions of success
Although people are not equal in all ways and their roles remain different, they can share a basic set of responsibilities and rewards as members of the same community. Continental Airlines' collective definition of success—on-time arrivals—and the rewards associated with it—the same small bonus to absolutely everyone—is a classic example of an inclusive, win-win goal. It is good for customers, good for financial performance, good for employees, and everyone can contribute. Similarly, investments in upgrading workplaces for all organization members, whether factories, classrooms, practice fields, fitness facilities, or offices, sends a message about inclusion.

Leaders remind people of their obligations to support their teammates. Gestures of inclusion and responsibility seem tricky in professional sports, where there are wide discrepancies in salaries and big monetary prizes. Yet, teams that want to win do not seem to let stars get away with prima-donna behavior for long. Stars are expected to lift others to a higher standard of play; they are expected to share opportunities for glory on the field with the rest of the team, especially in practice sessions. As a consequence, the team ends up with more depth—and with more options, if stars are incapacitated. That is why the New England Patriots could enjoy a fifteen-game winning streak and the 2004 Super Bowl victory despite player injuries. Chicago Cubs' pitcher Matt Clement always felt that Dusty Baker was behind him and the rest of the team. "If someone is having bad day, Dusty wants others to pick him up," Clement said. When the Eagles' star quarterback Donovan McNabb had a series of bad games, head coach Andy Reid asked everyone to support him and to raise their own level of play. After a loss in which team chemistry seemed to have fizzled, Connecticut's Geno Auriemma called in players individually to remind them of their responsibilities to support one another.

The work itself is the first and most important source of cohesiveness for winning teams, but when people can see one another in other settings, they often feel more comfortable counting on teammates in a pinch. To Anson Dorrance, the fifteen minutes at the beginning of practice when the players on the North Carolina women's soccer team socialized while they warmed up were both utterly wasted and utterly necessary.

Initiative, Imagination, and Innovation

Confidence is enhanced when it is clear that people are empowered to take action, to solve problems, to voice their ideas, to create innovations. Accountability keeps people focused on the details of execution, while initiative keeps their heads above the fray so they can make split-second decisions about responding to the twists and turns of the play or search for new ways to create the future.

Leaders can develop tools, channels, rewards, and permission for the people around them to take initiative by:

Opening channels for new ideas
To keep fueling cycles of success, leaders welcome proposals from any position. They seek them, fund them, praise them, and provide a support system to sponsor them, as with the senior executive sponsors Gerhard Schulmeyer established for Siemens-Nixdorf's change agents. To show how important it is for people to think about and develop their ideas, the BBC set aside time for open discussion and brainstorming. Leaders who guide winning streaks believe in people and in people's power to make a difference, and that helps propel the streak. "When I went after him with a project, an idea, an inquiry, whatever it may be," Saide Kuzeyli said of Garanti Bank CEO Akin Öngör, "I knew he would think it would be good for the bank. I knew that he would say yes. If this isn't confidence, then what is?"

Treating people as experts in their own work
Giving people on the front lines and on the field leadership responsibilities and input into decisions pays dividends. Leaders start by removing organizational impediments that slow the action or stifle innovation, from "cutting the crap" in meetings to creating "instant checkbooks" for getting things done. They empower people with information and trust them to make decisions or adjustments on the field, when the game is in motion and the action cannot stop. On winning teams, people are seen as professionals who know their own world best. At SBLI, Vikki Pryor upgraded performance of people who were barely contributing by giving them more, not less, responsibility. At Continental, Deborah McCoy transformed the environment by letting pilots hire pilots, flight attendants hire flight attendants. Billy Beane of the Oakland Athletics found that players knew things that were very useful for managerial decisions, such as the inside word on players the team might be seeking in a trade or experience hitting against particular pitchers, so he talked to the

players as professionals. This was not participatory leadership for its own sake, but a pragmatic realization of the value of frontline knowledge. "It's not so much that they need to feel part of decisions. For me, they are a resource," he said.

Encouraging small wins and grassroots innovations

Awakening initiative starts with encouraging people to work on projects that they value, that involve factors they can control, that are connected to key tasks, and that serve as demonstration projects to stimulate more ideas. People work hardest on things that matter to them and make a difference to their own success—or change the way they experience work. A high proportion of the BBC's new ideas through One BBC and Making It Happen involved workplace cosmetics or staff amenities, but that same environment also produced bigger wins in the form of new programs and schedules emanating from unexpected places. Christophe Kopke, head of Daimler-Chrysler South Africa, awakened initiative in a passive, negative, strike-prone, and unproductive work force by asking them what they valued, and then supporting them in building a Mercedes for Nelson Mandela.

In business, streams of innovations make it possible to stay ahead of the competition, by increasing the value delivered to customers. Continental Airlines benefited from "firsts" in all domains, even when the industry was declining and air transportation was a commodity: the most flexible schedules for flight crews and an online trip-trading site; the first service in Washington's Reagan National Airport after 9/11; the first airline certified to carry pets from the United States to the UK. All these were the products of the imaginations of people in a range of functions. For nonprofit organizations, innovation stretches scarce resources, improves and extends services, and attracts donors. Jackie Jenkins-Scott guided Dimock Community Health Center back from the brink of death to a vibrant, nationally recognized facility with twenty times the number of programs and ten times the budget, by stimulating the imagination of her board and staff.

In any endeavor, initiative can be the game-winning edge. In sports, even small innovations can change the game by making teams less predictable to their opponents. Athletic director Paul Dee said that the Miami Hurricanes' head coach, Larry Coker, encouraged the coaching staff under him to be imaginative and come to him with ideas, which made the team more successful: "If you bring in fresh ideas and you allow other people to come up with ideas, there may not be a total change but a subtle shift so that other teams can't predict with certainty your actions, which then gives you the edge. Fresh thinking doesn't allow the defense to catch up quite so quickly."

EXTERNAL CONFIDENCE: ENSURING STAKEHOLDER AND PUBLIC TRUST

Leaders live on the boundaries. They connect people to tasks, members of the team to one another, and the whole system to the world outside the borders of the organization. The ultimate work of leaders lies in the connection between their groups and the wider network that provides support, loyalty, revenues, or capital. Leaders must prove to those in the wider circle that their investments are warranted.

Winning streaks are associated with the growth of external networks of customers, fans, audiences, sponsors, partners, and investors, and with closer relationships with public officials. Winners gain a variety of monetary and nonmonetary advantages from their external connections, which ensure a flow of talent, resources, market intelligence, and public support to fuel the momentum of a winning streak. Leaders must continue to prove every day that the organization is worthy of this support.

External confidence rests on more than the mere fact of winning. Confidence is based in part on *how* results are achieved, because that provides signs and signals about the likelihood of success in the future. Accountability, collaboration, and initiative are cornerstones of confidence because they both make continued success more likely and suggest a responsibility to the wider network outside. In losing teams, declining organizations, and failing countries, the people in charge have generally stopped exercising accountability and collaborative leadership, and the ensuing weaknesses affect external investors and the public. Support has been eroded not only by poor performance but by losers' behavior that repels customers, investors, or fans, who feel they cannot count on the organization to deliver winning performance in the future.

Turnaround leaders must rebuild the foundations for external confidence—that they will be accountable to stakeholders, work with them more collaboratively, and take actions to make improvements before they are forced to do it. Consider how important it was for each turnaround team in this book to restore external confidence by repairing and rebuilding stakeholder relationships. (And how one otherwise exemplary leader stumbled.)

To turn around Continental Airlines, Gordon Bethune, Greg Brenneman, and Larry Kellner had to restore financial integrity and do something about the worst customer service in the industry. Jim Kilts had to plug holes in Gillette's investor relations and trade relations caused by overpromising and underdelivering. Steve Luczo and Bill Watkins had to show investors that they could reduce the costs of Seagate's warring silos that consumed resources without getting a sufficient return. Jackie Jenkins-Scott of Dimock Community Health Center had to show the bankruptcy courts, donors, and a range of community institutions that the center could take initiative to deliver services with secure funding. Public school leaders had to build credibility with elected officials, school boards, parents, neighborhood groups, and the press by showing that stakeholders' goals and needs would help shape plans for turning around low-performing schools. Jeffrey Lurie and Joe Banner had to win fans and public support for the Philadelphia Eagles' turnaround before securing public financing for a new stadium. Garanti Bank took on responsibilities for the Turkish government in rescuing a failed bank during the 1994 financial crisis. Nelson Mandela not only had to replace a nonrepresentative government with one that promised to represent all the people, but he had to convince international businesses, foreign investors, and South Africans in exile that South Africa could shift to a winning cycle.

BBC leaders were acutely conscious of the need to nurture external confidence or suffer the consequences. As an organization with a government charter, funded by the public, and operating in a highly charged political environment, yet needing to protect journalistic independence, the BBC's existence and survival depended not simply on audience share against commercial competition but heavily on public approval and the belief of government officials—themselves a politically divided group—that the BBC was using license-payers' money in the public interest. The Hutton Inquiry following the suicide of David Kelly, the British scientist who had served as an anonymous informant for a BBC News broadcast making an allegation about Blair administration intelligence about weapons of mass destruction in Iraq, was a dramatic example of how easy it was for a BBC mistake to jeopardize external confidence.

Despite public outcries more supportive of the BBC than of the government, Greg Dyke acknowledged responsibility by resigning—itself a step in restoring external confidence—to draw a line under the incident to permit the BBC to move forward. But Hutton's report was not the only investigation of the BBC. BBC News had been scrutinized in 2002; former *Financial Times* editor Richard Lambert authored a report for the government about how to strengthen it. Another review had questioned whether BBC Interactive, the multimedia division, had used its power to monopolize the Internet to the detriment of commercial content. And there were others, a constant flow of probes and questions.

Although few people operate in quite as controversial, politicized environment as the BBC's, the BBC story is a reminder to leaders in every sector to weigh the external appearances and consequences of all actions, however justified those actions seem internally.

Delivering external confidence guarantees a solid future and, as we saw in winning streaks, results in greater self-determination because stakeholders trust the organization.

External confidence seems easy to obtain in boom years. Investors and fans like to win, and sometimes they do not look too closely at the reasons for winning and whether the cornerstones of confidence are strengthening or crumbling. Economic booms sometimes hide underlying weaknesses, as the rising tide lifts all boats, even leaky ones. Bust years, in contrast, make weaknesses, especially deteriorating accountability, all too apparent, because weak, directionless, or irresponsible groups cannot survive.

As I worked on this book, many large institutions were challenged by crises of confidence, especially in business. Each crisis was accompanied by a loud call for leadership to restore that confidence by meeting ever-higher standards. A large number of corporate financial scandals in the United States (Enron, Tyco, Adelphia), Europe (Ahold, Skandia, Parmalat), and elsewhere put the spotlight on the need to improve corporate governance and develop new rules for oversight and disclosure. On a September 2000 *Business Week*/Harris poll, more than 80 percent of Americans agreed that "business has gained too much power over too many aspects of American life." On a 2002 *Wall Street Journal*/NBC poll, fully 70 percent indicated that they did not trust the word of brokers and corporations, and one-third said they had "hardly any confidence" in big-company executives—the highest proportion in more than three decades.

When the cornerstones of confidence crumble and external confidence deteriorates, the work of leaders is made that much more challenging. It can take much longer to restore that confidence than it does to solve financial and operational problems. Leaders face the Humpty-Dumpty problem, that it is very easy to break the egg but very hard to put it back together again. Once promises are broken, it can take many years before any further promises will be believed.

Crises of confidence reflect failures of leadership, and they occur in every sector, including school systems, nonprofit organizations, government agencies, and religious institutions, as well as for-profit businesses. The typical pattern has become depressingly familiar, regardless of the sector in which it occurs: Mistakes and failures are covered up rather than confronted, information is restricted, communication externally as well as internally becomes defensive, contact is minimized, and initiative shuts down, stifling dissent and problem solving. This seemed to be the pattern that caused a massive loss of confidence in the Catholic Church following revelations that abusive priests had been protected by church leaders and a pattern of abuse covered up for many years. Discovery of the problem began in the United States and soon reverberated through Catholic countries around the world. The Boston archdiocese, a division of the world's wealthiest religious establishment, had to sell its property, including the former cardinal's residence, to pay for an $85-million settlement to victims. In Ireland, the government was helping the Church with a $200-million victims' settlement.

Financial investors are joining customers, consumers, and the general public in wanting to hold leaders to even higher standards. Over 90 percent of 25,000 citizens of twenty-three countries reported on a Millennium Survey that they want companies to focus on more than profitability. Two-thirds of American consumers, in another survey, said they felt more trust in a product aligned with social values. By the end of 2003, over $2.14 trillion was invested in the United States in social investment funds, representing a growth of 6.5 percent from 2001, while the broader universe of all professionally managed portfolios declined 4 percent in the same period of the stock market bust. Criteria for investments included screens for alcohol, tobacco, gambling, defense/weapons, animal testing, environment, human rights, labor relations, employment equality, and community investment and/or community relations.

This was a global trend, appearing in all advanced market economies. Japan's Keidanren, the Japanese Federation of Economic Organizations, issued a Charter for Good Corporate Behavior. In October 2001 the Association of British Insurers, whose members control one-quarter of the UK stock market, published new guidelines asking companies to disclose any significant risks to short- and long-term value from social, environmental, and ethical factors. The *Financial Times* called this a significant shift for investors who had traditionally seen social responsibility as an extraneous distraction.

Organizations associated with social causes increasingly gain goodwill benefits that enhance financial performance, from brand enhancement to employee recruitment and retention. Gillette grouped its corporate philanthropy under the name "Gillette Face Forward." The Miami Hurricanes developed programs for at-risk youth. The Philadelphia Eagles' foundation for children helped the franchise garner an award as Pennsylvania's most philanthropic corporation. But the Eagles were involved in community service because this was what Jeffrey Lurie and Joe Banner believed in, as the right thing to do. The Eagles Youth Foundation did not get much local publicity, and it was not a factor in the negotiations for public financing of a new stadium; indeed, the Eagles agreed to donate another $1 million to a city charity as part of the stadium deal.

Confidence cannot be bought, it must be earned. Confidence does not grow because of giveaways that are just superficial— lipstick on a bulldog that doesn't change the nature of the beast. It is earned not through side activities but at the core of the enterprise—how the money is made or the victory secured in the first place. Trust is earned through the actions of leaders in guiding the daily work of the organization, in carrying out its core business. The presence of accountability, collaboration, and initiative increases external confidence that problems will be solved, crises resolved, disasters kept from escalating. The absence of those cornerstones of confidence erodes public trust.

In early 2004, the public crisis of confidence *du jour* involved the situation in Iraq. Despite weak international support, Iraq was invaded by the U.S. and UK with a smattering of allies, Saddam Hussein was toppled, and victory was declared. But in the aftermath of the official war, the long march of nation-building was proving much harder than the bold stroke of military force, and the entire situation was beginning to resemble a losing streak.

In the United States, confidence in President Bush had declined precipitously by March 2004. Speaking to the Council on Foreign Relations on March 5, U.S. Senator Edward M. Kennedy accused President Bush of "manipulation and distortion" to build the case for an invasion, making a point-by-point comparison of White House statements before the war in Iraq and the available intelligence to argue that the president had misrepresented facts about Iraq's weapons and terrorist links. Investigations were underway of both U.S. and British intelligence (a pyrrhic victory for Greg Dyke and the BBC). Within Iraq itself, the occupying forces faced escalating violence and doubts about their nation-building efforts— although I heard from friends in the military about progress in some areas at rebuilding Iraqi institutions. In the rest of the Muslim world, as Admiral Lowell Jacoby, head of the Defense Intelligence Agency, told the Senate Intelligence Committee on February 24, support for the U.S.-led war on terrorism had plunged even in countries considered friendly, fueling radical groups and increasing opposition to pro-U.S. regimes.

Was this an accelerating death spiral with all the anger, blame, revenge-seeking, and negativity of a losing streak? If so, it would be increasingly hard to shift the cycle to a more positive mode without new leadership, for all the reasons I outlined in Chapter 6.

Whatever subsequent events will reveal, including whether the American electorate votes for a new president to lead a turnaround, it is clear that restoring public trust in U.S. leaders will rest on rebuilding the three cornerstones of confidence: accountability— facts on the table, a more open dialogue about how to improve performance; collaboration across partisan divides and with international allies; and initiative, through investment in new economic opportunities and encouragement of small wins—achievements in local areas to make people feel hopeful about future success.

CHOICES, CHOICES, CHOICES

Heads of teams, airlines, schools, manufacturing companies, media organizations, hospitals, religious denominations, and nations define a culture of winning or losing, success or failure, by the choices they make in their messages, personal examples, and formal programs:

- Whether to make decisions in secret behind closed doors, or to use transparent processes involving open debate and dialogue
- Whether to restrict the flow of information, or to expose facts and support abundant communication
- Whether to blame problems on enemies and sinister forces, or to seek solutions by taking actions under one's own control
- Whether to act unilaterally, or to seek collaborators
- Whether to fuel partisan division, or to stress collective goals that unite people
- Whether to underscore suspicion and mistrust of groups that are "different," or to promote mutual respect and relationships
- Whether to feed desires for revenge, or to encourage initiatives for improvement
- Whether to concentrate resources at the center, in the hands of elites, or to invest in numerous small wins in many places by many people
- Whether to use fear to justify decisions, or to emphasize sources of hope

Which end of the scale a leader chooses sets the standards for negative or positive behavior, restricts or opens opportunities for action, depresses energy or raises spirits, and influences how much people are willing to invest. Secrecy, blame, revenge, unilateral action, partisan division, and motivation by fear are, of course, the stuff of losing streaks. Sending messages (explicitly or implicitly) that those phenomena are acceptable, and exemplifying them in policy and practice, tilts the odds toward slipping into decline and losers' habits. This limits the capacity to solve problems and erodes confidence at all levels, from self to system, internally and externally.

Leaders who guide winning streaks make a different set of choices, toward positive, inclusive, empowering actions that build confidence. By believing in other people, they make it possible for others to believe in them. Working together, they increase the likelihood of success, and of continuing to succeed.

12

Winning Streaks, Losing Streaks, and the Game of Life

I WROTE THIS BOOK NOT ONLY TO SHOW TEAMS, COMPANIES, COMMUNI-
TIES, AND COUNTRIES HOW TO CULTIVATE BETTER LEADERSHIP. I ALSO
HAD A GRANDER GOAL: TO HELP MORE PEOPLE IN MANY WALKS OF LIFE
find the confidence to win whatever game they're playing—to gain
life lessons from the winning streaks, losing streaks, and turnarounds that I have described.

By now, the secret of winning should be clear: *Try not to lose
twice in a row.*

I admit that sounds a little facile. But that's exactly what confidence brings: the resilience to bounce back from defeat to victory—
in business, in sports, in professions, in politics, or in life.

Confidence does not guarantee that you will win every single
time (unless you are from Concord, California, and play football for
De La Salle High School—but even then you have to work hard at
it). Too many surprising events, unlucky breaks, acts of nature,
angry sacred cows, competitors who rise to the occasion, or unfortunate injuries can interfere with winning to make it possible to
win each and every game forever. But what confidence does make
more likely is that accountability, collaboration, and initiative will
kick in to shape positive expectations for the next round. Feeling
that they can uncover weaknesses and transcend them, winners are
more likely to analyze problems and face them head-on, communicate and cooperate with those whose support they need, and take
initiative to make adjustments or try innovations. People with con-

fidence feel they can count on themselves, count on other people, and count on shaping events. They can lose and still return to winning.

Confidence motivates people to put in extra effort, to stretch beyond their previous limits, to rebound from setbacks, or to play through injuries anyway. People with confidence stay in the game no matter what. Duke's Mike Krzyzewski called this the principle of "next play." "Don't take what you did in this play to the next play—positive or negative," he told us. "If you develop a culture that is built on next play, collective responsibility, and care, when a loss or a mistake occurs, you are more apt to suffer it together, and get on with the next thing with more of a positive outlook. We say we will never lose two in a row."

PERSONAL WINNING AND LOSING STREAKS

The language of winning and losing that I use throughout this book belongs to sports. Sports has a great deal in common with life—Chicago Cubs manager Dusty Baker declared that everything that's in society is in his team and vice versa, except that his players have a whole lot of ability to play baseball—but sports is just a small slice of life. In sports, as in political campaigns, courtroom battles, or competition for a share of any fixed market, every game produces winners and losers. But even in sports, there are multiple definitions of success and failure, including the odd fact that some perennially losing teams can still win financially (e.g., the Los Angeles Clippers in professional basketball).

In other pursuits, "winning" and "losing" are often complex, overlapping, or blurred. Success in life has many meanings, and a win for one does not have to be at the expense of another. That is the broader way I think about winning streaks and losing streaks—they are shorthands for repeated success or failure at achieving goals.

In my research, I deliberately focused on the extremes—those with long traditions of winning or losing—to make the patterns as clear as possible. But those extremes constitute a relatively small number of people, teams, or organizations. In my surveys, I was more likely to hear from successful companies and teams than from unsuccessful ones, but only a subset reported that they were successful all the time or failed all the time. Even some of the companies, schools, and community organizations I used as examples of organizational turnarounds were not completely awful before, and not completely perfect afterwards. There is a great deal of middle ground.

Most people—including the majority of my survey respondents—fall into that vast middle territory of "win some, lose some." Being equidistant between the best and the worst is not a disaster, but it does not inspire confidence either. And it is an unstable state. One young professional, thinking about her own so-so career, described that middle state to me as "hovering," or "on hold." Which direction was she headed? Was she accumulating strength, or was she slowly deteriorating? Were the cornerstones of confidence getting firmer, or were they crumbling underneath her? My view was that unless she set goals and went all-out to accomplish them—almost anything that could be defined as winning in her world—she would slide into the demoralizing state of losing more than winning.

Confidence guides many personal decisions about what to do next. Individuals run a mental calculation to determine whether the system around them will support them or let them down, whether their personal investment of time, energy, effort, ideas, or emotional commitment will produce positive results or bring disappointment. Winners decide that it is worth the extra push, because the push will pay off. But if someone concludes that there's no point in trying, that he might as well be late or skip practice altogether, that other people will only let him down, that no one is interested in an imaginative idea, etc., etc., then the outcome is foreordained. The self-fulfilling prophecy is fulfilled. He will lose, and lose again.

Weakening accountability, deteriorating relationships, and disappearing initiative are signs that there is further trouble ahead.

Secrecy, denial, blame-shifting, scorn for others, avoidance of contact, and turf protection provoke similar reactions in other people, and the cycle of decline begins. As others shut off the flow of information and contact, as others react by pointing fingers across territories, as others similarly express scorn for people in the system, everyone feels punished. These responses make it harder to solve problems—whether in bankrupt businesses, failing inner-city schools, deteriorating communities, Third World countries, losing teams, or the ordinary life circumstances of average individuals who hit a bump in the road.

My teenaged friend Robert was on a personal losing streak, a classic downward spiral, as his performance in math got worse and worse. He had started at a new school in his junior year of high school and was surprised at how different and how much harder the math classes were. He received a failing grade on the first math test. He started to lose confidence, and he slid into losers' behavior. The first failing grade was embarrassing, so he didn't talk to his parents about it. He couldn't wait to leave math class, and he didn't want to see the teacher, either. He shut the door at home. He said he was studying math, but it began to seem too overwhelming. When his parents discovered halfway through the school year that he was failing math, Robert blamed the teacher for unfair treatment of kids like himself who came from a different background. The teacher gave him extra homework to help him catch up, but that just made Robert feel more ashamed and made math more distasteful. He began to think of himself as someone who couldn't do math and brooded over whether he should go to college. He withdrew from his friends, because they all seemed to be adjusting well and making college plans. He lost energy and started sleeping longer, so his parents told him he wasn't trying hard enough. That made him feel that no one understood him, and he began to neglect his other subjects. Robert's response to his first small failure was making significant failure seem inevitable.

My physician friend Linda started her career on a happier path, a personal winning streak. When she established her practice, she had a series of early successes that built her reputation, and she found ways to publicize them. She exuded confidence. As her reputation grew, she attracted more patients, she could hire others to help her, she could influence the policies of the local hospital and get preferential treatment, she was asked to serve on community boards, she could use her contacts to raise money to start a health-related nonprofit. Leaders of the community expressed their confidence in Linda. Each success encouraged her to approach more senior people to join her. She ran community meetings that people attended at first because of her personal magnetism, but later they came because everyone else did; they liked being part of the network Linda had created. She often appeared in the local newspaper. When the nonprofit stumbled, and there could have been questions about where all that money was going, the press treated her gently, let her tell her story, and left it at that. Everyone assumed that someone like Linda obviously knew what she was doing, and whatever it was must be right.

But Linda began to slip, too. It wasn't a failing grade that started her slide, but the stubbornness of the nonprofit's financial problems, accompanied by a bitter divorce. She was angry and ashamed. She doubted herself. She felt surrounded by a culture of failure, so she became critical and punishing to those running the nonprofit, and they started to leave. The exit of key staff caught the attention of the press, and the local newspaper ran an exposé. For the first time in her life, she felt like a victim. She blamed her ex-husband, she blamed her employees, she pushed her young sons to do chores and criticized the results. She spent less time in her office, she avoided board meetings, and she drove people away. Others lost confidence in her, and that further damaged her self-confidence.

Robert and Linda were fortunate to have people around them who served as their "turnaround leaders." For Robert, it was his parents. I had given them a summary of my conclusions about the dangers of losing streaks, and they decided to discuss the pattern with their son. They presented him with their analysis in a matter-of-fact way that avoided blame, and they ended what Robert felt was punishment. They pointed to his talents (writing and organizing community service) and interests (history and politics). They bought him clothes, an investment that increased his pride in his appearance, but insisted on regular room cleaning and daily extra math drills. They asked his teacher for drills that Robert could practice whenever he had free time, but not too much to feel onerous. Robert set his own goals for small steps he could take to improve his math performance and also act on his other interests. "Team Robert" was convened, complete with a funny membership certificate his mother designed, to cheer him on—his father, his uncle, and two trusted friends, who agreed to get together before watching Sunday sports matches on television. Robert's self-confidence increased in school, and he became more interested, energetic, and—eventually—better at math.

For Linda, it was a second-husband-to-be who acted as a coach and problem-solver. Linda's fiancé was an active, energetic entrepreneur who had built the successful technology company he headed. Every time she tried to say "let's stay home," he said "let's go out." He dragged her out of the house to community events. He stood by her side and told others how happy he was to find someone with Linda's talents, which, of course, reminded her in public of her strengths. He helped her with a turnaround plan for her practice and for the nonprofit, which included forming an external advisory committee. When she hesitated to call potential advisers, he volunteered to do it. After the marriage, Linda's family started a tradition of monthly family conferences at which adults and children alike talked about their accomplishments the previous month and their hopes for the month ahead. Linda became more cheerful and positive at home and at work, and soon people once again flocked to join her causes.

Turnarounds are proof that people can change. Despite the power of cycles to shape behavior, the influence of leaders can change it. Teacher Bruce Walker turned a ninth-grade troublemaker into Booker T. Washington High School's student role model by eleventh grade. At Garanti Bank in Turkey, as Akin Öngör increased pride by investing in new facilities, managers who had once come to work without a business suit bought new clothes, cut their mustaches, and lost weight. The sunny smiles Seagate employees saw after Steve Luczo and Bill Watkins's turnaround had taken hold were found on many of the same faces that had been contorted with anger a few years earlier. The accountable people who join hands to perform mini-miracles in the aftermath of a turnaround are often the same people who were once resentful victims or distrustful turf-protectors under the old regime. That's why I could find so many people at Gillette, the BBC, or Continental Airlines who were in both the "before" and "after" pictures and could describe both states. Failed leaders at the top were long gone, but the middle and lower ranks contained many long-term people, once long-suffering citizens complaining about a losers' culture, but now proud to be on a winning team.

Human behavior is propelled by cycles but not confined by them. People can get swept up in the momentum, but they can also fight against it. That's why it is possible to learn a great deal about winning from losing.

LEARNING ABOUT WINNING FROM LOSING: THE ROLE OF CHARACTER

The only good thing about losing is that it sounds an alarm bell. If people hear the wake-up call and heed it, losing can shake them out of complacency and into action—the way a mild heart attack might propel someone to diet and exercise, or a financial setback might trigger scrutiny of taken-for-granted assumptions about the business.

The point at which people have the most control is at the time of the first losses, when the first signs that something is slipping become apparent. That's the time to avoid panic, resist the temptation to neglect the foundations (like skipping practices or letting relationships slide), and definitely not get dragged down by denial. Later, when a streak has hardened, a cycle is in motion, and patterns are established, it is much more difficult to change course. But the first setbacks represent a choice point: whether to firm up the cornerstones of confidence—a sense of personal responsibility, respect for others, the desire to do something to make a difference—or to slip into self-defeating behavior.

Confidence is an expectation of a positive outcome, but what happens when outcomes are negative? The dividing line between winning streaks and losing streaks is the choice of behavior in response to setbacks. Every game has fumbles, every winning team is sometimes behind, every successful company must respond to crises (such as the national blackout that challenged Continental Airlines) or handle errors (such as the Seagate engineer's $10-million mistake). Former South African president Nelson Mandela set the world-class gold standard for dealing with troubles in a positive way. Despite twenty-seven years in prison, he maintained his strength, built his support system, and educated other leaders in anticipation of someday leading his country. And when he came to power, he focused on reconciliation rather than revenge.

"Not every failure or loss is devastating. It is part of the building process," observed "Coach K" of the winning Duke men's basketball team. Nearby, Gail Goestenkors, coach of the winning Duke women's basketball team, reflected on her number-one team's loss to the Connecticut Huskies in February 2003 (a story I told in Chapter 2). "Sometimes you have to learn lessons the hard way, and that's what we did," she said. "We were down twenty at halftime. We learned a lot from that about some of our weaknesses, and I think that's a great thing. We were much more intense post-UConn." (And they won.)

That decision to build rather than retreat, to rally rather than get discouraged, involves viewing setbacks through an optimistic lens, as an opportunity to learn and move on. Optimists assume that negative events are temporary glitches rather than the permanent state of affairs that pessimists see, and that setbacks are due to specific causes that can be identified and fixed. It's more likely that pessimists will hold superstitions about a "curse of the Bambino"

(Boston Red Sox), or "June swoons" and "ninety-five years of negative thoughts" (Chicago Cubs), putting events in the permanent,
fixed, and unchangeable column—which means there is no point in
trying to change them. Although recent research has claimed to
find optimism/pessimism genes, and some psychologists present
these approaches as fixed dispositions, Martin Seligman, the guru
of optimism/pessimism, believes the opposite: that people can be
taught to use an optimistic approach. Dusty Baker, the Cubs' manager, would certainly agree. "You can condition people to win and
think lucky, just like you can condition people to lose or think unlucky," he said.

That's what can-do optimists such as Gordon Bethune of
Continental Airlines or Elsie Bailey of Booker T. Washington High
School believe, and that's what winning coaches preach to their
teams when they face losses. Putting events in perspective, staying
calm under pressure, and remembering responsibilities to other
people helps prevent panic and keeps the mood positive. This requires as much discipline as the development of technical skills.

"You have to turn a negative into a positive. You have to defeat
defeat. To do this you have to believe in what you do, even when
you lose," Andy Reid, the Philadelphia Eagles head coach, declared.
He said this from the comfortable vantage point of having turned a
loss of the first two games of the 2003 season into a streak of eight
subsequent wins when we spoke to him in his office. (The winning
streak soon extended to eleven games, though not a championship.) Those two initial losses were highly visible and major
blows. The Eagles' first loss occurred on the opening-day celebration of the opening of the new stadium, Lincoln Financial Field,
when the eyes of Philadelphia, if not the country, were on the
Eagles. The next game was on national television. Imagine living
through most people's worst nightmare: failing when the greatest
number are watching.

Throughout the games, it was important that Reid and star quarterback Donovan McNabb stay calm. "The two of us are under the
microscope. Everyone watches us," Reid said. "If we are out of con-

trol, it affects everyone. That calm has to be innate. The game is going to reach extreme highs and lows." It was not just a brave façade when the television cameras were on them, and the public was watching. "The players will call coaches out if they are putting on an act," Reid said. "The veteran guys know I won't waver, so they won't waver." McNabb explained, "Mentally we stay on course. We get our chins up, go to practice, and get things done."

McNabb was recruited not just for athletic prowess but for character. Andy Reid said he would select a lesser talent with character over a better athlete without it. The Eagles' owners described character in terms of the respect McNabb showed to others, his maturity and steadiness. They attributed it to an inner security that stemmed from his childhood. "The Philadelphia media and fans can be brutal. What would amaze the outside world is how important it is, and how much Donovan is affected by having two parents married to each other all his life and close, loving relationships among his family," Eagles president Joe Banner said. McNabb drew on that confidence during the early weeks of the 2003 season, when he was not playing well. He had to contend with attacks from right-wing commentator Rush Limbaugh, who called McNabb an overrated beneficiary of the NFL's desire for black quarterbacks. (That racist remark got Limbaugh fired from his slot on ESPN television.)

Character is a term used often by successful people and organizations in my research. Gordon Bethune at Continental and Steve Luczo at Seagate eliminated managers who did not have it. Elsie Bailey, principal of Booker T. Washington High School, looked for it in new teachers and administrators. Anson Dorrance, coach of the North Carolina women's soccer team, also chose players with character over those with innate talent who lacked it. He looked for young women whom he considered to have the right psychological makeup to support teammates in an accountable way. That's how he selected Jordan Walker, whom he once called one of the least athletic players he had ever seen, and why she became team captain. Billy Beane, general manager of the Oakland A's, described a player of several years earlier who didn't play a great deal but had a huge impact because of his character. "He was a guy that players would listen to because he had a lot of physical presence to him and had won before and had a lot of energy, and he brought a dynamic off the field and into the dugout that seemed to have a great influence on the players."

Character is shaped by values. Values can be taught and communicated. They can be reinforced by reminders of responsibilities to the wider world. I asked Donovan McNabb about the large photos and tributes to Martin Luther King, Mother Teresa, and Jonas Salk in the lobby of the Eagles' headquarters and fitness center. "When a player walks into NovaCare and sees so many great leaders that are non-athletes, it says a lot," he replied. "That life is not all about football, it's about leaders who have done wonders for the universe. That's the thought process that Mr. Lurie and Mr. Banner want us to have."

Development of character was about the only explanation we could find for De La Salle High School's amazing record of never losing a football game—a 151-game winning streak (and counting) over twelve undefeated seasons for a world's record well ahead of number two, and long streaks of thirty and forty unbroken wins before that. As a Christian Brothers school, De La Salle's goal was to produce "men of integrity." Long-serving head football coach Bob Ladouceur also taught the senior religion seminar. In his religion class he guided a wide-ranging discussion of current social and ethical issues. In football he emphasized both the fundamentals of blocking, tackling, and running, which needed to be drilled day after day, and the intangibles of teamwork, responsibility, accountability, honesty, toughness, heart, and fortitude, which emanated from character.

Despite awful facilities (a dank, dark locker room infested with mice and cockroaches), tough academic requirements, a diminishing number of fans at home games, stringent discipline for the occasional player who violated an ethical rule (it had last happened two years before our interviews), and a schedule that increasingly featured tough, nationally ranked teams, the work ethic was strong. Perhaps character began with the coach. Ladouceur was so reticent, it took repeated calls to get him to agree to an interview, and the interview had to take place during his break to ride his exercise bike; he talked while pedaling steadily. He certainly did not appear to be looking for a college coaching job (he had led the De La Salle team for twenty-four years); he was totally focused on execution and on being the best high school coach that he could be.

Whether innate, nurtured in a secure childhood, faith-based, or taught by leaders and their values, character helps people make positive rather than negative choices when confronted with losing, and those positive actions make recovery and return to a winners' path more likely. People with character have internalized—embedded in themselves—the three cornerstones of confidence: accountability, collaboration, and initiative. When the going is tough, they are able to draw on those internal supports. They behave accountably in finding the strength for extra effort so as to live up to responsibilities. They behave collaboratively by reaching out to other people and seeking mutual support. And they show initiative by finding steps that can be taken through things that they control, that can make a difference, however small.

Dig Deeper, Find the Roots, Work Harder: The Spirit of Personal Accountability

"When the chips are down, you can count on a person of character to dig a little deeper," Andy Reid said. "They will work through adversity. They will buckle down and eventually win." De La Salle's athletic director, Terry Eidson, said about the winning football team, "I don't know if it's a culture of winning; it's more of a culture of effort and commitment." He felt that what made them different was the commitment of the players, because the school nurtured hard work and commitment in every endeavor.

Commitment comes from high internal standards—the desire to achieve excellence in whatever the pursuit, and regardless of the outcome. Digging deeper, all the way to the roots, is a way to find those internal standards, and to find the courage to examine whether they are being met. It's possible to win while playing badly, and to lose while playing well. For Anson Dorrance, Geno Auriemma, and many others, the party line was that getting beaten by a better opponent was different from losing. As long as the team was playing at the highest level, it would resume winning. The point is that the standard is internal, as Bob Ladouceur of De La Salle indicated: "I don't talk about other teams—how to get up for other team's strengths—too much. I talk about what we need to do, what can we do right now. And I've got some weaknesses on our team that we need to work on."

Finding those standards means being willing to face the truth, to be honest with oneself. Understanding what is happening makes it possible to avoid being victimized or feeling like a victim. Seeking the truth, seeking the feedback, seeking the negative information is the first step toward improvement. Duke's Mike Krzyzewski joined Gillette's Jim Kilts in emphasizing truth-telling as a high value. "You can win without playing great. You tell the team the truth," Coach K said. "Okay, we won and we need to do these things better— we were fortunate and the team we played maybe wasn't ready to play us. In other words, deal with the truth." The facts are the keys to knowing what to do the next time.

Knowledge and effort help people go on rather than give up. Perseverance is the willingness to stay in just a little longer, run just a few more steps, practice just a little harder, try just one more time. The difference between success and failure is often how long people give it before they give up. Recall my favorite law of management and life, which I set forth in Chapter 3: "Everything can look like a failure in the middle." Winners redefine setbacks as detours en route to success, and they redouble their efforts to find a way around the obstacles. That's why Connecticut's Geno Auriemma designed practices that were tougher than games. That's why Steve Luczo, Bill Watkins, and Doug DeHaan at Seagate believed that stretch goals spur innovation and build pride, so that people discover they are capable of doing much more than they thought possible at first. That's why the best teams and the best organizations are known for thorough preparation and extremely hard work.

Reach Out, Draw Closer, Seek Support:
The Spirit of Personal Collaboration

One of the best things winners can do when facing a loss that feels personal is not to think of themselves at all, but to think first about others. I don't know how Andy Reid really felt inside while watching the Eagles go down to crushing defeats in their first two games, but his first instinct was to acknowledge his responsibility to the team by remaining steadfast and supportive. Reactions such as anger or sulking would be inherently selfish and would drive people further apart.

Nelson Mandela, of course, exemplified reaching out, both as a revolutionary and as a statesman. He relied on close colleagues during his years of imprisonment, sought international support for his cause, and worked to befriend former enemies after his release. Seeing virtues in others, rather than emphasizing their faults, brings them closer. The culture of pride that surrounds winners comes from admiration and respect for others' talents. Akin Öngör and Saide Kuzeyli had high standards and did not tolerate those who resisted change, yet I was struck by how much they drew people to them by praise and recognition.

When in trouble, find a partner. Avoiding the loser's temptation to shut down and withdraw helps restore the ability to win. It's easier to do together what seems impossible alone. After Connecticut's loss to Villanova, Geno Auriemma led the women on the Huskies team to examine whether they had stopped caring about one another, whether they had started to go it alone rather than relying on their teammates. People without a set of teammates to help them weather difficult times do not have to suffer in isolation; they can look for support, any support, and build their own mini-network. Ulrike von Manteuffel at Siemens-Nixdorf reached out to her peers, and when she hit a corporate obstacle, a co-worker whom she barely knew offered to send a petition to the CEO.

For those who reach out to help others, reciprocity kicks in—*Give, and you shall later get.* When Donovan McNabb was dropping balls at the beginning of the 2003 season, the people around him took on a piece of the responsibility and increased their level of play to help him through a difficult time.

People can be remarkably generous when approached directly; they are even flattered to be asked. Even in the culture of warring factions that characterized pre-turnaround Continental, and even during the demoralized years at the BBC, people at lower levels who were insulated from the turf battles above them did favors for one another. At Peabody Elementary School, which had no tradition of parental involvement and a large number of students from single-parent families, new principal Marty Pettigrew got fathers to help with school security just by asking. Reaching out can sometimes uncover surprising resources.

When people come to respect one another, and feel respected, they do not want to disappoint their teammates. David Heffernan, offensive lineman for the 1983 championship Miami Hurricanes and an avid fan of subsequent teams, declared that the work ethic does not come from coaches but from peers. "It's when you are terrified of looking into the eyes of your teammates and letting them down in some way. When the players can push each other, that is when you get a ton of success."

Find Attainable Steps, Focus on What You Can Control: The Spirit of Personal Initiative

Just do something! When faced with problems, winners are willing to move forward and to take risks, even to risk being wrong. They favor action over passivity, looking ahead over looking back, and they are willing to admit mistakes and move on. At his first day at Gillette, new CEO Jim Kilts called himself "often wrong, never uncertain." Coach K also espoused the ability to make immediate change and not worry about ego, if it turns out something was wrong. "Instant corrections help you stop losing and maybe keep winning," he said.

After the Eagles lost the first two games of 2003, Andy Reid eliminated the fancy maneuvers and went back to basics, to work on the obvious things that needed improvement. "I'm in the boat with all of those mistakes we made," he said. "I control this stuff, the fundamentals. When things go south like this, you tell the team, 'It's time to take off the tuxedoes and put on the blue jeans. Let's go to work!' It's all about not pushing too hard to get it all back too quickly. Some players are thinking, 'I've got to make a play.' No! Just do your job—nothing extra. I preach that you have to put yourself in a position to make a play; don't try too hard to make it happen. That doesn't work; when you're down, you can't force it, no matter how much you feel like you need to."

Forcing it is what losers try to do. I found it poignant that some of the athletes on the 2003 Prairie View A&M football team said before the season began that this might be their year to win a championship, even though the team had not won more than a half-dozen games in fourteen years; leaping ahead to think about the championship, instead of taking it one game at a time, was too big a leap—and indeed, the Panthers continued to lose, perhaps in part because Coach Whittington pushed them too hard, beyond the attainable goals they controlled. If it helps to have a vision, or a BHAG ("big hairy audacious goal"), as some management gurus recommend, that grand vision needs to be tucked away in the back of the mind when players go out on the field to perform a move at a time, or they make the mistake I make in tennis, when I stop watching the ball at game point because I'm already mentally celebrating the win (and then I miss the shot). Instead, it is better to work on the "fifteen-minute competitive advantage," which I named after a Woody Allen short story about the most effective invaders of Earth from outer space, who were not light years ahead of us, but only fifteen minutes ahead. That is, seek step by step progress a little faster or a little smarter.

"You can't jump the process because you were in the title game last year. In order to win you can't jump any stages," observed Miami Hurricanes' assistant head coach Art Kehoe. "We make such a big point of living in the moment, of being just mindful of what you're doing today," said Gale Valley, assistant coach of the Duke women's basketball team. "That's how you live with the pressure. That's how you enjoy the journey, because you can't worry about the NCAA tournament when you're starting to work out in September and October, starting to play games in November and December." The Cubs' Dusty Baker set goals for batches of games: take two out of three-game series, at least split a four-game series, win eight out of ten on a ten-game road trip, win fifteen games per month. His strategy of dividing big goals into attainable steps helped the 2003 Cubs go one game at a time into a winning season and the playoffs.

People cannot jump stages in other endeavors, either. As much as CEOs and politicians long for the bold stroke of the policy pen that will ensure prosperity or peace forever, as much as the dieter wishes the extra weight could come off in a week, as much as American presidential candidates wish they could be anointed without campaigning, as much as adolescents wish they could leap into adult fame and fortune without intense effort in the intervening years, winning is just not possible without a long march. Long marches take place step by step by hard-working step. But the good news is that every single person can make a difference in a long march. A vital part of Continental Airlines' return to health was the discovery by people at every level that there was something they could do to make a difference in on-time performance.

Even when problems seem overwhelming, when circumstances seem uncontrollable, that's when winners focus on whatever they *can* control—how prepared they are, how hard they work, how many steps they can take. This is the practical power of positive thinking, as captured in clichés about making lemonade when life provides lemons. Jackie Jenkins-Scott was a good lemonade maker who found hidden assets in her turnaround of an inner-city health center. Where predecessors had seen old buildings, she saw a historic landmark. Where others saw an impoverished African-American population, she saw a musical tradition that could be turned into an appealing fund-raiser attracting the whole Greater Boston community.

Small steps, small accomplishments, a hurdle at a time, can have big impact. Small wins can improve the odds of achieving the next big success. Geno Auriemma focused his women's basketball team's attention on the small, unseen things that helped win the game, such as a rebound that somebody grabbed at a crucial time. It is those little things on the part of everyone that separate a win from a loss. That's why City Year, the American national service organization of young people that Nelson Mandela embraced as a model for South Africa, begins every meeting with "ripples": an opportunity to tell a personal story about a recent accomplishment or sign of success, however modest, that sends out a "tiny ripple of hope" to remind everyone that taking action is worth it. Celebration of the small wins creates confidence that bigger goals can be attained.

RISING TO THE OCCASION AND WALKING ON WATER

Throughout this book we have seen numerous self-reinforcing cycles. Those on winning streaks seem to get all the advantages—adulation, career opportunities, good deals, benefits of the doubt, fewer rules and restrictions—while those on losing streaks miss out. It is easy to feel on top of the world as a winner (and risk entering the danger zone of arrogance and complacency), but to feel at the bottom of the scrap heap when facing setbacks. Losing streaks, decline cycles, big institutional forces, and unsupportive systems certainly arouse negative emotions and tempt people toward losers' behavior; yet practically no one is utterly powerless. Even if individuals do not control their circumstances, at least they do have a measure of control over their responses to those circumstances. And so they have the potential to break the cycle by refusing to indulge in losers' behavior or slip into losers' habits. They can tilt the cycle in their favor by practicing winners' approaches and winners' behavior: accountability, collaboration, and initiative.

If people look positively at themselves and the hidden value of their assets, they are more likely to discover strengths that they can cultivate. If people look positively at others, those people are more likely to come through for them. And if people look positively at the opportunities any situation provides to take even a small step, they are more likely to find that their actions make a difference.

The values statement for the North Carolina women's soccer team expresses the foundations of individual confidence for anyone playing the game of life: "We don't whine. We work hard. The truly extraordinary do something every day. We choose to be positive. When we don't play as much as we would like, we are noble and still support the team and its mission. We don't freak out over ridiculous issues or live in fragile states of emotional catharsis or create crises where none should exist. We are well led. We care about each other as teammates and as human beings. We play for each other. And we want our lives (and not just in soccer) to be never-ending ascensions."

From the simplest ball games to the most complicated business and political situations, the common element is a basic truth about people: People rise to the occasion when they have the confidence to do it.

Sir Isaac Newton said about his own scientific accomplishments: "If I have seen further, it is by standing on the shoulders of giants." He was referring to his predecessors who laid the foundation, but I like the meaning of this for everyone who gets a boost from those around them.

This truth holds for business executives, national politicians, and community leaders who rely on the actions of thousands of people beneath them to achieve lofty goals, or for individuals (like my friends Robert and Linda) who are lifted by their families to see new possibilities for success. Even athletes, whose height and talents can make them seem like giants, are standing on the shoulders of others—the team that surrounds them, the organization that guides the team, the leaders who define the context, and the external network of all those other people who cheer them on, invest in their success, and, indeed, make the game itself possible. We can applaud remarkable achievements of individuals while remembering that they are not succeeding, or fumbling, alone.

In losing streaks, it seems as though talent has disappeared and decline is inevitable—or else why would the workers, the managers, the politicians, the players let the situation continue to deteriorate? The opposite appears to be at work in winning streaks—that individuals can perform miracles, that they do indeed walk on water. But every water walker needs the stones to make it possible to move across the water.

Knowing that what's underneath will hold you and help you rise to victory is the essence of confidence.

Notes

8   *Overconfidence* Dan Lovallo and Daniel Kahneman, "Delusions of Success: How Optimism Undermines Executives' Decisions," *Harvard Business Review*, July 2003: 56–63.

8   *And for nonrandom activities* Although the idea has roots in the work of earlier sociologists, Robert K. Merton shaped the concept of the self-fulfilling prophecy, which he introduced in an article in the *Antioch Review* in 1948 and refined in his book *Social Theory and Social Structure* (Glencoe, IL: Free Press,1949).

9   *Statistically, each player* T. Gilovich, R. Vallone, and A. Tversky, "The Hot Hand in Basketball: On the Misperception of Random Sequences," *Cognitive Psychology* 17 (1985): 295–314. S. C. Albright, "A Statistical Analysis of Hitting Streaks in Baseball," *Journal of the American Statistical Association* 88 (1993): 1175–83. Stephen Jay Gould, "The Streak of Streaks," *New York Review of Books* 35 (1988): 8–12.

10   For a sampling of the many views of self-fueling spirals, see Dana H. Lindsley, Daniel J. Brass, and James B. Thomas, "Efficacy-Performance Spirals: A Multilevel Perspective," *Academy of Management Review* 20, no. 3 (1995): 645–70; Scott Snook, "Winning and Losing Streaks in Professional Football: A Study of Self-Fueling Spirals in Team Effectiveness," unpublished manuscript, Harvard University Department of Psychology, January 1995; and Kim S. Cameron, Jane E. Dutton, and Robert H. Quinn, eds., *Positive Organizational Scholarship* (San Francisco: Berrett-Koehler, 2003).

13   *Teams compete for the glory* Emma Herbert prepared a detailed and highly informed analysis for me about winning streaks and losing streaks in international test cricket from 1980 through 2003, drawing on win-loss records and extensive press commentary. This account is derived from her report.

15   *"Where and when did it all go wrong?"* H. Davies, "Oh Why Are Ingerland So Bad?" *Independent On Sunday*, 31 October 1999.

16   *"most hated man in America"* Aaron Bernstein, *Grounded: Frank Lorenzo*

and the Destruction of Eastern Airlines (New York: Simon & Schuster, 1990).

16   On the costs of the Northeast blackout, see Associated Press, "Report on Blackout to Be Released Today," *New York Times*, 19 November 2003, 3:18 p.m., on nytimes.com http://www.nytimes.com/aponline/national/AP-Blackout.html (accessed 19 November 2003).

22   *deliberately varied range of sports* Many others have used sports as a proxy for leadership and teamwork in business or politics and have pointed out the differences among sports. For example, Robert W. Keidel called football a metaphor for hierarchical control, baseball for autonomy of organizational parts, basketball and soccer for voluntary cooperation. Keidel, *Game Plans: Sports Strategies for Business* (New York: Dutton, 1985); and "Team Sports Models as a Generic Organizational Framework," *Human Relations* 40 (1987): 591–612. My sports research, however, was designed to capture phenomena that occurred across sports, despite obvious differences in the games themselves and in competitive rules.

34   *The Huskies were off the scale* Daniel L. Fulks, *Revenues and Expenses of Division I and II Intercollegiate Athletics*, http://www.ncaa.org/library/research/i_ii_rev_exp/2002/d1_d2_revenues_expenses.pdf (accessed 28 July 2003). Wendy Parker, "Analysis: The Top Five; UConn the Class of Women's Programs," *Atlanta Journal-Constitution*, 1 February 2003.

39   *causality can run in the opposite direction* This is supported by what social psychologists call the "fundamental attribution error"—the common but often flawed assumption that success is due to our own skills but that failure is due to bad luck. Shelley Taylor has written about the positive role self-deception can play in helping people cope with stressful situations, in *Positive Illusions: Creative Self-Deception and the Healthy Mind* (New York: Basic Books, 1989).

39   *"self-efficacy"* Albert Bandura, "Self-Efficacy: Toward a Unifying Theory of Behavioral Change," *Psychological Review* 84 (1977): 191–215. On the stretching experiment: R. S. Weinberg, D. Gould, and A. Jackson, "Expectations and Performance: An Empirical Test of Bandura's Self-Efficacy Theory," *Journal of Sports Psychology* 1 (1979): 320–31.

40   *Pygmalion Effect* Robert Rosenthal and Lenore Jacobson, *Pygmalion in the Classroom: Teacher Expectation and Pupils' Intellectual Development* (New York: Irvington Publishers, 1992), an update of a book first published in 1968.

45   *Winning begets winning* A study comparing fifty-three high- or low-performing sales teams in a major retailer found a clear relationship between the good mood of leaders and group performance, with each serving as both cause and effect. Jennifer George, "Leader Positive Mood and Group Performance: The Case of Customer Service," *Journal of Applied Social Psychology* 25 (1995): 778–94.

45   *"Primitive emotional contagion"* Elaine Hatfield, John T. Cacioppo, and Richard L. Rapson, *Emotional Contagion* (Cambridge, England: Cambridge University Press, 1994). On facial expressions: Sigal G. Barsade, "The Ripple Effect: Emotional Contagion and Its Influence on Group

Behavior," *Administrative Science Quarterly* 47 (2002): 644–75. On mimicry: Roland Neumann and Fritz Strack, " 'Mood Contagion': The Automatic Transfer of Mood between Persons," *Journal of Personality and Social Psychology* 79 (2000): 211–33. On pleasant feelings and rapport: Janice R. Kelly and Sigal G. Barsade, "Mood and Emotion in Small Groups and Work Teams," *Organizational Behavior and Human Decision Processes* 86 (September 2001): 99–130.

46   *everyone played better* On the effects of positive or negative emotions: Barsade, ibid. The cricket study: P. Totterdell, "Catching Moods and Hitting Runs: Mood Linkage and Subjective Performance in Professional Sport Teams," *Journal of Applied Psychology* 74 (2000): 848–59. Other studies have found that positive emotions predicted improvements in supervisor evaluations: Barry M. Staw, Robert R. Sutton, and I. Pellod, "Employee Positive Emotion and Favorable Outcomes at the Workplace," *Organization Science* 5 (1994): 51–71. It appears that pleasant feelings associated with good moods, rather than elevated energy levels, raise productivity: T. A. Wright and Barry M. Staw, "Affect and Favorable Work Outcomes: Two Longitudinal Tests of the Happy-Productive Worker Thesis," *Journal of Organizational Behavior* 20 (1999): 1–23. See also Barbara L. Frederickson, "Emotions and Upward Spirals," in Kim S. Cameron, Jane E. Dutton, and Robert H. Quinn, eds., *Positive Organizational Scholarship* (San Francisco: Berrett-Koehler, 2003): 163–75.

46   *Liking one another* Albert V. Carron, Michelle M. Colman, Jennifer Wheeler, and Diane Stevens, "Cohesion and Performance in Sport: A Meta Analysis," *Journal of Sports & Exercise Psychology* 24, no.2 (June 2002): 168–88.

46   *Because they feel committed* J. R. Larson, P. G. Foster-Fishman, and T. Franz, "Leadership Style and the Discussion of Shared and Unshared Information in Decision-making Groups," *Personality and Social Psychology Bulletin* 24, no. 5 (1998): 482–95.

47   *They feel a sense of belonging* Richard M. Ryan and Wedward L. Deci, "Self-Determination Theory and the Facilitation of Intrinsic Motivation, Social Development, and Well-being," *American Psychologist* 55, no. 1 (2000): 68–78.

48   *teammates who care* Anthony J. Amorose and Thelma S. Horn, "Intrinsic Motivation: Relationships with Collegiate Athletes' Gender, Scholarship Status, and Perceptions of Their Coaches' Behavior," *Journal of Sports & Exercise Psychology* 22, no. 1 (February 2000): 63–84.

48   *The Vision of a Champion* This is the title of Anson Dorrance's book (Ann Arbor, MI: Ann Arbor Press, 2002).

50   *A rival coach once said* S. L. Price, *Sports Illustrated,* 7 December 1998.

53   *human resource practices* Jeffrey Pfeffer, *The Human Equation* (Boston: Harvard Business School Press, 1998).

56   *Wider networks* Mark Granovetter, "The Strength of Weak Ties," *American Journal of Sociology* 78 (May 1973): 1360–80.

59   *more continuity, fewer disruptions* Jeffrey Pfeffer and Alison Davis-Blake studied the turnover of coaches in the National Basketball Association from 1977 to 1981; they found that whether succession disrupts or im-

proves performance depends on a coach's prior experience and competence. There is more disruption if succession occurs in the middle of the season and the new coach comes from outside, but less disruption if new coaches resemble previous ones. In short, continuity makes succession less disruptive. Pfeffer and Davis-Blake, "Administrative Succession and Organizational Performance: How Administrator Experience Mediates the Succession Effect," *Academy of Management Journal* 1986 (1): 72–83. Another study of NBA teams found a high correlation between winning percentage and longer tenure of the head coach: Shawn L. Berman, Jonathon Down, and Charles W. L. Hill, "Tacit Knowledge as a Source of Competitive Advantage in the National Basketball Association," *Academy of Management Journal* 45 (1, 2002): 13–31.

59   *Owners, boards of directors* Andrew Van de Ven and D. Polley, "Learning While Innovating," *Organization Science* 3, no. 1 (February 1992): 92–115.

62   *It is even a little mundane* Daniel Chambliss, "The Mundanity of Excellence: An Ethnographic Report on Stratification and Olympic Swimmers," *Sociological Theory* 7 (Spring 1989): 70–86.

65   *For example, a developing country* Dietrich Dorner, *The Logic of Failure*, translated by Rita Kimber and Robert Kimber (New York: Henry Holt/Metropolitan Books, 1996).

65   *Potential leaders* Warren Bennis and Robert Thomas, *Geeks and Geezers: Leadership for a Lifetime* (Boston: Harvard Business School Press, 2002).

66   Bethune quote Gordon Bethune, with Scott Huler, *From Worst to First* (New York: Wiley, 1998), 149–50.

67   *It doesn't take a rocket scientist* The more complex the system, the greater the possibilities for "normal accidents," as sociologist Charles Perrow termed them. Perrow, *Normal Accidents: Living with High-Risk Technologies* (New York: Basic Books, 1984). See also Diane Vaughan, *The Challenger Launch Decision* (Chicago: Univ. of Chicago Press, 1997).

67   *Kanter's Law* The "law" about failure in the middle is from Rosabeth Moss Kanter, *Evolve!: Succeeding in the Digital Culture of Tomorrow* (Boston: Harvard Business School Press, 2001), chapter 9.

68   *The situation will get worse* Dietrich Dorner conducted simulations of decision making in complex situations, in which participants played such roles as mayors of towns or leaders of developing countries, identifying differences between "good" participants, whose actions improved conditions, and "bad" ones whose decisions caused things to get worse. Dorner, *The Logic of Failure.*

68   *It's not mistakes* Barry M. Staw, Lance E. Sandelands, and Jane E. Dutton, "Threat-Rigidity Effects in Organizational Behavior: A Multilevel Analysis," *Administrative Science Quarterly* 26, no. 4 (December 1981): 501–24.

72   *"delusional optimism"* Dan Lovallo and Daniel Kahneman, "Delusions of Success: How Optimism Undermines Executives' Decisions," *Harvard Business Review,* July 2003: 56–63.

72   *oversimplification* David Dunning, Dale W. Griffin, James D. Milojkovic, and Lee Ross, "The Overconfidence Effect in Social Prediction," *Journal of Personality and Social Psychology* 58, no. 4 (1990): 568–81.

72   *overshooting* Mark Simon and Susan M. Houghton, "The Relationship Between Overconfidence and the Introduction of Risky Products: Evidence from a Field Study," *Academy of Management Journal* 46, no. 2 (2003): 139–49.

74   On the importance of broken windows and other such small signs of decay, in influencing effort and commitment, see James Q. Wilson and George L. Kelling, "Broken Windows," *The Atlantic Monthly* 249 (March 1982): 29–38. This was based on Wilson's analysis as reported in his *Thinking About Crime* (New York: Basic Books, 1975). Kelling later wrote, with Catherine Coles, *Fixing Broken Windows* (New York: Free Press, 1996).

74   *Chernobyl* Dorner, *The Logic of Failure*, 33–34.

74   *groupthink* Irving L. Janis, *Victims of Groupthink: A Psychological Study of Foreign Policy Decisions and Fiascoes* (Boston: Houghton Mifflin, 1972).

76   On tuning in to changes in the environment, see Kanter, *Evolve!*, chapter 9, and www.changetoolkit.com.

77   On lapses and denial, see Albert O. Hirschman, *Exit, Voice and Loyalty: Responses to Decline in Firms, Organizations, and States* (Cambridge, MA: Harvard University Press, 1970), 1.

78   *silent filters* Edgar Schein, *Organizational Culture and Leadership* (San Francisco: Jossey-Bass, 1992).

78   *"competence traps"* Barbara Leavitt and James G. March, "Organizational Learning," *Annual Review of Sociology* 14 (1988): 319–40; Dorothy Leonard-Barton, "Core Capabilities and Core Rigidities: A Paradox in Managing New Product Development," *Strategic Management Journal* 13 (1992): 111–25.

78   On denial as impression management, see Andrew Van de Ven and D. Polley, "Learning While Innovating," *Organization Science* 3, no. 1 (February 1992): 92–115.

78   *a tendency to oversimplify* Giovanni Gavetti and Daniel Levinthal, "Looking Forward and Looking Backward: Cognitive and Experiential Search," *Administrative Science Quarterly* 45, no. 1 (March 2000): 113–37; and Daniel A. Levinthal, "Adaptation on Rugged Landscapes," *Management Science* 43, no. 7 (July 1997): 934–50.

78   On politics and cognitive limitations, see Robert Burgelman, "Fading Memories: A Process Theory of Strategic Business Exit in Dynamic Environments," *Administrative Sciences Quarterly* 39 (March 1994): 24–56.

78   *When companies lag* Rosabeth Moss Kanter, *Evolve!*, chapter 3.

80   On bankruptcies of British companies, see John Argenti, *Corporate Collapse: The Causes and Symptoms* (Maidenhead, UK: McGraw-Hill, 1976).

80   *Continental Airlines* Greg Brenneman, "Right Away and All at Once: How We Saved Continental," *Harvard Business Review*, September–October 1998: 2–12.

80   *public school officials hid data* M. Rodekohr, "Adjustments of Colorado School Districts to Declining Enrollments," unpublished doctoral dissertation, University of Colorado at Boulder, 1974.

80   *Houston school district* Diana Jean Schemo, "Questions on Data Cloud Luster of Houston Schools," *New York Times*, 11 July 2003.

80   On defensiveness and cover-ups, see Chris Argyris, *On Organizational Learning* (Malden, MA: Blackwell, 1999), second edition.

93   *"learned helplessness"* L. B. Alloy, Christopher Peterson, L. Y. Abramson, and Martin E. P. Seligman, "Attributional Style and the Generality of Learned Helplessness," *Journal of Personality and Social Psychology* 46 (1984): 681–87. Christopher Peterson, Steven F. Maier, and Martin E. P. Seligman, *Learned Helplessness* (New York: Oxford University Press, 1993).

96   *Lou Piniella* Major League Baseball Advanced Media, L.P., "MLB.com: The Devil Rays: Manager and Coaches," MLB.com, http://tampabay.devilrays.mlb.com (accessed December 23, 2003).

96   *"Losing beats you down"* Pat Jordan, "Winning Used to Be Everything," *New York Times Magazine*, 20 July 2003.

96   *The atmosphere in Tampa Bay* Ibid.

98   *Powerlessness corrodes* Rosabeth Moss Kanter, *Men and Women of the Corporation* (New York: Basic Books, 1977).

98   *Conversations about losing* Harvard psychologist David Perkins called these discussion traps "brownian motion" (jumping around too much from topic to topic) and "down-spiraling" (getting stuck in arguments for the sake of arguing, becoming more negative and more polarized as the conversation proceeds). Perkins, *King Arthur's Round Table: How Collaborative Conversations Create Smart Organizations* (New York: Wiley, 2003).

99   *Losers, compared with winners* About 30 percent of the losers, compared with only 8 percent of the winners, on my business survey reported that their companies never or rarely communicated the facts about their situation often and to most everyone, and 53 percent of the losers but only 14 percent of the winners said that their companies always or often tended to be secretive, with small groups making decisions behind closed doors.

100   *Losing teams frequently fired their managers* William A. Gamson and Norman Scotch, "Scapegoating in Baseball," *American Journal of Sociology* 70 (1964): 64–70.

100   On Just for Feet v. Saatchi & Saatchi, see Carrick Mollenkamp and Kelly Greene, "Sneaker King Wound a Path to Chapter 11," *Wall Street Journal*, 3 November 1999.

101   *Attack and blame* In addition, losing is depressing, and depression is associated with greater irritability. That fact all by itself accounts for some of the negativity. Irritability makes people picky, dissatisfied, more critical.

101   *Criticizing performance* Jean-François Manzoni and Jean-Louis Barsoux, *The Set-Up-to-Fail Syndrome* (Boston: Harvard Business School Press, 2002).

102   On cultures of pride producing innovation and cultures of mediocrity suppressing it, see Rosabeth Kanter, *The Change Masters* (New York: Simon & Schuster, 1983).

102 *Among the high school groups* Nearly 42 percent of the losers compared with 25 percent of the winners always or often wonder whether certain players deserve to be on the team. One clear reason for this isn't talent, it's whether people are willing to work.

104 *"self-focus"* Chu-Min Liao and Richard S. W. Masters, "Self-Focused Attention and Performance Failure under Psychological Stress," *Journal of Sports & Exercise Psychology* 24, no. 3 (September 2002): 289–305.

105 *But trusting only in yourself* Perkins, *King Arthur's Round Table.*

106 *More than twice as many people* For internal rivalries the survey percentages are 44 percent for losers versus 20 percent for winners; for absence of cross-company teams, 38 percent for losers versus 8 percent for winners. Also, 55 percent percent of the winners said they never had internal rivalries, and 73 percent always or often used cross-company teams, compared with only 36 percent of the losers.

106 On the effect of "star" behavior, see Anne Donnellon, *Team Talk: Listening Between the Lines to Improve Team Performance* (Boston: Harvard Business School Press, 1996).

107 *Envy* Michelle K. Duffy and Jason D. Shaw, "The Salieri Syndrome: Consequences of Envy in Groups," *Small Group Research* 31 (2000): 3–23.

107 *Lack of contact and localized decisions* Claude M. Steele, "Contending with Group Image: The Psychology of Stereotype and Social Identity Threat," *Advances in Experimental Social Psychology* 34 (2002): 379–440.

108 *"defensive pessimism"* Julie K. Norem and Nancy Cantor, "Defensive Pessimism: Harnessing Anxiety as Motivation," *Journal of Personality and Social Psychology* 51 (1986): 1208–17.

109 *helplessness . . . hopelessness* More than twice as many losers as winners on my sports survey (23 percent versus 11 percent) and over three times as many losers as winners on my business survey (41 percent versus 13 percent) said they felt helpless; and twice as many losers as winners on the sports survey (41 percent versus 22 percent) and more than four times as many losers as winners on the business survey (42 percent versus 9 percent) felt hopeless, saying that there were too many things stacked against them.

109 *Pessimists see problems* Martin E. P. Seligman, *Learned Optimism* (New York: Knopf, 1991). Jane E. Gillham, Andrew J. Shatte, Karen J. Reivich, and Martin E. P. Seligman, "Optimism, Pessimism, and Explanatory Style," in Edward C. Chang, ed., *Optimism and Pessimism* (Washington, DC: American Psychological Association, 2002): 53–75.

110 *Emotional contagion* Mood linkage seems greater for positive emotions and for groups of people who identify with one another, but the contagion of negative emotions leads to less cooperation, heightened conflict, and lower ratings of task performance by oneself and others. Kelly and Barsade, "Mood and Emotions in Small Groups and Work Teams," *Organizational Behavior and Human Decision Processes.*

110 *Negativity reduces energy* Burnout contagion has been found among schoolteachers, especially when teachers susceptible to influence communicated frequently about work-related problems; see Arnold B.

Bakker and Wilmar B. Schaufeli, "Burnout Contagion Processes Among Teachers," *Journal of Applied Social Psychology* 30, no. 11 (2000): 2289–2308. Sports psychologists found that coaches experienced burnout and exhaustion when they felt trapped; see Thomas D. Raadeke, Tracy L. Granzyk, and Anne Warren, "Why Coaches Experience Burnout: A Commitment Perspective," *Journal of Sports & Exercise Psychology* 22, no. 1 (February 2000): 85–105.

111 *Failure becomes a self-fulfilling prophecy* Researchers have shown a tendency for self-fulfilling prophecies to play a more important role among low achievers and people with low socioeconomic status (as well as among people who seek predictability and are not motivated to be accurate), and to last longer over time for low achievers (or losers) than for high achievers; A. E. Smith, L. Jussim, and J. Eccles, "Do Self-fulfilling Prophecies Accumulate, Dissipate, or Remain Stable over Time?" *Journal of Personality and Social Psychology* 77 (1999): 548–65.

113 *Billy Beane* I loved Michael Lewis's book about the Oakland Athletics, *Moneyball: The Art of Winning an Unfair Game* (New York: Norton, 2003), but all the quotes from Beane and his colleagues in this book are from my own team's original interviews (with thanks to Scott Hildula).

115 *harder to get opportunities* This is why the poor can get poorer, even if they try to work their way out of poverty. They often face more problems with fewer resources to deal with them, so they must spend more time just on basic survival. David K. Shipler tells a revealing (and moving) story about a hard-working but low-paid woman too poor to afford to get her teeth fixed, which then perpetuates her poverty because missing teeth and badly-fitted dentures made her less desirable to employers, so she was stuck in low-wage jobs with no prospects for promotion and high turnover. Shipler, *The Working Poor: Invisible in America* (New York: Knopf, 2004).

117 *75 percent of the African-American teachers* This figure comes from Frank Jackson, an alumnus dubbed the "unofficial historian of the school," as quoted in John Maher, "Purple Pain: Defeat Today Would Complete the Fall of Prairie View from Proud National Football Power," *Austin American-Statesman*, 30 September 1995.

118 *a strike by most of the sixty-five players* Tom Weir, "Striking by Opposite Views at Prairie View," *USA Today*, 14 February 1989.

118 *"permanently failing organizations"* Marshall W. Meyer and Lynne G. Zucker, *Permanently Failing Organizations* (Newbury Park, CA: Sage, 1989).

120 *The worst moment* Lorraine Kee Montre, "Keeping the Faith: Prairie View Scrambles for Money After 0–65 Basketball-Football Mark," *St. Louis Post-Dispatch*, 18 March 1992.

120 *One writer* Mark Blaudschun, "Lost on Prairie," *Boston Globe*, 3 October 1992.

121 *"It hurts"* Ira Berkow, "College Football: More Students Than Athletes, as the 44 Losses Prove," *New York Times*, 11 November 1994.

121 *Going to games underfed* John P. Lopez, "A Will to Win: Tired of Losing, Prairie View Remains Proudly Hopeful," *Houston Chronicle*, 31 August 1994.

123 *Player superstitions* Jennifer Frey, "At Prairie View, Losing Fosters a Winning Attitude," *Washington Post,* 1 October 1995.

128 *A committee of representatives* Texas Higher Education Coordinating Board, "Priority Plan to Strengthen Education at Prairie View A&M University and at Texas Southern University," October 2000.

132 *a charge Whittington disputed* W. H. Stickney Jr., "Firing 'Ridiculous,' Says Ex-PV Coach," *Houston Chronicle,* 10 December 2003.

137 *Institutional forces* J. Ross and Barry Staw, "Expo 86: An Escalation Prototype," *Administrative Science Quarterly* 31 (1986): 274–97.

138 *In one study* Donald C. Hambrick and Richard A. D'Aveni, "Large Corporate Failures as Downward Spirals," *Administrative Science Quarterly* 33 (1 March 1988): 1–23.

138 *Weakness led to flawed decisions* Donald C. Hambrick and Richard A. D'Aveni, "Top Team Deterioration as Part of the Downward Spiral of Large Corporate Bankruptcies," *Management Science* 18 (1992): 1445–66.

145 *"putting lipstick on a bulldog"* This phrase was introduced in Kanter, *Evolve!*

154 *Cornerback Troy Vincent* Dan Pompe, *The Sporting News,* 1 January 2001.

162 On bold strokes versus long marches, see Rosabeth Moss Kanter, Barry Stein, and Todd Jick, *The Challenge of Organizational Change* (New York: Free Press, 1992), chapter 14.

165 *The old leadership group* Brenneman, "Right Away and All at Once: How We Saved Continental," *Harvard Business Review.*

165 *"pluralistic ignorance"* This term was coined by social psychologist Floyd Allport in the 1920s to describe a widely held false belief about others' knowledge. People were not themselves ignorant in the ordinary sense of not knowing, but their understanding of what others knew was incorrect. Floyd H. Allport, *Social Psychology* (Boston: Houghton Mifflin, 1924). Also see Hubert J. Gorman, "The Discovery of Pluralistic Ignorance," *Journal of History of the Behavioral Sciences* 22 (1986): 333–47.

166 *a gap between knowing and doing* Jeffrey Pfeffer and Robert Sutton, *The Knowing-Doing Gap: How Smart Companies Turn Knowledge into Action* (Boston: Harvard Business School Press, 1999).

166 On the performance of new CEOs, see Rakesh Khurana, *Searching for a Corporate Savior* (Princeton, NJ: Princeton University Press, 2002). On the performance of new managers and coaches, see Oscar Grusky, "Managerial Succession and Organizational Effectiveness," *American Journal of Sociology* 69 (July 1963): 21–31; Gamson and Scotch, "Scapegoating in Baseball," *American Journal of Sociology;* Pfeffer and Davis-Blake, "Administrative Succession and Organizational Performance: How Administrator Experience Mediates the Succession Effect," *Academy of Management Journal.*

172 On how turnaround leaders can find resources to reinvest and influence beliefs that change is possible, see W. Chan Kim and Renee Mauborgne, "Tipping Point Leadership," *Harvard Business Review* (April 2003): 61–9, which features William Bratton's turnarounds of police departments.

Kim and Mauborgne identify four tasks: overcoming cognitive (beliefs), resources, political, and motivational hurdles to change.

174 On divided management and the Wilson firing, see Ken Peters, "Mighty Ducks Fire Ron Wilson as Coach," *Associated Press Newswires*, 20 May 1997; Karen Crouse, "Capitals Coach Wilson Brings Big Ego Back to Ducks' Pond," *Pittsburgh Post-Gazette*, 14 December 1997. On the Page firing, see Beth Harris, "Ducks Coach Page Fired after 10 Months," *Associated Press Newswires*, 15 June 1998. On negative attitudes, see Maureen Delany, "A Sorry Effort for Anaheim," *Press-Enterprise*, 20 December 1997.

174 *The Ducks hit bottom* John Blanchette, "Ex-Chiefs Coach has Mighty Ducks on a Mighty Roll," *Spokane Spokesman-Review*, 11 February 2003.

179 *a legacy of mistrust* Social memories of broken trust can endure for centuries, perpetuating enduring ethnic conflicts, as in Northern Ireland or the Balkins; Perkins, *King Arthur's Round Table*.

210 *Early in the Continental Airlines turnaround* Brenneman, "Right Away and All at Once: How We Saved Continental," *Harvard Business Review*.

210 On optimism and health-related dangers, see Lisa G. Aspinwall and Susanne M. Brunhart, "What I Do Know Won't Hurt Me: Optimism, Attention to Negative Information, Coping, and Health," in Jane E. Gillham, ed., *The Science of Optimism and Hope: Research Essays in Honor of Martin Seligman* (Radnor, PA: Templeton Foundation, 2000), 163–200. On proactive coping and adjustment to college life, see Lisa G. Aspinwall and Shelley E. Taylor, "Modeling Cognitive Adaptation: A Longitudinal Investigation of the Impact of Individual Differences and Coping on College Adjustment and Performance," *Journal of Personality and Social Psychology* 63 (1992): 989–1003. On coronary bypass recovery, see M. F. Scheier, K. A. Matthews, J. F. Owens, G. J. Magovern, R. C. Lefebre, R. A. Abbott, and C. S. Carver, "Dispositional Optimism and Recovery from Artery Bypass Surgery: The Beneficial Effects on Physical and Psychological Well-being," *Journal of Personality and Social Psychology* 57 (1989): 1024–40. On use of feedback to improve, see Lisa G. Aspinwall and Shelley E. Taylor, "A Stitch in Time: Self-Regulation and Proactive Coping," *Psychological Bulletin* 121 (1997): 417–36. On attacks on self-worth, see L. B. Alloy, L. Y. Abramson, L. A. Murray, W. G. Whitehouse, and M. E. Hogan, "Self-referent Information-processing in Individuals at High and Low Cognitive Risk for Depression," *Cognition and Emotion* 11 (1997): 539–68.

211 *Leaders can also provide safe havens* Amy C. Edmondson, "Psychological Safety and Learning Behavior in Work Teams," *Administrative Science Quarterly* 44 (1999): 350–83. The idea of psychological safety first appeared in Edgar Schein and Warren Bennis, *Personal and Organizational Change via Group Methods* (New York: Wiley, 1965).

218 *an organization is just a vast series of conversations* J. D. Ford argues that the state of an organization can be defined by its network of conversations, in "Conversations and the Epistemology of Change," in W. A. Pasmore and R. W. Woodman, eds., *Research in Organizational Development and Change* 12 (Stamford, CT: JAI Press, 1999): 1–39.

230 *Running an airline* Gordon Bethune with Scott Huler, *From Worst to First*.

241 *four kinds of actions* These are similar to Richard Hackman's five enabling conditions for team success: It must be a real team with compelling direction, an enabling structure (meaningful tasks, explicit norms), a supportive context (collective rewards and information), and expert coaching. Richard B. Hackman, *Leading Teams: Setting the Stage for Great Performance* (Boston: HBS Press, 2002). The difference in my analysis is that I am talking about the ability to collaborate across boundaries as well as work in a formal team.

243 *Group cohesiveness* Albert V. Carron, Michelle M. Colman, Jennifer Wheeler, and Diane Stevens, "Cohesion and Performance in Sport: A Meta Analysis," *Journal of Sports & Exercise Psychology* 24, no. 2 (June 2002): 168–88.

245 *Teams that produce innovations* Kay Lovelace, Debra L. Shapiro, and Laurie Weingart, "Maximizing Cross-functional New Product Teams' Innovativeness and Constraint Adherence," *Academy of Management Journal* 44 (August 2001): 779–83.

245 *the consistency principle* When people experience "cognitive dissonance" stemming from a discrepancy between their behavior and their attitudes, they are often likely to change their attitudes to match the new behavior. Leon Festinger, *A Theory of Cognitive Dissonance* (Evanston, IL: Row, Peterson, 1957).

247 *When people feel understood* M. Korsgaard, D. Schweiger, and H. Sapienza, "Building Commitment, Attachment, and Trust in Strategic Decision-making Teams: The Role of Procedural Justice," *Academy of Management Journal* 38 no. 2 (1995): 60–84. Amy C. Edmondson, Michael A. Roberto, and Michael D. Watkins, "A Dynamic Model of Top Management Team Effectiveness: Managing Unstructured Task Streams," *Leadership Quarterly* 14 (2003): 297–325.

248 *The police ward surrounding the school* On crime, see Beverly Steward, "Crime Thrives on Targets of Opportunity: Police Cite 'Ignorance of Victims,'" *Memphis Commercial Appeal*, 26 March 1992. On poverty, see Aimee Edmondson, "An Open or Shut Case—Tradition, Politics Keep Underused Schools Alive," *Memphis Commercial Appeal*, 9 February 2003.

256 On self-direction as a human desire, see Albert Bandura, "Self-Efficacy: Toward a Unifying Theory of Behavioral Change," *Psychological Review*.

272 *This was improvisational theater* Rosabeth Moss Kanter, "Strategy as Improvisational Theatre." *Sloan Management Review* 43, no. 2 (Winter 2002), derived from Kanter, *Evolve!*, chapter 4.

274 *"appreciative inquiry"* David Cooperrider of Case Western Reserve University is the father of this concept. See David L. Cooperrider and Diana Whitney, *Appreciative Inquiry* (San Francisco: Berrett-Koehler, 2000); and David L. Cooperrider and Leslie E. Sekerka, "Toward a Theory of Positive Organizational Change," in Cameron, Dutton, and Quinn, eds., *Positive Organizational Scholarship*.

282 "Kaleidoscope thinking" is my term for finding creative new

approaches—a more dynamic metaphor than "out-of-the-box thinking" because a kaleidoscope suggests that there are many ways to shake the fragments of ideas into new patterns. This idea is developed in Kanter, *Evolve!*, and in Kanter, "Kaleidoscope Thinking," in S. Chowdhury, ed., *Management 21C: Someday We'll All Manage This Way* (London: Financial Times/Prentice Hall 2000), 250–61.

282 *That's almost a textbook formula* For my model of systemic change called the "change wheel," see Kanter, *Evolve!*, chapter 8, and on the Web at www.changetoolkit.com.

289 *Start with small wins* For a similar idea, see Karl Weick, "Small Wins: Redefining the Scale of Social Problems," *American Psychologist* 39, no. 1 (January 1984): 40–49.

291 *the 1995 Rugby World Cup* Press accounts of the game include Anton Ferreira, "Mandela Leads South Africans in Celebrating Rugby Win," Reuters, 24 June 1995; Chris Rea, "Nelson and His Nation on Top of the World," *Independent on Sunday*, 25 June 1995; Huw Richards, "Rugby World Cup—Triumph for a New Society," *Financial Times*, 26 June 1995.

293 Mandela biographical information is taken from Nelson R. Mandela, *The Illustrated Long Walk to Freedom* (London: Little Brown, 1994), 52, 55. Rough Guides U.S. Ltd., "South Africa—Sharpeville: 1994–1999," from Yahoo!Travel, http://travel.yahoo.com/p-travelguide-820227-south_africa_sharpeville-i (accessed 14 July 2003).

294 *"I have fought"* Mandela's statement is from " 'I Am Prepared to Die,' " Nelson Mandela's statement at the opening of the defense case in the Rivonia trial, Pretoria Supreme Court, 20 April 1964, http://www.anc.org.za/ancdocs/history/ mandela/1960s/rivonia.html, last accessed 1 August 2003. Botha's quote that follows is from Anthony Sampson, *Mandela: The Authorized Biography* (New York: Vintage Books, 2000), 452–53.

297 Facts about South Africa and apartheid are from Library of Congress, "South Africa—A Country Study," http://lcweb2.loc.gov/frd/cs/ zatoc.html (accessed 14 July 2003).

298 *Mandela had to walk a tightrope* Rough Guides U.S. Ltd., "South Africa—The Mandela Years."

300 *Although nineteen of the twenty-five members* Ibid.

300 Mandela's criticisms of the press and his quote are from Sampson, *Mandela*, 517–19.

301 *Of the estimated 21.7 million voters* Library of Congress, "South Africa—A Country Study." Rough Guides U.S. Ltd., "South Africa—The Mandela Years."

301 *Mandela's desire for input* Sampson, *Mandela*, 93–94.

302 *over 4 million copies of the draft constitution* Catherine Barnes and Eldred De Klerk, "South Africa's Multi-party Constitutional Negotiation Process," *Accord* (an International Review of Peace Initiatives), no. 13 (December 2002), http://www.c-r.org/accord/peace/accord13/samul.shtml (accessed 14 July 2003).

302 *The government had imparted a sense* Library of Congress, "South Africa—A Country Study."

303 *On April 10, 1993* The Hani story and its aftermath in the following paragraph is based on Sampson, *Mandela*, 461–62.

304 *Truth and Reconciliation Commission* Charles Haupt and Charles Malcolm, "From Hell to Hope: An Organizational Case Study of the Truth and Reconciliation Commission (TRC) in South Africa," from the International Society for the Psychoanalytic Study of Organizations, 2000, http://www.ispso.org/Symposia/London/2000haupt-malcolm.htm (accessed 14 July 2003).

305 *the TRC encouraged an atmosphere of openness* Sampson, *Mandela*, 522.

305 *Joe Slovo* Ibid., 521.

305 *After two and a half years* Rough Guides U.S. Ltd., "South Africa—The Mandela Years."

305 *"We must regard"* Sampson, *Mandela*, 524.

306 Graca Machel quote Ibid., 525.

306 For the structure of the delegation, see ibid., 418. For the structure of the government: Library of Congress, "South Africa—A Country Study."

307 *"enormously patient"* Sampson, *Mandela*, 425. In 1927, with the death of his father, Nelson Mandela was placed in the care of the acting chief of the Thembu clan, Jongintaba Dalindyebo. Growing up as a boy in the royal household, Mandela witnessed firsthand the decision-making process of the chief and elder tribesmen.

307 *"whites are fellow South Africans"* Mandela, *Long Walk to Freedom*, 181.

307 *"Those that do not know"* Sampson, *Mandela*, 471.

307 *"They'll come right in the end"* Ibid., 514.

308 *"We can neither heal nor build"* Ibid., 516.

309 *1995 to 1999 annual percentage growth* National Economic Development and Labour Council, "NEDLAC Agreements and Reports" (1999), http://www.nedlac.org.za/docs/agreements/index.html (accessed 14 July 2003).

309 *free compulsory education* Rough Guides U.S. Ltd., "South Africa—The Mandela Years."

309 *"Spare a thought"* Mamphele Ramphele, "When Will the Real Debate on Employment Equity Begin?" *Monday Paper* (University of Cape Town), http:///web.uct.ac.za/depts/dpa/monpaper/98-no5/equity.htm (accessed 14 July 2003).

309 *the Employment Equity Act* Thabo Kobokoane, "Employment Equity on Track Despite Criticism," *Business Times*, 18 October 1998, http://www.sundaytimes.co.za/98/1018/news/news10.htm (accessed 14 July 2003).

310 For data on black firms' listings on the JSE, see National Economic Development and Labour Council, "NEDLAC Agreements and Reports" (2000), http://www.nedlac.org.za/docs/agreements/index.html (accessed 14 July 2003). For data on black firms' market cap, see National Economic Development and Labour Council, "The Nedlac Socio-Economic Development Trends Bulletin: Annexure" (June 2002), http://www.nedlac.org.za//research/bulletin/2002/june/annexure.html (accessed 14 July 2003). On delivery of essential services, see Government Communication and Information System (GCIS), "Government's Mid-term Report to the Nation: Speeding up Provision of Services (International Marketing Council, February 2002), http://www.gcis.

gov.za/ docs/ publications/midterm/mdtrm02_7_8.pdf (accessed 14 July 2003). On educational progress, see The World Bank Group, "World Development Indicators" (information obtained from single-user CD-ROM by WDI Database Search Query) (Washington, DC: World Bank, 2003).

311 *The gap between the highest and lowest earners* National Economic Development and Labour Council, "Nedlac Agreements and Reports." Wage gap data from 1997 report; blacks in senior management positions from 2000 report; housing budget from 1999 report. Health-care data from *The Second Kaiser Family Foundation Survey of Health-Care in South Africa* (publication no. 1513) (Menlo Park, CA: Henry J. Kaiser Family Foundation, August 1999).

313 *Mandela told the crowd* Sampson, *Mandela,* xxiii.

313 *Foreign investment* Figures come from the Economist Intelligence Unit Country Data, EIU Data Services (New York: Bureau van Dijk Electronic Publishing) (accessed 24 November 2003).

313 *At his inauguration in 1994* Richard Stengel, "The Long Walk of Nelson Mandela," interview by John Carlin, *PBS Online* (1999) http://www.pbs.org/wgbh/pages/frontline/shows/mandela/interviews/stengel.html (accessed 14 July 2003). On entrenched leadership in neighboring countries, see Martin Meredith, *Our Votes, Our Guns* (New York: Public Affairs Press, 2001).

314 *Mbeki clasped Mandela's hand* Charlayne Hunter-Gault, "Mandela Gets Rousing Send-off as Mbeki Takes Office," *CNN.com,* 16 June 1999, http://www.cnn.com/WORLD/africa/9906/16/s.africa.mbeki/ (accessed 14 July 2003).

315 *"the kind of leader who not only transforms"* James Joseph, "Strengthening Democracy by Strengthening Leadership," speech at the Leadership Triangle Awards Dinner, Durham, North Carolina, 17 October 2002, http://www.leadershiptriangle.com/programs/Speeches/amb_james_joseph.html (accessed 14 July 2003). For definitions of hard and soft power, see Joseph S. Nye Jr. *Soft Power: The Means to Success in World Politics* (New York: Public Affairs, 2004).

315 *BBC commentator Brian Walden* Andre Brink, "Nelson Mandela," *Time: Leaders and Revolutionaries,* http://www.time.com/ time/time100/leaders/ profile/mandela.html (accessed 14 July 2003).

317 *A political scientist* Arthur A. Goldsmith, "Risk, Rule, and Reason: Leadership in Africa," *Public Administration and Development* 21 (2001): 77–87.

318 *George Washington* Leonard White, *The Federalists* (New York: Macmillan, 1961), 6.

319 *"accidental chiefs"* Dean Keith Simonton, "The Vice-presidential Succession Effect: Individual or Situational Basis?" *Political Behavior* 7(1985): 79–99.

320 *In eighteen of twenty-two U.S. presidential elections* Harold M. Zullow, "Pessimistic Rumination in American Politics and Society," in G. M. Buchanan and M. E. P. Seligman, eds., *Explanatory Style* (Hillsdale, NJ: Erlbaum, 1995), 187–208.

320   *In 1988, optimism* Ibid.

333   *the charisma of leadership* Charisma can take the form of "institutional-ized awe," in which anyone representing the group can be imbued with moral authority by virtue of the values of the enterprise that he or she represents. Rosabeth Moss Kanter, *Commitment and Community* (Cambridge, MA: Harvard University Press, 1972).

344   *Business Week* poll: BusinessWeek/Harris Interactive, "How Business Rates: By the Numbers," *Business Week*, 11 September 2000. *Wall Street Journal* poll: Gerald F. Seib and John Harwood, "Rising Anxiety: What Could Bring 1930s-Style Reform of U.S. Businesses?" *Wall Street Journal*, 24 July 2002.

344   *the Humpty-Dumpty problem* Perkins uses a similar image in *King Arthur's Round Table*.

345   *Millennium Survey* This survey was conducted by Environics Inter-national in 1999, in collaboration with the Conference Board in the United States and the Prince of Wales Business Forum in the UK. Other surveys are cited by Business for Social Responsibility (www.bsr.org). Social Investment Forum is the source for the investment figures (www.socialinvest.org/areas/news/120403release.htm). The *Financial Times* observation appeared on 24 October 2001. Other data are found in Rosabeth Moss Kanter, "Rising to Rising Expectations," *Worldlink: The Magazine of the World Economic Forum*, January 2002.

357   *Optimists assume* For the differences between optimists' and pessimists' explanations of events, see Gillham, ed., *The Science of Optimism and Hope;* and Jane E. Gillham, Andrew J. Shatte, Karen J. Reivich, and Martin E. P. Seligman, "Optimism, Pessimism, and Explanatory Style," in Chang, ed., *Optimism and Pessimism.* For a discussion of the teaching of optimism, see Martin E. P. Seligman, *Learned Optimism.*

Acknowledgments

I am grateful to many people who provided valuable help when it was needed, from early stages to final manuscript.

Glenn Hutchins, one of the brains behind SilverLake Partners, introduced me to Seagate, and at just the right moment, he and his wife Debby held a dinner party on Martha's Vineyard that included two owners of major professional sports franchises I wanted to see. Stanley Litow, Robin Willner, Sasha Dichter, and Ann Cramer of IBM, whose path-breaking work on IBM's Reinventing Education initiatives is helping transform K-12 public education worldwide, gave me the chance to put my leadership and change tools online (*www.reinventingeducation.org*) and to interact with school system leaders; Dot Neale was helpful in Memphis. Daniel Isenberg, a venture capitalist in Israel, introduced me to Akin Öngör in Istanbul. Henry Louis ("Skip") Gates Jr. introduced me to comedian Chris Tucker. Phyllis and Eli Segal introduced me to Jim Joseph, former U.S. Ambassador to South Africa, as I was considering telling the story of Nelson Mandela's presidency.

At the World Economic Forum in Davos, Switzerland, I met numerous CEOs and even Nelson Mandela through the years, but the 2001 meeting's gem was Anthos Yannakou, who invited me to South Africa for a lecture tour on behalf of CSIR, starting another ball rolling there. Back home, longtime friends Donna Shalala, former U.S. Secretary of Health and Human Services and now president of the University of Miami, and Nannerl Keohane, then-president of Duke University, opened doors to their athletic programs. Alan Greer, Peter Klein, and *Miami Herald* publisher Alberto Ibarguen were also helpful.

As the core ideas for this book were being developed, they received a trial run before highly diverse audiences in many fields and on many continents. That gave me confidence (so to speak) that the ideas could travel widely and have universal relevance. Among the most memorable of those audiences were Bill Gates's CEO Summit at Microsoft; managers of a major American retail chain; leaders of Girl Scout troops and councils from every region; European customers of a large software company; women entrepreneurs and small business owners; global managers of Japanese and Korean companies; American college and university administrators; British politicians and policy makers convened by the UK's Economic and Social Research Council; and directors of national associations ranging from women's basketball coaches to religious interfaith councils to medical professionals.

Not everything I did made it into this book, but a discussion with Home Depot executives and later a breakfast with CEO Bob Nardelli in Atlanta came at just the right moment in the development of my ideas about leadership of turnarounds, as did conversations with Novartis CEO Daniel Vasella and WPP Group chairman Sir Martin Sorrell.

I am perhaps even more grateful to the many friends who immediately started seeing the relevance to their own personal lives and careers. For obvious reasons I cannot name them here, but those more personal conversations grounded the research in themes that could resonate with ordinary individuals as well as with those in leadership roles.

I think that people learn best through stories, so I tell a great many memorable ones in this book. I believe that the most useful ideas are grounded in a deep understanding of how the world actually works. That is why I value getting out into the field, talking with people in their own settings. I also want to collect enough information from enough places to permit comparisons, later using large-sample surveys to check whether my findings can be generalized across different situations. I enjoy the construction of a mosaic composed of many observations of reality for which I can find an illuminating new pattern. And it is a lot of fun to hire bright people, assemble a big team, and tackle an ambitious project (but less fun, I confess, to go into seclusion to do the writing).

Just about every word quoted in this book was said directly to me and/or my research associates on field visits. Hundreds of interviews (over 300) and thousands of hours of observations were conducted by me and my team, often with access to archives or company documents. Most of the research took place starting in September 2002, but a few projects had earlier origins. All this work was made possible by funding from the Harvard Business School Division of Faculty Research and Development and the support of Dean Kim Clark and many faculty colleagues, for which I am very grateful.

I was fortunate to have an incredible research team, and especially lucky to have Douglas Raymond as team captain (which was appropriate, as that was also his rank when he completed his tour of duty in the U.S. Army); Doug's intelligence, character, optimism, and sense of fun were a gift every day. Micki Heskett (a talented, insightful member of what I jokingly call my "alumni association" of former research associates) was willing to set aside some of her own work to conduct interviews, as was the charming and knowledgeable Corrie Dretler. David Leopold did great spadework to find the best winning and losing streaks in sports. Scott Hildula, a California marketing expert and former sportswriter, became a virtual team member, traveling for some sports interviews. Kevin Morris handled public schools and sports teams, before returning to his native New Zealand.

Euvin Naidoo, who grew up in South Africa and returned there after Harvard, tirelessly pursued facts about Nelson Mandela, drafting the wonderful case that was the basis for my story. Emma Herbert, who hails from England, taught me just about everything

I know about cricket. Eliza Moody jumped in toward the end and did a bit of nearly everything with enthusiasm, intelligence, and helpful attention to details. Willa Reiser and Ariel Shoresh served as my assistants during early stages of the project; Cheryl Daigle added her consummate professionalism and infectious charm in this role in the later stages. Other talented people were research associates for pieces of this complex endeavor and have my heartfelt thanks: these include Lyn Baranowski, Brooke Bartletta, Brad Karmiol, David Lehrer, Maximilian Martin, John McGuire, Afroze Mohammed, Ryan Raffaelli, Jane Roessner, and Jim Weber. Jay Chrepta kept me up-to-date on news about some of the organizations in the project. Analysts at Baker Library helped with database searches.

Two online surveys were conducted with the help of *SchoolSports* magazine (thanks to Jim Kaufman, Jon Segal, and Eli Segal), *Business 2.0* magazine (Josh Quittner), and the Massachusetts Biotechnology Council (Janice Bourque and Cynthia Fisher) and Software Council (Joyce Plotkin). The Harvard Business School IT group got the polls up and running effectively; Ariel Shoresh was a great interface. Sarah Woolverton crunched large amounts of data with skill, found just the right summary statistics, set up websites so I could view findings easily, and documented the statistical significance of differences between winners and losers. Although I do not reference all the numbers in the book, they are available in the archives thanks to Sarah's efforts.

Of course, I owe a great deal to all the people in the companies, sports teams, schools, hospitals, and other organizations who generously provided the benefit of their experience. I cannot name all of them here, but I hope they will enjoy seeing their names later in the book (except for those who preferred anonymity). But I want to single out some people who not only welcomed us on their premises (in some cases using me as an adviser), but also came to Harvard to speak with my MBAs and the Harvard community: Akin Öngör, Saide Kuzeyli, and Tuba Koseoglu of Garanti Bank; Gail Snowden of Fleet Bank; Greg Dyke, Stephen Dando, and Susan

Spindler of the BBC; Dr. Craig Feied of Washington Hospital Center; Jim Kilts, Peter Klein, and Ned Guillet of Gillette; Mike Cook of Deloitte and Touche; Ivan Seidenberg of Verizon; and Steve Luczo of Seagate.

Special thanks are due to the friends and colleagues who read first drafts and provided wise, thoughtful comments, including Cheryl Batzer, Max Batzer, Connie Borde, Michael Brown, Jane Dutton, Alan Khazei, Rakesh Khurana, Wick Sloane, and Scott Snook. Scott Snook also joined me for a visit to Andy Reid at the Philadelphia Eagles; en route, he shared insights from years of teaching leadership at West Point before he came to Harvard. Tom Stewart, editor of *Harvard Business Review,* and senior editor Julia Kirby encouraged the development of some of the first findings into an article for the June 2003 issue, "Leadership and the Psychology of Turnarounds."

In addition, I had productive conversations at various stages with John Barnhill, Warren Bennis, Carolyn Cohen, Alan Dershowitz, Daniel Galvin, David Gergen, Swanee Hunt, Linda Paresky, Clyde Phillips, Laura Roosevelt, Charlie Silberstein, Maureen Strafford, Gerri Sweder, and Michael and Randy Wertheimer. Lisa Foster shared thoughts on writing (and if there is ever *Confidence: The Major Motion Picture,* I want Gary *Sleepless in Seattle* Foster to produce it). Marsha Feinberg wanted me to dedicate the book to "the Feinberg children, without whom it would have been written faster," but in fact all of the Feinbergs contributed energy and spirit (as did all of the Dretlers).

I have left for last five people (and one dog) most closely connected to me in the final stages of translating ideas to book form. Ande Zellman was amazing in her graciousness and generosity, sharing the benefit of considerable experience at major magazines and newspapers to provide editorial counseling about revisions; her dedication, professionalism, and encouragement were invaluable, especially because she has many demands on her time as a consultant on media innovations. Cathy Turco scrutinized the first draft and suggested useful edits and references to relevant studies, lending her considerable intelligence on her own time, which was above and beyond. John Mahaney, executive editor at Crown, understood the project from the start, which was itself extremely important, and provided very helpful guidance at many stages.

Regardless of his location, my son Matthew Stein (officially Matthew Moss Kanter Stein) is my favorite sports expert, political analyst, and computer help desk. (He performed a few rescues via long-distance instructions.) My husband, Barry Stein, who is very astute and knows a great deal about most subjects, did a million things to support this effort (including saving the hard drive, talking about ideas, giving me pep talks, and entertaining Browser, our cute cocker spaniel, so she wouldn't be under whatever spot I set up the laptop). He can't be thanked nearly enough, but this is a start.

Index

About the Author

Rosabeth Moss Kanter is an internationally known business leader, bestselling author, and expert on strategy, innovation, and leadership for change. She holds an endowed chair as the Ernest L. Arbuckle Professor of Business Administration at Harvard Business School. She advises major corporations and governments worldwide, as well as a range of smaller business and community organizations. *Confidence* is her sixteenth book. Her award-winning bestsellers include *Men & Women of the Corporation, The Change Masters, When Giants Learn to Dance,* and *World Class: Thriving Locally in the Global Economy.* In 2001 she received the Academy of Management's Distinguished Career Award, its highest award for scholarly contributions, for her impact on management thought, and in 2002 received the World Teleport Association's Intelligent Community Visionary of the Year Award.

Considered one of the most prominent business thought leaders in the world, she has received twenty-one honorary doctoral degrees and over a dozen leadership awards, and has been named to lists of the "50 most influential business thinkers in the world" (ranked in the top ten), the "100 most important women in America," and the "50 most powerful women in the world." A dynamic speaker, she has shared the platform at major events with prime ministers, presidents, and CEOs in many countries. She cofounded Goodmeasure Inc., whose consulting clients have included some of the world's best companies; Goodmeasure has developed electronic Web-based versions of Kanter's leadership and change tools, to help embed them in the daily work of organizations (www.changetoolkit.com). She serves as a senior adviser to IBM's award-winning Reinventing Education initiative and is partnering with IBM to bring her leadership models to K-12 education reform (www.reinventingeducation.org).

She joined the Harvard Business School faculty in 1986 from Yale University, where she held a tenured professorship from 1977 to 1986; previously, she was a Fellow in Law and Social Science at Harvard Law School and taught at Brandeis University. In 1997–1998 she led the Business Leadership in the Social Sector (BLSS) project at Harvard Business School, including CEOs, senators, and governors in dialogue about public-private partnerships for change. From 1989 to 1992 she also served as editor of the *Harvard Business Review*, which was a finalist for a National Magazine Award for General Excellence in 1991.

Her public service activities include the board of judges for the Ron Brown Award for Corporate Leadership given at the White House; the board of overseers for the Malcolm Baldrige National Quality Award; the U.S. Secretary of Labor's Skills Gap committee of the 21st Century Work Force Council; the Massachusetts Governor's Economic Council (for which she co-chaired the International Trade Task Force); and, currently, the Massachusetts Convention Center Authority board. A Fellow of the World Economic Forum, she has served on corporate, pension fund, civic, and nonprofit boards, including City Year, the national urban youth service corps that was a model for Americorps and is expanding internationally, first to South Africa.

An avid sports fan, tennis player, and dancer, she lives in Cambridge, Massachusetts, with her husband, son, and a very cute cocker spaniel. She walks to her office at Harvard along the Charles River in Boston and gets to ocean beaches in Miami and Martha's Vineyard whenever she can.